SUCCESSFUL
SOUND SYSTEM OPERATION

Other TAB Books by the Author

No. 2606
$24.95

SUCCESSFUL SOUND SYSTEM OPERATION

F. ALTON EVEREST

TAB BOOKS Inc.
Blue Ridge Summit, PA 17214

FIRST EDITION
FIRST PRINTING

Copyright © 1985 by TAB BOOKS Inc.
Printed in the United States of America

Library of Congress Cataloging in Publication Data

Everest, F. Alton (Frederick Alton), 1909-
Successful sound system operation.

Includes index.
1. Electro-acoustics.   2. Sound—Recording and
reproducing.   I. Title.
TK5981.E94   1985   621.389′3   85-17343
ISBN 0-8306-0306-9
ISBN 0-8306-0206-2 (pbk.)

Front cover: clockwise from top right: courtesy of Community Light and Sound,
Chester, PA.; the three other photographs are courtesy of Altec Corporation, Oklahoma City, OK.

Contents

SUCCESSFUL
SOUND
SYSTEM
OPERATION

Introduction

THE KEY LINK IN THE AUDIO CHAIN IS NOT the microphone, the amplifiers, the loudspeaker, or even the acoustics of the space. The key link is that person we shall call the operator, the one responsible for the effective functioning of the system as a whole. This person is the key to success, whether the audio system is a sound reinforcement system in a church or a school, a home high-fidelity setup, or a recording studio, personal or professional. The efforts of the expert designer and dedicated manufacturer are lost if their audio equipment is improperly used.

This book is written specifically for this key person, the operator. The game plan is to provide this person with basic background material in acoustics, electronics, and that very commonly used but often abused concept, the decibel. Then comes what every audio person dearly loves, equipment. The emphasis is on how various microphones and loudspeakers work, what goes on inside amplifiers, mixers, and sound processing devices, and how to use them intelligently. Using audio equipment with little understanding of what goes on inside is an invitation to disaster, embarrassing disaster. Only analog equipment is considered, although one chapter is devoted to the digital revolution that is upon us.

The audio system operator will find this book of greatest value when used with other books I have written such as *Acoustic Techniques For Home and Studio* (1984, 2nd edition), *The Master Handbook of Acoustics* (1981), and *Handbook of Multichannel Recording* (1975), all published by TAB BOOKS, Inc.

The phrase, "no man is an island," surely applies to writers of books such as this. My dependence on the work and writings of others is recognized all through this book by references to the literature, and I wish to express my thanks to these authors and researchers for their massive contributions upon which the great advances in audio of the past century are based. Thanks are also due to the many manufacturers of audio equipment who have provided photographs and other data.

Chapter 1

Sound Waves

S OUND WAVES CAN OFTEN BE HEARD, BUT otherwise give little evidence of their presence to our other senses. How do they get from one point to another? How are they produced in the first place? If we were able to get out hands on them and see them, perhaps some of the mystery surrounding them would disappear. It is really aggravating that something so basic to audio systems is so ephemeral and ghostlike. and yet, radio waves are even more intangible, so maybe we are not so bad off after all. At least let us look at sound with the idea of removing some of the mystery surrounding it so that we will be able to handle it more intelligently in our sound systems.

1.1 HOW SOUND TRAVELS

Sound travels in air, in water, in solids such as wood and steel. The ocean is full of sound: whales and porpoises communicating with each other, tiny shrimp snapping their claws, croakers serenading each other on summer evenings as well as mechanical noise generated as the surf pounds on the rocks and the wind disturbs the surface. Strike a railroad rail and the sound travels great distances, the sound traveling through the steel arriving at a distant point even before the sound in air arrives. In a modern high-rise building the noise of heel taps, doors slamming, plumbing, and elevators travels throughout the building through the steel and concrete frame with practically no attenuation.

Sound must have a solid, liquid, or gaseous medium in which to travel and all such media share two absolutely necessary qualities: elasticity and inertia. Elasticity in the medium means that it can be compressed and once the compressing force is released its original shape tends to be restored. Inertia is associated with the density of the medium and wherever there is mass there is the tendency for the mass, if moved, to keep moving, and if stationary, to stay put.

Sound in air is most common to us. To get a grip on just how sound travels in the air medium we must focus our attention on the tiniest air particles and the role they play in the process. Let us assume that a loudspeaker cone is our source of sound. As the cone moves outward the air particles immediately in front of it are forced forward increasing the air pressure ever so slightly and when it moves back a partial vacuum is formed. Without worrying right now how the sound is really radiated, let us focus our attention on a single particle well out in front of the loudspeaker, on the medium itself. In Fig. 1-1 we trace the movement of a single particle of air as the sine disturbance goes by. At time t_1 we find the air particle moved to the right to d_1. At time t_2 it is moved to d_2, and so on. But at t_5 the air particle has moved to d_5, the extreme deflection caused by the distant loudspeaker. In moving to the right the particle has pushed against other particles tending to crowd them together. Work has been done on this particle to get it to move. It has inertia and it "wanted" to stay in it s equilibrium, resting position. It also has elasticity and it now reverses direction and heads back toward its resting position. When it reaches it at t_{10} it does not skid to a halt, but rather keeps on going to the left past the resting position because of its inertia. The elastic forces now tend to slow its leftward travel and at t_{15} it reaches its leftward extreme and starts back toward the resting position. If all this seems to be similar to a ball on a rubber band it is because it is a manifestation of the same forces at work, elasticity and inertia.

So much for one lone air particle. As there are four hundred billion billion molecules in one cubic inch of air, it is time for us to back up and get a better perspective. In Fig. 1-2 the lines represent either long rows of air particles or a sectional view of sheets of them acting under the influence of this same sound wave going by. During the compression cycle, the rows or sheets of air particles are pushed closer together and during the rarefaction cycle they are spread apart. The small arrows a and b represent the equal but opposite forces associated with the compression and rarefaction, respectively. The fact with that a and b point toward each other means that the air particles between them tend to be compressed, thus moving the peak of the compression cycle slightly to the right. Voila! This is what makes the sound wave move to the right! The interesting part is that the sound wave goes on, but the air particles do their shimmy close to home. Did you ever see the wind effect on a wheat field ripe for harvest? The wave travels across the field, but each head of wheat just waves back and forth.

In talking about sound waves we are talking about air pressure variations. A barometer measures air pressure, but is not much good to us

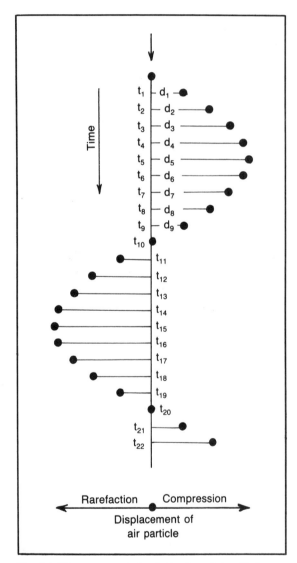

Fig. 1-1. The movement of a single air particle with time as a sine-wave disturbance passes by.

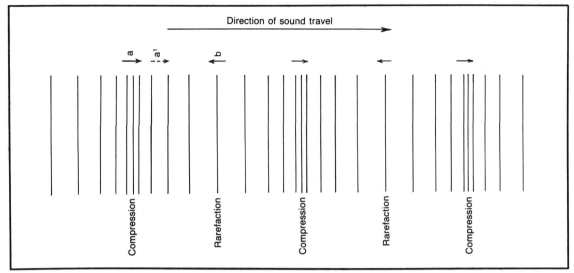

Fig. 1-2. Rows of air particles engaged in the propagation of sound. The arrows pointing to the right represent compressed regions, arrows pointing to the left represent rarified regions. Arrows pointing toward each other also indicate regions in which compression occurs. The broken arrow indicates the slight progression to the right of the compression peak, which constitutes the progression of the wave to the right.

to measure sound pressure. The sound pressure fluctuations ride along on top of the prevailing atmospheric pressure. The atmospheric pressure is the dc component, as it were, and the sound fluctuations the alternating component. The magnitude of the sound fluctuations associated with faint sounds just audible to the human ear is something like five billion times smaller than the atmospheric pressure. We shall leave the barometer to its normal task of measuring the slowly varying atmospheric pressure, and use the microphone to measure the sound ripples superimposed on it.

1.2 DESCRIBING SOUND WAVES

In the air particle discussion and in Fig. 1-1 we have assumed a simple sine wave. Sine waves are important, they are the basic component of all periodic waves, yet our speech and music signals are of complex shape. The distance between comparable positions on the compression cycle or the rarefaction cycle of Fig. 1-2 is called the wavelength. This is a very important concept to which we will be continually referring. It is evident that the speed of propagation of sound determines how

much the compression peaks are spread out. Wavelength and speed of sound are related as follows:

$$\text{Wavelength} = \frac{\text{speed of sound}}{\text{frequency}} \qquad \textbf{Eq. 1-1}$$

Speed of sound is close to 1,130 ft/sec in air (about 700 mi/hr). Thus wavelength in feet can be obtained by dividing 1,130 by the frequency of sound in hertz (cycles/second). Using this simple expression we can figure that at 20 Hz the wavelength of sound is 56.5 ft. At the opposite end of the audible spectrum, 20 kHz, the wavelength is only 0.0565 ft or about 5/8 inch. In the middle of the spectrum, if you can accept 1,000 Hz as the middle, the wavelength of sound is 1.13 ft. The graph of Fig. 1-3 is a convenient way of finding the wavelength of sound in air at a given frequency, or finding the frequency if the wavelength is known.

1.3 DIFFERENT WAVEFRONT SHAPES

The location of the sound source with respect to our point of observation or measurement affects the form of the wavefront. For example, in Fig. 1-4 a point source radiates sound in all directions and the wavefronts are spherical. If the source is more

3

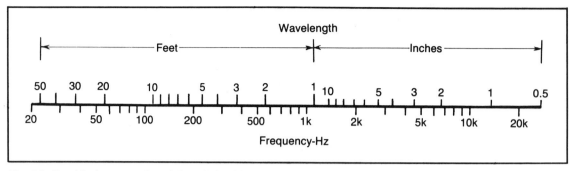

Fig. 1-3. Graphical presentation of the relationship between frequency and wavelength of sound traveling in air.

distant, only a segment of the spherical wavefront affects our observation, and the wavefront, while curved, has much less curvature as shown in Fig. 1-5. If the sound source is moved to infinity, the tiny portion of the wavefront affecting our obser-

vation is composed of essentially plane waves as in Fig. 1-6.

1.4 STANDING WAVES

While we are on the general subject of waves,

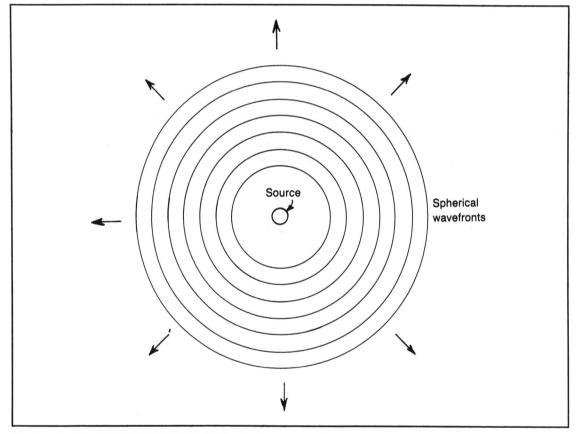

Fig. 1-4. A point source radiates sound energy or spherical wavefronts.

4

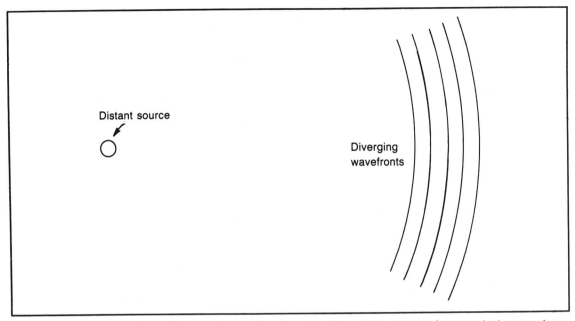

Fig. 1-5. When the source of sound is some distance from the point of observation, the wavefronts tend to become planes.

the phrase "standing waves" comes to mind. Does sound stand still to make a standing wave? Does its speed of 1,130 ft/sec slow down to a standstill? No, none of the basic laws of sound are repealed. Standing waves just appear to be standing still. Let us consider sound in the enclosed space pictured in Fig. 1-7. Further, we must simplify the very complex situation of sound in small rooms in order to

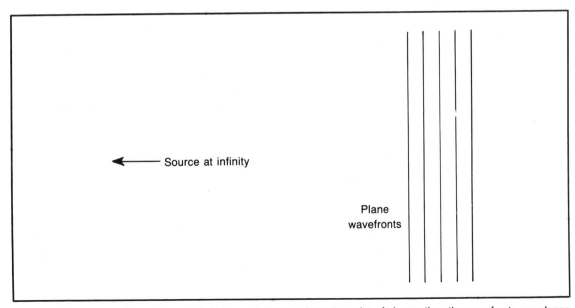

Fig. 1-6. If the source of sound is an infinitely great distance from the point of observation, the wavefronts are planes.

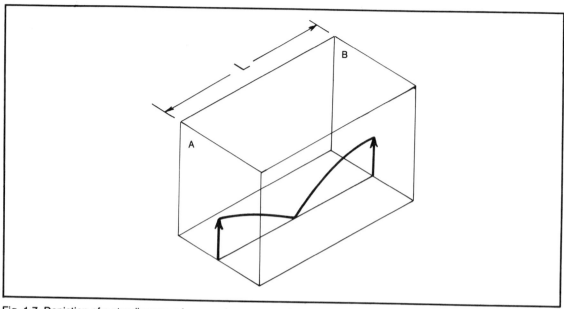

Fig. 1-7. Depiction of a standing wave in an enclosure caused by the space between two opposing parallel walls, A and B, coming into resonance when the wavelength of the sound is twice the length L. This is comparable to an organ pipe closed at both ends.

get at the bottom of the principles involved by first considering only the ends A and b of the room of Fig. 1-7. If this room has a length L = 20 ft it comes into a sort of resonance condition at a certain frequency, much as an organ pipe closed at each end. This frequency can be determined from:

$$\text{Frequency} = \frac{\text{speed of sound}}{2L}$$

$$= \frac{1130}{2L}$$

Eq. 1-2

For the L = 20 ft above, this frequency is 1130/(2) (20) = 28.25 Hz. At this frequency the sound pressure in the room is distributed as suggested by the heavy line of Fig. 1-7, high at each end and zero at the center of the room. We are, of course, neglecting the effect of the other four room surfaces in this discussion. The sound pressure distribution of Fig. 1-7 results only from the two parallel end walls, A and B. Walls A and B are also resonant at whole number multiplies of this frequency. Figure 1-8 shows the sound pressure distribution at 2 × 28.25 = 56.5 Hz. The right and

left walls are another parallel pair. They are also resonant at a frequency of 1130/2L where L is the distance between them. They are also resonant at whole number multiplies of this frequency. The same is true of the ceiling and floor which constitute another resonant system of the same type. These are called axial modes because they are active along the axis of each pair of plane, parallel walls. The axial modal frequencies of the three axial sets are intertwined up through the audible spectrum.

If we assume that in the room of Figs. 1-7 and 1-8 the width is 16 feet 5 inches and the height is 14 feet 5 inches we can easily calculate the frequency of the lowest axial mode for the length, width, and height from Eq. 1-2. By multiplying each lowest frequency by 2, 3, 4, 5 . . . etc. the series for each can be determined. These frequencies of the axial resonances are plotted in Fig. 1-9(A), (B), and (C) for the three axes of the room and in Fig. 1-9(D) all frequencies are combined. In the latter we can see that the axial resonance frequencies are reasonably well distributed which is the result of a bit of prescience in optimizing the room proportions in advance. Reflecting on the opposite condi-

6

tion we note that in a cubical room the three families of frequencies would coincide, resulting in extra high response at these coincident frequencies but with wide gaps in between.

The three series of axial modal frequencies are the simple part, there is much more to this room resonance business. In addition to the axial modes there are the tangential modes which involve four surfaces of the room and the oblique modes that involve all six room surfaces. And, of course, there is a series of frequencies for each of the three families. The axial modes are the more powerful, but the tangential and oblique modes play an important part in filling in the spectrum between the axial modes which makes for a smoother room response. One of the secrets of designing good audio rooms, especially studios, control rooms, and listening rooms, is to select room proportions that distribute all three families of resonance frequencies as equally s possible, avoiding piling up of many modes at one frequency or in one narrow range of frequencies.

Experiment: The above room must be considered "acoustically small" because the

modal resonance frequencies are relatively far apart below about 300 Hz. By using Eq. 1-2: (a) what is the lowest resonance-supported frequency of a room having a smallest dimension of 10 ft? (b) what is the lowest frequency for a large auditorium having 100 ft as its smallest dimension?

1.5 BENDING SOUND WAVES

For this discussion we go outdoors. Let us assume an expert crew has been assigned the job of installing a high quality sound reinforcement system for a gig in an open field. The loudspeakers are carefully aimed to cover the audience. Environmental effects can move the loudspeaker beams up and down and sideways. For instance thermal gradients result when the air near the ground is warm and the air above is cold, a common condition after sundown. Sound travels faster in the warm air than in the cold and the result is a refraction effect which bends the beam upward as in Fig. 1-10(A). If the cooler air is near the ground and the warm air above the beam is bent

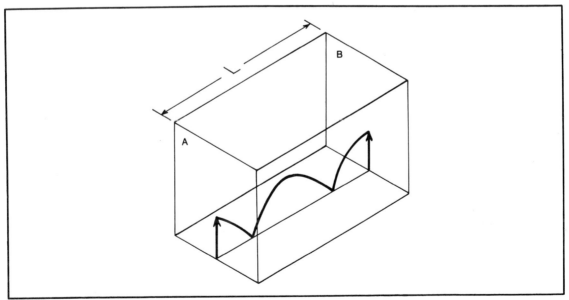

Fig. 1-8. The same space of Fig. 1-7 is also resonant at twice the frequency of the condition prevailing in Fig. 1-7. Resonances also occur at all whole number multiples of the basic frequency.

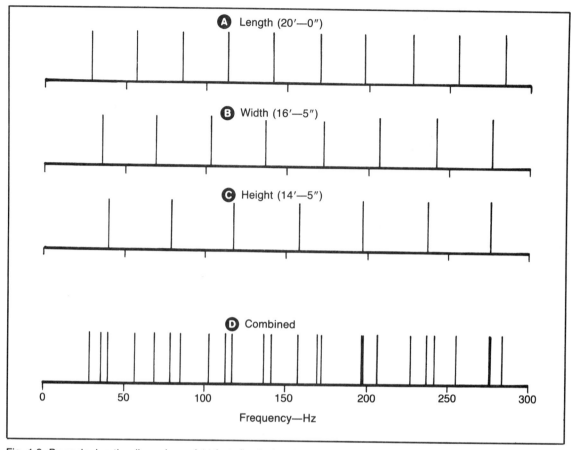

Fig. 1-9. By assigning the dimensions of 14 feet, five inches by 16 feet, five inches by 20 feet to the room of Fig. 1-7. resonance frequencies of all three pairs of opposing, plane, parallel walls can be calculated from Eq. 1-2. Those frequencies below 300 Hz for the length, width, and height of the room are shown in the top three plots. All three are combined in the bottom plot. The favorable distribution of these modal frequencies is the result of choosing favorable room proportions. These are the axial modes. Although not shown, tangential and oblique modes would also be present, tending to fill in the space between the axial modes and smoothing the room response in this way.

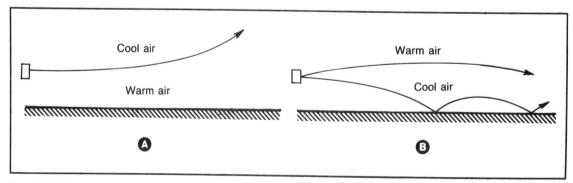

Fig. 1-10. The effects of vertical temperature gradients. (A) warm air below and cool air above refracts the sound upwards. (B) With warm air above and cool air below, sound is refracted downward.

downward as in Fig. 1-10(B). This condition results in sound carrying great distances and sometimes even results in dead spots at ground level. Thermal gradient effects may even be observed indoors. For example, gymnasiums that are used as auditoriums are often heated with ceiling mounted space heaters. Extreme temperature differences between floor and ceiling are often produced in such situations. A loudspeaker mounted at a height two thirds of the way up to the ceiling would have its beam bent downward by the temperature gradient. This effect might be great enough to reduce the sound level at the back seats substantially. Let us apply some numbers to this example. Let us take an extreme case in which the air temperature near the ceiling is 100 degrees F. and the air temperature near the floor is 60 degrees F. The speed of sound at 100 degrees is 1163 ft/sec and at 60 degrees is 1118 ft/sec, a difference of 45 ft/sec. This amounts, in more familiar terms, to a speed differential of about 31 miles/hr as compared to 762 mi/hr for 1118

ft/sec, a difference of about 4%. It would be a rather complicated problem in physics to trace out the bent path of the beam, but at least we see the possibility of temperature gradients explaining some of the unusual effects observed.

Wind can also affect sound transmission . After all, if the little air particles involved in passing a sound disturbance on its merry way are moving 30 mi/hr in the direction of sound travel, the sound is going to get there just that much faster. If the sound bucks a headwind, it is slowed down. With an outdoor sound reinforcement system, a cross wind can bend the loudspeaker beam as shown in Fig. 1-11A. A 20 mi/hr crosswind is the equivalent of 30 ft/sec. The not-to-scale vector diagram of Fig. 1-11B shows the 1130 ft/sec speed of sound traveling from the loudspeaker and the 30 ft/sec crosswind acting at right angles to it. The resultant diagonal arrow represents the resultant vector of the two speeds.

Another wind effect is caused by velocity gradients. If the wind velocity well above the ground

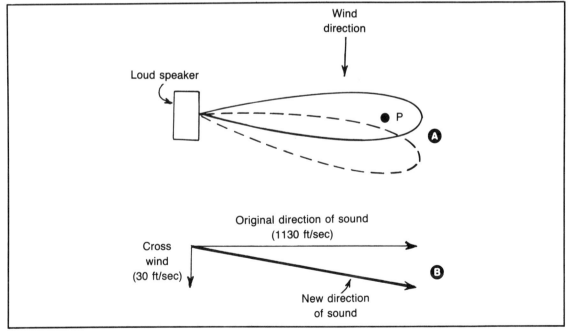

Fig. 1-11. Horizontal wind velocity gradient refracts sound horizontally. With a crosswind as indicated, an observer at 0 might experience a significant reduction in sound level from the loudspeaker due to the crosswind. The resultant direction of the loudspeaker beam would be the vector sum of the velocity of sound along the main axis of the loudspeaker and the wind velocity at right angles to it.

is 30 mi/hr, it will be much slower down close to the ground because of the friction and obstacles encountered. This could result in a loudspeaker beam aimed in the direction the wind is flowing being bent down toward the ground, similar to temperature effects.

1.6 SOUND WAVES AROUND CORNERS

The noise of traffic on freeways is becoming a problem to those living nearby. High concrete block walls are being built to protect the residences from the noise. If these walls were 100% effective, there would be no freeway noise behind them. Our common experience tells us that the noise levels behind the walls may be reduced, but not eliminated. Why? The answer is all wrapped up in an effect called diffraction. Refraction (examined in the previous section) sounds like diffraction, but we must keep the two effects separate in our minds because they are entirely different. If the wall height is great compared to the wavelength of the sound being considered, the wall is quite effective as a barrier. For the long wavelengths of low frequency sound, however, the wall is not large in comparison to the wavelength of sound. In Fig. 1-3

we see that the wavelength of 20 Hz sound is over 50 ft. At this frequency the usual wall is small compared to the wavelength of sound and the wall is not a very effective barrier. Low frequency sound is diffracted into the shadow zone behind the wall. The upper edge of the wall becomes a new source of sound, radiating into this shadow zone.

What does a freeway wall have to do with our sound systems? Well, diffraction enters into both. In Fig. 1-12 we can see the effect of a 3-foot cube of some solid substance placed between a sound source and a microphone. Amazingly enough, this cube acts as an acoustical amplifier as the sound pressure on the far side is greater than the incident sound pressure. The frequency response of this particular amplifier, however, is not very smooth as shown by the graph of Fig. 1-12. The diffraction around a sphere, however, is quite smooth once it reaches the +5 or +6 dB level. In fact, our heads are solid enough to create an amplification (by diffraction) of sound pressure at one ear of the sound falling on the opposite ear. Some of the wiggles in the measured response of loudspeakers are due to the diffraction of sound at the edges of the cabinet as shown in Fig. 1-13. These edges act as secon-

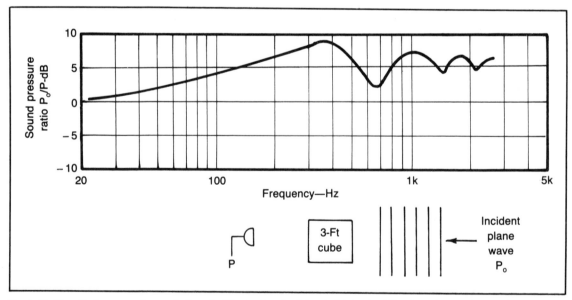

Fig. 1-12. The effect on sound transmission of a 3-foot cube of solid material due to diffraction. An actual acoustical amplification effect can be produced in this way (Adapted from Reference 1).

10

dary radiators of sound, which combines with the main sound radiated. The wiggles result from the delay associated with the longer path of the diffracted component as we shall see in the next section. If the loudspeaker is mounted flush with a baffle, the edges are eliminated along with their diffraction effects. We must be aware of the possibility of diffraction effects because they are everywhere, although normally of modest magnitude. When the manufacturers of sound absorbing materials have their products measured in reverberation chambers a standard 8 × 9 ft sample is laid on the floor. Absorption coefficients greater than 100% are regularly measured and the reason is that, because of edge diffraction, the sample appears acoustically larger than the physical dimensions.

1.7 COMBINING A WAVE WITH ITS OWN REFLECTION

The expression "comb filter" is becoming very common in audio literature and it is high time that it is widely recognized because its effects are everywhere. As the direct wave from a source falls on a microphone, the placement of physical objects nearby is usually such as to produce one or more

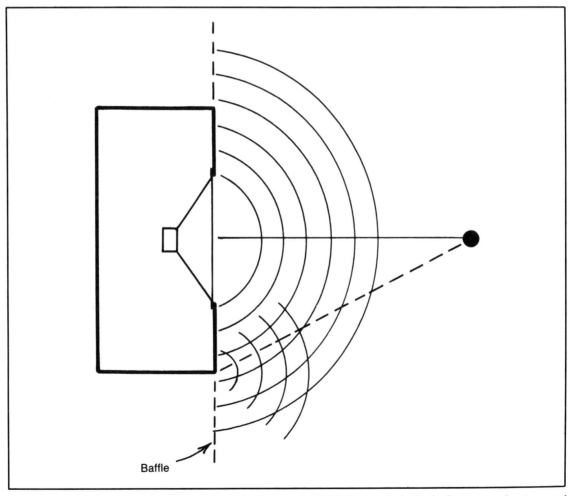

Baffle

Fig. 1-13. Diffraction of sound from the edges of the loudspeaker cabinet can put wiggles in the measured response of the loudspeaker due to combination of the direct wave with the diffracted waves.

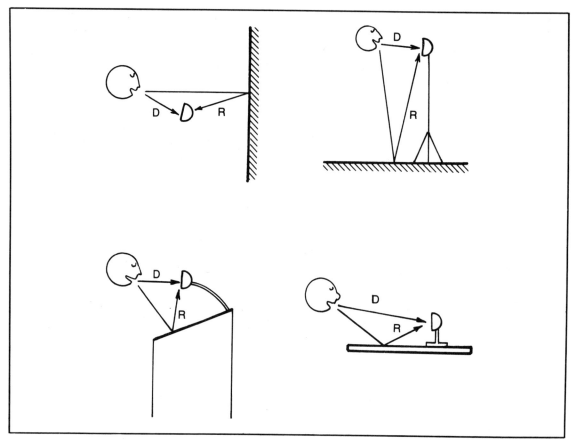

Fig. 1-14. Four of the numerous ways of creating coloration of sound due to acoustical comb-filter effects.

reflections that also fall on the microphone. These sound pressure signals are then combined acoustically and the microphone diaphragm is actuated according to their vector sum. That word "vector" is the secret of the whole effect, for it describes the relative timing of the several components. You see, the reflection invariably travels a longer path and comes to the microphone at some time slightly later than the direct component. The situations of Fig. 1-14 will stir common emotions in the breast of every hi-fi buff and audio engineer. These reflection paths vary in length. The longer ones are reasonably forgiving, but when the delays are under 10 milliseconds or so the reflections can degrade sound quality greatly. Acoustical comb filter effects are discussed in detail in another of the author's books (Ref. 2).

Experiment: Start your tape recorder and while you are speaking steadily into the microphone walk slowly toward a hard wall until your head and the microphone are close to the wall. Play back this selection and note the roughness of your voice when you get close to the wall.

References
1. Muller, G.G., R. Black, and T.E. Davis, 1938. "The Diffraction Produced by Cylindrical and Cubical Obstacles and by Circular and Square Plates," *Jour. Acous. Soc. Am.*, Vol. 10, No. 1, p. 1.
2. Everest, F. Alton, 1982. *The Master Handbook of Acoustics*, Chapter 5, "Acoustical Comb Filter Effects", TAB BOOKS Inc. Blue Ridge Summit, PA 17214.

Chapter 2

Basics of Electricity

ELECTRICITY AND SOUND ARE INSEPARABLY locked together in practical audio systems of all kinds. By means of various types of transducers (microphones, loudspeakers, etc.) sound disturbances in the air are changed to electrical signals, or electrical signals are changed to sound. It is therefore necessary that we have a working familiarity with electrical circuits. The person who does not have such a working knowledge is beset on every turn with mystery piled upon mystery. A sure way to become obsolete today is to adopt a superficial approach to some of these basic things. We shall cover the basics of electricity in this chapter, distinguishing it from electronics in the next chapter, which is dominated by circuits and solid-state devices.

2.1 ELECTROSTATICS

When electrostatics is mentioned, one can be excused if visions of cat's fur, hard rubber rods, pith balls, Wimshurst machines, and hair standing on end come to mind. These staples of the physics 101 lecture demonstrations and science fairs are today pushed into the background by other experiences closer to home. When I scoot out of the front vinyl-covered seat of our ancient Buick on a dry day with the car keys in hand, I have formed the habit of firmly gripping the ignition key and touching it to the door latch before swinging the door closed. Otherwise I receive a hefty shock. Like Pavlov's dogs, I learn in time. Or have you noticed how dust clings to the phonograph record? Or how hard it is to get the plastic bag open at the supermarket or how stikum tape seems to have a life of its own? One of the most convincing experiments in electrostatics is trying to throw one of those plastic peanuts used in packing into the waste basket. It might cling to the hand, or it might go in a big curve and stick to the outside of the wastebasket! The saddest event in the life of an audio person may be zapping a field-effect transistor (FET) or an expensive integrated circuit by a spark as it is being plugged into the socket.

We shall consider the electron theory of matter, but only briefly. The atoms making up all substances have a structure consisting of nuclei, intimately associated with positive charges of electricity, called protons, surrounded by some sort of cloud of negative charges of electricity called electrons. The positive and negative charges are normally in an electrically balanced state. The electrons are reasonably free to move about and may be actually removed from substances by such means as rubbing the hard rubber rod previously mentioned by a cat's fur (with or without the cat in it). The protons are relatively heavy and they account for most of the mass of the atom. The proton is some 1800 times heavier than the electron. Free electrons account for most electrical activity. If a body has an excess of electrons it is said to be negatively charged, and if it has a deficiency of electrons it is said to be positively charged. Many other basic components of matter, such as neutrons and positrons, have been found, but they play a minor role in electrical phenomena. We can say that all matter appears to be electrical in nature. When a rubber rod is rubbed with a cat's fur, electrical charges are not generated, in the true sense of the word, they are merely separated by the frictional effect.

2.2 ELECTRICAL POTENTIAL

Electric fields surround electrical charges and it takes work to move an electric charge in such a field. A force is required to move such a charge and the amount of work is determined by the product of the force and the distance through which the charge is moved. By definition, the electrical potential between two points A and B is the amount of work that must be done on a unit positive charge in moving it from A to B. Electrical potential is measured in volts.

2.3 ELECTRICAL CAPACITANCE

When two conductors are separated by a dielectric, a capacitor is formed. The unit of capacitance is the farad which is such a large unit that microfarads is more a size to our liking. Capacitance depends on the nature of the dielectric, the size of the plates, and the distance between the plates. In a later section, the rules for adding capacitors in series and parallel will be discussed.

2.4 ELECTRIC CURRENTS

If an electrical potential is maintained between points, an electric current will flow if the two points are connected by an electrical conductor. Thus we see that a current flow is composed of a flow of electrons to equalize the difference of potential. Here is a source of great confusion in many minds. By convention, the "flow" of electricity is from high (+) to low (−) potential in a conductor. The true nature of electrical current flow is not too well understood, but it has been established that a flow of current in metallic conductors is chiefly a drift of negatively charged electrons (−) moving from low potential to higher potential (+) in an electric field. In spite of the knowledge that electrons, which constitute current flow, really flow from low potential to higher potential, the convention wins out as far as everyday practice is concerned. In other words, we take the direction of current flow from the positive pole to the negative pole even though, way back in our minds, we know that electrons really go in the opposite direction. This is something one just has to remember and follow blindly. Figuring things out on the basis of electron flow will really confuse one.

2.5 ELECTROSTATIC DEVICES: ELECTRETS

The principles of electrostatics have been applied to microphones, loudspeakers, and earphones, yielding some of the highest quality transducers available. The condenser (or capacitance) microphone is a good example. Figure 2-1 will help us to understand how the condenser microphone works. The diaphragm and the backing plate are closely spaced. The backplate is maintained at a positive potential with respect to the diaphragm by a polarizing voltage, commonly 48 volts. The diaphragm and the backplate constitute a capacitor which varies in capacitance as the diaphragm moves in response to the sound pressure variations. With a constant polarizing voltage, the movement of the diaphragm results in a proportional signal voltage superimposed on the polarizing voltage. As

14

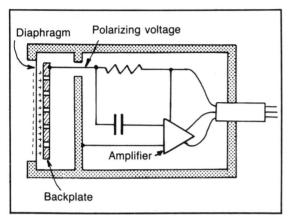

Fig. 2-1. Major features of a condenser microphone. A polarizing voltage (commonly 48 volts) charges the backing plate positively. The diaphragm forms the other plate of an air-dielectric condenser. Sound waves falling on the diaphragm cause it to move, which results in a signal voltage that is amplified.

shown in Fig. 2-1, this fluctuating signal voltage is applied to the input of an amplifier. Actually, this amplifier is more an impedance changing device than a gain device because the very high impedance of the condenser microphone is best reduced for the microphone cable run.

The electret microphone of Fig. 2-2 is similar in many ways to the standard condenser microphone. The difference lies in the method of polarization. Instead of the external polarizing voltage of the normal condenser microphone, the electret diaphragm is made of a dielectric material such as polyester or fluorocarbon. The diaphragm is very thin (typically 0.25 to 0.5 thousandth of an inch) and is coated with an optically thin metallic coating on one side. This diaphragm is then permanently charged by being heated and subjected to a high voltage field as it slowly cools. The polyester may be Mylar™ and the fluorocarbon may be Teflon™ (tradenames of E.I. du Pont de Nemours & Co., Inc.). Permanent charges on the electret of the order of 200 volts are possible. The question that invariably arises is, "How long will such charges be maintained?," because the sensitivity of the microphone is at stake. Tests made by Bell Labs indicate a 30 year life for fluorocarbon electrets without preconditioning and 1,000 years for those

properly aged and polyester electrets are even better!

Electrets have been known for over 50 years, but their widespread application in audio has taken place since about 1970 (Ref. 1). Electret microphones have many advantages over conventional condenser microphones: among them are (a) elimination of external bias voltage, (b) lower noise, (c) freedom from solid-borne noise due to low mass, (d) sensitivity independent of size and shape (e.g., hearing aids), and (e) adaptability to directional arrays. Electret microphones have turned out to be useful in a wide variety of basic scientific research applications. They can be made flat over 7 octaves (the ear covers about 10 octaves) and are especially useful in infrasonic (down to 0.001 Hz or one cycle every 17 minutes!) as well as ultrasonic applications (to 200 MHz in solids and liquids). An electret transducer detected infrasonic disturbances of the Saturn V rocket over 600 miles away.

Electrostatic earphones are far superior to the old magnetic type. They employ both the externally polarized and the self-polarized principles of operation. Figure 2-3 shows their general construction. The diaphragm is supported between two perforated fixed electrodes. The signal voltage is stepped up by a transformer and applied to the two fixed electrodes. The charges on these electrodes,

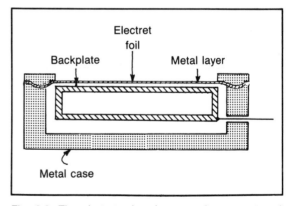

Fig. 2-2. The electret microphone requires no external polarizing voltage. The electret diaphragm of polyester or fluorocarbon material has a thin metallic coating on one side. By subjecting it to a high potential as it slowly cools the charge is retained indefinitely. In other respects the electret microphone is a normal condenser microphone.

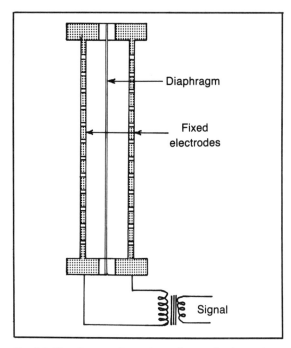

Fig. 2-3. The electrostatic earphones have a diaphragm fixed between two fixed electrodes. The charges on these electrodes, varying with the signal, cause the diaphragm to vibrate in a push-pull action. The diaphragm may be polarized as an electret or externally polarized.

varying with the signal, interact with the charge on the diaphragm causing the diaphragm to move in accordance with the signal. This diaphragm is very thin (2 to 4 microns thick) and is polarized either permanently, in electret form, or by an external polarizing voltage. A sort of push-pull action is imparted to the diaphragm. When the audio signal is positive on the left fixed electrode, it is at the same instant negative on the right fixed electrode. If the diaphragm is charged negatively, it is attracted to the left electrode as it is being repelled by the right electrode. In this way the diaphragm follows faithfully the audio voltage, transducing electrical variations to sound pressure variations. One of the problems with the old magnetic type of earphone is that the massive diaphragm results in poor transient response. Also they are plagued with breakup of vibrational modes of the diaphragm because the magnetic driving force is applied only to the center of the diaphragm. The electrostatic earphone

diaphragm has more of a piston action. Figure 2-4 is a photograph of commercially available electret headphones.

Electrostatic loudspeakers, while very expensive, offer important quality advantages (Fig. 2-5). One advantage is that of having a plane vibrating surface rather than a cone.

2.6 ELECTROMOTIVE FORCE

The electrical age was ushered in with wet cells of various kinds decorating the laboratories. A zinc plate and a copper plate immersed in a sulphuric acid solution was typical of such cells. If the copper electrode (the positive terminal) and the zinc (the negative terminal) are connected by an external conductor, a current will flow. The chemical action maintains a difference of potential between the two metal electrodes. Eventually the zinc will be consumed and require replacement. This voltaic cell sets up a potential difference between the two electrodes which is called the electromotive force or emf. Strictly speaking, there is a difference between the emf of the cell and the potential difference, even though both are measured in volts. If the measuring instrument draws any current, the measured potential difference will be lower than the emf. The only way the measured potential difference and the emf would be equal would be to use an electrostatic or other type of voltmeter which draws no current.

Wet cells went out with high-buttoned shoes and gates-ajar collars. The dry cell or dry battery is widely used today. The "dry" is a misnomer, it should be "moist." "Battery" implies several cells connected together but is also used to denote a single cell. The dry cell relies on chemical action to sort out the charges leading to a potential difference that can sustain a current flow in an external circuit, which can accomplish many useful things for us. The construction of a typical dry cell, whether C, D, penlite, or other, is shown in Fig. 2-6. The zinc case of the cell is the negative electrode (the cathode) and the carbon rod is the positive electrode (the anode). The electrolyte in one form of this cell is a mixture of powdered carbon and manganese dioxide moistened with am-

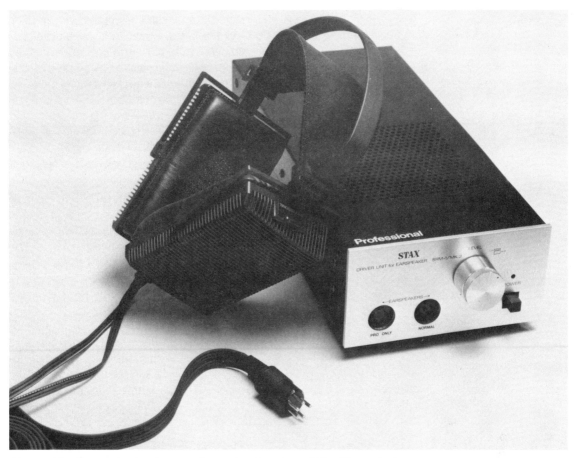

Fig. 2-4. The Stax professional earspeaker system (courtesy of Stax Kogyo, Inc.).

monium chloride. Such a cell produces an open circuit emf of 1.5 volts. The mercury cells produce an emf of 1.35 volts. As the cell delivers current the zinc is disintegrated and it is not rechargeable. For voltages greater than 1.5 volts (e.g., 9 V.) several cells are packaged together. These cells are not generators of electricity, but only separators of charges through chemical means, transforming chemical energy to electrical form.

2.7 ELECTROMAGNETICS

Rowland, a historical figure in electricity, proved conclusively that electric charges in motion constitute an electric current. By rotating a charged, insulated disk at a very high speed he ws able to detect a magnetic field. This established once and for all not only the idea that moving charges constitute a current flow but that the current flow is always accompanied by a magnetic field. Magnetic fields are everywhere about us. The earth is one huge magnet. The strange forms taken by the corona of the sun indicate that magnetic forces are at work there as well. We must be alert to the fact that no matter how minute the electric current, even if only a single unit charge is moving, a magnetic field is present.

The permanent magnet of Fig. 2-7 shows the magnetic lines of force in the time-honored way. If a piece of white paper were laid over this magnet and iron filings were scattered on the paper, the filings would line up along lines such as these. The

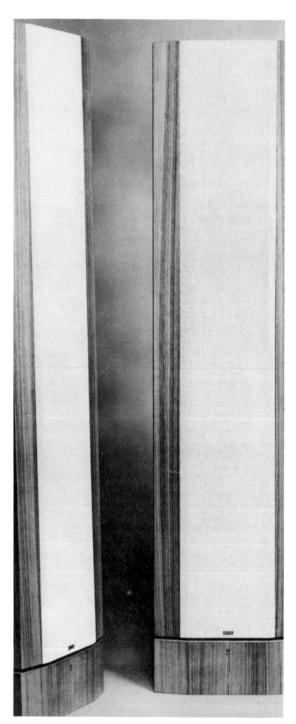

Fig. 2-5. The Stax electrostatic loudspeaker Model ULS-F83. (Courtesy Stax Kogyo, Inc.)

lines really show the direction of the magnetic field at various positions. These lines, often called flux lines, emanate from the north pole of the magnet and are completed through the south pole and the body of the magnet itself. Thus the magnetic circuit, in this case, involves the air path and the magnet itself in series. There is an analogy to *Ohm's law* applicable to magnetic circuits. It states that *magnetic flux* is equal to *magnetomotive force* divided by *reluctance*. Although we are not going to dwell upon magnetic circuits, some of these terms are familiar because of their application to loudspeaker drivers.

2.8 MAGNETIC EFFECTS OF STEADY CURRENTS

We have seen that a conductor carrying an electric current has a magnetic field associated with it. A handy rule to jog the memory on the direction of the flux around a conductor is the right hand rule of Fig. 2-8. By encircling the wire with the right hand and pointing the thumb in the direction the current is flowing, the fingers indicate the direction of the lines of force. This is called the right-hand screw rule. If this conductor carrying a current were placed in the magnetic field between the two fixed pole pieces of Fig. 2-9, a force due to the interaction of the two fields would act on the conductor in the direction of the arrow. The direction of current flow in the conductor is symbolized by another arrow, the tail feathers of which are the + sign as a direction of current flow away from the reader is indicated. The point of this arrow indicates current flow toward the reader.

Not to be confused with profane gestures, the left hand rule shown in Fig. 2-10 shows the relative directions of magnetic flux, current flow in the conductor, and the resultant force acting on the conductor.

2.9 MAGNETODYNAMICS

If, instead of the single conductor, a single loop of wire, such as in Fig. 2-11, were placed in the magnetic field, a torque would be produced. The current flowing in the coil goes away from the

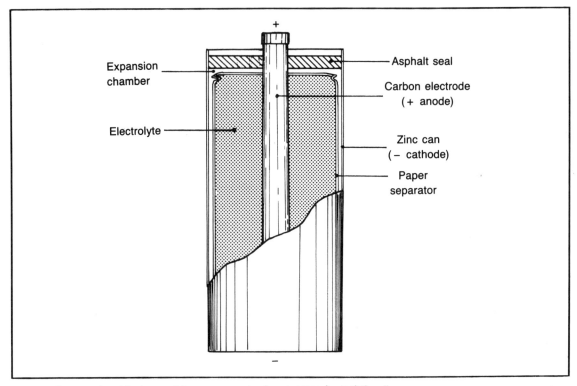

Expansion chamber

Electrolyte

+

Asphalt seal

Carbon electrode (+ anode)

Zinc can (– cathode)

Paper separator

–

Fig. 2-6. Constructional features of the common dry (more properly, moist) cell.

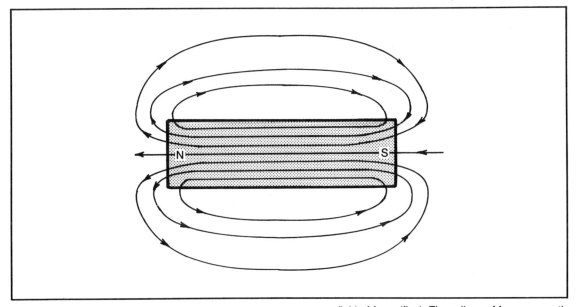

N   S

Fig. 2-7. The magnetomotive force of a permanent magnet creates a field of force (flux). These lines of force are partly in the metal of the magnet and partly in air.

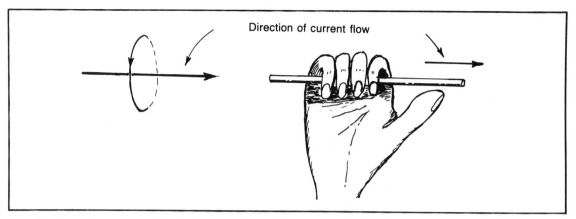

Fig. 2-8. The righthand screw rule helps to remember the direction of the lines of force when the direction of current flow in a conductor is known.

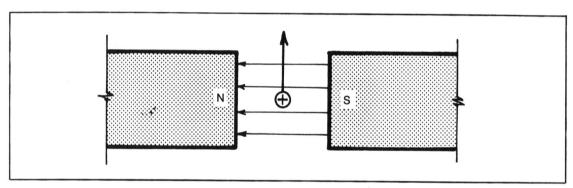

Fig. 2-9. A conductor carrying an electric current has a force acting on it when placed in a magnetic field. With the current flowing in the conductor away from the reader and with the magnetic field of the direction shown, the force on the conductor is downward.

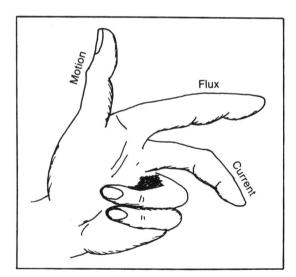

Fig. 2-10. The lefthand rule shows the relationship between the direction of current flow, the direction of magnetic flux, and the direction of the force acting on the conductor.

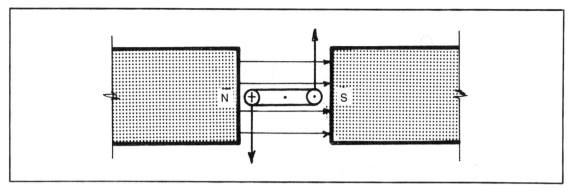

Fig. 2-11. A torque is produced when a single-turn loop of wire carrying a current is placed in a magnetic field.

observer in the left conductor and toward the observer in the right conductor. The force resulting from the interaction of the two magnetic fields acts downward on the left part of the single-turn coil and upward on the right part creating a torque tending to rotate the coil around its center. With some carefully timed switching of the direction of the current flowing in the coil (commutating), we have an electric motor.

We have seen that a side thrust results if a conductor carrying a current is placed in a magnetic field. The converse of this is that a conductor moved in a magnetic field will have a current induced in the conductor. The direction of flow of this induced current is the opposite to that of the motor action of Fig. 2-9. In Fig. 2-12, if the conductor is moved upward through the magnetic flux, the current induced in the conductor will flow in a direc-

tion away from the observer, into the page. The right hand generator rule applies in this case as shown in Fig. 2-13, again showing the relationship of the directions of current flow, magnetic flux, and motion for the generator case. Here again, much like Fig. 2-11, a dc electric generator can be built by rotating a coil of wire in a magnetic field assisted by some timely switching (commutating).

2.10 DC CIRCUITS

There seems to be a law of nature that the results of any activity are directly proportional to the amount of effort expended and inversely proportional to the opposition encountered. So it is with electricity. This is an excellent description of Ohms's Law. We have seen that a potential difference between two points will cause a current to

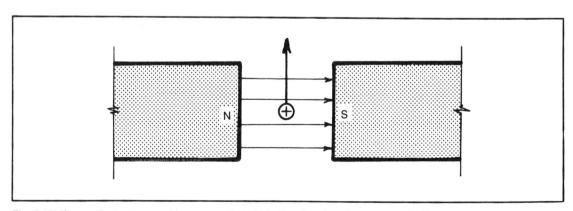

Fig. 2-12. If a conductor is moved in a magnetic field in the direction shown, an emf will be induced in the conductor tending to make current flow in the conductor away from the reader.

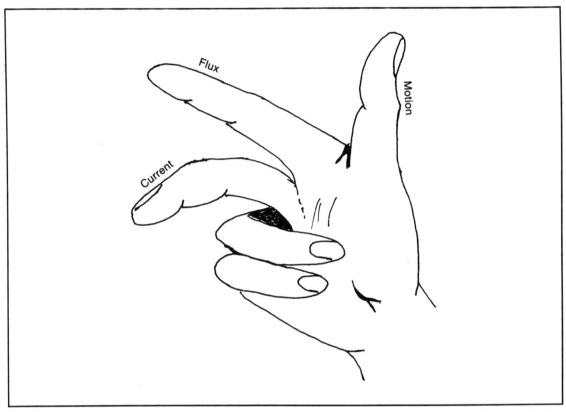

Fig. 2-13. The righthand generator rule shows the relationship between the direction of the magnetic field, the direction of movement of the conductor, and the direction of the induced current.

flow to equalize that potential difference if a conducting path is provided. In Fig. 2-14 we see a resistance with a current of I amperes flowing through it. A potential drop of V volts occurs across this resistance. The relationship between the potential difference in volts, current flow in amperes, and resistance in ohms is expressed in Ohm's Law. Three forms of this simple relationship are shown in Fig. 2-14. These are, of course, three forms of the very same expression, the form being used that best fits the particular knowns and unknowns in the problem at hand. Let us say that the current flowing is I = 2 amperes and that the resistance has a value of 10 ohms. What is the potential drop across the resistance? The V = IR expression is selected because it is V that is unknown. By substituting, V = (2) (10) = 20 volts. Now that all three values are known, we can test the consistency of the three expressions: I = V/R = 20/10 = 2 amperes, R = V/I = 20/2 = 10 ohms and V = IR = (2) (10) = 20 volts.

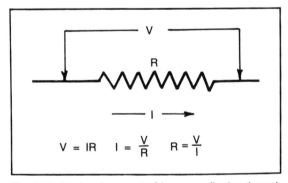

$$V = IR \quad I = \frac{V}{R} \quad R = \frac{V}{I}$$

Fig. 2-14. An electric current of *I* amperes flowing through a resistance of *R* ohms causes a voltage drop across the resistance of V = IR volts. The three forms of Ohm's Law are shown.

Figure 2-15 forces us once more to distinguish between emf (electromotive force) and difference in potential. In this circuit is a battery with an external resistance connected across it. By placing an ammeter in the circuit we find that a current of I amperes flows. This current, flowing in a simple series circuit, flows through both the battery and the resistance. If the battery voltage were measured before the resistance was connected and that measurement was made with a voltmeter which drew no current itself (such as an electrostatic voltmeter) the measurement would yield the true emf of the battery. As soon as a current flows through the battery, however, the voltage at its terminals would not be the emf because all batteries have an internal resistance and a current flowing would cause a voltage drop to occur across this battery resistance. The true emf of the battery, E, is equal to the sum of the voltage drop across the resistance and the voltage drop across the internal resistance of the battery.

There will be much further consideration of this principle in later chapters. The battery in this case is the source and it has an internal resistance. The resistance can be considered as the load the source works into. It is important in many applications to consider the *impedance* of the source as well as the impedance of the load, but we are getting ahead of ourselves as we have not yet discussed impedance.

2.11 RESISTANCES IN SERIES

In Fig. 2-16 three resistances are connected in series. The current flowing in the circuit flows through all three elements of the circuit. The voltage applied to the circuit is equal to the sum of the three potential drops. The current that flows is equal to the applied voltage divided by the sum of the three resistances. Because the same current flows through all of the resistances of a series circuit, the total resistance is simply the sum of the individual resistances.

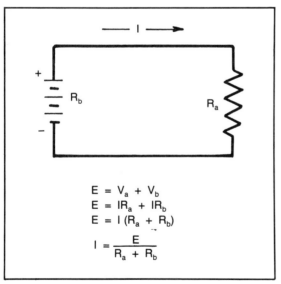

$$E = V_a + V_b$$
$$E = IR_a + IR_b$$
$$E = I(R_a + R_b)$$
$$I = \frac{E}{R_a + R_b}$$

Fig. 2-15. If the voltage of the battery is measured before the resistor is connected across it, and this voltmeter is, say, an electrostatic voltmeter, which draws no current, the true emf of the battery will be obtained. Connecting the resistor across the battery causes a current to flow. This current reduces the voltage at the battery terminals because of the voltage drop across the inevitable internal resistance of the battery.

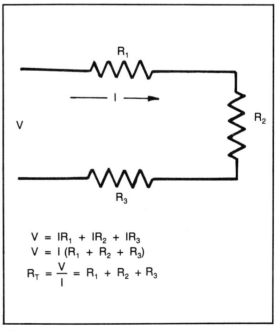

$$V = IR_1 + IR_2 + IR_3$$
$$V = I(R_1 + R_2 + R_3)$$
$$R_T = \frac{V}{I} = R_1 + R_2 + R_3$$

Fig. 2-16. A voltage applied to three resistors in series is equal to the sum of the voltage drops across the three resistors. From this we conclude that the total resistance of resistors in series is the sum of the individual resistances.

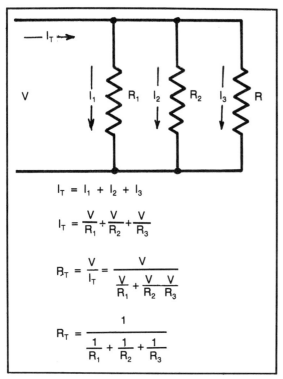

$$I_T = I_1 + I_2 + I_3$$

$$I_T = \frac{V}{R_1} + \frac{V}{R_2} + \frac{V}{R_3}$$

$$R_T = \frac{V}{I_T} = \frac{V}{\dfrac{V}{R_1} + \dfrac{V}{R_2} \dfrac{V}{R_3}}$$

$$R_T = \frac{1}{\dfrac{1}{R_1} + \dfrac{1}{R_2} + \dfrac{1}{R_3}}$$

Fig. 2-17. In the case of resistors in parallel, it is the applied voltage that is common to all the resistors. From this it can be determined that the total resistance of resistors in parallel is the reciprocal of the sum of the reciprocals.

2.12 RESISTANCES IN PARALLEL

The case of resistances in parallel is illustrated in Fig. 2-17. In this case the same current most assuredly does not flow through all the resistances. The current in the supply line branches into three components and joins together again for the return. The parameter that is common to all three resistances in the parallel case is that the voltage V is the same across each resistance. The current flowing in each resistance, according to Ohm's law, is the voltage divided by the value of resistance and each branch of the circuit would have a different current flowing in it if the value of the resistances are different. The total combined resistance of the three resistors in parallel is found by taking the reciprocal of the sum of the reciprocals as shown in the last expression of Fig. 2-17. Reciprocals are messy to do by hand, but they are easy with the

1/X button on the hand-held calculator. As an exercise, let us find the combined resistance of 150 ohms, 500 ohms, and 96 ohms connected in parallel. The steps are as follows on the simplest calculator: punch in 150 and hit the 1/X button which gives 0.00666666 and store this. Punch in 500, the reciprocal of this is 0.002, so add this to the value in memory. Punch in 96, the reciprocal of which is 0.0104167, add to that in memory. Recalling the sum of these three reciprocals from memory gives 0.0190833 and the reciprocal of this, the answer, is 52.40 ohms. In other words, the three paralleled resistances act, as far as the external part of the circuit is concerned, as though they are a single resistance of 52.40 ohms.

2.13 RESISTANCE NETWORKS

We shall be considering circuits of many resistances connected in all sorts of ways to form impedance matching "pads," or networks, as well as networks to attenuate the signal a known amount without upsetting the circuits. Figure 2-18 shows a historically significant Wheatstone Bridge circuit that is very much alive and well today used in measuring resistance, capacitance, and inductance.

There are some very handy rules for analyzing resistance networks of any degree of complexity. The first is called *Kirchhoff's Point Law*. Taking the top corner of the Wheatstone bridge circuit of Fig. 2-18, this law simply states that at this or at any other branching point of a network the total current entering the point is equal to the total current leaving that point. One can assume directions of current flow and if the assumption is wrong, the answer will come out with a minus sign. The second is called *Kirchhoff's Loop Law* which says that the voltage drops around any closed path are equal to zero. With these two laws, applied diligently and correctly, complex networks can be solved. But we must move on as we are not in the business of solving complex networks right now, only interested in seeing how all these things hold together for a better view of networks as a whole.

2.14 ELECTRICAL POWER

Power in electrical circuits is measured in

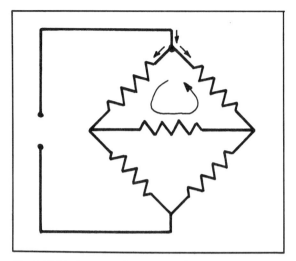

Fig. 2-18. Resistors may be connected into networks of many types. This is the Wheatstone Bridge circuit commonly used to measure R, L, and C values. Such networks can be solved by application of Kirchhoff's Laws.

watts. In dc circuits power is simply the product of the voltage applied to a circuit and the current flowing in that circuit. A voltage of 9 volts applied to a resistor of 180 ohms causes a current of 0.05 amperes or 50 milliamperes to flow. The power dissipated in the resistor is then EI = (9) (0.05) = 0.45 watt.

The same general relationship holds for ac circuits, except instantaneous values of power may be found by multiplying instantaneous values of voltage by the corresponding instantaneous values of current. Practically speaking, this does not help us very much because our meter readings in ac circuits usually give us rms values, not instantaneous. To calculate power in ac circuits the angular relationship between voltage and current must be taken into consideration. Power in ac circuits may be found from:

$$\text{Power} = E\ I\ \text{Cos}\ \Theta \qquad \textbf{Eq. 2-1.}$$

where

Power =	in watts
E =	rms voltage, volts
I =	rms current, amperes
Θ =	angle between voltage and current
cos Θ =	power factor

It is interesting to note that the cosine of 90 degrees equals zero. This means that a pure inductance or a pure capacitance consumes no power. In practical circuits, however, some resistance is always present for work to be done. Perhaps you have noticed large capacitors perched atop power poles. If there are many motors on a line, a heavy lagging current will be drawn. The power company hangs these capacitors across the circuit to bring the current more into phase for more efficient use of their lines and other equipment. This is called power factor correction.

2.15 MAGNETIC FIELDS

We have seen that an electrical current flowing in a conductor causes a magnetic field to be set up around it. We have also learned that a conductor moving in a magnetic field has an emf induced in it. The reverse action of a changing magnetic flux also induces a voltage in a conductor. This induced voltage (called the emf of self-induction) is always in a direction to oppose the change. This opposing effect is present (although slightly) even in a short, straight piece of wire but is much greater in a coil of wire having many turns such as shown in Fig. 2-19A. Many turns of wires are wound on a cardboard or other non-metallic form. The magnetic flux of a single turn is indicated, and, by the right hand screw rule, we even know the direction. The same current flows through all the turns and the magnetic field of each turn adds to that of the others resulting in the composite field of the air-core coil.

In Fig. 2-19B a core of soft iron or other magnetic material is placed in the coil. This results in a much more intense magnetic field. With the same current flowing in the identical coils of Fig. 2-1A and 2-19B the same magnetomotive force prevails. The amount of magnetic flux resulting depends upon the opposition encountered. With the air core of Fig. 2-19A, the opposition is greater than with the soft iron core of Fig. 2-19B, hence the magnetic flux density is greater in the latter.

2.16 BACK EMF IN INDUCTORS

Lest an important detail be overlooked, let us repeat the idea that an emf induced in a conductor by a magnetic field by cutting lines of force (either by moving the conductor or the field) is always in the direction to oppose the change. In Fig. 2-19A the magnetic field around one of the turns induces a voltage in other turns as it changes. As the flux

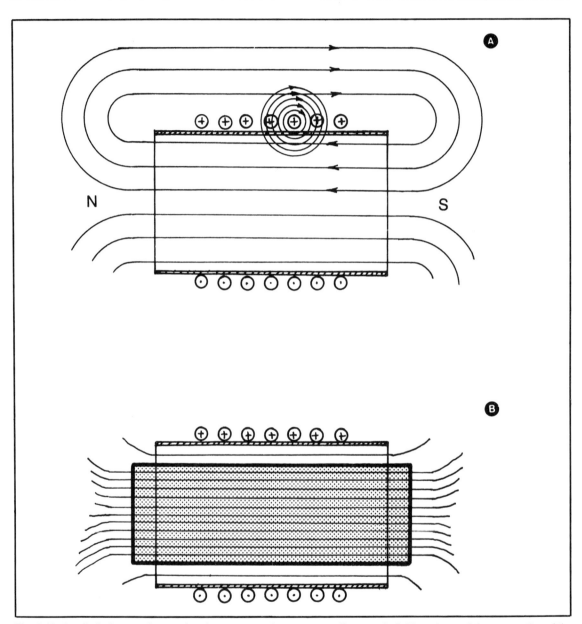

Fig. 2-19. A coil of wire carrying an electric current produces an overall magnetic field made up of the summation of the magnetic fields produced around each wire. The magnetic form of ''Ohm's Law'' states that the lower the opposition to the magnetic flux, with a given magnetomotive force, the greater the flux produced. Therefore, introducing a soft iron core results in a denser magnetic flux.

increases, this voltage is induced in one direction and as it decreases the sign of the induced voltage reverses. This back emf can be compared to a storage battery being charged. The potential difference of the battery charger must be great enough to overcome the opposing emf of the storage battery and have a bit more to force charging current through the internal resistance of the battery.

2.17 ALTERNATING CURRENT

The concept of direct current is easily grasped, flowing steadily in one direction like water in a garden hose. The concept of alternating current is a bit more opaque. How is it possible to do useful work with electric current that can't make up its mind which direction to flow? Doesn't current flowing in one direction half the time and half the time in the opposite direction cancel out any worthwhile effect? These are quite logical subliminal suspicions in the mind of the novice. The fact is that current creates an instantaneous voltage drop across a resistor directly proportional to the instantaneous current flowing. The current flowing in this resistor also causes it to heat up. In like manner, alternating current generators and motors are constructed so that useful work is done. First, let us look at the alternating current generator.

A highly simplified alternating current generator is shown in Fig. 2-20. It consists of a single turn of wire arranged with slip rings and brushes so that contact with the single turn is maintained as it is rotated. This single turn of wire is rotated in a magnetic field produced by a permanent magnet. As we saw in Section 2.9, moving a conductor in a magnetic field induces a voltage in it. This single turn generates a voltage that is proportional to the rate at which the flux lines are cut. This means that if the single turn were stationary, as shown in Fig. 2-20, no voltage would be induced in it at all. To examine what happens to this single turn of wire during one revolution, we shall imagine that we are taking instantaneous voltmeter readings at intervals during the single revolution while the single turn of wire is moving constantly.

At the 0 degree position both the top and bottom parts of the single turn are traveling parallel to the flux lines, hence, zero voltage is induced in the turn of wire. At the 45 degree position both sides of the single turn are cutting flux lines. Application of the right-hand generator rule of Fig. 2-13 discloses that the direction of conventional current flow is as indicated by the arrow head and point, toward the reader in the top conductor, away from the reader in the bottom conductor. As the conductors are cutting the flux lines at an angle, the magnitude of the voltage induced is less than that at the 90 degree position where the conductors are cutting lines at right angles. From 180 to 315 degree positions, what was the top conductor is now on the bottom and the polarity of the voltage induced has reversed. A plot of the induced voltages is shown at the bottom of Fig. 2-20. One cycle of alternating voltage has been generated as the single turn has made one revolution. We now see the intimate relationship between a wire loop rotating in a uniform magnetic field and the sine wave of induced voltage. The sine wave is also a manifestation of simple harmonic motion, such as that which a weight on a rubber band exhibits, or the sound wave generated by the back and forth movement of a loudspeaker diaphragm.

The simple generator of Fig. 2-20 has all sorts of possibilities. For instance, if the coil being rotated had many turns, the voltage induced in the individual turns would be summed, resulting in a higher voltage output. If two such coils were mounted 90 degrees to each other and rotated, two cycles of sine wave would be generated at each revolution or, stated differently, the frequency would be doubled.

The concept of frequency is probably well understood by most readers. However, for those who may be a bit hazy on the subject Fig. 2-21 has been prepared. Figure 2-21A shows a sine wave with a period of 0.10 second, i.e. one cycle is completed in this time. If 0.10 is more properly taken to be seconds/cycle rather than simply seconds, the reciprocal of 0.10 seconds per cycle is 1/0.10 = 10 cycles per second, which is a unit of frequency. Frequency is generally a more useful form than period and frequency is measured in cycles per second or

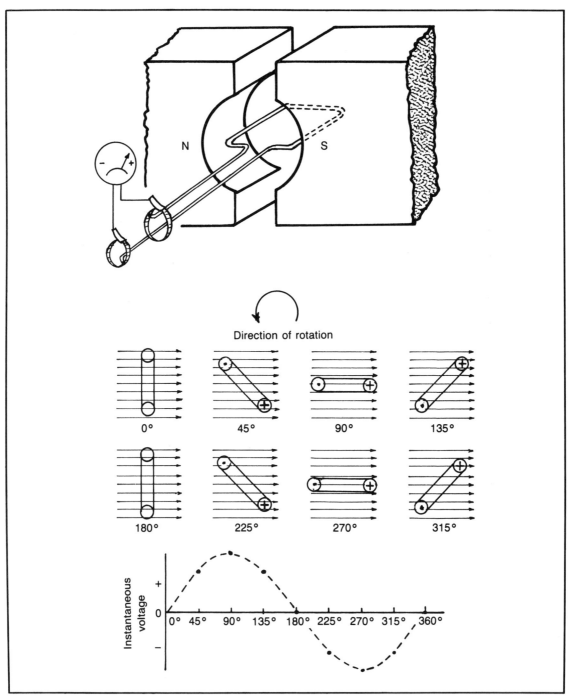

Fig. 2-20. A highly simplified electrical generator composed of a single turn loop of wire rotating in a magnetic field. The slip-ring arrangement makes possible continuous contact with the loop irrespective of its position. Instantaneous voltages induced at various positions of the loop are plotted to form the sine wave. This is a generator of alternating current. Multiple coils and a commutating (switching) system is required for a dc generator.

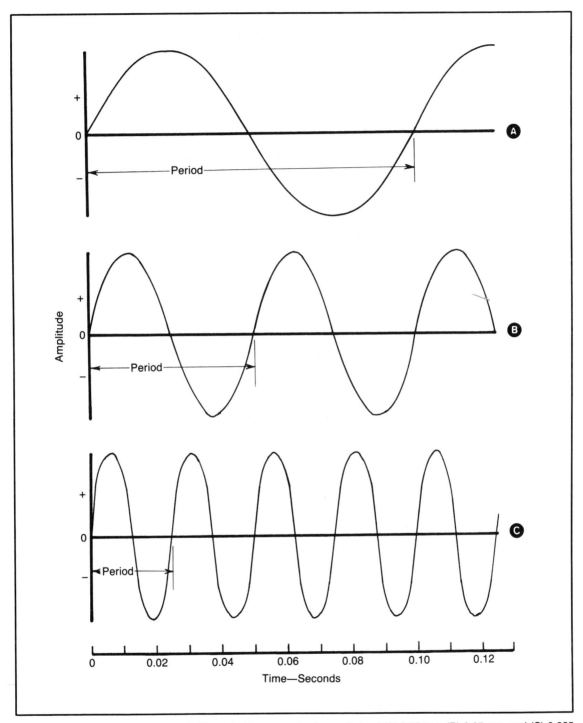

Fig. 2-21. The concept of frequency is illustrated by waves having periods of (A) 0.10 sec, (B) 0.05 sec, and (C) 0.025 sec. These translate to frequencies of (A) 10 Hz, (B) 20 Hz, and (C) 40 Hz.

Hertz. In Fig. 2-21B a sine wave with a period of 0.05 second is portrayed. As the period is half that of (A), its frequency is doubled: 1/0.05 = 20 Hz. A third example is given in Fig. 2-21C of a sine wave with a period of 0.025 second, which can be translated to the more familiar frequency form by taking the reciprocal: 1/0.025 = 40 Hz.

2.18 SINE TERMINOLOGY

In measuring voltage or current with commonly available instruments it is important to know what type of instrument is being used because different types of instruments respond differently to ac. The sine wave of Fig. 2-22 will serve to illustrate this. If a cathode-ray oscilloscope shows a wave like this figure, it is evident that the easiest thing to read off would be the peak or the peak-to-peak value. The ac voltmeter in your test set is probably a dc instrument equipped with a rectifier that changes the ac voltage with its positive and negative excursions to positive excursions only. The meter then reads the average value of these positive pulses. However, we usually are interested in the effective or rms value so the voltmeter is probably calibrated in terms of rms values. So things are really mixed up. If you desire the true rms value, and the wave

being measured in a sine wave, there is no problem for the reading will be reasonably accurate. But the rms calibration holds only for sine waves and is inaccurate for any periodic wave other than the sine wave.

The rms designation stands for *root-mean-square*. Referring to Fig. 2-21A, let us find the rms value of this sine wave. First, take the ordinate (height) readings for each 0.005 second time interval for both the positive and negative portions of the cycle. Next, square each ordinate reading. Then add up all the squares and take the square root of the sum and you have the rms value of this particular wave. This is exactly what root-mean-square means. It is significant because it is the effective value. One ampere of ac flowing through a resistor heats the resistor exactly the same as one ampere of dc. In calculating power in ac circuits, the rms value of current must be used.

In addition to peak and peak-to-peak values, Fig. 2-22 shows the effective and average relationship as well. For the sine wave these are all interrelated according to the following:

$$\text{rms} = (0.707)\,(\text{peak})$$
$$\text{rms} = (1.1)\,(\text{average})$$

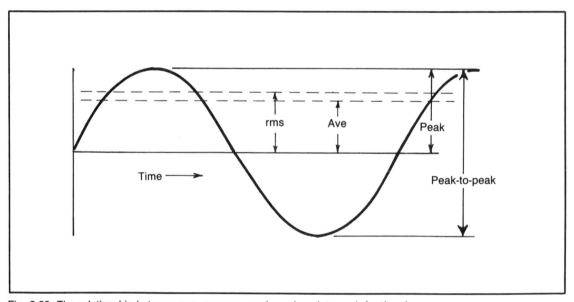

Fig. 2-22. The relationship between rms, average, peak, and peak-to-peak for the sine wave.

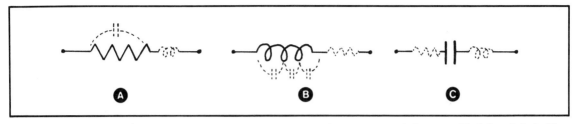

Fig. 2-23. There is no such thing as a pure resistance, pure capacitance, or pure inductance. Each is polluted with a little bit of the other two. Fortunately, at audio frequencies these stray effects may usually be neglected.

peak = (1.414) (rms)
peak = (1.57) (average)

2.19 BUILDING BLOCKS OF ALL CIRCUITS

We have studied R, L, and C. R is resistance in ohms. L is the inductor and its inductance is measured in henrys. C is the capacitor whose capacitance is measured in farads or microfarads.

There is no such thing as a pure resistance, inductance, or capacitance, each has a little of the other two in it as shown in Fig. 2-23. For example, every resistor has a point-to-point difference of potential in it as a current flows through it and this means a bit of distributed capacitance. Further, we have learned that a magnetic field springs to life whenever charges move (current flows). Every inductor has some resistance in the wires making up the inductor and these wires will be at different potentials, which means that a capacitance is formed. The capacitor also has resistance and inductance as well as capacitance. At radio frequencies the tiny amount of capacitance and inductance in a resistor, the resistance and capacitance of an inductor, or the resistance and inductance of a capacitor can have major consequences. At audio frequencies, however, we ordinarily do not have to worry about the incidental stray effects.

2.20 REACTIVE ELEMENTS

Alternating current problems would be a cinch if we had only resistance to deal with. Inductance and capacitance tend to complicate our lives and there is no escaping them. Nor is there any need to fear them if a few basic principles are mastered early in the game. Figure 2-24 compares the different way R, L, and C act in a circuit. The ac voltage E is applied to a resistance in Fig. 2-24A, the current I that flows is in phase with the applied voltage. That is, the current starts at zero with the voltage, reaches a peak the same time as the voltage, goes through the next zero as the voltage does, etc. The time relationships of the two are identical.

In Fig. 2-24B we have the same ac voltage applied to a capacitor. As the voltage is going through zero, its rate of change is maximum and the charges (current) flowing into the capacitor is maximum. When the voltage is maximum, its rate of change is zero as its direction is changed and at this point the charges flowing into the capacitor would be zero. Following through other parts of the cycle we find that the current into the capacitor is maximum when the voltage is going through zero (maximum rate of change) and the current into the capacitor is zero when the voltage is maximum (rate of change is zero). We note that the ac current in a capacitive circuit leads the voltage by 90 degrees. The capacitor acts as an opposition to flow in what is called capacitive reactance, which is measured in ohms.

The inductive circuit of Fig. 2-24C also has current flow out of phase with the applied voltage. Remember induced voltage? When the current flowing is changing at a maximum rate, the voltage is at a maximum and when the current rate of change is zero (as it goes through a peak) the induced voltage (equal to the applied voltage) is zero. Thus we see that the current lags the applied voltage by 90 degrees in the inductive circuit. Inductive reactance is an opposition to the flow of current as is capacitive reactance and it also is measured in ohms.

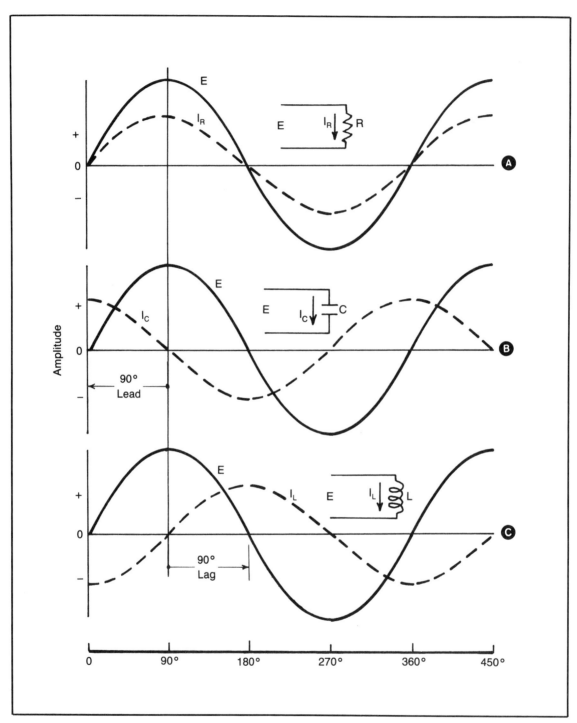

Fig. 2-24. Taking voltage as the reference, current through a resistance is in-phase with the voltage, current through a capacitance leads the voltage by 90 degrees, and current through an inductance lags the voltage by 90 degrees.

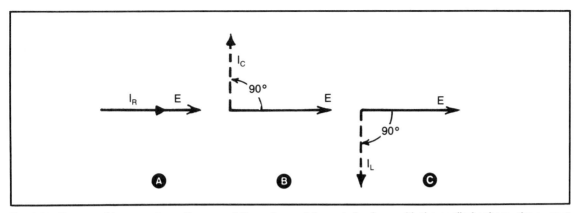

Fig. 2-25. Expressed in vector form, the current through a resistance is in-phase with the applied voltage, the current through a capacitance leads the applied voltage by 90 degrees, and the current through an inductance lags the applied voltage by 90 degrees.

The above discussion involves degrees, but these angles are plotted horizontally in what may seem to be a bit unnatural to some readers. The three sketches of Fig. 2-25 treat angles in the more traditional polar form. We take the applied voltage as the basis for these sketches for, after all, it is the common element in the three circuits of Fig. 2-24. In Fig. 2-25A, representing current flow in a resistor, the current is in phase with the applied voltage and this representation is the exact equivalent of Fig. 2-24A. In Fig. 2-25B the capacitive current leads the voltage by 90 degrees, taking counter-clockwise rotation as positive. This is the vector equivalent of Fig. 2-24B. In like manner, the inductive current of Fig. 2-25C lags the reference voltage vector by 90 degrees and this is the equivalent of Fig. 2-24C.

2.21 VECTORS AND IMPEDANCE

We have now seen the effect of inductance and capacitance in a circuit carrying alternating current. A phase angle is introduced and as long as it is pure capacitance and pure inductance, the phase angle is 90 degrees. Taking the vector diagrams of Fig. 2-25 and neglecting a few intermediate steps in the interest of simplification, we arrive at the impedance diagrams of Fig. 2-26. The components of impedance are resistance and reactance, and reactance comes in two forms, inductive and capacitive, all three measured in ohms. The two reactances impede the flow of current only when it changes, whether it be a transient change or whether it is constantly changing as in an alternating current. For the alternating current case, inductive reactance is:

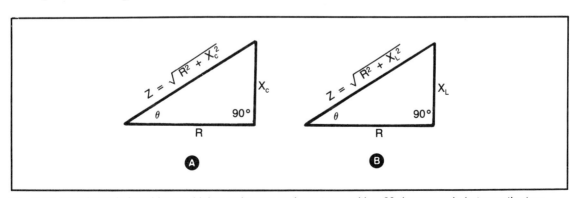

Fig. 2-26. Impedance is found by combining resistance and reactance with a 90 degree angle between the two.

$$X_L = 2\Pi fL \qquad \textbf{Eq. 2-2}$$

and capacitive reactance is:

$$X_C = 1/(2\Pi fC) \qquad \textbf{Eq. 2-3}$$

where

X_L = inductive reactance, ohms

X_C = capacitive reactance, ohms

f = frequency, hertz

L = inductance, henrys

C = CAPACITANCE, farads

Once the reactances are calculated from Equations 2-2 and 2-3 we are in a position to compute impedance by reference to Fig. 2-26. In Fig. 2-26A the right angle relationship between R and X makes possible solving the triangle with the familiar rule, "the square on the hypotenuse is equal to the sum of the squares on the other two sides." Resistance and inductive reactance is similarly related in Fig. 2-26B. There is always a 90 degree relationship between resistance and pure reactance but the angle

Θ varies as R and X varies. This angle is called the phase angle, the angle between the applied voltage and the current flowing in the circuit.

As an example, let us assume a resistance of 100 ohms connected in series with a capacitor having a capacitance of 1 microfarad and we are interested in what happens at 1,000 Hz. The capacitive reactance from Eq. 2-3 is: $1/[(2)\,(\Pi)\,(1,000)\,(1 \times 10)] = 159$ ohms. The impedance of the combination is then:

$$Z = \sqrt{100^2 + 159^2} = 187.8 \text{ ohms} \qquad \textbf{Eq. 2-4}$$

2.22 RLC CIRCUITS

Leaving the mathematical approach, let us inspect a real circuit composed of a resistance and an inductance in series as shown in Fig. 2-27A. A voltage E is applied to this circuit. A perfect voltmeter (i.e., one having infinite internal impedance, which takes no current to operate it) is connected across the resistance, another across the inductance, and a third across both of them. It is evident that the voltage measured by V is equal to the sum of V_R and V_L. But there is this 90 degree

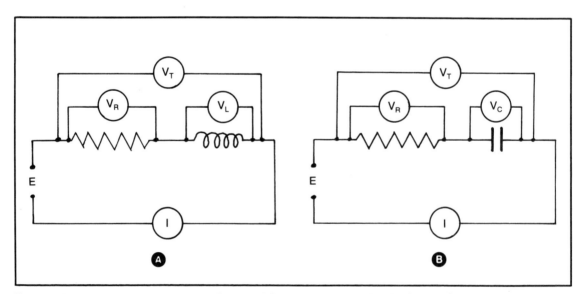

Fig. 2-27. The voltmeter reading across the RL or the RC combination is not the simple sum of the separate voltage read across the individual elements because of the 90 degree phase shift in the reactive elements.

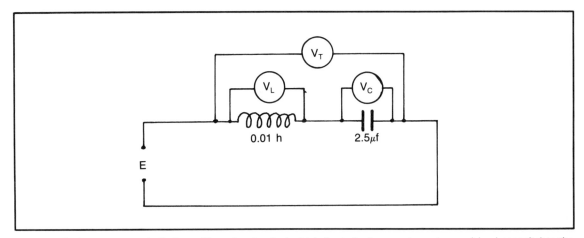

Fig. 2-28. Series resonance is that condition of a circuit at which the inductive reactance is equal (and opposite) to the capacitive reactance. Maximum current will flow at series resonance.

angle between V_R and V_L which the voltmeters do not show. V_T is not the simple arithmetic sum of V_R and V_L but the vector sum as shown in Fig. 2-26B. The series circuit of a resistance and a capacitance shown in Fig. 2-27B acts the same way, except that the current flowing leads the voltage applied. There is a right angle relationship between V_R and V_C.

2.23 SERIES RESONANCE

When an inductance and a capacitance are connected in series, as in Fig. 2-28, some interesting things happen. The capacitive reactance decreases as the frequency is increased while the inductive reactance increases with frequency as shown in Fig. 2-29. For an inductance of 10 millihenrys and a capacitance of 2.5 microfarads the reactances are equal at about 1,000 Hz. They are not only equal, but they are of opposite sign, one tending to cancel the other. This creates what is called a resonance condition. At this frequency of 1,000 Hz the impedance of the series circuit of Fig. 2-28 is zero if there is no resistance in the circuit. Of course, there are no perfect inductors or capacitors, so there would be some resistance which would be the only thing limiting current at this resonance frequency. We conclude, then, that with series resonance, the impedance of the circuit is minimum at resonance.

2.24 PARALLEL RESONANCE

In Fig. 2-30 the same 10 millihenry inductance and 2.5 microfarad capacitance are connected in parallel. Again they come into a resonance condition at 1,000 Hz, but quite different things happen. Below resonance the inductive branch has a low reactance, hence it will draw a large, lagging current. At frequencies above resonance, it is the capacitive branch that has the low reactance, drawing a large current leading the applied voltage. In between these two extremes, at resonance, the lagging current taken by the inductance and the leading current taken by the capacitance are equal. As they are 180 degrees out of phase, they neutralize each other. The current is very small at resonance, which is another way of saying that the impedance of the parallel resonant circuit of Fig. 2-30 is very high, the opposite of the series resonance circuit. Series and parallel resonant circuits are used in both audio circuits and in radio frequency circuits and their complementary characteristics are important arros in the quiver of the circuit designer. This book is not for circuit designers, but for circuit users, but the user must have some appreciation of what the various circuit elements do individually and working together. As a summary of resonance effects and as an aid to the memory, Fig. 2-31 brings together these various effects with respect to impedance, current flow, and

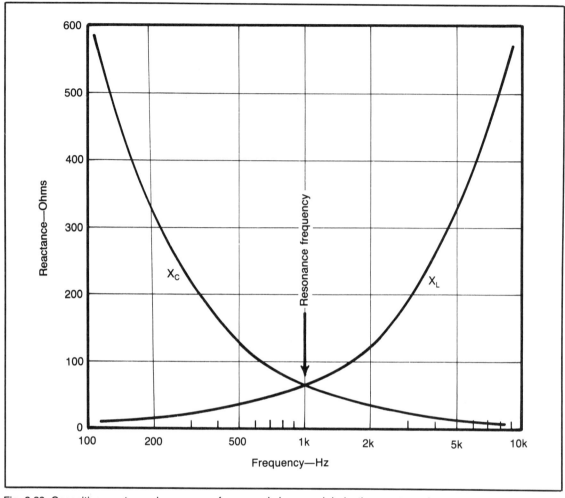

Fig. 2-29. Capacitive reactance decreases as frequency is increased, inductive reactance increases as frequency is increased. Impedance is minimum and current is maximum at series resonance where the two reactances are equal.

the phase angle between the applied voltage and the resulting current.

2.25 ELECTRICAL/MECHANICAL ANALOGS

It helps to get a physical picture of what happens in our audio circuits. Resistance in electrical circuits has its analogy in mechanical circuits as friction. Friction opposes motion, just as resistance opposes current flow. Inductance can be likened to mass which has inertia and capacitance can be likened to compliance or spring-like action. In microphones, loudspeakers, and phonograph

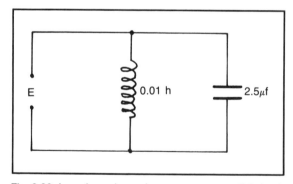

Fig. 2-30. Impedance is maximum across a parallel circuit at resonance and current flow is minimum.

36

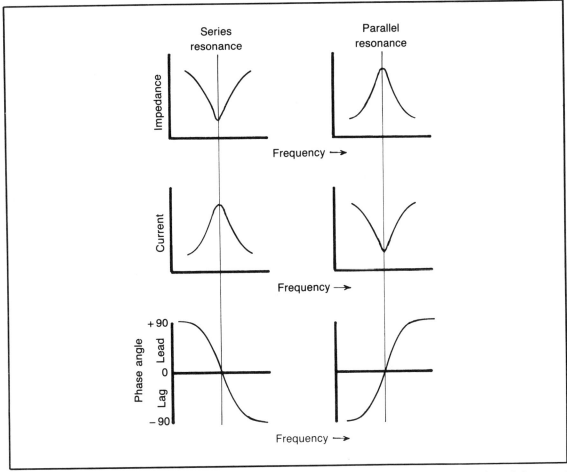

Fig. 2-31. A summary of what happens to impedance, current, and phase angle in series resonant and parallel resonant circuits.

pickups there are the electrical parameters and there are the mechanical parameters with electrical analogs and mechanical analogs being quite interchangeable. While we are at it we should also bring in the whole acoustical analog family as well. A cavity of air is springy, acting like a capacitor. A panel of glass fiber acts like a resistance, absorbing sound by changing it to heat. A loudspeaker cone and its driving coil has mass and therefore has inertia. The electrical, the mechanical, and the acoustical systems all work together and can be analyzed by constructing analogous models. One system can be translated into either of the other two.

2.26 IMPEDANCE MATCHING

Like the thought expressed in the old song about heaven, "everybody talkin' about it ain't going there." In audio circles the idea of impedance matching is confronted on every side, but not too many know the why and wherefore of it. It is a vital concept that becomes a handicap if not fully understood. The matching of the impedance of one machine with another is necessary for the maximum transfer of power from one circuit to another. In audio, maximum transfer of power is important at the point where power amplifiers are joined to loudspeakers, but in many other parts of audio circuits, the matching of impedances is not only unnecessary but downright disadvantageous. Let us consider such a situation.

In Fig. 2-32A the source in the black box has the regulation two terminals. This source might be the output of a mixing console or a dynamic microphone, or what have you. The important thing is that a valuable signal appears at these two terminals that must be protected and conserved. This source has an internal resistance of 150 ohms in series with its open circuit signal voltage. The 150 ohm load of Fig. 2-32B is now connected to the two terminals of the source. This is strict matching of impedances, 150 ohms to 150 ohms. It is evident that half the voltage generated by the source is going to appear across its own internal resistance of 150 ohms and half across the 150 ohm load. Impedances are matched, but we have lost half our precious voltage. In a later chapter we shall see that this means we have lost 6 dB of signal which would put the signal just that much closer to the noise level.

Another approach is illustrated in Fig. 2-32C. Here the load is made to be of high resistance in what is commonly called a bridging arrangement. Now 99.8% of the open circuit voltage generated by the source appears across the load resistor and we have recouped practically all of the 6 dB lost

in Fig. 2-32B. This bridging arrangement is widely used where power transfer efficiency is of no concern, but conservation of source signal voltage is vital.

2.27 IMPEDANCE CHANGING WITH TRANSFORMERS

Transformers produce a change of voltage between primary and secondary, but the power on each side remains the same except for a very small loss. In Fig. 2-33 a transformer is pictured which has N_1 turns on the primary and N_2 turns on the secondary. If an ac voltage V_1 is applied to the primary, a voltage V_2 appears at the secondary winding. The voltage step up or step down is directly proportional to the turns ratio. This makes sense, remembering that the emf induced in a single turn adds to that induced in other turns.

In using the transformer as an impedance changing device, we are interested in what an impedance R_1 connected to the primary looks like when viewed from the secondary side. Normally, R_1 is set by the equipment connected to the primary. The analysis for this is given in Fig. 2-33. We start with the assumption that the power in both primary and secondary sides of the transformer is the same for the transformer produces no power.

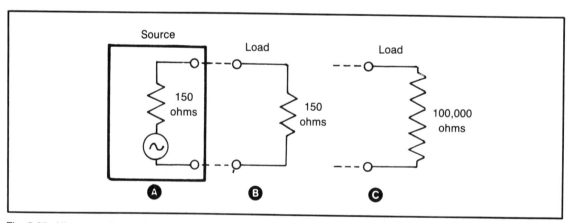

Fig. 2-32. All sources (e.g., microphones) have an internal resistance. Matching this with a load of the same resistance assures maximum transfer of power, but power is of no consequence in low-level circuits. Loading the source with a load of equal resistance results in a loss of half the voltage, or 6 dB. The bridging load at (C) captures 99.8% of the source generated emf. Where efficient transfer of power is important (e.g., between power amplifier and loudspeaker) the (A-B) condition is proper.

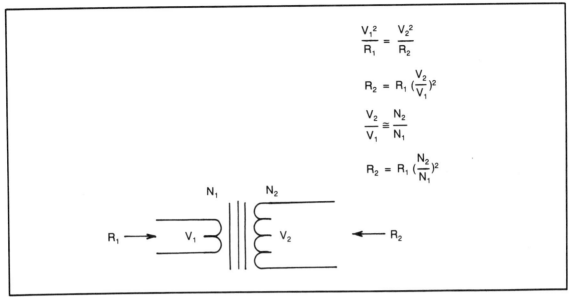

$$\frac{V_1{}^2}{R_1} = \frac{V_2{}^2}{R_2}$$

$$R_2 = R_1\left(\frac{V_2}{V_1}\right)^2$$

$$\frac{V_2}{V_1} \cong \frac{N_2}{N_1}$$

$$R_2 = R_1\left(\frac{N_2}{N_1}\right)^2$$

Fig. 2-33. Transformers may be used as impedance changing devices.

After a couple of simple mathematical moves we see that R_2 is equal to R_1 multiplied by the square of the turns ratio (or the square of the voltage ratio). This is a very usable concept. Let us illustrate by an example. Let us assume that Fig. 2-33 is a picture of a transformer coupling a microphone of 150 ohms to the input of a preamplifier. After some voltage measurements on the transformer we determine that the voltage ratio (and hence the turns ratio) is 8/1, that is, applying 1 volt to the primary yields 8 volts on the secondary. The impedance looking back into the secondary then becomes 150 ohms multiplied by the square of 8 or 64, which gives us a value of R_2 of 9,600 ohms.

Transformers have advantages as well as disadvantages. They are excellent for isolating one circuit from another, such as a single-ended grounded circuit from a balanced ungrounded circuit. However, they do introduce some distortion, which may be a factor in critical circuits. Also, such coils of wire require massive shielding to keep them from picking up hum and radio frequency interference. With the advent of solid-state devices, however, we have entered into a new era of flexibility of changing impedances of circuits without recourse to transformers, and transistor circuits, in general, pick up less interference because of their low impedance.

References

1. Sessler, G.M. and J.E. West, 1973. "Electret Transducers: A Review," *Jour. Acous. Soc. Am.*, Vol. 53, No. 6 (June), pp 1589-1600. An excellent review with 90 references to the literature.

Chapter 3

Basics of Electronics

S OLID STATE IS IN; VACUUM TUBES ARE OUT. This, in a nutshell, is the revolution that has taken place in the field of electronics during the past few decades. Nor is it any great comfort when it is pointed out that the cat-whisker/galena crystal radio receiver of the 1920s was a forerunner of the solid-state devices of today. In spite of the conviction of a small band of die-hard audio purists that vacuum-tube amplifiers sound better than modern solid state amplifiers, both types have their own special types of distortion and solid-state amplifiers are constantly being improved in quality. Solid state has won the battle in audio and is rapidly taking over the radio-frequency field as well. The modern radio or television transmitter is solid state all the way up to the giant final amplifier and it will not be long before that, too, is relegated to the museum.

3.1 SEMICONDUCTORS

Electrical conductors such as copper, aluminum, and gold have one characteristic in common: they have many free electrons in their crystalline structure. When a potential difference is established at the two ends of a conductor, these loosely bound drifting electrons constitute an electrical current flow. We recall that conventional current flow is opposite to the direction of drift of these electrons as carriers of charge. Insulators do not have these free electrons, or at least very few such electrons are available to produce an electrical current. Semiconductors are just what the word implies, neither conductor nor insulator, but a new class of solid-state material in-between the two in its conductive qualities.

Germanium and silicon are two semiconductor materials of very great significance to us because transistors are made of them. Transistors now dominate the electronics industry. Their small size is translated into compact, lightweight, portable consumer equipment as well as sophisticated professional gear. They are so very small that little space is required for devices utilizing them. Power supply requirements are modest because transistors require so little electrical energy for them to function.

Low power consumption means heat radiation problems are minimized. Also, transistors are rugged devices capable of functioning in hand-held equipment or during a rocket blast-off.

When germanium and silicon are "doped" with very small quantities of impurities, their conductive qualities are increased dramatically. An impurity of 1 part of antimony in 100 million parts of germanium results in something like a 20-fold increase in conductivity. Both germanium and silicon have four so-called valence electrons which are loosely bound to the atom in the crystal structure. In the undoped material, what electrical conduction there is depends upon these loosely bound electrons. When an impurity having five valence electrons, such as antimony or arsenic, is introduced to germanium or silicon having four valence electrons, some interesting things happen. Many more free electrons are available as charge carriers and the conductivity of the material increases greatly. Something equally interesting but somewhat different happens when an impurity having three valence electrons, such as boron or gallium, is added to germanium or silicon. In this case a shortage of electrons exists and a new concept of electrical conductivity is introduced which states that when an electron is missing, a positively charged "hole" is produced which is free to move about. This hole carries a positive charge whose drifting constitutes an electrical current flow even as electron drift does.

In the case of doping with the five-valence material, there is an increase in the number of free electrons. Germanium or silicon doped in this way produces an N-type semiconductor. The N-type semiconductor is illustrated in Fig. 3-1 with a preponderance of free electrons. Doping with the three-valence electron material produces a preponderance of positively charged holes and yields what is called the P-type semiconductor, illustrated in Fig. 3-2.

In Fig. 3-3 a battery is connected across a P-type semiconductor. The positive holes are repelled by the positive charge of the battery, but attracted to the negative side of the semiconductor. The negative charges supplied by the battery combine with the holes, neutralizing them. New holes are then formed in the P-type material and these new holes move toward the negative side of the semiconductor where they in turn are neutralized by negative charges from the battery, and so on. This process constitutes a current flow through the semiconductor.

3.2 THE NP JUNCTION

The NP junction, illustrated in Fig. 3-4, is formed when N-type semiconductor material is joined to some P-type semiconductor. When a battery is connected so that the negative pole of the battery is connected to the N-type material and the positive pole is connected to the P-type material, current will flow. To understand this current, we

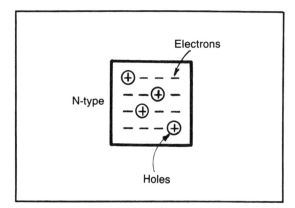

Fig. 3-1. The N-type semiconductor with a preponderance of free electrons.

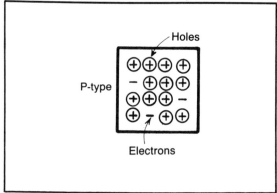

Fig. 3-2. The P-type semiconductor with a preponderance of positively charged "holes."

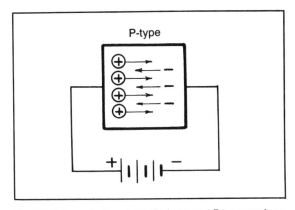

P-type

Fig. 3-3. When a battery is applied across a P-type semiconductor the positive "holes" are repelled by the positive battery terminal and attracted to the negative. The negative charges supplied by the battery combine with the holes, neutralizing them. New holes formed move toward the negative pole where they are neutralized. This constitutes a current flow through the semiconductor.

must sort out the holes and the electrons. When the battery is connected the electrons of the N-type material drift toward the positive pole and the holes drift toward the negative pole. In the vicinity of the junction the electrons neutralize the holes and more electrons, supplied by the battery, flow into the N-type semiconductor to replaced those neutralized

at the junction. In the P-type material new holes are also created to replace those neutralized at the junction and this releases new electrons, which move toward the positive pole.

Notice that the negative side of the battery is connected to the N-material and the positive side of the battery to the P-type. N to N, P to P. This is no accident, but part of the official labelling which can be an aid to our memory. When this N to N and P to P condition prevails, the current flowing is called forward bias.

3.3 THE NP JUNCTION: REVERSE BIAS

What happens if the polarity of the battery of Fig. 3-4 is reversed to that of Fig. 3-5? The electrons in the N-type semiconductor are attracted toward the positive face of the N-type material and the positively charged holes in the P-type semiconductor are attracted to the negative side of the P-type material, and nothing much happens. There is now little neutralization of the holes by the electrons in the vicinity of the junction and the whole process of the forward bias case comes to a halt and very little current flows. This is called the reversed bias condition.

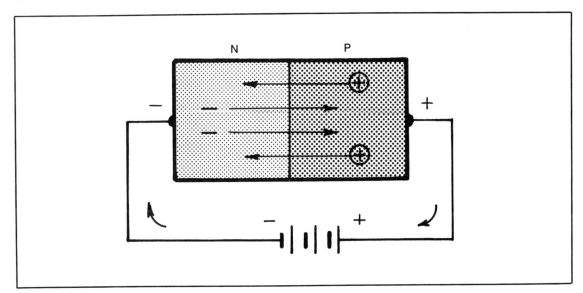

Fig. 3-4. The NP junction is formed by joining N- and P-type semiconductor material. When the negative battery pole is applied to the N material and the positive pole to the P material, the current flowing is called forward bias.

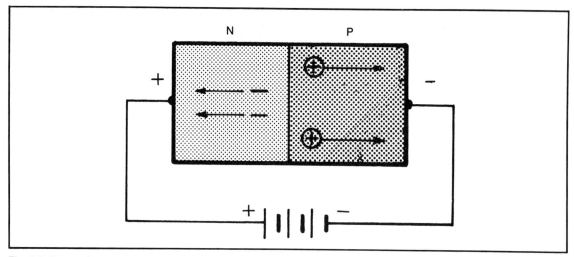

Fig. 3-5. Reversing the battery polarity from that of Fig. 3-4 results in very little current flowing. The NP junction is a rectifier and can serve as a detector in radio receiver circuits. This is called a junction diode.

3.4 THE NP JUNCTION: RECTIFIER/DETECTOR

The reversal of the polarity of the applied voltage between Figs. 3-4 and 3-5 means the difference between current flowing and no (or very little) current flowing. If ac voltage is applied across an N-P junction, current will flow half the time and a pulsating direct current results. In this way the N-P junction can serve as a detector in radio receiver circuits. This is the so-called junction diode such as shown in Fig. 3-6.

3.5 THE ZENER DIODE

If the junction diode is stressed with a very large voltage in the reverse direction, a breakdown results in a very large increase in current for a very

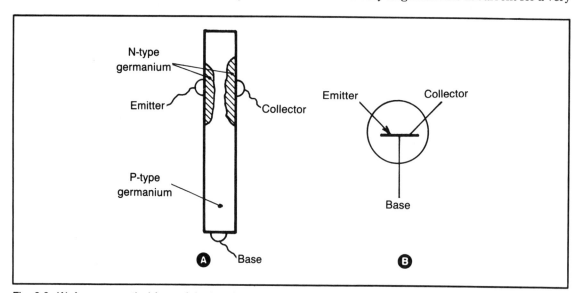

Fig. 3-6. (A) A more practical form of the junction diode. (B) The accepted symbol for the junction diode.

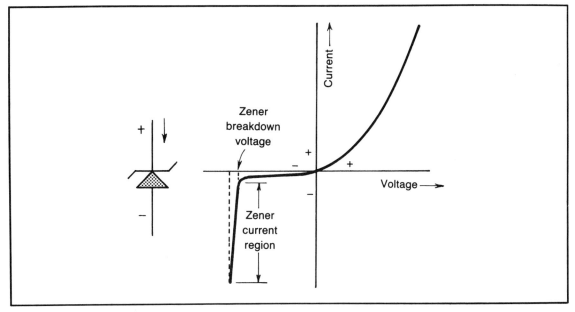

Fig. 3-7. If a large voltage is applied to an NP junction a breakdown results in a large increase in current for a very small change in voltage. Zener diodes, designed to operate in the Zener region, are valuable as voltage reference devices.

small change in voltage. This is pictured in the graph of Fig. 3-7. When the voltage is increased in the negative direction the breakdown results in a very steep portion of the characteristic curve. In this Zener current region, the current flow is very sensitive to small changes in the negative voltage applied. If this Zener effect occurs in a standard junction diode, it would go down in flames. The Zener diodes are designed and manufactured to operate in this region and are very valuable as voltage reference devices. A Zener diode rated at 5.5 volts tends to hold the voltage across it at 5.5 volts over a wide range of current flowing through it in spite of what Ohm's Law says. The symbol for the Zener diode is shown in Fig. 3-7.

3.6 THE JUNCTION TRANSISTOR

The form of the junction transistor is illustrated

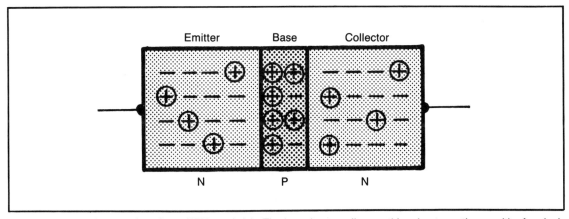

Fig. 3-8. The junction transistor is an NPN sandwich. The base is normally very thin, about one thousandth of an inch.

in Fig. 3-8. It is formed by a sandwich of N-type and P-type semiconductor material. The NPN transistor is shown in Fig. 3-8, the left and right outside materials being N-type and the central part P-type semiconductor. This central part, called the *base*, is very thin, about one thousandth of an inch thick. The N-type material on one side is called the *emitter*, and that on the other the *collector*.

The PNP junction transistor is just what the letters suggest, the thin section of N-type material forming the junction with P-type material on each side of it.

3.7 HOW THE NPN TRANSISTOR WORKS

To put the transistor to work, connections are made as shown in Fig. 3-9. The negative terminal of one battery is connected to the emitter of N-type semiconductor material and the positive terminal of a second battery is connected to the collector. The base is connected to the remaining two terminals of the batteries. Because the negative terminal of the battery is connected to the N-type material, a forward bias condition (conductive to current flow) exists. If the collector were made negative, no current would flow but current does

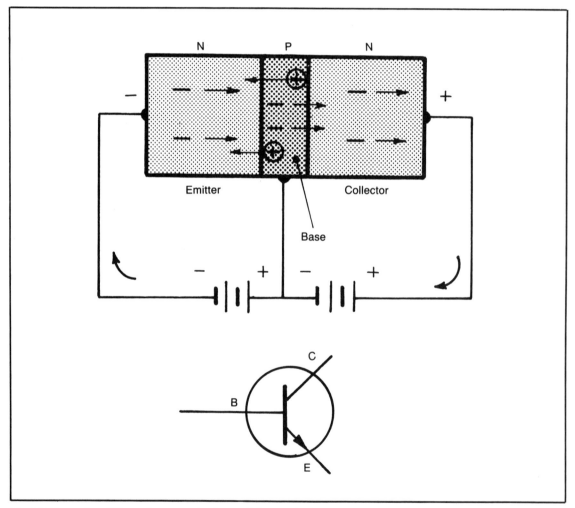

Fig. 3-9. To put the NPN transistor to work a forward bias results from connecting the negative battery pole to the emitter. Electrons of both emitter and collector flow toward the positive pole.

flow with the positive polarity indicated in Fig. 3-9. The electrons of both emitter and collector flow toward the positive pole, those from the emitter going through the very thin base material. This NPN arrangement allows current to flow with the battery polarities shown.

We are now close to a workable transistor amplifier. In Fig. 3-10 a microphone has been connected between emitter and base through a transformer that allows ac to be applied to the transistor. This ac signal voltage is superimposed on the dc bias of the battery causing the emitter voltage to vary above and below the bias point. As the signal voltage goes positive, it reduces the negative voltage applied to the emitter. As it goes negative, it adds to the emitter voltage. The current through the NPN transistor is thus varied as the emitter voltage is varied by the signal input. The transformer in the collector circuit couples some output device, such as a loudspeaker, to the transistor. The signal in the collector circuit is stronger than that in the emitter circuit and we have a functioning amplifier.

3.8 HOW THE PNP TRANSISTOR WORKS

The PNP arrangement, as shown in Fig. 3-11, can also be used as an amplifier. The principal difference is that battery polarities are reversed. This, of course, reverses the direction of current flow, but the same amplifier action results. The positive holes in the emitter are repelled by the positive emitter voltage, flowing through the very thin base toward the negative terminal. The electrons in the emitter flow toward the positive terminal forming new holes on the way.

The forward bias in the emitter circuit causes current to flow readily in the emitter-base input circuit. The reverse bias of the collector means that little current flows in the collector-base circuit. Another way of stating it is that the collector-base circuit has a high resistance. Fluctuations of signal voltage in the emitter-base circuit cause fluctuations in collector-base current. Although this current is relatively small, it can flow through a high load resistance creating a high output signal voltage. In this way a small voltage change in the input circuit can result in a large signal voltage in the output circuit which is a way of saying that the voltage amplification is great.

3.9 TRANSISTOR AMPLIFIER CONFIGURATIONS

There are two basic arrangements of the N-type and P-type semiconductor materials, the NPN

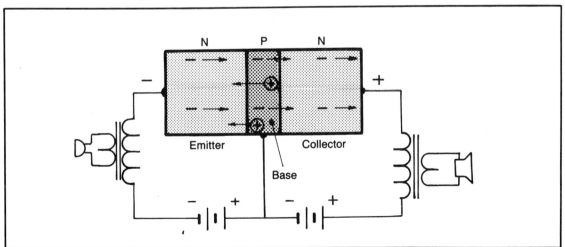

Fig. 3-10. If an ac voltage is superimposed on the dc emitter bias of an NPN transistor, the signal voltage varies above and below the dc bias voltage on the emitter. The current through the transistor varies accordingly, but the collector current is stronger than that in the emitter resulting in amplification.

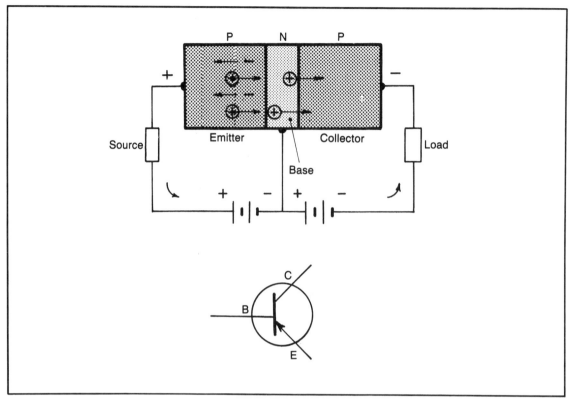

Fig. 3-11. The PNP transistor is also an amplifier. With reverse bias the collector-base current is low but flowing through a high load resistance can produce a large output voltage.

and the PNP. For each of these there are three possible circuit configurations. Either the base, emitter, or the collector may be the element common to both the input and output circuits. This makes a total of six possible transistor amplifier arrangements. These six are shown in Fig. 3-12. Of course, the battery polarity must be adapted to the configuration used. These six configurations provide a diversity of characteristics to the circuit designer as suggested by Table 3-1. A typical amplifier circuit utilizing the common emitter configuration is shown in Fig. 3-13.

3.10 FIELD-EFFECT TRANSISTORS

Junction transistors considered previously are bipolar types and their operation depends on two types of charge carriers, electrons and positive holes. Two junctions were involved with the basic transistor, one utilizing forward bias and the other reverse bias. The *field-effect transistor* (FET) differs considerably from the junction transistor in that it is a unipolar device having only a single charge carrier. The FET is noted for its high input impedance, which is even higher than that obtained with vacuum tubes. One on the types of FET in very wide use today is the *metal-oxide semiconductor* (MOS) which accounts for the acronym MOSFET. The MOSFET uses a metal-gate electrode separated from the semiconductor material as shown by Fig. 3-14. This gate electrode is actually one plate of a capacitor, the other plate being the P-type substrate and the metal oxide is the dielectric between them. The action of the MOSFET is through the dielectric field. A current flows between the drain and the source, which is controlled by the amount of negative bias applied to the gate electrode. The input circuit of the MOSFET, i.e., the gate, draws no current because

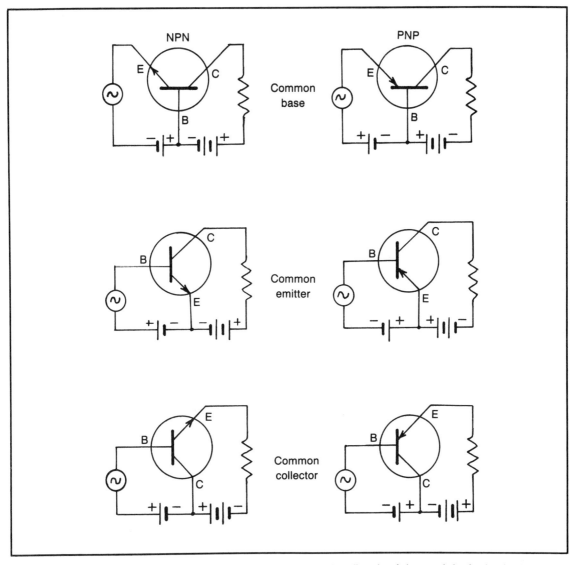

Fig. 3-12. The six combinations of transistor circuit configurations provide a diversity of characteristics for the circuit designer.

Table 3-1. Comparison of Transistor Types.

	Common Base	Common Emitter	Common Collector
Phase reversal between input and output?	No	Yes	No
Input Impedance	Low	Moderate	High
Output Impedance	High	Moderate	Low
Voltage gain	High	High	Less Than 1

49

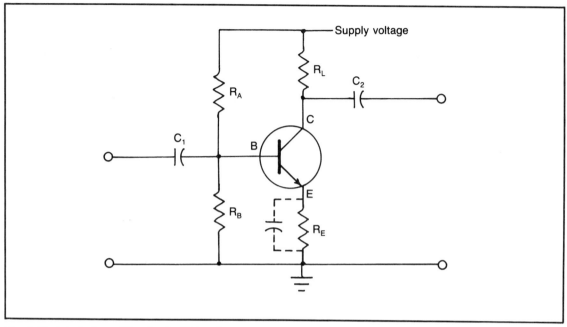

Fig. 3-13. A typical amplifier circuit utilizing the common emitter configuration.

of the negative voltage applied to it. This results in an input resistance of the order of thousands of megohms. The signal voltage applied to the gate controls the electrostatic field across the N-type semiconductor and through it the drain-source current. As the input signal voltage on the gate varies, the drain-source current varies accordingly through change of the size and extent of the depletion region.

A typical MOSFET amplifier circuit is shown in Fig. 3-15. This MOSFET is of the common source (comparable to the common emitter) type. It is also characterized as N-channel. If it were P-channel the polarity of both batteries would have to be reversed, otherwise its operation would be the same but dependent upon holes as carriers. There is a phase reversal between the input and the output in the circuit of Fig. 3-15. The input capacitance is of the order of 1 to 5 picofarads. The output impedance is in the range of 4 to 200 ohms.

3.11 INTEGRATED CIRCUITS

The development of the transistor was soon followed by integrated circuits, circuits which are built-up on silicon chips as the transistors are formed. This was the beginning of micromin-iaturization undreamed of before. Integrated circuits have become so complex that we are going back to one of the very early ones to get one simple enough to serve as an example. Figure 3-16 shows the circuitry embodied in the Radio Corporation of America CA3020 universal linear integrated circuit. This is a stabilized, multipurpose, wide-band, direct-coupled audio amplifier which gives a preamplifier, phase-inverter, driving stage, and power amplifier. It operates on a supply voltage of 3 to 9 volts. With a +9 volt supply, it is capable of delivering about a half watt of power to a loudspeaker.

A functional block diagram of what happens inside the CA3020 is shown in Fig. 3-17. An input amplifier may be used either as a buffer amplifier for isolation or for the realization of gain. This feeds a differential amplifier/phase splitter, which provides a balanced signal to apply to the output power stage. How is such an integrated circuit used? Figure 3-18 shows the few external components and connections to make a practical audio amplifier.

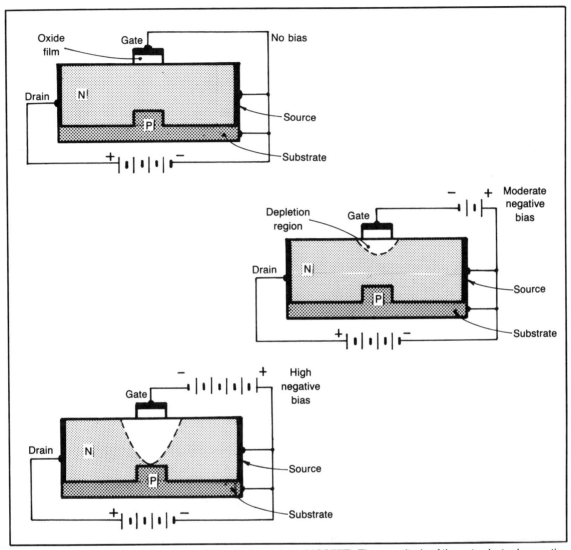

Fig. 3-14. The metal-oxide semiconductor field-effect transistor (MOSFET). The magnitude of the gate electrode negative bias controls the amount of current between drain and source. The very high impedance of the MOSFET input gate circuit lends it to certain circuit applications.

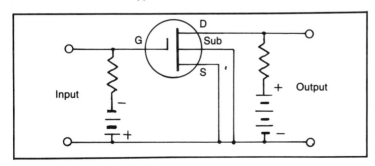

Fig. 3-15. A typical MOSFET amplifier circuit.

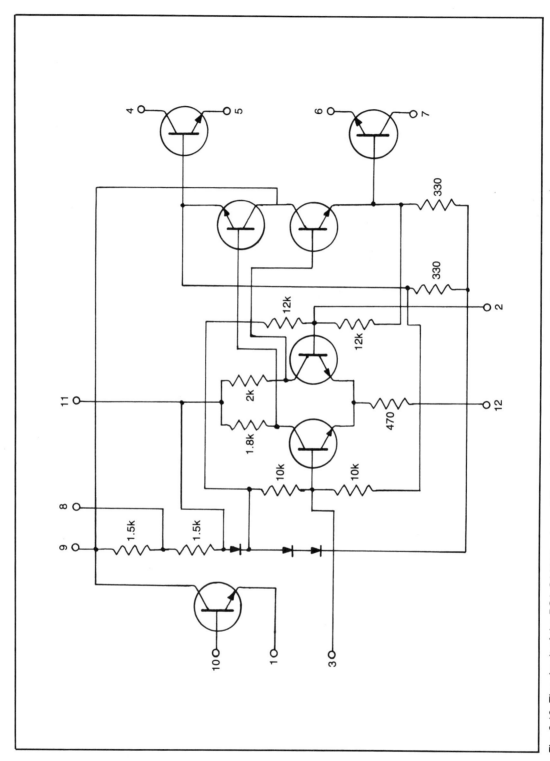

Fig. 3-16. The circuit of the RCA CA3020 universal linear integrated circuit. It is a preamplifier, phase inverter, driving stage, and power amplifier capable of delivering 1/2-watt to a loudspeaker.

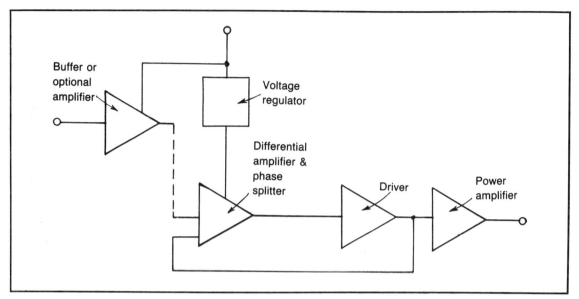

Fig. 3-17. A functional block diagram of the RCA CA3020 integrated amplifier circuit.

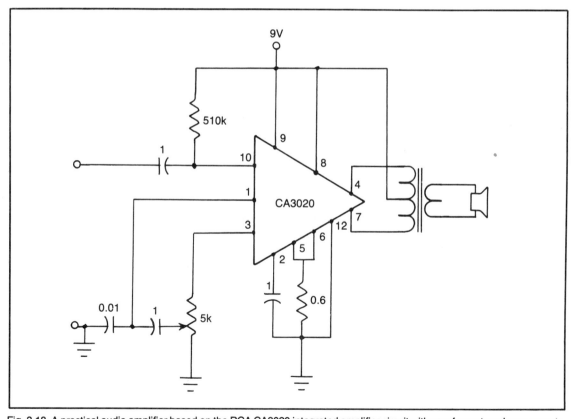

Fig. 3-18. A practical audio amplifier based on the RCA CA3020 integrated amplifier circuit with very few external components.

As mentioned, the CA3020 is a pioneer in a field that has seen much growth since it first saw the light of day. A vast horde of integrated circuits (ICs) are available, which, with a minimum of external components, can be used as oscillators, frequency counters, signal processors, noise-reduction circuits, and amplifiers in audio work and now ICs are covering radio-frequency applications as well. The computer revolution has been made possible by integrated circuits of amazing complexity. In the future we may expect further growth in the IC industry as well as expansion of the capabilities and reduction of size and power requirements of the IC units.

Chapter 4

That Demon the Decibel

THE BEL IS THE LOGARITHM OF A POWER ratio and the decibel is 1/10 of a bel. This statement is to audio what the laws of the Medes and the Persians were to the ancient Middle East. There is no escaping the decibel in audio and it is one of the most maligned and misused concepts. It is not a unit of quantity, such as apples, amperes, oranges, and ohms. It is, just like the man said, the logarithm of a ratio of two powers. Now, that implies that we know what logarithms are and what is meant by ratios. The purpose of this chapter is to remove some of the mystery from this decibel concept and make of it a beloved, familiar, and useful thing.

4.1 WHAT ARE LOGARITHMS?

There are many different number systems, each being most useful in selected areas, none equally useful in all areas. Take the arithmetic system, for instance. It is probably based on counting fingers and toes and, when these proved insuf-

ficient, notches in sticks and knots in a string took over. Even when simple addition was augmented by subtraction and division the limitations of the arithmetic system were evident in the scientific age. The decimal system fits ten fingers and ten toes and goes far beyond this as the decimal point shifts to the right and the left to handle very large and very small numbers.

Another system which has proved very useful in modern usage is the exponential system. Let us take powers of ten for an example. The simple expression 10 to the 14th power (10^{14}) means that there are 14 zeros to the right of the decimal point. In contrast, writing out those 14 zeros would be quite messy. Going the other way, 10 to the -14th power (10^{-14}) conveniently represents a very small number in a minimum space with a minimum of exertion. Logarithms are related to the exponential system.

The number 100,000 can be represented in the exponential system as 10 to the 5th power (10^5). The logarithm to the base 10 of 100,000 is 5. The logarithms of other selected numbers are:

1	$= 10^0$, therefore log 1	$= 0$
10	$= 10^1$, therefore log 10	$= 1$
100	$= 10^2$, therefore log 100	$= 2$
1,000	$= 10^3$, therefore log 1,000	$= 3$
1,000,000	$= 10^6$, therefore log 1,000,000	$= 6$

Get the idea? Even if you forget, all you have to do is to pull out the hand-held calculator, punch in the number in question, punch the log button and read off the answer. In fact, this is the only practical way to find the logarithm of a number falling in the cracks between nice even numbers such as those listed above. We know the logarithm of 100 and 1,000, but what is the logarithm of 655? Easy. Punch in 655 on the calculator, punch the log button, and read off 2.8162413. What this means is that the logarithm (from now on let's just abbreviate logarithm to log) of 655 is equal to 10 raised to the 2.816 power ($10^{2.816}$). From the tabulation above we see that the log of 100 is 2 and the log of 1,000 is 3 so it is logical to expect that the log of 655 would lie between these two, which 2.816 does. This procedure works equally well with calculators based on reverse Polish notation or those of the garden variety scientific calculator. We conclude that logarithms are nothing more or less than powers of ten. That is why we call these logs to the base 10. It is possible to have logarithms to any base desired. In fact, your calculator has buttons both for "log" and for "ln." The log designation applies to logs to the base ten, the ln designation to so-called Naperian or natural logarithms which are to the base 2.7183.

4.2 WHAT IS A DECIBEL?

The bel was so named in honor of Alexander Graham Bell (1847-1922). We have already stated the definition of a bel as the logarithm of the ratio of two powers, and the decibel as 1/10 of a bel. Thus, the definition of power level in decibels is:

$$\text{Power Level} = 10 \log \frac{\text{power 1}}{\text{power 2}} \qquad \textbf{Eq. 4-1}$$

As an example, let us say we measure a power of 27 watts, what is the power level in decibels? Everything depends upon what we take as power 2, the reference power. Later such reference quantities will be discussed in more detail, but, for the moment, let us take 1 watt as our reference power. The power level then becomes 10 log 27/1 = 14.31 decibels.

In electrical work voltages or currents are the most commonly measured parameters, not power. In acoustics, sound pressure is the most accessible parameter which is measured with the sound level meter, not energy density or sound intensity. Electrical power is proportional to the square of voltage or current and in acoustics sound intensity is proportional to the square of sound pressure. Therefore, if voltage, current , or sound pressure are measured, a new form of Eq. 4-1 must be used to change these quantities to power-like quantities. By introducing a squared value, the 10 in Eq. 4-1 then becomes a 20:

$$\text{Sound pressure level} = 20 \log \frac{\text{pressure}}{\text{ref. pressure}} \qquad \textbf{Eq. 4-2}$$

$$\text{Voltage level} = 20 \log \frac{\text{voltage}}{\text{ref. voltage}} \qquad \textbf{Eq. 4-3}$$

These two statements cover most measurements commonly encountered in audio work. It must be remembered, however, that the 10 log form covers power and that power ratios are the very basis of the decibel expression. Because most measurements are made of sound pressure or electrical voltage, the 20 log form is the more commonly used. This should not be allowed to obscure the face that power ratios are the basis of the decibel and that the 20 log changes our sound pressure or voltage measurements to power-like quantities.

Reference quantities in common use include:

For sound pressure level.......20 micropascal
For audio power level.............1 milliwatt
Sound power level................1 picowatt
Voltage...............................1 volt

The graph of Fig. 4-1 shows the relationship

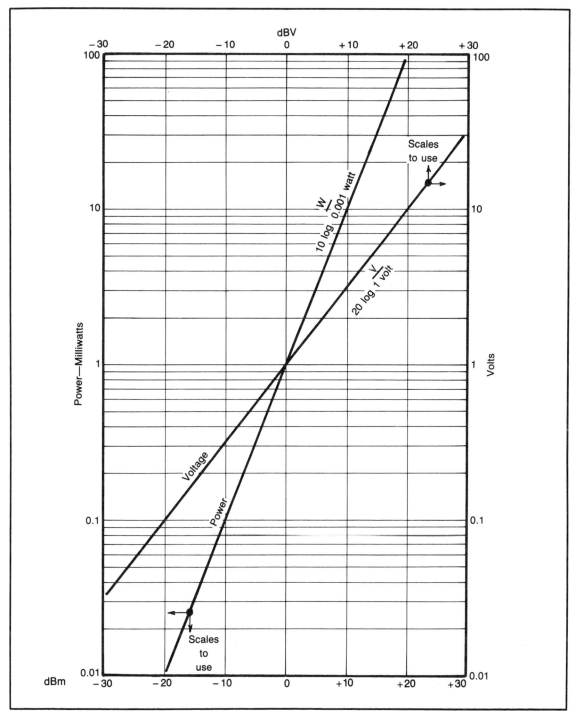

Fig. 4-1. Graphical representation of decibels calculated on both the voltage and the power basis. Reference level for voltage is one volt: reference level for power is one milliwatt.

of the 10 log and the 20 log forms. The power graph is based on the reference of 1 milliwatt using the bottom and the left scales. The voltage graph takes 1 volt as reference and uses the top and right-hand scales. Both lines cross at the reference values of 1 milliwatt and 1 volt.

For professional loudspeakers a "sensitivity" specification is often given. It may be something like this: 88 dB (1 watt, 10 feet) or 90 dB (1 watt, 1 meter). For instance if the sensitivity of a certain loudspeaker is 88 dB (1 watt at 10 feet), putting 100 watts into this unit would produce 88 + 10 log(100/1) = 88 + 20 = 108 dB at 10 foot distance. The 10 log form is used because watts are involved.

What would be the sound pressure level 45 feet from the above loudspeaker? This is a very common problem and to find the answer we must remember that sound (in free space, at least) follows the inverse square law. That square gives us a clue that the 20 log form should be used. For 100 watts input to the loudspeaker, the sound pressure level at 45 feet would be 108 dB − 20 log(45/10) = 108 − 13. = 95 dB. This would be approximate because indoors or even outdoors near the reflecting earth surface the inverse square law is not followed precisely.

Another pertinent application of the decibel is in microphone specifications. The AKG D-125E cardioid dynamic microphone has a sensitivity rating in the catalog of 1.9 millivolts per pascal which has no decibels involved. Along with this form of sensitivity rating is another one, − 54.4 dBV for a sound pressure of 1 pascal. The − 54.4 dBV is equivalent to the 1.9 millivolts: 20 log(0.0019/1) = − 54.4 dBV in which the reference is 1 volt. The reference for acoustical measurements is 20 micropascal, the threshold of human hearing. What is the loudness level of a sound having a pressure of 1 pascal? We can find the sound pressure level of 1 pascal: 20 log(1/0.000020) = 93.98 dB which is quite a loud sound compared to other more familiar sounds in Fig. 4-2.

4.3 WHY USE DECIBELS?

Decibels are logarithmic and they are of such

value to us for the simple reason that human senses are more or less logarithmic in their responses. Our senses respond to stimuli over an amazingly wide range. Let us imagine we are observers at a Saturn rocket blastoff. The sound pressure measured was 100,000 pascals. This is close to one atmosphere. Instead of the little wiggles of normal sound pressure superimposed on atmospheric pressure, this noise comes close to modulating atmospheric pressure completely. This is an overpowering sound, damaging to human ears. But the human ear can also respond to sounds closer to the footfalls of a cat or the rustling of leaves. In fact, the reference sound pressure used in acoustical measurements is taken as the threshold of human hearing, 20 micropascal. The ratio of 100,000 pascals to 20 micropascals is 500 million. The sound pressure level of the big noise is then 20 log 500,000,000 = 174 dB.

Fechner's law (1860) states that every time we double the power of a sound we increase the sensation of loudness by a constant amount. This emphasizes the importance of ratios. It takes something like the logarithmic decibel to express such a tremendous range of sensitivity without getting crunched by the large numbers. Figure 4-2 lists several recognizable noise conditions, each with its sound pressure level, to show how these levels in decibels are far more convenient to work with than the large numbers of the previous paragraph.

4.4 THE VU METER

There are real and ersatz VU meters. The real ones are built to follow the standard specifications of "Standard Volume Indicator" (USA, C-16.5, 1961). This standard specifies that a 0VU reading be obtained when 1.228 volts is applied to the meter. One VU (volume unit) is taken as the equivalent of one dB. This standard meter has carefully controlled ballistics which determine the time it takes to reach the peak on a suddenly applied signal, its overshoot, and time to recover when a signal is removed. Such instruments are expensive and cost limits their use in budget equipment. Many cheaper volume indicators have "VU" printed on their faces, but this does not mean that they are standard.

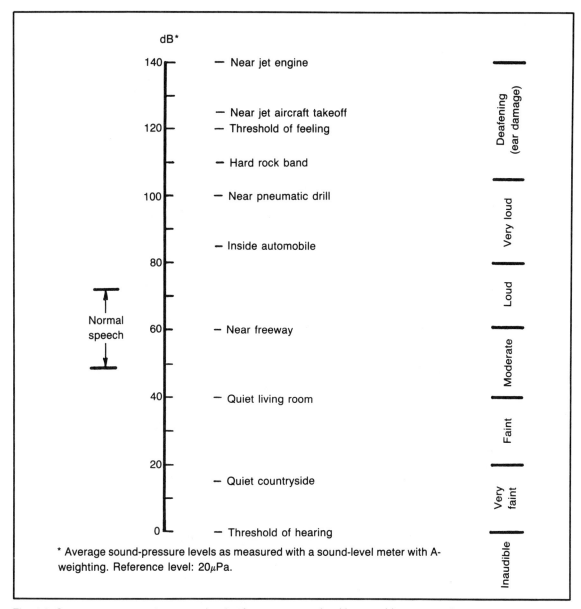

Fig. 4-2. Some average sound-pressure levels of common sounds with normal human reactions as to loudness. Note that the reference for the decibel scale is the threshold of human hearing.

The big problem is to avoid clipping and other distortions on program peaks. The standard VU meter is not a peak-reading instrument but it responds to sudden peaks in a standard and uniform way. The appearance of LED (light-emitting diode) type of peak indicators on consumer as well as pro-fessional equipment has lessened the need for standard meters, but the averaging characteristics of a meter are still important in monitoring.

4.5 GAIN AND THE dB

There is a great temptation to measure the voltage applied to an amplifier and the voltage at the output, take the log of the ratio, multiply by 20 and say, "The gain of this amplifier is so many dB." Strictly speaking, this is incorrect because the input impedance and the output impedance are different. Remember? The dB is based on a power ratio and if the input and output impedances differ, the goal posts have been shifted in the middle of the game.

Now that the thoughts of the above paragraph

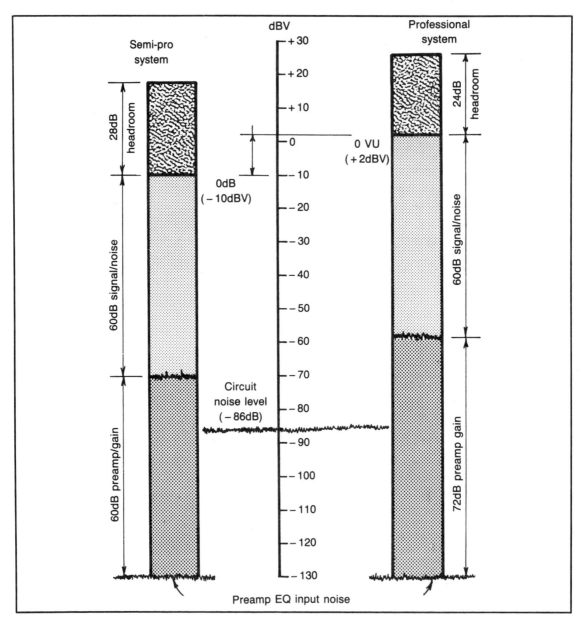

Fig. 4-3. A comparison of semi-professional and professional sound mixing consoles based on certain assumptions discussed in the text. The zero levels are 12 dB apart, thus the professional equipment provides line feeds 12 dB higher than the semi-professional equipment.

have been dutifully recorded, it must be admitted that most contemporary equipment is voltage and not power limited and will put out the same voltage into a wide range of impedances. Because of this, the dBV is useful for voltage ratios irrespective of impedance. Also, there is no denying the convenience of expressing voltage ratios in terms of decibels even if impedance do differ. However, the person involved does well to know the technical fallacy involved. A transformer is not an amplifier, yet do not be too disturbed to hear someone refer to a transformer having a "gain" of so many dB, just flash a knowing smile.

4.6 THE PITFALLS OF ZERO LEVELS

The zero levels of different pieces of audio equipment yield output voltages that are quite different. The budget mixer and the fancy control consoles often have quite different zero levels. Figure 4-3 illustrates a reasonably typical comparison between what we will call semi-professional and fully professional mixing consoles. It is assumed that both use high quality microphone preamplifiers having equivalent input noise of − 130 dBV. The semi-professional equipment employs single-ended amplifiers and 15-volt power supply while the professional system uses differential amplifiers and 22-volt supply. Both systems have the same signal-to-noise ratio because it is dominated by microphone thermal noise. With the assumptions given, the semi-pro gear gives 4 dB more headroom with the prospect of more hum and radio frequency interference because of the single-ended approach. The professional gear gives 12 dB higher line-level feeds. Thus the two zero levels are quite different. This comparison (based on John Roberts treatment in Ref. 1) does not mean that the semi-pro gear could not provide good results, only that the grass-roots quality is better in the professional equipment and the line-level is higher.

4.7 SOME HANDY MEMORY JOGGERS FOR DECIBELS

■ Doubling the power of an amplifier will increase its output only 3 dB (10 log 2 = 3 dB). Cutting the power of an amplifier to half reduces its output by 3 dB (10 log 0.5 = − 3 dB).

■ Doubling the voltage in a circuit represents a 6 dB increase. (20 log 2 = 6 dB). Reducing the voltage in a circuit to half represents a 6 dB decrease (20 log 0.5 = − 6 dB).

■ If the distance from a sound source is doubled, the sound pressure level is reduced approximately 6 dB. The word "approximately" is necessary because the inverse square law is based on spherical divergence in free space and our practical problems are indoors, with many reflecting surfaces, or outdoors near the reflecting earth surface. However, this rule of thumb, "6 dB per distance double" is helpful as a guide. If the distance to a sound source is cut in half, the sound pressure level would increase approximately 6 dB.

■ Most people would consider a sound pressure level increase of 10 dB to be "twice as loud." A decrease of sound pressure level of 10 dB would be interpreted by most people to be "half as loud."

■ The minimum change in sound level discernible to the human ear is about 1 to 3 dB depending on frequency and level.

References

1. Roberts, John, 1983. "Exposing Audio Mythology," *Recording Engineer/Producer*, Vol 14, No 6 (Dec), pp 19, 20.

Chapter 5

Perception of Sound

T O SAY THAT THE EAR IS AN AMAZING IN-strument is about as trite a statement as one can imagine. In a long and checkered career I have had many, many experiences which underline the "amazing" part of that statement, trite as it may sound. For example, working with bats over an extended period at Moody Institute of Science revealed that the hearing of a bat we named "Icky Micky" eclipsed even that of the human ear, in many ways at least. Blindfolded, he avoided collision with obstacles, banking his wings vertically to fly between two closely spaced bars, all with the aid of his sonar pulses sent out and echoes from the bars received by his big, pointed ears. Icky Micky operated at a frequency of about 32 kHz which is far outside the range of human ears. Another astounding manifestation of the bat's echo-ranging ability is to observe such obstacle avoidance in the presence of what must be one of the highest background noise conditions imaginable - a hundred thousand other bats flying around in a cave, each emitting its own steady stream of ultrasonic pulses

in, presumably, the same frequency region.

Sitting in the anechoic chamber or "dead room" at UCLA, after an hour or so in such quiet surroundings, isolated from all the "busy" noises of life to which we become so accustomed, new sounds become apparent. One's heart throbs become very audible. Finally, a rushing sound becomes audible—the sound of agitated air molecules striking the eardrum. This is the threshold of hearing. It would do us no good to have hearing sensitivity greater than this because air molecular movement noise would mask all fainter sounds.

In studying sounds of biological origin in the sea one is impressed that the croakers of Chesapeake bay, like the croakers off Santa Monica Pier in the Pacific, make a raucous racket during summer evenings. It is best heard with the aid of a hydrophone, but sometimes it is so loud that it penetrates the air-water boundary making it audible to the unaided ear. There is also the tiny snapping shrimp whose single snap of the pincer is so feeble, but a population of millions raised such an underwater din during World War II as to shield submarines sneaking into harbors. A big spectral peak in the 20-25 kHz region reduced the ability of sonar equipment to pick up ping echoes. Nor will I ever forget our first encounter with whale sounds about 300 miles from San Diego, off the continental shelf. Ghostly an ghastly moans and creaks were heard, as if Davey Jones were having a bad stomach ache. It was years later that they were definitely identified. But all these sounds in the sea! Surely they serve some purpose and there must be ears to hear them, just like the bird songs and other animal sounds on dry land.

Man's sense of hearing, like that of the animals on land and sea, is a fascinating study and for the person interested in audio it is a required subject. We are so familiar with our instruments that measure volts, amperes, frequency, sound pressure, and other parameters with such ease that we are somewhat taken aback to realize that our sense of hearing is a psychoacoustical and psysiological sense, not directly accessible to such meter readings. For example, it is easy to measure the sound pressure level of a sound with a sound level meter. How loud will it sound? Loudness is over in another realm. And so it is with the discernment of pitch and its relationship to what the frequency meter says. In this chapter we shall treat some of the aspects of the perception of sound by humans. The anatomy of the ear will be missing except where an understanding of its structure affects our study of how it works.

5.1 THE OUTER EAR

The outer ear consists of the pinna and the auditory or ear canal which terminates at the eardrum. The pinna is that external flap which serves a purpose far beyond the simple collection of sound as we shall see in a later section. In women it can be a beautiful pearl-like shell and in men can elicit comments like, "What are you listening for?"

The auditory canal acts like a resonant pipe, like an organ pipe open at one end and closed at the other. Such pipes have the interesting characteristic of "amplifying" sound pressure. A pipe a quarter of a wavelength long with one end closed will have zero (or very low) pressure at the open end and high pressure at the closed end. Although it is somewhat irregular, rather than smooth like an organ pipe, it acts acoustically like a pipe about 0.7 cm in diameter and 3 cm long. The result is shown graphically in Fig. 5-1. There is little acoustic gain at low frequencies, but in the vicinity of 2-3 kHz there is a 20 dB gain. The fascinating thing about this is that speech frequencies also peak in the 2-3 kHz region. It is almost as though this auditory canal were sized for the very job to be done.

Actually, only about half of the 20 dB gain can be attributed to the quarter wave pipe explanation (Ref. 3). A nearly spherical dense object like the human head (no pun intended) also serves to diffract sound. This diffraction effect has about a 5 dB contribution, depending upon the direction of arrival of the sound. Other contributions to this effect come from the trumpet bell effect of the opening to the auditory canal, etc. This 20 dB is not a power amplification because only passive elements contribute to it. However, the eardrum is responsive to pressure changes acting on it and it receives full benefit of this 20 dB peak.

5.2 THE MIDDLE EAR

Movements of the eardrum are transmitted to the oval window of the inner ear through the action of three tiny bones linked together, the hammer, the anvil, and the stirrup, so-called because of their shape. The hammer is attached to the eardrum and the footplate of the stirrup is attached to the oval window of the middle ear.

These three bones contribute to an amazing feat, that of matching the acoustic impedance of the air acting on the eardrum to the water-like liquid of the inner ear against which the oval window works. the shouting of one sitting in a boat can scarcely be heard by a driver close by but beneath the surface. The massive impedance discontinuity between air and water reflects the voice energy and very little penetrates into the water. The mechanism of the middle ear solves the problem of air to water transmission of sound energy in an efficient

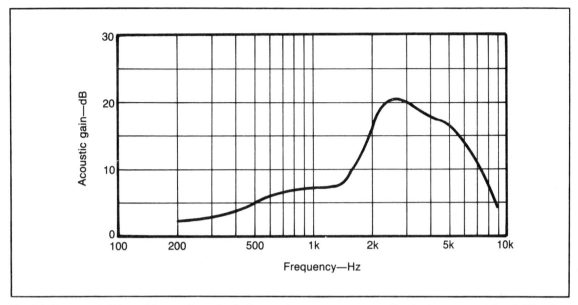

Fig. 5-1. Pressure build-up at the eardrum due to the quarter-wave resonance effect in the ear canal, head diffraction, and other effects. The peak occurs, fortuitously, at the important speech frequencies. (After Shaw, Ref. 3.)

way. First, the area of the eardrum (80 sq mm) is much greater than that of the oval window (3 sq mm). The leverage advantage of the three earbones is as much as 1:3. These two effects solve the problem of matching sound in air to sound in the fluid of the inner ear. How efficient is it? Well, an eardrum movement of molecular dimensions gives a threshold perception of sound. It is almost as though the middle ear mechanics were designed to achieve peak performances for greatest hearing acuity.

Attached to the three middle ear bones are two tiny striated muscles, one attached to the hammer near the eardrum and the other to the stirrup near the oval window. As these muscles contract, the stiffness of the bones linkage system is increased. This increase in stiffness, of course, affects their acoustical function of transmitting eardrum vibrations to the oval window of the inner ear. Below about 1 kHz the transmission through the three bones is stiffness controlled, hence the effect on transmission is greatest. Above 1 kHz there is essentially no effect. When sounds greater than about 75 dB sound pressure level fall on the ear, these muscles contract in a way that reduces the

transmission of vibrations of the ear bones. This action is illustrated in Fig. 5-2. The two graphs of Fig. 5-2A show what happens at frequencies below 1-2 kHz. As sound pressure is increased above the 75 dB level the transmission of sound through the three bone linkage is progressively reduced. This affects the frequency response for frequencies below 1 kHz as shown in the lower graph of Fig. 5-2A, reducing transmission of low frequencies without affecting frequencies above 1-2kHz. The graphs of Fig. 5-2B show that for frequencies above 1 kHz there is essentially no effect in either transmission or frequency response.

The muscles attached to the earbones of the middle ear serve to protect the ear from damage from the low frequency components of very loud sounds in what amount to automatic gain control (AGC) action. This action is too slow to protect the ear from very fast, intense impulses, however, which means that the ear is subject to damage from such sounds, which are rare in nature, but common in industrial plants. Another interesting result of this muscle action of the middle ear is that it improves the perception of complex sounds such as speech in the presence of high-level low-frequency

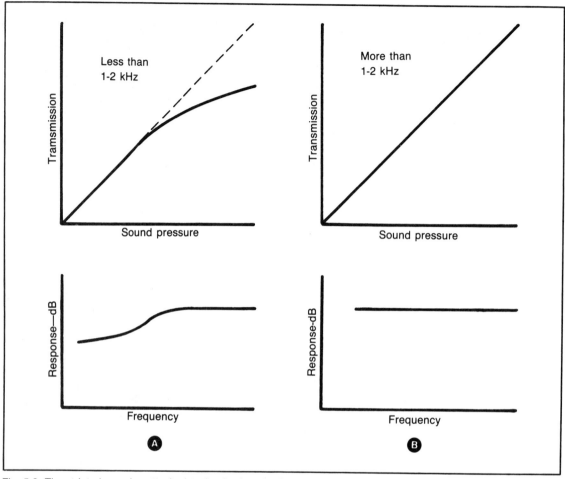

Fig. 5-2. The striated muscles attached to the tiny bones of the middle ear provide an automatic gain control function. This effect is active primarily below 1-2 kHz affecting low-frequency response for the lower frequencies as shown in (A). There is little effect above 1-2 kHz as shown in (B).

sounds. These low-frequency sounds tend to mask the higher-frequency sounds. By this AGC action the intelligibility of speech in noisy surroundings is improved. There are other more obscure salutary effects of this muscular action of the middle ear bones.

5.3 THE INNER EAR

We shall now leave the middle ear to see what happens to the sound vibrations transmitted to the oval window fo the inner ear by the hammer, anvil, and stirrup with their muscular attachments. Remember the path of sound transmission: air con-

duction in the outer ear canal to the eardrum, mechanical conduction of eardrum vibrations through the middle ear bones, to the oval window of the inner ear. the very rough schematic drawing of the inner ear of Fig. 5-3 will help us to follow the sound path in the inner ear.

There are two windows facing the air-filled middle ear on one side and the fluid of the inner ear on the other, the oval window to which the stirrup bone is attached, and the round window. the round window serves as a sort of pressure release.

The water-like fluid of the inner ear is essentially noncompressible. As the oval window is moved inward against this fluid by the earbone action, something must "give." It is the function of the round window to relieve the pressure resulting from oval window action.

The cochlea is coiled up like a snail shell, embedded deep in the temporal bone of the skull. In Fig. 5-3 this cochlea is unrolled for us to better understand its acoustical function. It is divided into three compartments, illustrated by the section A-A, the scala vestibula, the scala media, and the scala tympani. The upper edge (that is, upper in the drawing, not particularly in the head) of the scala tympani is called the basilar membrane, very important because on this membrane is attached the organ of corti, which is the neural sensory organ that changes mechanical vibrations of the basilar membrane into nerve impulses, which are sent on to the brain for analysis and perception. There are some 30,000 sensory neurons in man's ear. These are associated with the so-called hair cells which are the subject of intense current research activity.

Referring back to Fig. 5-3, the vibrations of the stirrup bone of the middle ear are transmitted via the oval window to the fluid of the cochlea. A complicated wave action is set up in such a way that hair cells nearest the oval window respond to high frequencies and those at the other end of the basilar membrane respond to low frequencies. This

amounts to a spectral analysis of the complex sound entering the ear. Hair cells distributed along the basilar membrane are connected to fibers of the auditory nerve and the greater the excitation of the hair cells, the greater the signals sent on to the brain. We shall see later, however, that the effective bandwidth of this portion of the sound analyzing system of the inner ear is not narrow enough to account for the amazing analytical ability of the hearing system. This entire inner ear system, in which structure and function are so closely related, seems almost as though it were specifically designed for the job to be done.

5.4 PITCH AND FREQUENCY

Our frequency meters measure what we call frequency, the number of oscillations per second. The psychoacoustical analog of frequency is called pitch. There is a rough proportionality between physical frequency and psychoacoustical pitch, but it is not exact and it varies with the level of the sound falling on the ear. Investigators have noticed that a low-frequency tone appears to drop in pitch as intensity is increased while the pitch of a high-frequency tone seems to rise as intensity is increased. Figure 5-4 illustrates this effect (Ref.4). Two tones of slightly different frequency were presented alternately to the observer. He adjusted

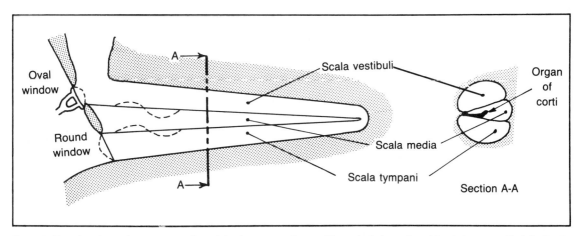

Fig. 5-3. Rough schematic representation of the inner ear of man. The spiral-shaped cochlea is here unrolled, better to see the acoustical action. The inner ear is filled with a water-like fluid. The footplate of the stirrup actuates the oval window, setting up a standing-wave condition on the basilar membrane, high frequencies peak near the oval window end, low frequencies near the apex. The hair cells of the organ of Corti send neural signals to the brain through the auditory nerve.

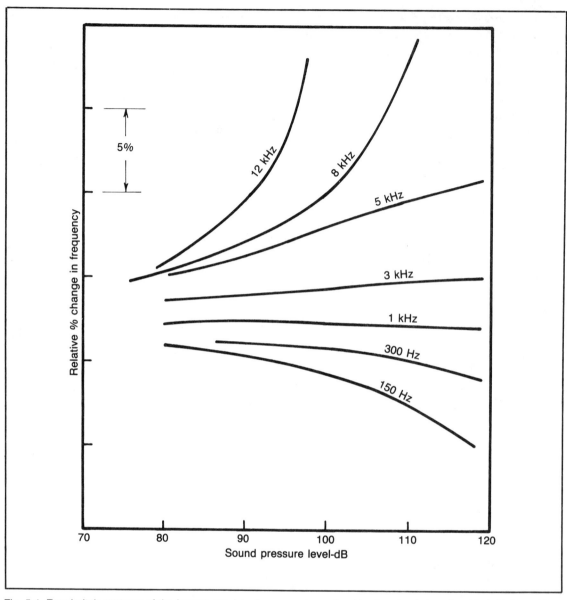

Fig. 5-4. Equal pitch contours of the human ear. Low-frequency tones tend to drop in pitch as level is increased, high-frequency tones tend to increase in pitch as level is increased. Midband frequencies, so important to speech, vary very little with increase in level. (After Stevens, Ref. 4.)

the intensity of one of the tones until the pitch of the two was equal. The curves of Fig. 5-4 are equal-pitch contours which show the relation of pitch to intensity. It shows that tones in the middle range are relatively unaffected by changes in level, but that low or high tones are considerably affected.

It is very interesting that at 3 kHz, where the ear is most sensitive, there is minimum change of pitch with intensity.

If two tones are presented in succession to the ear, it is found that there is an amazing ability to detect small differences in frequency. At 1 kHz, for example, a difference of 3 Hz can be detected. This amounts to a difference of only 0.3 percent! This is called frequency discrimination, discriminating between two tones separated in time. Frequency resolution, or frequency selectivity, is the subject of the next section.

5.5 TIMBRE AND SPECTRUM

We commonly analyze complex sounds with real time analyzers or wave analyzers and the result is a graph showing the distribution of spectral energy throughout the range of audible frequencies. This reveals the peaks and valleys of sound energy. The ear, as we have seen, is also an analyzer of sound. The perception of this analysis by the ear, however, gives us an impression of what is called the timbre of the sound. For example, a violin tone is a complex periodic wave composed of fundamen-

tal and overtones. The ear is very keen in giving a perception of the quality of the tone, which is, in the final analysis, an appraisal of the relative strengths of the overtones with respect to the fundamental. A Stradivarius violin gives an A tone which sounds different than the A tone of a cheap violin. This difference lies in the relative strengths of the overtones.

In 1940 Fletcher introduced the concept of the critical band to explain the analytical ability of the human hearing mechanism. Fletcher found that only a narrow band of noise was effective in masking a tone. He called this band the "critical band." The width of this band is 15 percent to 20 percent of the stimulus frequency. The 1/3 octave filters used so widely in audio analyzing and equalizing equipment have a bandwidth of 23 percent. These 1/3 octave filters thus have a certain

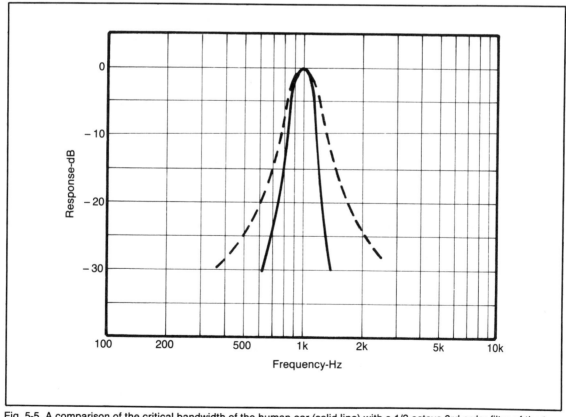

Fig. 5-5. A comparison of the critical bandwidth of the human ear (solid line) with a 1/3 octave 3rd order filter of the type commonly used in real time analyzers. (After Patterson, Ref. 5.)

psychoacoustical basis for their selection for such equipment. The shape of a typical 1 kHz critical band filter and a 1/3 octave filer are compared in Fig. 5-5 (Ref.5).

A set of 1/3 octave filters are arranged so that the 3 dB down points of adjacent filters coincide. In other words, a good 1/3 octave equalizer might have 27 filters to cover the audible spectrum. There are far more critical bands active over the audible range of frequencies. In fact, the critical bands are continuous rather than adjacent to each other. The critical band seems to be related to the individual hair cell and there are many hair cells. If a tone is presented to the ear, there is a critical band centered on that tone, no matter where it is on the frequency scale. If the tone is moved over 1 Hz, the critical band also moves over that amount. The physiological filters of the human hearing mechanism are seen to be infinitely more complex and detailed than a 1/3 octave filter set to which they are often compared.

5.6 LOUDNESS

Basic to an audio person's understanding of the functioning of the hearing system is the family of equal-loudness contours of Fig. 5-6. Fletcher and Munson did the early work in this area but the contours shown were obtained by the meticulous refinement of Robinson and Dadson which have been adopted as a standard (Ref.6). Let us take the 60 phon contour as an example. Note that it crosses 1 kHz at a sound pressure level of 60 dB. This is the definition of the phon: the loudness level of a 1 kHz tone at any sound pressure level. Loudness level is still a physical unit, but it is a step on the way to relating sound pressure level and loudness. This 60 phon contour reveals the sound pressure level required to make tones of various frequencies sound as loud as the 1 kHz tone. These equal-loudness contours tell us that the ear is less sensitive at low frequencies than at kHz. For instance, for a loudness level of 60 phons, a 30 Hz tone must be at a level of 89 dB, or 29 dB higher than a 1 kHz tone to sound as loud as the 1 kHz tone. The contours above 1 kHz go through some "wingdings" but the average deviation from the 1 kHz values

generally are less than plus or minus 10 dB.

The equal loudness contours of Fig. 5-6 explain several effects commonly observed by audio workers. When the hi-fi is turned down to accommodate the neighbors, bass is lost. The loudness control, designed to adjust the highs and lows for the playback level used, is a good idea, but impractical. There are too many variables in loudspeaker characteristics, room acoustics, etc. to enable the loudness control to adhere to these equal-loudness contours with any accuracy. These contours also explain why sound mixers in recording studios like to monitor at excessively high levels—at a level of 110 dB the contours are flatter than they are at 70 dB (but oh!, what is happening to those ears!).

Loudness level in phons, as mentioned above, is a step in relating sound pressure level (a physical quantity) to loudness (a psychophysical quantity). Experiments have been run with listeners who were asked to judge when a sound is twice as loud or half as loud as another sound. Taking the arbitrary definition of loudness of a 1 kHz tone as being 1 sone when the loudness level is 40 phons, we have one point on a graph relating loudness in sones to loudness level in phons. Experimenters have found that observers seem to estimate that if a 1 kHz tone is doubled in loudness, its level is 10 dB higher than before. If it is judged to be half as loud, it is 10 dB lower in level. Plotting the arbitrary point of a loudness of 1 sone at a loudness level of 40 phons, by calling the twice-as-loud level 2 sones and thehalf-as-loud level as 0.5 sone, we have three points on a new loudness versus loudness-level graph. We will not go into this further, but it is through such reasoning that one must go in translating sound level meter readings to subjective loudness.

The method of obtaining loudness (sones) from loudness level (phons, related to sound pressure level through Fig. 5-6) is illustrated in Fig. 5-7. The spectrum of the signal to be studied must be broken down into bands. The sound pressure level of each band in dB must be translated to phons, which, in turn, must be translated to sones. Sones may be added, so by summing the loudnesses in sones of the various bands, the overall subjective loudness

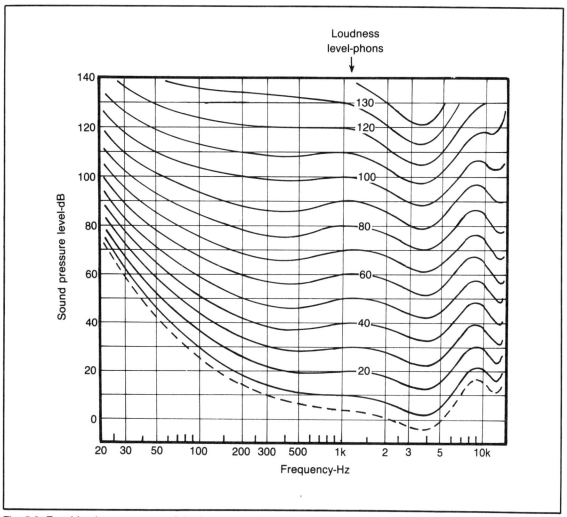

Loudness
level-phons

Fig. 5-6. Equal loudness contours of the human ear. These curves are the inverse of the frequency responses of the ear for different sound-pressure levels. The ear is shown to be relatively insensitive to lower frequencies. The broken line is the threshold of hearing. The top curves are close to the threshold of feeling and pain. These equal loudness contours were obtained by Robinson and Dadson and have been accepted as a standard. (Ref. 6.)

of the original signal represented by the spectrum can be estimated. That word "estimated" is important. Of the various systems for carrying out the general process indicated, they do not agree too well with each other and none are completely satisfactory.

Have the commercials ever seemed to be much louder than the average program level as you listen to the radio or television? The public seems to be continually saying that they are, the broadcasters

usually say they are not. There have been many attempts to devise a monitoring instrument that would indicate average subjective loudness rather than simple, physical VUs. Typical of the many attempts to devise such a meter is that of Bauer and his colleagues at CBS Laboratories (Ref.7), which has found limited, but far from universal, acceptance.

If two tones fall within the same critical band, they are combined on a power basis. If they are in

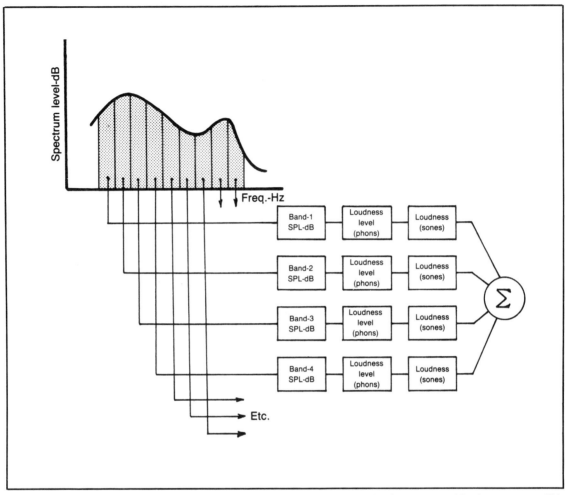

Fig. 5-7. There is a great gulf fixed between sound-level meter readings and loudness as a subjective response. This sketch illustrates the method currently used to get a meter reading that correlates with subjective loudness. The spectrum must be broken down into bands. The sound-pressure level of each band must then be operated on once to get to loudness level in phons (a physical quantity), then operated on again to get loudness in sones which may be added together. It has been found that a sound-level meter reading with A-weighting correlates quite well with loudness as experienced by humans. (See Ref. 7.)

different critical bands, the way to combine them to get combined loudness is to determine the loudness of each in sones and then add the sones. For very rough estimation, loudness may be considered approximately proportional to the 0.6 power of the sound pressure. If we are listening to a random noise, increasing the bandwidth does not increase loudness until the critical bandwidth is exceeded. As other critical bands are excited, loudness increases.

5.7 SPATIAL ORIENTATION

How do we sense the direction from which sounds arrive? Delving into this reveals even more of the genius of our ear-brain hearing system. In a basis sense, sound direction is sensed through the comparison of data gathered by our two ears, but not entirely. Some data gathered by a single ear can result in sensing direction.

With a sinusoidal signal arriving at the head pictured in Fig. 5-8 at the 45 degree angle, two cues are presented for sensing the direction of arrival. First, the intensity of sound falling on the near ear is higher than that falling on the farther ear. This effect is frequency dependent because the head offers more of a shadow to sound of higher audio frequencies than the lower frequencies. At frequencies at which the head dimension is small compared to the wavelength of the sound there is practically no shadow effect. Second, there is a time difference cue between the two ears. The sound arriving at the farther ear is delayed with respect to the near ear.

In Fig. 5-8 the approximate diameter of the human head is 9 inches or 0.75 ft. The head has a diameter of one wavelength at a frequency of 1130/0.75 = 150 Hz. This frequency appears to be the dividing line between intensity dominating and phase (timing) effects dominating. Below about 1500 Hz phase/timing is more important, above this frequency amplitude is more important.

Experiment: listen to the sound of a small portable radio to become familiar with the general quality. Hold the radio close to the left ear while a finger plugs the left ear. The sound you hear passes around the head before entering the right ear. Note that the low frequencies are most prominent because the sound bends readily around the head while the high frequencies cast a deep shadow at the right ear. The head acts like a low-pass filter.

It is interesting that near the transistion zone between time and amplitude dominance near 1500 Hz our ability to detect the direction of arrival of sound is rather poor. It seems that when both time and amplitude cues are present our directional sense is inferior to having only one cue.

It is possible, at least with a bit of training and experience, to tell the direction of arrival of sound

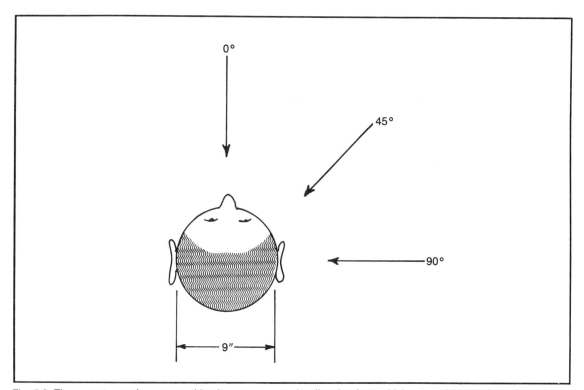

Fig. 5-8. There are two main cues used by the ear to sense the direction from which a sound comes, intensity and time delay. The ear closer to the sound source receives a higher level of sound, the far ear receives sound later than the near ear.

with only one ear. This works primarily on the high-frequency content of the sound, especially for frequencies greater than 6 kHz. Batteau (Ref. 8) performed an interesting experiment with two artificial ears (pinnae) with microphones in them held in place at the normal separation by a rod, not a head. The signal from each microphone was amplified and connected to stereo-type headphones. Reasonably accurate azimuth and elevation judgements were possible with the sensation that the sounds were out in space and not in the head as is common with headphones. The artificial pinnae were then removed and the experiment repeated with the bare microphones with very erratic results. It appears that frequency response variations due to comb-filter effects between the sound entering the ear canal directly and reflections from the folds of the pinna account for monaural directional ability as well as augmenting the time/amplitude cues.

5.8 WHEN IS AN ECHO NOT AN ECHO?

As we are listening to reproduced music in a normal environment, we naturally consider the loudspeaker as the source of what we hear. While this is true in an ultimate sense, actually the sound striking our ears arrives by many paths because of reflections from the surfaces of the room. In a simplistic sense, each such reflection could be considered an echo, yet they do not sound like echoes. Why? The answer is found in a consideration of the magnitude of the delay of the reflected component. Let us break these delays down into several categories to better understand this echo business.

A normal living room having the dimensions 20-feet by 14-feet by 8-feet has a volume of 2,240 cubic feet and a surface area of 1,104 square feet. The so-called "mean free path" or average distance sound travels between reflections in this room is then 4V/S or about 8 feet. As sound travels 1.13 feet in one millisecond, the average reflection is delayed about 9 milliseconds. Reflections from the floor, ceiling or near walls might be as low as a few milliseconds and multiple reflections up in the hundreds of milliseconds, but the multiple reflections get weaker with each reflection so we can say that

the reflections that really count in this room might lie in a range of something like 1 to 100 milliseconds. Some very interesting characteristics of the ear come into play for delayed reflections (echoes?) falling within this range, characteristics that have great significance for those interested in audio.

Back in 1854 Joseph Henry, first director of the Smithsonian Institution, performed a simple, yet elegant, experiment that revealed how the ear-brain system reacts to delayed reflections. He struck his hands sharply together to produce an impulsive sound and listened to echoes returned from the face of a building. He found that when he was less than 30 to 40 feet from the building he heard no echo when his hands were struck together, yet it was obvious that strong reflected impulses fell on his ears. He concluded that sound must be delayed 1/20th to 1/16th of a second before the ear could hear the reflection as an echo. This translates to delays of 50 to 60 milliseconds. A number of researchers dipped into this subject to one degree or another, but it was 100 years later that a German graduate student by the name of Haas studied the effect in a way particularly applicable to practical audio problems. This became known as the *Haas Effect*, although psychologists and physiologists know it as the *procedence effect*.

Haas arranged two loudspeakers to form an angle of 45 degrees with the observer who was directed to adjust an attenuator until the sound from the loudspeaker that emitted the "direct" sound was the same as that emitting the "delayed" sound (Ref. 9). The results are shown in Fig. 5-9. He found that for delays in the 5 to 20 ms range the sound from the delayed loudspeaker had to be boosted under 10 dB before it sounded as loud as that from the undelayed loudspeaker. What this actually means is that sound arriving at the ear within 20 or so milliseconds after the direct sound is fused with the direct sound and does not sound like a discrete echo. In fact, the apparent level of the sound is increased and a generally pleasant character is imparted to it, which we have come to associate with indoor sound as contrasted to dry outdoor sound.

74

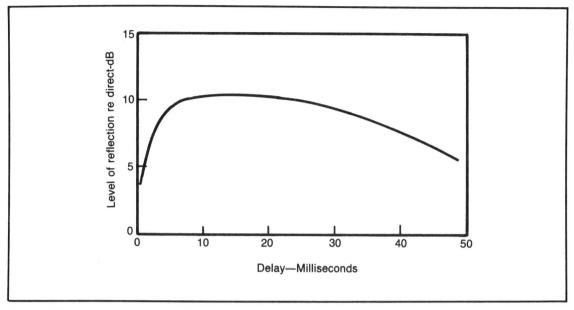

Fig. 5-9. With delays between 1 and 20 ms, the delayed sound is fused or integrated with the direct sound with no echoes being perceived. For delays greater than 20 ms, the delayed signal begins to be perceived as a discrete echo. (After Haas, Ref. 9.)

For sound delayed more than 20 or 25 milliseconds, a discrete echo begins to appear and when the delay exceeds 50 milliseconds the echo is very prominent with detrimental effects on speech intelligibility.

The whole pattern of delayed sound may then be divided into three sections: (1) delays less than 1 millisecond, (2) delays from 1 millisecond up to 25 or so milliseconds, and (3) delays greater than 25 milliseconds.

While relatively unimportant in regard to the fusion of sound, delays less than 1 millisecond are very important in regard to perceiving the direction from which sound comes. The comb-filter effects resulting from the combination of the sound entering directly into the ear canal with sound reflected from folds of the pinna are associated with delays in the order of microseconds. The "law of the first wavefront" tells us the direction from which a sound arrives, even in a small room in the presence of many reflections.

The second category is very important in audio engineering. In the fusion zone a reflection of normal strength does not appear subjectively as something apart from the direct sound. Only if the amplitude of the delayed sound is increased 10 dB or more is it perceived as an echo. This condition prevails only under the artificial conditions of a test setup, because reflections lose strength in distance travelled and upon reflection unless some focusing surfaces are present. Therefore, in this fusion zone of reflections delayed 1-25 milliseconds the direct sound appears to be reinforced with a modest change in timbre and, in certain situations, the apparent width of the source may be increased.

The third category is that in which definite discrete echoes appear, which can be very disturbing. However, even in category (2) it is always a matter of relative levels. If the signal delayed 10 milliseconds is 20 dB higher than the direct, the fusion effect can be overcome and an echo perceived. With a sound component delayed 100 milliseconds, if the echo level is 30 dB or more below the direct, the echo will not be audible. Discrete echoes in this category commonly occur in large auditoriums with highly reflective rear walls. Problems also arise with sound reinforcement systems in large spaces incorporating supplementary distributed loudspeakers under a balcony. Digital time delay devices are used to delay the signal fed to the distributed loudspeakers with the delay adjusted so that persons seated under the balcony receive sound from the main cluster and from the supplementary loudspeaker within the fusion zone.

The above boundaries of the fusion zone are somewhat dependent upon the character of the signal. The results for music are somewhat different from those for speech. It turns out that the syllables of speech or the musical stacatto interval are directly involved in determining the onset of disturbing echoes. For example, English speech averages about 5 syllables per second or about 200 milliseconds between syllables. Cox (Ref.10) has pointed out that the maximum tolerable delay is invariably close to one third of the syllable interval for speech or the stacatto interval for music. One third of 200 milliseconds is 67 milliseconds, which would be well into a serious echo condition in Fig. 5-9.

5.9 HEARING AND LISTENING

Hearing is being aware that a sound stimulus has actuated the ear mechanism. Listening emphasizes paying attention to what is heard. This attention might be for pure enjoyment of the music or for conscious analysis of structure of the music, or simply for the detection of flaws. Those in the audio field have many occasions to direct the full force of one's concentration on obscure components of the sound such as distortion or noise. One marvels at the highly developed ability of the experienced sound mixer to detect details of the sound inaudible to the untrained bystander. Can such skill be imparted by training?

There have been a few notable efforts to train people in the art and science of listening with discernment. Bell Labs developed a series of 78 rpm disc recordings in about 1926 for the purpose of training workers in the telephone industry. These demonstrated the effect of suppressing certain frequency ranges on speech and music, transmission through an overloaded amplifier, the fundamentals and overtones of common musical instruments, phase distortion of long cable circuits, noises, ef-

fect of echoes on speech and music, etc. (Ref. 11).

About 1977 a modern effort toward training in listening was made by Nippon Columbia Co., Ltd. of Tokyo. These "Audio Technical Records" were quite exhaustive, covering such topics as the effects of frequency range on the signal, channel separation (cross talk), wow and flutter, dynamic range, distortion, and many others. Most of the records of the original set are not available today. (Ref. 12)

In 1982 the writer produced a ten lesson set entitled "Critical Listening" designed primarily for the novice but including material of interest on a wider basis. Such topics are covered as estimation of frequency, estimation of sound-level changes, frequency-response irregularities, fundamentals and harmonics, distortion, reverberation, signal/noise ratio, and voice colorations due to comb-filter effects (Ref. 13).

No efforts of this type can hope to replace actual experience but they can accelerate the process of acquiring a keen sense of sound analysis. After all, such training methods merely subject the trainee to listening experiences obtainable in practice, but in an accelerated and organized order.

5.10 HEARING CONSERVATION

The most important tool the audio person has in the toolbox is a keen sense of hearing. By keen, I do not mean exceptional sensitivity or absolute pitch, but normal hearing trained in analysis and discrimination. Why is it that we think nothing of wearing eye glasses to correct visual deficiencies but would be aghast at a sound mixer wearing a hearing aid? Viewed objectively, that hearing aid could very well bring a major improvement in the quality of the job. All those engaged in audio work of any form should have their hearing acuity checked periodically, always asking for a copy of the audiogram for the personal file so that trends may be detected.

High sound levels can be very damaging to hearing. Mixing sound in the monitoring room of a recording studio at levels around 100 dB can result in serious and permanent damage to the hair cells of the inner ear. After such a session a temporary threshold shift is often noted but permanent

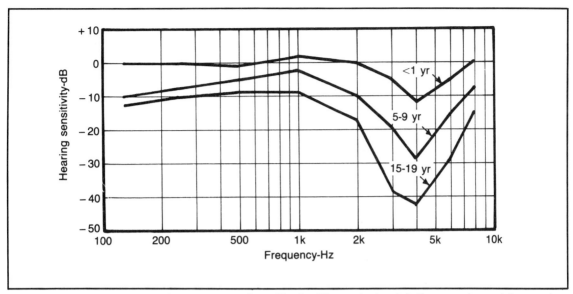

Fig. 5-10. Hearing loss induced by long exposure to jute mill noise. The greater loss is in the general speech frequencies. Similar hearing losses can be expected by sound mixers and others subjected to high-level rock music or other sound. The jute mill workers were subjected to sound levels of 87-102 dB. (After Taylor, et al, Ref. 14.)

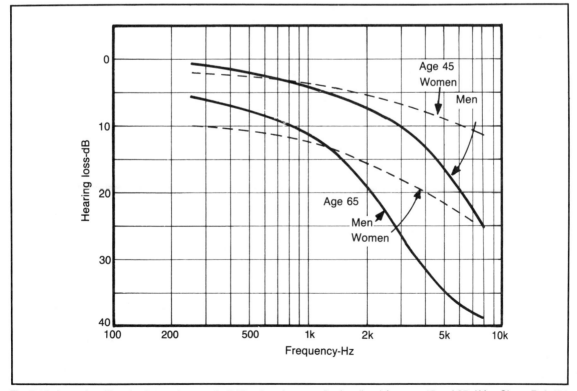

Fig. 5-11. Age-related hearing losses for men (solid lines) and women (broken lines) for ages 45 and 65. (After Olson, Ref. 15.)

damage can also result. The accumulation of research data on the effects of high level rock music on hearing is rather fragmentary at this time. However, there is a classic paper on the effects of jute mill noise on the hearing of the workers (Ref. 14). Some of the results of this study are shown in Fig. 5-10 covering environmental noise levels of 87-102 dB. Those subjected to this noise for a year or less experienced a permanent hearing loss of 10 dB at 4 kHz. Those subjected to this noise level for 5-9 years were found to have about a 20 dB loss at 4 kHz as compared to the average low frequency level. Those working 15-19 years under these conditions were found to have about a 30 dB loss at 4 kHz. Those working with high level rock music might very well expect some such loss as this. It is a very serious prospect to contemplate something like a 2 dB loss per year in the important region of the audio spectrum.

So much for losses traceable to working under high sound levels. There is another inevitable hearing loss associated with growing older. This loss is illustrated in Fig. 5-11 (Ref. 15). The upper pair of curves is for age 45, the lower pair for age 65. Men seem to have the greater loss and this may be due to their working in noisier environments than women. On the average, men can expect a loss of 25 dB at 8 kHz at age 45 and a loss of 35 dB at age 65.

Human hearing is the only component of the audio chain that cannot be replaced, take good care of yours.

References

1. Pickles, James. O., 1982. *An Introduction To The Physiology of Hearing,* Academic Press, Inc., New York. = An excellent general reference.

2. Moore, Brian C., 1982. *An Introduction To The Psychology of Hearing,* Academic Press, Inc., New York, 2nd edition. An excellent general reference.

3. Shaw. E.A.G., The External Ear, In *Handbook of Sensory Physiology,* Vol 5/1 (eds. W.D. Keidel and W.D. Neff) pp 455-490, Springer, Berlin. As described by Pickles, Ref. 1.

4. Stevens, Stanley Smith and Hallowell Davis, 1983. *Hearing, Its Psychology and Physiology,* 1938. Republished by Am. Inst. of Physics, NY. Page 71.

5. Patterson, Roy. D., 1970. "Auditory Filter Shapes Derived With Noise Stimuli," *Jour. Acous. Soc. Am.,* Vol 53, No 9 (Mar). pp 640-654.

6. Robinson, D.W. and R.S. Dadson, 1956, "A Re-Determination Of The Equal Loudness Relations For Pure Tones," *Brit. J. Appl. Phys.,* Vol 7, pp 166-181.

7. Bauer, Benjamin B., Emil Torick, and Richard G. Allen, 1971. "The Measurement of Loudness Level," *Jour. Acous. Soc. Am.,* Vol 50, No 2, Part 1 (Aug) pp 405-414.

8. Batteau, D.W. 1967,"The Role Of The Pinna In Human Localization," *Proc. Roy. Soc. B.,* Vol 168, pp 158-180.

9. Haas, Helmut, 1972. "The Influence Of A Single Echo On The Audibility of Speech," *Jour. Audio Engr. Soc.,* Vol 20, No 2 (Mar) pp 146-159.

10. Cox, John Charles, 1981. "The Effect Of A Single Echo On The Intelligibility of Speech And Music," Master of Science Thesis, Dept. of Elect. and Computer Engr., University of Colorado.

11. Information supplied by History Services Department, Bell Laboratories.

12. Information supplied by Nippon Columbia Co., Ltd., Overseas Business Operations Division, No. 14-14, Akasaka 4-chome, Minato ku, Tokyo, Japan, through the courtesy of Mr. Steve Tygret of Pacific Broadcasting Association and Mr. Teppei Kado, both of Tokyo.

13. Everest, F. Alton, 1982. "Instruction In Critical Listening," presented at the 72nd convention of the Audio Engr. Soc., (Oct), preprint #1890. Critical Listening albums are available from *Mix Magazine,* 2608 Ninth St., Berkeley, CA 94710. Phone (415) 843-7901.

14. Taylor, W. et al, 1965. "Study Of Noise and Hearing In Jute Weaving," *Jour. Acous. Soc, Am.,* Vol 38.

15. Olson, Harry F., 1972. *Modern Sound Reproduction,* Van Nostrand Reinhold Co., pg 325.

Chapter 6

Sound Reinforcement

O NE-ON-ONE PRESENTS NO PROBLEM, BUT AS soon as the need to communicate with a large group of people arises, there are problems. The weakness of the human voice was a severe limitation in the days before electronic gear was available. In the ancient Roman and Greek amphitheaters the performers spoke loudly and what the unaided voice could not communicate, exaggerated gestures did. (Is this why people from this part of the world gesticulate so?) Stentor, a Greek herald in the Trojan war, is said to have had the voice of fifty men (that's 17 dB), and from him we get the word stentorian, which is the kind of a voice needed for addressing large groups outdoors.

Coming indoors, the situation is helped somewhat. The walls and ceiling tend to contain the energy of the talker's voice so that larger groups may hear. With this containment, however, came problems of reverberation and echo. Various means were employed to improve the situation. Placing the talker on a platform helps some as the attenuation through the audience is reduced. Visiting Christ Church in London I do not remember the ser-

mon but I was impressed by two things. One was the way this lovely church was overpowered by the massive, monolithic BBC structure across the street. The other was that the pastor spoke from a high pulpit that was equipped with a handsomely shaped reflecting surface over the pastor's head. There was no need for sound reinforcement for an audience of such modest size as long as the talker enunciated clearly and spoke loudly.

Today, audiences of 2,000 are common and the demand for larger and larger meeting halls grows. Not only this, but there is an accompanying demand for halls that serve many different purposes, which brings conflicting acoustical problems. In this chapter on sound reinforcement we shall look at the various types of systems from the point of view of the operator who must have an understanding of the general principles involved in design and testing to operate any system intelligently. Of course, we are talking not about the "knob twister" type of individual, but the person who can come up with good solutions when confronted by unusual problems.

6.1 FACTORS AFFECTING INTELLIGIBILITY

Speech is a quite complicated signal and understanding it is likewise complicated. First we must get a picture of the speech signal itself in such a way that the audiophile or audio engineer can make comparisons with the familiar ground of other signals. Although we scarcely think of it in our normal activities, speech is made up of many different components. The nasal sounds are just what the word implies, sounds made in the nose. The consonants are the hard sounds found at the beginning and end of many words. The consonants on the end of the words bat, ban, bad must be understood clearly or we are unable to distinguish between these words and others similar to them. These consonants are 20 to 30 dB lower in level than average speech, which complicates the apprehension of the words. The consonant frequency range extends from 250 hertz to about 3,000 hertz. The sibilants are entirely in the high frequency range and we are familiar with them because of the piece of equipment used to control them, the de-esser. The four formats are regions of concentrated sound energy, sufficiently distinguished from each other to require separate identification. They are even lower in level than the consonants.

When it comes to understanding words, either you do or you don't. This makes understanding words a good way to measure the effectiveness of any communication system. There is the talker and the listener and in-between is the communication link, whether an expanse of air carrying sound waves, complicated by the acoustics of the space if indoors, a telephone line, or satellite system girdling the globe. The basic method is simply to speak words into one end of the system and see how many of them the listener at the other end hears correctly. Of course, the word list is carefully made up by experts. Sometimes single syllables are used instead of words. If 100 words are spoken the listener gets 87 correct, it is said that the articulation index is 87%.

It was found by Peutz (Ref. 1) that vowels are more readily perceived, that understanding consonants is the critical, determining factor in weighing the effectiveness of a sound reinforcement system. The "articulation loss of consonants" has been found to be a good measure of speech intelligibility and has become the accepted criterion in predicting the performance of a sound system on the drawing board. A summary of extensive psychoacoustical measurements commonly used in sound reinforcement design is shown in Fig. 6-1. These graphs, which apply to the reverberant sound field, reveal the restricted conditions under which good speech intelligibility can be attained. Peutz states that for articulation loss of consonants below 10%, speech intelligibility is very good. Above 15% intelligibility requires good listeners, good talkers, and/or high interest in the message.

In Fig. 6-1 the effects on intelligibility of background noise and reverberation are summarized. If articulation loss of consonants is limited to 10 percent to 15 percent the operating range is limited to high signal-to-noise ratios are relatively absorbent spaces. This underlines the importance of adequate acoustical properties of the space and proper directivity of the loudspeakers (Ref. 2).

6.2 SOUND FIELDS IN AUDITORIUMS

When a loudspeaker is energized in a large church sanctuary or auditorium a sound field is built up as the switch is closed. The building up process stops when the power supplied to the loudspeaker is just sufficient to supply the losses as sound is absorbed by the various surfaces of the space. To increase the general sound level in the room, the volume control must be advanced so that the loudspeaker supplies more power. This is analogous to the dependence of the speed of an automobile on the accelerator setting. The sound field, however, is not uniform throughout the room. We expect it to be highest near the loudspeaker, but what happens elsewhere? It is important to designer and operator alike to understand the character of this sound field.

As the distance from the sound source is increased, three specific regions are encountered, each dominated by different acoustical effects. Figure 6-2 identifies these three as (1) the near field, (2) the free field, and (3) the reverberant field. In the immediate vicinity of the loudspeaker, the beam being radiated "is just getting organized," so to speak. The direction of the velocity of the air particles is not yet fully in line with the direction of the beam. In this region measurements are uncertain, unpredictable, and inadvisable. It is for this reason that the sensitivity specification provided by the loudspeaker manufacturer is given as a sound pressure level at 1 meter (or other distance) for 1-watt power input to the loudspeaker.

Next comes the free field region of Fig. 6-2 in which the sound field acts as though the loudspeaker is in free space. In a typical room, the free field region does not extend very far, but as far as it does the sound level falls off at 6 dB per distance double as dictated by the inverse square law.

At greater distances reflections from the various surfaces of the room soon submerge the di-

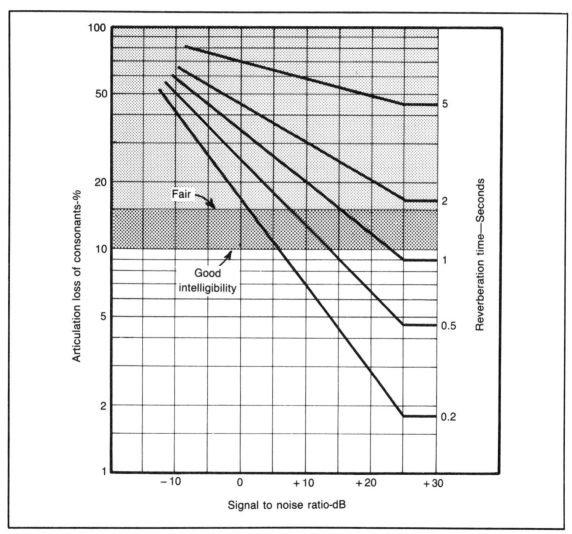

Fig. 6-1. Articulation loss of consonants in the reverberant sound field and with background noise, as a function of the signal-to-noise ratio for different reverberation times. The percentage of articulation loss of consonants must be below 15% for adequate speech intelligibility. Intelligibility is essentially perfect for 10% articulation loss of consonants. Such intelligibility criteria limit the acceptable reverberation times and background noise conditions. (After Peutz, Ref. 1.)

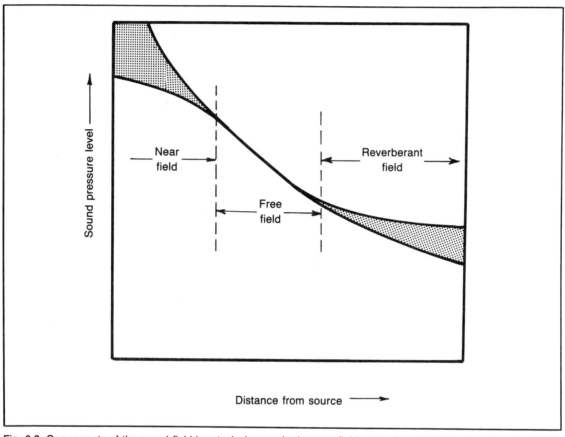

Fig. 6-2. Components of the sound field in a typical room. In the near field, very close to the loudspeaker, the field is partially unorganized. The free field section is characterized by sound falling off according to the inverse square law (6 dB per doubling of the distance). The reverberant field is dominated by reflected energy and falls off slowly with distance.

rect sound and dominate the sound field and the reverberant field region of Fig. 6-2 prevails. The transition point is defined as that point at which the direct sound of the free field and the indirect sound of the reverberant field are equal. This means that the separation between them is 3 dB. In this reverberant field the sound pressure level falls off very slowly with increasing distance from the source, rarely more than 2 or 3 dB per distance double or even less in very large spaces. The level of the reverberant field depends on the sound absorption in the space. With highly reflective surfaces the reverberant field level is high, in very dead spaces it is low.

Now that the regions are defined, let us consider the specific example shown in Fig. 6-3. This

particular loudspeaker has a sensitivity of 100 dB sound pressure level at 1 meter for 1-watt input. This is our starting point on our odyssey of exploration of the sound field. As the distance from the loudspeaker is increased the sound pressure level decreases at a rate of 6 dB per doubling of the distance. Without reflecting surfaces (i.e., in free space) the sound would continue to follow this rate of decrease. In our practical hall, however, the rate of fall off of sound pressure decreases, the curve tends to flatten as the reverberant field is entered. Persons seated in this reverberant field receive sound dominated by reflections and not sound direct from the loudspeaker.

It is well to mention at this point that in small rooms it may not be possible to get far enough away from the loudspeaker to observe a reverberant field. In other words, a reverberant field may not exist, or exist only partially.

As we move away from the loudspeaker we soon reach a point known as the critical distance. At this point the level of the free field and that of the reverberant field are equal. This means that the combination of the two is 3 dB higher than either one alone. At distances from the loudspeaker less than the critical distance the 6 dB per distance double rule applies. At distances greater than the critical distance the reverberation field, made up of reflected contributions from the room surfaces, dominates and the sound pressure level tends to flatten off.

6.3 THE GOOD SOUND REINFORCEMENT SYSTEM

There are certain requirements a sound reinforcement system should meet before it can be judged a "good" system. For one thing, the signal should be well above the prevailing background noise level. Background noises usually have a spectrum that falls off as frequency is increased. Speech and music spectra have this general shape also, al-

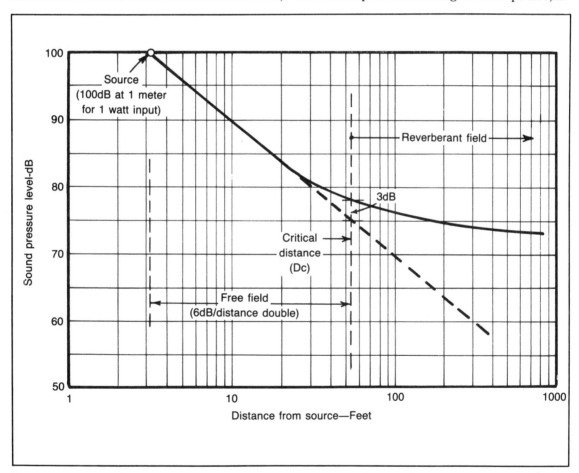

Fig. 6-3. A practical representation of the sound fields of Fig. 6-2 with a loudspeaker having a sensitivity of 100 dB at 1-meter with a power input of 1-watt. The straight line portion follows free field rules (6 dB per doubling of the distance). The reverberant field is dominated by energy reflected from the room surfaces and falls off slowly as distance from the source is increased. The critical distance is defined as that distance at which the direct and the reverberant fields are equal, i.e., 3 dB apart.

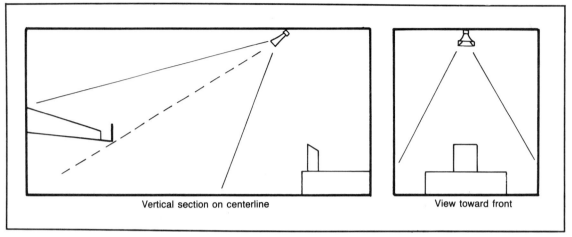

Fig. 6-4. A single loudspeaker cluster is used in the high-level system considered to be the best solution to most church and auditorium situations. The cluster commonly employs direct-driven cone units for the low frequencies and horns for the high frequencies.

though the rate of fall off may vary considerably. Experienced sound system designers and sound contractors have stated that the signal of a good system should be at least 25 dB above the background noise at the important midband frequencies.

A good sound reinforcement system must also radiate a close approximation of the signal entering the microphone. This is the requirement of quality and it involves frequency response and distortion as well as subjective qualities such as "*naturalness.*"

"*Understandability*" is another important subjective term which has to do with the faithfulness with which the different speech components are treated. The vowels of speech give little trouble, it is the consonants that determine the understability of the speech passing through the system.

For a sound reinforcement system to be classified as good it must perform well in signal-to-noise ratio, fidelity, and understandability.

6.4 CENTRAL CLUSTER SYSTEMS

There are many advantages in having the sound radiators at a single point in sound reinforcement systems for churches and auditoriums for general usage (Fig. 6-4). If this single cluster is located above the head of the one speaking, everyone in the audience facing the podium automatically places the podium and the loudspeaker cluster in the vertical plane in which human localizing ability is poorest. If the sound reaches both ears with the same amplitude and at the same time, one cannot tell whether the source is behind, above, or ahead. The result is the impression that the sound from the loudspeakers is coming from the person speaking at the podium. On the other hand, placing the loudspeaker(s) elsewhere tells the auditor that sound is coming from both the one speaking and one or more loudspeakers.

Another advantage of the single cluster radiating system is that of sound quality. The cluster is made up of different types of units, each designed to handle a part of the audible spectrum with maximum efficiency and quality. For example, the low-frequency radiator is usually mounted in a large box carefully designed for optimum functioning of the driver. The midrange- and high-frequency units are also optimized to handle their own restricted band. The power amplifiers commonly associated with such a system are of high quality, often separate amplifiers for each portion of the spectrum are used.

It is desirable to concentrate the sound energy radiated on the audience area and to minimize the portion falling on the walls and other reflecting surfaces. It is possible to exercise good control of the distribution of sound energy with horns used in single point radiating installations. Furthermore, the directional patterns of such horns are reasonably constant with frequency. This type of installation is also suitable for electronic equalizations, which further improves available gain and reduces the feedback howling hazard.

6.5 DISTRIBUTED SYSTEMS

In the single cluster system, the sound is radiated from essentially a single point at high level. There are situations in which no suitable location for such a cluster exists. Perhaps the ceiling is so low that the cluster would be too close to the microphones on the platform, which would result

in too low available gain and high feedback howling tendenices. Sometimes owners rebel at the idea of sacrificing appearance for good sound. In such cases, strictly as a second-best solution, an approach is used involving many low level loudspeakers. One such distributed loudspeaker approach for a church is shown in Fig. 6-5. Here the loudspeakers are incorporated into the light fixtures, at least in the open part of the sanctuary. The spacing between units is carefully adjusted for adequate coverage. Figure 6-6 shows a similar distributed system utilizing column loudspeakers spaced along the walls. There are many other types of situations forcing the designer to use the principle of many low level sources to achieve adequate coverage. A very common application is in rooms having low, lay-in, suspended ceilings for which there may be no alternatives.

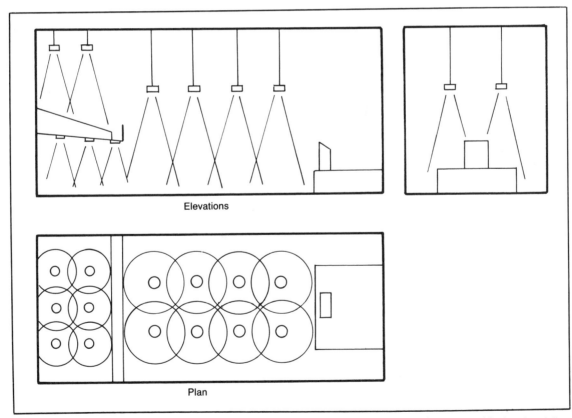

Elevations

Plan

Fig. 6-5. A distributed sound reinforcing system in which high-quality loudspeakers are incorporated in the chandeliers in the open part and in the ceiling under the balcony.

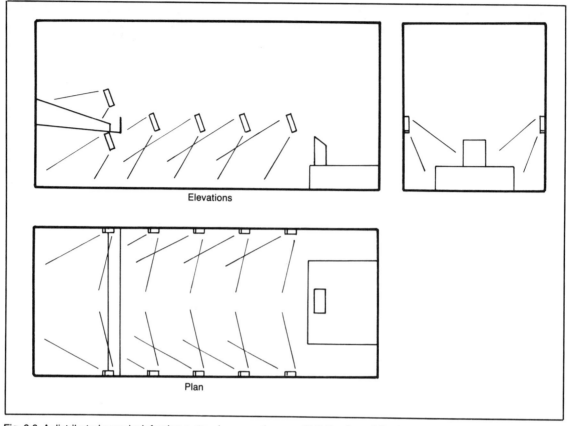

Elevations

Plan

Fig. 6-6. A distributed sound reinforcing system incorporating a multiplicity of carefully aimed column loudspeakers mounted along the walls. Delay devices are usually required for satisfactory intelligibility in such systems.

6.6 COLUMN LOUDSPEAKERS

In this section the column loudspeaker is defined as a simple line array of individual direct radiator cone loudspeakers mounted close together. The directional characteristic in the horizontal plane is simply that of a single isolated unit, which means that it is not very directive at the low frequencies, but quite directive at high frequencies. This results from the fact that at low frequencies (long wavelengths) the cone diameter is essentially a point source, but at high frequencies the cone diameter is large compared to the wavelength. In very rough terms a column 6 feet long might have a 25 degree vertical pattern and a 120 degree horizontal pattern. Because such columns are relatively inexpensive, they are widely used and abused. They dominate the do-it-yourself, home

brewed type of systems and, as frequently used, often yields indifferent or downright poor results. Used in the right way with full knowledge of their strengths and weaknesses columns are an important resource.

Figure 6-7 illustrates one problem with column loudspeakers, that of directivity. Considering a single column operating alone, this figure shows how the frequency response varies over the audience area. The frequency response on the centerline is the best it has to offer. It cannot be said to be flat because, among other things, its mounting affect its low-frequency radiation efficiency. Compared to an isolated column, mounting the column against a flat wall would increase its low-frequency response by 3 dB because it is now radiating into a half sphere rather than a full sphere.

Mounted in a corner would add another 3 dB to its low-frequency response as it radiates into a quarter sphere. Mounted at the intersection of three surfaces (e.g., two walls and ceiling) a third 3 dB is added to its low-frequency response as it radiates into an eighth sphere. In this way the column's response on axis may vary according to its mounting. At a seat located 45 degrees from the axis the high frequency response falls off because of the beaming action at higher frequencies. At progressively greater angles from the axis the highs fall off even more.

In the usual column installation, more often than not two columns are used in a split configuration, one on either side of the podium as shown in Fig. 6-8. This arrangement brings in another problem that is not exclusive to the column but would appear with any spaced loudspeakers radiating the same signal from a common amplifier. This is phase interference, or *"comb filter" effect,* so-called because its response resembles the teeth of a comb if plotted on a linear frequency scale. Let us consider the comb filtering at seats A and B of Fig. 6-8, one located on the 5 and the other on the 1 millisecond delay contour. At seat A the sound from the right loudspeaker arrives 5 milliseconds later

than that from the left loudspeaker. The same delay exists at seats all along this 5 millisecond contour. A similar situation exists at seat B and all along the 1 millisecond contour. Of course, another family of equal-delay contours exists on the right half of the audience area as well.

The response throughout the seating area goes through alternating peaks and dips up through the audible spectrum. As frequency is increased there is first a 6 dB peak as the two signals combine in phase. This is followed by a cancellation as the signals from the two loudspeakers are 180 degrees out-of-phase, or in *phase opposition.* These dips are theoretically infinitely deep, but practically 30 and 40 dB dips are routinely observed. The frequency at which the dips and peaks occur depends upon the delay. A delay of 1 millisecond places the first dip at 500 hertz and the spacing between adjacent dips or peaks is 1 Kilohertz. A delay of 5 milliseconds places the first dip at 100 hertz with successive dips and/or peaks 200 hertz apart. The big dip at 500 hertz at seat B will have a very substantial effect on quality of voice or music. The effect of the closer spaced peaks and dips of the 5 millisecond delay will be somewhat less than the greater spacing of the 1 millisecond case. It is seen

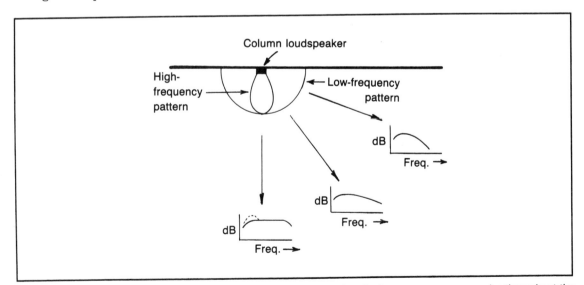

Fig. 6-7. A basic problem with the traditional column loudspeaker is that the frequency response varies throughout the area it covers. The on-beam response is the best, although the mounting can affect the low-frequency response 3-9 dB. At 45 degrees off axis the high-frequency response drops. Farther off axis the high-frequency response can be very low.

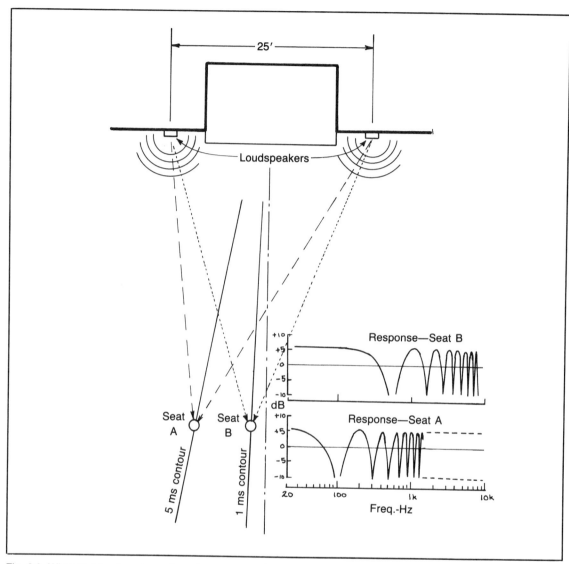

Fig. 6-8. When two loudspeakers of any type are energized with the same mono signal, phase-distortion or comb-filter effects can seriously degrade the frequency response, especially through the central section. At seat A the sound from the right loudspeaker lags that from the left loudspeaker,5 milliseconds. Down through the spectrum as the two coherent signals are in-phase they combine to increase the level 6 dB. When they are out-of-phase, cancellation occurs. The same effect takes place at seat B, although the 1-millisecond delay shifts the location of the peaks and dips. These effects add to the response variations described in Fig. 6-7.

that the greatest effect of comb filtering will be down the central part of the room. The closely spaced peaks and dips resulting from great delays are less audible. Blessed is the church with a split loudspeaker system that has a center aisle. The ushers may be bothered by the swish-swishing sound effects as they walk through different short delay contours, but this is one case where the aisle seats are not necessarily the best. Note that these comb-filter effects are superimposed on the response variations inherent in the simple column radiator shown in Fig. 6-7. In Chapter 9 modern improvements on the line array loudspeaker are described that minimize the effects of Fig. 6-7, but the comb filtering of Fig. 6-8 exist with any type of loudspeaker.

6.7 EFFECT OF MULTIPLE OPEN MICROPHONES

If a second microphone is adjusted to the same level as the first one in a sound reinforcement system, the margin of gain before the system goes into feedback howling is reduced 3 dB. As the number of open microphones is increased, the available gain before feedback is further reduced according to the graph of Fig. 6-9. A marginal system is fast degraded by employing a number of microphones in the pickup. A well designed system is required to allow deployment of the number of microphones commonly used in modern music.

6.8 OPERATING CLOSE TO FEEDBACK

In 1955 Snow clearly demonstrated the detrimental effects of operating a sound system close to the point of feedback. At feedback the system acts as an oscillator. If the system gain is increased to a point near feedback, the decay time of signals in the room is increased and the response becomes ragged. In a room having a decay time of 3 seconds, the sound system operating within a few dB of feedback can result in an apparent reverberation time of as much as 4 times 3 seconds. Stability

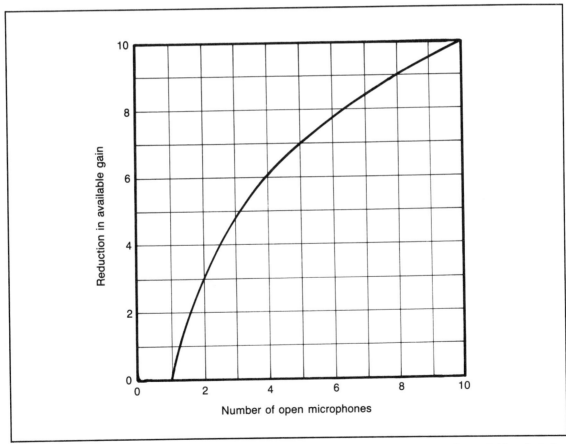

Fig. 6-9. When more than a single microphone is opened in a sound reinforcement system, the available gain before feedback is decreased. Two open microphones degrade the situation 3 dB. If N = the number of open microphones, the system will be degraded 10 log N dB, as shown in the above curve.

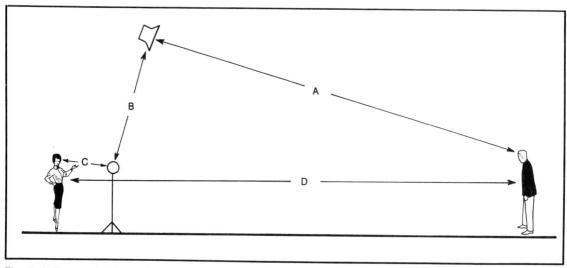

Fig. 6-10. The crucial dimensions of a typical sound reinforcement system. With both microphone and listener in the reverberant sound field, dimension C becomes the determining factor in how much gain there will be before feedback howling sets in. Halving this distance adds 6 dB to available gain. Clip-on microphones make many marginal systems usable when greater microphone distance leads to howling.

is restored as the gain is reduced. Obviously, working too close to the feedback point is undesirable. In the design of systems, a 6 dB allowance is recommended by the experts (Ref. 3). This feedback allowance adds to that required for multiple open microphones. It takes a well designed system to meet these factors and still have enough available gain to operate satisfactorily.

6.9 BASIC PARAMETERS OF SOUND REINFORCEMENT

Without getting into the complexities of sound reinforcement system design (which should always be left to consultant or qualified sound contractor) let us consider the factors of a system which affect its operation. Figure 6-10 shows the four distances determining system performance. Sound on path A decreases in level approximately 6 dB for each doubling of the distance. Assuming the inverse square law applies, the decrease in level at 50 feet would be $20 \log (50/1) = 34$ dB less than at 1 foot distance.

Distance B between loudspeaker and open microphone determines the feedback point of the system. At feedback, the loop gain is unity.

The gain of the system is defined as the increase in level at the listener with the system turned on, over that produced by the talker with the system turned off. Distance C between talker and microphone and distance D between talker and listener are the crucial distances involved. It turns out that for the usual situation in the auditorium in which both the talker and the listeners in the audience are in the reverberant field the potential acoustical gain (PAG) of the system simplifies to the following statement:

PAG = 20 log (critical distance) – 20 log (distance C) – 6   **Eq. 6-1**

The critical distance in Eq. 6-1 is that described in Fig. 6-3 and distance C is that described in Fig. 6-10. The 6 dB tacked on the end is an arbitrary, but important, allowance to keep 6 dB away from the feedback point. Critical distance is fixed by the loudspeaker level and the reverberation characteristics of the room which leaves as the only variable in Eq. 6-1 the distance C, the distance from talker to microphone. If this distance is halved, 6 dB are added to the potential acoustical gain of the system. This is the reason why a marginal system might be workable with the talker using a clip-on microphone that would be totally unworkable with a greater microphone distance.

6.10 DELAY IN SOUND SYSTEMS

In Chapter 5 we learned of the fusion effect of the human ear, that a delayed replica of a sound arriving within 20 or so milliseconds of the original does not sound like an echo but rather is integrated with the original sound in a beneficial way. The fusion of the two increases the apparent level somewhat and results in a pleasant change in timbre. This principle is applied in sound reinforcement systems to correct echo problems stemming from multiple sources. Consider the situation of Fig. 6-11 in which the sound at the listener's position from the main loudspeaker travels a distance A and the sound from a closer supplemental loudspeaker travels a much shorter distance E. The time it takes sound to travel the distance A minus E is the time the sound from the main loudspeaker lags behind that of the closer loudspeaker. If the main loudspeaker is 80 feet away from the listener and

the closer loudspeaker is only 15 feet away, the sound from the main cluster arrives (80-15)/(1.13 ft/ms) = 57.5 milliseconds later. A glance at Fig. 5-9 tells us that this will sound like a discrete echo. The situation can be salvaged by delaying the sound from the closer loudspeaker so that it falls within the fusion range of Fig. 5-9. A delay of 50 milliseconds would cause the sound from the main cluster to arrive only 7.5 milliseconds after the local sound causing the two to be fused nicely. The digital delay lines commonly available today are ideal for this service.

6.11 THE 70-VOLT DISTRIBUTED SYSTEM

In sound systems designed for paging and background music a multiplicity of loudspeakers is involved. The traditional method of feeding power to these loudspeakers has been the 70-volt line. All of the loudspeakers in this system are powered by a central amplifier by way of the 70-volt line. This central amplifier is designed to give maximum power output at 70 volts, regardless of its power rating. With this voltage on the distribution line as a starting point it is possible to design transformers

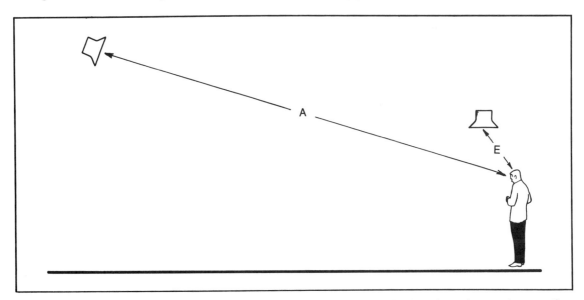

Fig. 6-11. A signal arriving over the short distance E from a close supplemental loudspeaker arrives much sooner than the signal over path A. If the delay exceeds the fusion zone of the ear, a discrete echo will be heard. An electronic digital delay placed in the close loudspeaker line can eliminate the echo by making the two sounds arrive at the listener within the fusion zone.

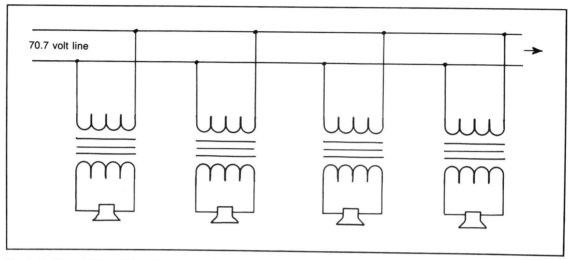

Fig. 6-12. The traditional 70-volt line approach to distributed systems for paging or background music. Each transformer is designed to supply a fixed amount of power to loudspeakers of a fixed impedance.

with 70-volt primaries to deliver a fixed power into the fixed impedance of each loudspeaker. Such a 70-volt system is pictured in Fig. 6-12. The design of such a system is simplicity itself. All that is necessary is to add up the powers to the loudspeakers to obtain the required amplifier power rating (Ref. 4).

One disadvantage of the 70-volt system is the necessity of a heavy power amplifier centrally located, which results in significant losses in the long lines. The cost of a heavy transformer at each loudspeaker is another disadvantage. The sound quality is deteriorated by these transformers, especially if their iron is limited to keep costs under control.

6.12 THE SIGNAL BIASED SYSTEM

In 1959 Heyser described a novel method of handling the power to a multiplicity of loudspeakers in a distributed system (Ref. 5). Although used in a few prototype systems, commercial availability of components has existed only since about 1979. J.W. Davis & Company (Ref. 9) now offers the Davis SBA Distributed Sound System™, an infinitely expandable, system as contrasted with the old 70-volt system.

The SBA system utilizes a special signal con-

taining the audio program plus a precisely generated bias voltage determined directly from the program signal and varying continuously with the level of the audio signal. The loudspeakers are connected to the master amplifier through a light duty, unshielded, three-wire cable (Fig. 6-13). Each loudspeaker has its own driver mounted on it, which is controlled by the bias received from the master.

The advantages of the SBA system include the elimination of power amplifier, transformers, racks, and heavy cable, as well as getting high fidelity sound. The SBA system is readily adapted to emergency use as batteries can be floated on the system. Further, the system is almost unlimited in expansion potential with the addition of occasional small supplemental power supplies (Refs. 6, 7). Photographs of the component parts of the SBA system are shown in Fig. 6-14A through 6-14D.

6.13 THE CONSULTANT AND THE SOUND CONTRACTOR

In large installations it is common for the architect or owner to engage a consultant in acoustics to review the tentative plans from the acoustical standpoint long before construction begins. This consultant might either undertake the design of the sound reinforcement system or work with an ex-

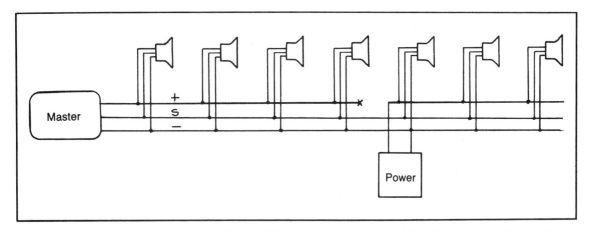

Fig. 6-13. The Davis SBA Distributed Sound System TM which overcomes many of the disadvantages of the traditional 70-volt system. The number of units which can be interconnected this way is virtually unlimited. The master unit supplies a special signal combining the audio signal and a bias voltage which varies with the signal. This combined bias/signal drives a small amplifier at each loudspeaker eliminating the transformers, centrally located power amplifier, and resulting in a more flexible system.

perienced sound contractor. In the more modest installation a sound contractor with the required training and experience could well handle the design of the system, the installation, the adjustment, and the qualification tests. The point here is that know-how is required far above that of the average resident electronic wizard. Satisfactory

sound seldom results from a budget sound reinforcement system installed by a well-intentioned, but inexperienced person.

References

1. Peutz, V.M.A., 1971. "Articulation Loss

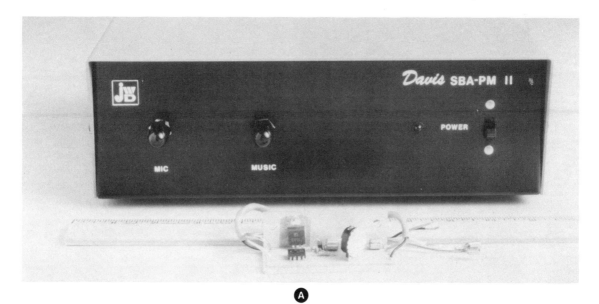

Fig. 6-14A. The component of the signal biased system as offered by J.W. Davis & Company. (front view).

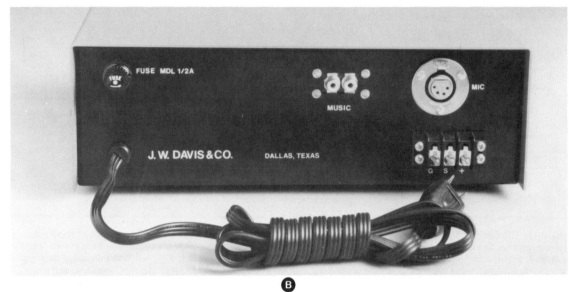

Fig. 6-14B. Back view of the SBA-PM master unit.

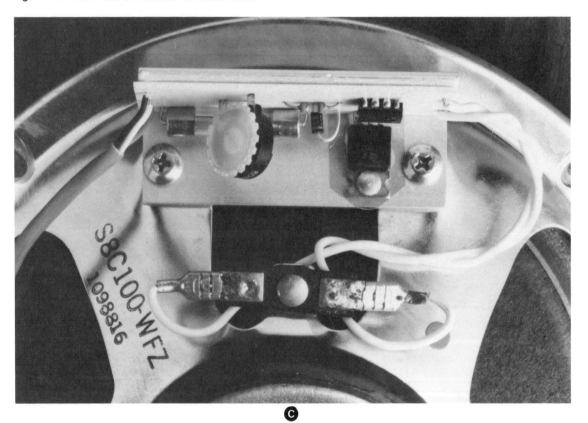

Fig. 6-14C. The SBA-R remote loudspeaker unit.

Fig. 6-14D. The SBA-P power supply used for long extensions of the system. The fidelity of the SBA system is excellent due to the direct-coupled circuit used.

Of Consonants as a Criterion For Speech Transmission in a Room," *Jour. Audio Engr. Soc.,* Vol 19, No 11 (Dec) pp 915-919.

2. Klein, W., 1971. "Articulation Loss of Consonants as a Basis For The Design and Judgement of Sound Reinforcement Systems," *Jour. Audio Engr. Soc.,* Vol 19, No 11 (Dec), pp 920-922.

3. Davis, Don and Carolyn, 1975. *Sound Systems Engineering,* Howard W. Sams & Co., Inc., Indianapolis.

4. Eargle, John, 1983. "Line Distribution Systems," *db The Sound Engr. Mag.,* Vol 17, No 1 (Jan) pp 14-15.

5. Heyser, Richard C., 1959. "A Signal Biased Output Tranformerless Transistor Power Amplifier," Presented at the Audio Engr. Soc. Convention, New York (Oct).

6. Adkins, Carl Dane, 1980. "A distributed System Concept," Presented at the 66th Convention of the Audio Engr. Soc., Los Angeles, (May) preprint #1627.

7. Davis, Don, 1979. "Signal Biased Amplification," *Sound & Comm.,* (Oct).

8. Freeman, B.A. and J.S. Sinclair, 1981. "Hearing Aids For The Elderly." *Aging: Communication Processes and Disorders,* D.S., Beasley and G.A. Davis, Editors, Grune and Stratton, Inc., New York.

9. J.W. Davis & Company, P.O. Box 26177, Dallas, TX 75226.

Chapter 7

Microphones—Types and, Characteristics

T HE MICROPHONE CAN BE CONSIDERED THE most critical link in the audio chain because of its basic determination of the quality of the signal entering the audio chain. No subsequent link in the chain can correct for inaccuracies introduced by the microphone, they can only degrade the signal further. The microphone is "up front," the transducer of the air pressure variations representing the audio signal into electrical variations, which is the audio signal in electrical form. There is good reason for focusing our attention on the microphone from the signal quality standpoint.

There are so many microphones available today that it is a difficult task for the uninitiated to select the best suited to present needs. Microphone types, directional pattern, impedance, power requirement, sensitivity, and efficiency tend to confuse the picture. The purpose of this chapter is to simplify this task, to emphasize the basic points and to provide a rationale for decision making.

7.1 DYNAMIC (MOVING COIL) MICROPHONES

In Chapter 2 we learned that a conductor mov-

ing in a magnetic field has a voltage induced in it. The longer the conductor, the faster it is moved, and the denser the magnetic flux, the greater is this induced voltage. This principle is the basis on which the moving coil, dynamic microphone of Fig. 7-1 is built. By attaching a coil to a diaphragm and positioning the coil in a magnetic field, the voltage induced in the coil will follow accurately the movement of the diaphragm.

We also remember the converse principle, that if a current flows in a conductor in a magnetic field, a force acts on the conductor. The loudspeaker operates on this principle, which emphasizes the close family resemblance between the dynamic microphone and the magnetic loudspeaker. In fact, loudspeakers commonly act also as microphones in some intercommunicating systems, and did you know that dynamic microphones can function as loudspeakers, as well? They may be a bit limited in their output, but all the pieces are there.

The voice coil of Fig. 7-1 is carefully formed to be as thin as possible so that the air gap of the magnetic circuit can also be small. This maximizes

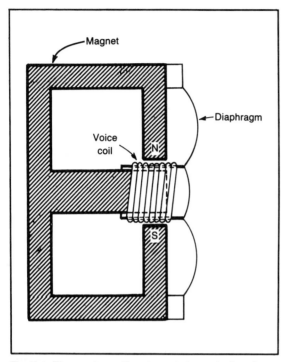

Fig. 7-1. The moving coil or dynamic type of microphone. The coil, affixed to the diaphragm, generates a voltage as it moves in the magnetic field. The voltage generated conforms closely to the movement of the diaphragm which, in turn, conforms to the air pressure changes of the audio signal actuating the diaphragm.

the intensity of the magnetic field in the gap, and thus the sensitivity of the microphone. The voice coil is made of very thin wire and the turns are glued together so as to be self supporting. The coil is then glued to the diaphragm and carefully centered in the gap. Air pressure fluctuations constituting the sound waves cause the diaphragm to move. This movement is imparted to the voice coil and an electrical replica of the sound pressure variations appear at the microphone terminals.

The air cavity behind the diaphragm is necessary to give the proper low-frequency response to the microphone. In some microphones the handle is made hollow to increase the volume of this cavity.

The impedance of typical voice coil is of the order of 10 to 12 ohms. A transformer is used to step this impedance up to the usual 150 ohms or so. The

feeble signal voltage is also stepped up in the process. In some dynamic microphones transformers step up the impedance to 30,000 ohms or so. These are classified as high-impedance microphones and their use is limited to short cable runs because of the tendency toward hum pickup.

The dynamic (moving coil) microphone is the most popular microphone in use today. There are several reasons for this popularity. It is very rugged microphone. Dynamic quality can be very high in well-designed units and the cost is modest. The response characteristics can be tailored to meet almost any need.

7.2 RIBBON MICROPHONES

Microphones employing the ribbon principle came into wide use in the early 1930s. Since that time they have been greatly improved and they are counted among the fine microphones available today. The ribbon microphone operates on the basis of a conductor, actuated by sound waves in air, having a voltage induced in it as it moved in a magnetic field. If this sounds like the dynamic microphone, well, it is similar. The form of the conductor in the two is quite different. A coil of wire moves in the magnetic field of the dynamic microphone. In the ribbon microphone, the ribbon serves both as the moving conductor and the diaphragm. A very lightweight corrugated aluminum ribbon is mounted between the pole pieces of the magnetic circuit as shown in Fig. 7-2. The mounting of the ribbon is such as to prevent the ribbon from ever touching the pole pieces. As the ribbon moves under the influence of minute air pressure fluctuations of the sound wave, a voltage is induced between the two ends of the ribbon. This voltage is stepped up as the impedance is increased by a transformer.

The ribbon microphone is sometimes referred to as a "pressure gradient" or "velocity gradient" microphone. The ribbon is not simply blown back and forth by the sound waves, it moves in response to difference in the pressure acting on the front and the rear of the ribbon, hence the "pressure gradient" term. Another way of putting this is that the ribbon responds to the difference in air velocity between the front and the rear of the ribbon.

Reproduction of sound by the ribbon microphone is accurate and highly detailed. The frequency response is wide range and its polar pattern is maintained throughout its frequency range. The ribbon microphone is noted for its warm and natural low-frequency reproduction. The lightness of the ribbon determines many of these favorable characteristics, but lightness and fragility tend to go hand in hand giving the ribbon microphone the early reputation of being vulnerable to outdoor wind damage and damage from powerfully popped "p's" and "t's." Modern manufacturing techniques have minimized such problems.

7.3 CONDENSER MICROPHONES

The sensitive element in the condenser or capacitive microphone is (surprise!) a condenser such as shown in Fig. 7-3. It may take a considerable amount of accompanying gear to complete the picture, but fundamentally such microphones are the acme of simplicity. Back in Chapter 2 it was

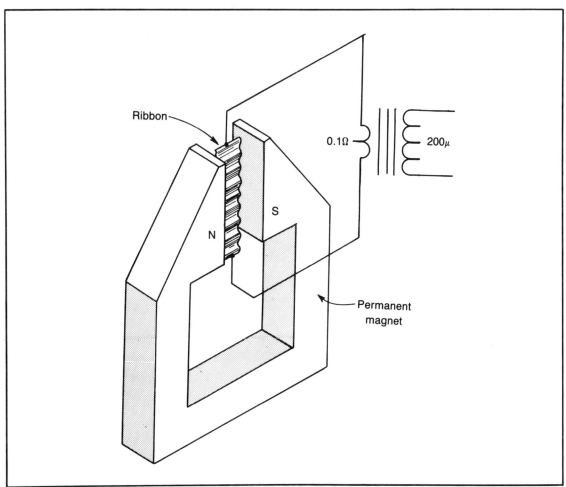

Fig. 7-2. The ribbon in the ribbon microphone serves both as diaphragm and moving conductor. This ribbon moves in response to pressure gradient or pressure differential on the two sides of the ribbon. The movement of the ribbon in the magnetic field generates the signal voltage. The pattern of the ribbon microphone is bidirectional with maximum response perpendicular to the plane of the ribbon and zero response in the plane of the ribbon.

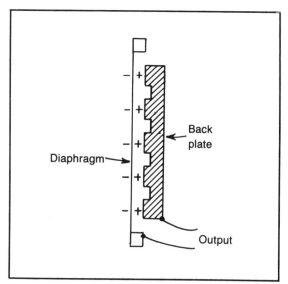

Fig. 7-3. The condenser microphone has a light, metallized diaphragm mounted close to a metal backplate, the two constituting a capacitor. A polarizing voltage charges this capacitor. As the diaphragm moves a voltage appears across the output proportional to the movement of the diaphragm. The electret condenser microphone requires no polarizing voltage because of the permanent charge placed on the electret diaphragm.

stated that the voltage appearing across two plates of a condenser is equal to the charge divided by the capacitance. The charge is constant, so movement of the diaphragm, which is one plate of the condenser, causes the voltage across the two plates to vary in direct proportion to the movement. The fixed backing plate assures that the movement of the very thin diaphragm (a few ten-thousandths of an inch thick) will not be impeded.

There must be a constant polarizing voltage between the diaphragm and the backing plate to maintain constant charge. This requires a special source of 45 to 60 volts, usually obtained through "phantom" powering to be described in detail in a following section. One type of condenser microphone which does nor require outside power is the electret condenser, which was described in Chapter 2 (see Figs. 2-1, 2-2).

Condenser microphones are used in precision sound-level meters and other types of acoustical measuring equipment. Their stability, wide and smooth frequency response, and their ability to measure high sound pressures have led to their selection for many measuring applications.

Condenser microphones have the lowest distortion of all types. The electret type of condenser must have a heavier diaphragm to maintain the charge and for this reason may not realize as low distortion as the phantom-powered type. Condenser microphones require a built-in preamplifier which helps their signal-to-noise ratio. The condenser microphone is noted for its flat frequency response and response to very high frequencies. Electret microphones are modest in cost, but true condenser microphones usually are at the top of the price list.

7.4 THE OMNIDIRECTIONAL PATTERN

In Fig. 7-4 an idealized microphone is shown simply as a diaphragm and a sealed air chamber. At the moment we do not care what type of operating principle it employs. Only one face of the microphone is available to the compressions and rarefactions of the impinging sound waves. If the wavelength of the sound is larger than the size of the microphone, waves arriving from the rear readily bend around to actuate the diaphragm. There would be a tendency for the high frequency, short wavelength sound arriving from the rear to "see" the diaphragm as being in a shadow zone. For all but these very high frequencies, the microphone pictured is equally responsive to sound from any direction.

The standard method of describing the directional properties of a microphone such as the one in Fig. 7-4 is through a polar plot of the type shown in Fig. 7-5. The heavy circle at 1.0 radius tells us that the microphone is equally responsive to sound arriving from any direction. The axis of the microphone is aligned with the 0 degree direction. Response of the microphone to sound arriving from the opposite direction is shown at 180 degrees. Response to sound arriving from the right is shown at 90 degrees, from the left at 270 degrees. The heavy circle describes full and uniform response to sound arriving from any direction.

This polar plot of Fig. 7-5 looks flat, but it should be considered, not as a circle, but as a sphere. In other words, consider the volume swept out by rotating the circle about the axis of the microphone. A truly omnidirectional microphone has a polar plot in the form of a sphere, with the same response fore, aft, off the port and starboard beams, above and below, to borrow a few nautical phrases.

7.5 THE BIDIRECTIONAL PATTERN

A sectional view of the ribbon microphone is shown in Fig. 7-6. The vertical ribbon is at A, the shaded pole pieces of the magnetic structure are at B and C. The entire instrument is encased in an acoustically transparent protective housing. As mentioned previously, the difference between the pressure (or velocity) of the air at the front and the rear of the ribbon is what moves the ribbon and gives output voltage. In Fig. 7-6 the sound is shown arriving from the right, but sound arriving from the left will have exactly the same effect if the microphone is symmetrical.

If the sound arrives from a direction in the plane of the ribbon (from the top or bottom of Fig. 7-6), there is no gradient, no difference between what strikes one side of the ribbon and what strikes the other side. Therefore, one cancels the other and there is zero response to sound arriving in the plane of the ribbon.

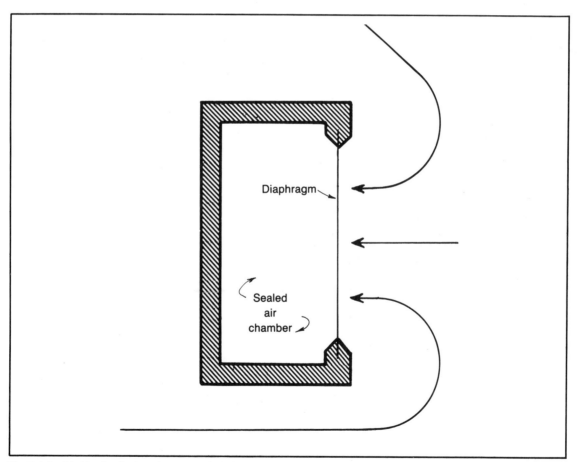

Fig. 7-4. In this idealized microphone a sealed chamber backs up the diaphragm. This is an omnidirectional microphone because sound arriving from any direction causes the diaphragm to vibrate. There is a shadow effect for very-high-frequency waves arriving from the rear.

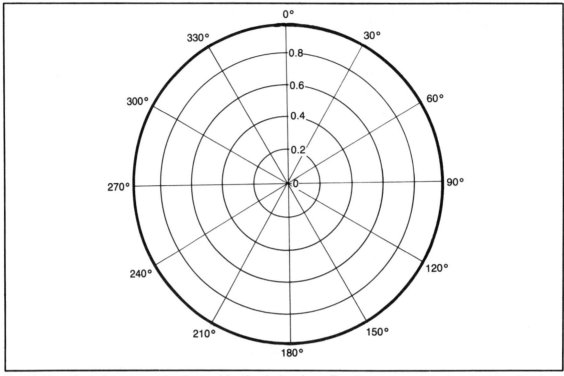

Fig. 7-5. The polar pattern representing the omnidirectional microphone. Zero degrees represents the axis of the microphone with the diaphragm pointed toward the 0 degree mark. This represents a sphere, not a circle on a flat plane.

This gives rise to the bidirectional pattern of Fig. 7-7. There is full response to sound arriving perpendicular to the face of the ribbon, either from the front or the rear. There is zero response to sound arriving at 90 or 270 degrees. In between these extremes the response turns out to be proportional to the cosine of the angle. For example, the cosine of 60 degrees is 0.5 and we see that the response if 0.5 in Fig. 7-7 at all the symmetrical 60 degree points.

Historically, the ribbon microphone was the primary source of bidirectional, figure-8 patterns. Today there are other ways of obtaining such a pattern. Through the use of acoustical or electrical networks, condenser or dynamic microphones may be made to have a bidirectional pattern.

7.6 THE CARDIOID PATTERN

The bidirectional pattern sometimes gives problems. For example, if a null is pointed toward

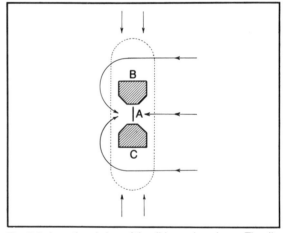

Fig. 7-6. A sectional view of the ribbon microphone. The ribbon is at A, mounted between two magnetic pole pieces B and C. Sound waves coming to the front and the rear of the ribbon create the pressure differential which actuates the ribbon and produces the voltage. Sound waves arriving in the plane of the ribbon are equal on both sides of the ribbon causing no ribbon movement, hence zero response from the ends.

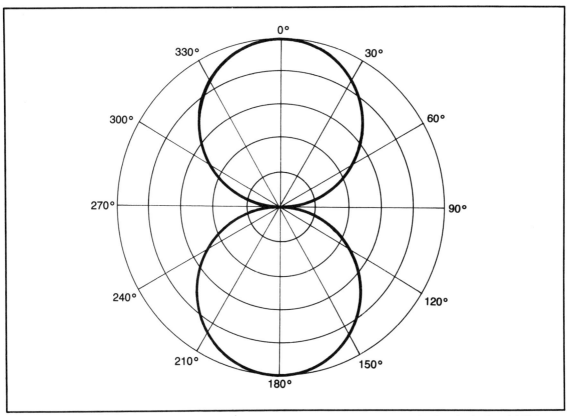

Fig. 7-7. The bidirectional pattern characteristic of the ribbon microphone. Full response is given in the 0 and 180 degree directions, zero response in the 90 and 270 degree directions. These are two spheres rather than two circles to represent the response of the ribbon microphone in three dimensions.

a particularly objectionable noise source to clean up the signal, the other null may reduce pickup from a desired source. It is sometimes awkward to manage a pair of nulls 180 degrees from each other. The cardioid pattern with its single null comes to the rescue.

The cardioid pattern gets its name from its heart-like shape. Producing a cardioid pattern is a mathematician's delight. In fact, even though we may not be too much attracted to math, we may dredge a little delight from the process. In Fig. 7-8 a circle of radium I have inscribed in it a bidirectional pattern having a radius of 1. By combining the omnidirectional pattern with the bidirectional pattern, a cardioid is produced. This can be done graphically, without recourse to the mathematics. At an angle of 30 degrees, for example, the distance

from the center of the polar diagram to the intersection with the bidirectional pattern at A is $= 0.866$. This adds to the circle radius of 1.00 at B to give the radius C of 1.866 units in length as a point on the cardioid pattern. At an angle of 60 degrees the distance to D ($+0.5$) is added to the radius E of the circle (1.00) to give the radius F of 1.5 units as the radius F on the cardioid pattern. At 90 degrees the bidirectional pattern adds nothing and the point G is simply the 1.00 units of the circle. The same process can be carried out for angles from 90 to 270 degrees remembering that the contribution of the bidirectional pattern now has a negative sign. At 180 degrees the cardioid response is -1 from the bidirectional pattern and $+1$ from the omnidirectional pattern, which gives a big fat zero for dead astern.

This cardioid pattern (heavy line of Fig. 7-8) is not in a single plane, but should be considered the three dimensional pattern obtained if the flat cardioid is rotated through 180 degrees. This gives a shape something like a toy balloon with the end dented. Figure 7-9 shows the cardioid pattern plotted to the same scale as Figs. 7-5 and 7-7.

7.7 PATTERN INTERRELATIONSHIPS

A null is not really a null if we take the word

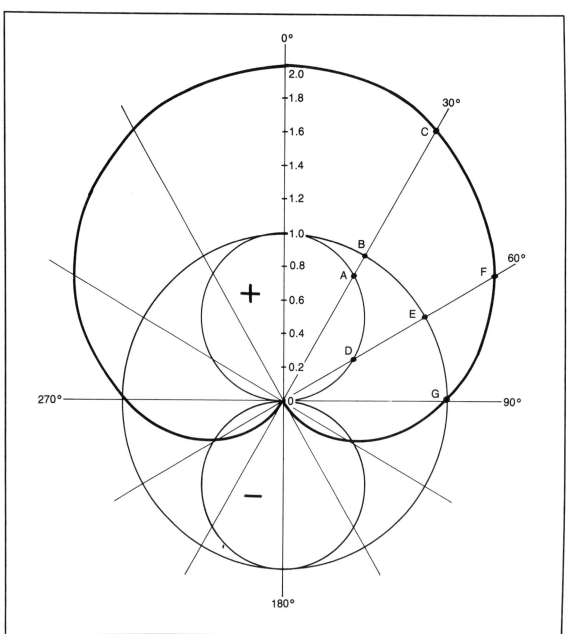

Fig. 7-8. The cardioid is produced by combining a bidirectional pattern with an omni pattern.

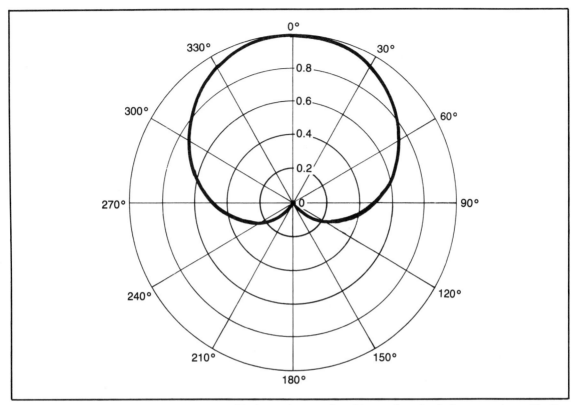

Fig. 7-9. A cardioid pattern, so-called because of its heart shape, reduced to a radius of unity for comparison with other patterns.

null to mean nil, nothing. However, it is a convenient word, well entrenched in audio lingo. Measured nulls may go down 20 dB or so, which in most practical cases gives some justification for doing violence to the Queen's English.

Table 7-1 shows the interrelationship between the omni and bidirectional patterns and the various cardioid and super-cardioid combinations in between (Refs.1,2). The last two lines of the table show how that particular pattern is built up from the sum of omni and bidirectional patterns. For the cardioid pattern, the omni portion is 0.5 and the bidirectional portion is 0.5 cos Θ. Adding these two portions for any angle gives the cardioid radius. Most hand-held calculators will give the cosine of any desired angle.

The first line of Table 7-1 gives the angular location of nulls. These are easily evaluated by finding the angle at which the cosine term of the last line is equal to the omni term above it.

The random energy efficiency (REE) of Table 7-1 is a convenient measure to use in comparing one pattern with another. It is a measure of how a microphone with the particular pattern responds to energy arriving from random directions. From the second line we see that the random energy efficiency of the omni pattern is 1.0, that of the cardioid is 0.33. The omni pattern responds equally to sound arriving from any direction while the cardioid pattern has minimum response at 180 degrees and far less than the omni between 90 and 270 degrees. We see, then, that the lower the REE value, the more directional is the microphone. This can be viewed in another way by taking the reciprocal of the square root of REE as done on the third line. Now we have a number that is a direct measure of working distance as compared to the omni rather than a fraction that is smaller for the more directive microphone patterns. The supercardioid patterns (1.93 and 2.0) are shown to work at greater distance from a source than any of the others. Interestingly, we note that the bidirectional and cardioid microphones have the same distance factor. This means that they respond to a diffuse field the same but accept energy from different directions.

The fourth line of Table 7-1 gives the directivity index which expresses directivity in terms of the number of decibels a given pattern is better than the omni pattern. This is probably the more useful indicator to the microphone user, as it is noted that the supercardioid will give 6 dB higher signal at 0 degrees than an omni microphone. However, of the three different ways of expressing directivity you may take your pick.

7.8 PROXIMITY EFFECT

The ribbon microphone, or any other microphone operating on the pressure gradient effect, exhibits what is called the *"proximity effect."* When such microphones are close to a sound source, such as a person talking or singing, the low-frequency response of the microphone is affected. Figure 7-18 illustrates the effect with a professional dynamic cardioid microphone, the Electro-Voice Model DS35. There is a boost at low frequencies at 10 dB or so when the sound source is very close to the microphone. At a more normal 2-inch distance the response is flat. When the source is more than two or three feet from the microphone, a smooth low frequency roll-off prevails. This variability of low-frequency response provides the user with great flexibility. Close talking this microphone gives warmth and strength to the voice but clarity may suffer somewhat due to the effect on high frequencies.

7.9 IMPEDANCE RELATIONSHIPS

A brief review of Section 2.26 and Fig. 2-32 is in order as impedance relationships affecting microphones are considered. Every microphone has an internal impedance in series with its open circuit generated voltage as shown in Fig. 7-11. This generated voltage is not measured at the microphone terminals with an instrument drawing current because this current would create and IR voltage drop across the internal impedance of the microphone. The voltage that would be measured would be the generator voltage less the voltage drop across the internal impedance of the microphone. It is this microphone generator voltage that we are interested in and conserving this feeble signal and protecting it from being lost in noise is our goal in deciding what amplifier load impedance should be

Table 7-1. Microphone Directional Patterns.

	Omni	Cardioid	Super-cardioid		Bidirectional
Nulls		180°	126.9°	109.5°	90°
REE	1.0	0.33	0.268	0.25	0.33
1/ $\sqrt{REE}$	1.0	1.73	1.93	2.0	1.73
10 log REE	0 dB	4.8 dB	5.7 dB	6.0 dB	4.8 dB
Omni	1	0.5	0.375	0.25	0
Bidir.	0	0.5 cos θ	0.625 cos θ	0.75 cos θ	1 cos θ

(After Ludwig, Reg 1 and Woram, Ref 2)

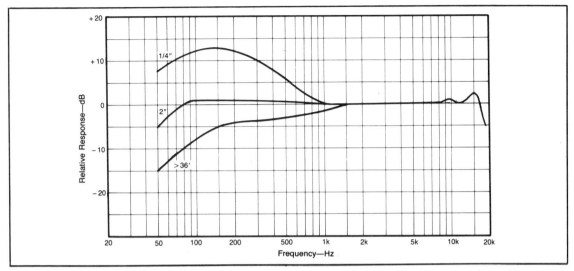

Fig. 7-10. An illustration of the proximity effect. The ribbon microphone and other microphones operating on the pressure gradient effect give a rise in bass response when the source of sound is very close. This figure shows the response of the Electro-Voice Model DS35 for source distances of 1/4 inch, 2 inches, and distances of 2 to 3 feet. This property of pressure gradient microphones is put to good use by performers to give body and strength for close talking, flat response for normal distances, and a falling low-frequency characteristic for more distant sources. Great flexibility of response is available by the simple expedient of varying distance to source.

connected to the microphone terminals.

There are two categories of microphones: those having low internal impedance and those having high internal impedance. High impedance microphones usually have unbalanced outputs with one of the two terminals grounded to the case and cable shield. This unbalanced arrangement, coupled with high impedance cable runs connecting the microphone to its amplifier, result in high hum and noise pickup. For this reason high impedance microphone use is limited principally to home and nonprofessional installations with cables of 15 feet length or less. Low impedance microphones are usually of the balanced type, that is, the two signal leads are isolated from case and cable shield to allow single-point grounding to avoid ground loops.

As mentioned in Section 2.26, the matching of microphone impedance to load impedance is required for maximum power transfer. With a microphone, voltage is the important parameter, not power. For this reason, capturing as much of the microphone generator voltage as possible is the goal. This is done by working the microphone into would be the generator voltage less the voltage drop

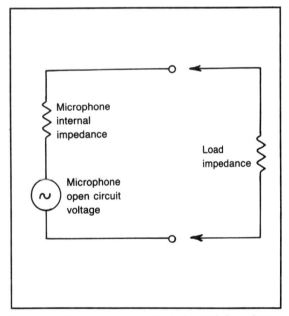

Fig. 7-11. All microphones have internal impedance. Matching impedances is important only for maximum transfer of power, which does not generally apply to microphones. Having the load impedance at least 10 times the internal impedance of the microphone assures maximum signal voltage transfer from the microphone to the preamplifier.

107

across the internal impedance of the microphone. It is this microphone generator voltage that we are interested in and conserving this feeble signal and protecting it from being lost in noise is our goal in deciding what amplifier load impedance should be connected to the microphone terminals.

There are two categories of microphones: those having low internal impedance and those having high internal impedance. High impedance microphones usually have unbalanced outputs with an impedance of at least 10 times the microphone impedance. Low impedance microphones have impedances of from 50 to 250 ohms. The $10 \times$ minimum would dictate impedances of 500 to 2500 ohms in mixer and amplifier inputs but 10,000 ohms is common.

7.10 MICROPHONE RATINGS

To compare one microphone with another may involve many things: cost, subjective evaluation of performance, frequency response curves, physical size and shape, etc. The sensitivity ratings of the microphones would also be considered. This rating is nothing more than a statement of how much output the microphone develops for a given sound pressure. Output may be considered on an open circuit voltage basis, or on a power basis.

In Europe (and microphones manufactured in Europe are common around the world) the open circuit voltage a microphone delivers when placed in a sound field of 1 pascal is the accepted form for specifying its rating. A sound pressure level of 94 dB corresponds to a sound pressure of 1 pascal. Thus a microphone might be rated as giving 5 millivolts when placed in a sound field of 1 Pa. The AKG C-460B pressure gradient condenser microphone is rated at 9.5 mV/Pa or -40.5 dBV. The latter is merely 0.0095 volt expressed in decibels below 1 volt.

The Electro-Voice Model DS35 dynamic cardioid microphone is rated for output level as follows: -60 dB (0 dB = 1 mW/10 dynes/sq cm). This is a power rating as milliwatts are involved. First, let us be reminded that 10 dynes/sq cm is exactly the same sound pressure as the 94 dB sound pressure level mentioned above. As the power reference is stated as 1 mW or 0.001 watt, the following statement can be written:

$$10 \log (P/0.001) = -60 \text{ dB}$$
$$(P/0.001) = 10 \text{ to the } -60/0.001 \text{ power}$$
$$P = 1 \text{ picowatt}$$

which is very small power. Knowing the impedance of the microphone is 150 ohms nominal it can be calculated that the output voltage of this microphone is 0.387 mV. For simplicity, the open circuit voltage method of specifying microphone sensitivity would seem to be better. This rating of the E-V DS35 mentioned above is for the condition of the microphone working into an impedance equal to its own. If it works into a higher impedance (say, 10 times higher) its voltage output would be doubled or 6 dB higher.

7.11 PHANTOM POWER

Condenser microphones of the electret type require no external powering because of the built-in polarization of the diaphragm. Conventional condenser microphones, however, must have a polarizing voltage to establish the charge between diaphragm and backing plate so that a signal voltage will be generated as the diaphragm moves. The usual method of supplying the condenser microphone element with dc power is shown in the circuit of Fig. 7-12. This is called "phantom" power because it is conducted over the signal leads with no adverse effect on the signal. The power supply positive terminal is connected to the center of matched resistors across the signal line. They are of high enough resistance so as not to disturb the impedance relationships of the line. Half the current from the power supply flows down each of the signal leads. The currents in the two halves of the microphone transformer secondary flow in opposite directions so that the dc current has no adverse magnetizing effect. From this transformer center-tap the positive potential goes by way of the field-effect transistor preamplifier circuit to the diaphragm and backing plate. A centertapped

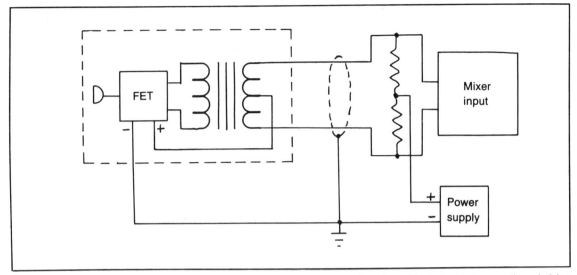

Fig. 7-12. A common method of supplying "phantom" power to a condenser microphone. Centertapping causes the polarizing current to flow in opposite directions in the transformer secondary, minimizing saturation effects.

transformer could also be used at the mixer end instead of a center-tapped resistance if transformer input to the mixer is used.

7.12 INTERFERENCE EFFECTS AT THE DIAPHRAGM

If diaphragm size becomes significant (say, an inch in diameter or more) interference takes place for sound arriving from off axis. Referring to Fig. 7-13, the wavefronts of sound arriving perpendicular to the surface of the diaphragm are all parallel to the diaphragm. The alternating condensations and rarefactions actuate the diaphragm in an accurate way. For short wavelength sound arriving at an angle to the axis of the microphone some portions of the diaphragm are under the effect of a condensation, while other portions are being affected by rarefactions. If the diameter of the diaphragm, the wavelength of the sound, and the angle of arrival are just right, half the diaphragm could be pushed inward while the other half is sucked outward by a rarefaction. A one-inch microphone has a diameter of one wavelength at 13.5 kHz. At this frequency, microphone response to sound coming from a 45 degree angle would be reduced as the diaphragm responds to

both a compression and a rarefaction at the same time. Microphone response to random sound at high audio frequencies is affected by this interference effect. The smaller the microphone diaphragm the less this effect will be.

For entertainment and other similar pickups, an effort is made to have the primary sound impinge on the microphone diaphragm at the 0 degree angle as shown on the polar diagrams. This minimizes this interference effect and tends to give the flattest response of the microphone. Sound arriving from off-axis angles tends to encounter a high-frequency drop-off.

7.13 WIRELESS MICROPHONES

The umbilical cord of the microphone has been cut by introduction of a radio frequency transmission link between the microphone and the recording of transmission equipment. Modern advances in the aerospace and computer industries have been applied to wireless microphone systems with the result of smaller size and better performance. Performers are accepting wireless microphones more readily because the unfortunate failures of the past are rare today.

Film and television production has been revolutionized as wireless microphones are hidden on performer giving exceptional freedom of movement. There are those who say this has elevated production values as more natural action is made possible. Others think the accompanying degradation of quality more than offsets the benefits realized. Some of the degradation of quality undoubtedly reflects budget limitations, which encourage a slap-happy attitude in recording and even directing personnel. Some of the degradation of quality may be attributed to lack of experience and/or training of recording personnel working with wireless microphones. To see this degradation of quality all one has to do is to compare sound quality of motion pictures made prior to about 1970 on television with the "made for TV" kind so prevalent today. Understandability of speech has fallen to abyssmal depths. The acceptance of irrelevant, disturbing environmental noises and the wheezing of performers as they walk through the woods is astounding. Clarity of speech should be evaluated as well as whether the signal makes the meter needle hit the pin. The sad part is that wireless microphone use is getting an undeserved bad reputation.

Two regions of the radio-frequency spectrum are used for wireless microphones. The VHF systems operate in the 175 to 216 MHz region, which are also used by television, and the channels available depend on locality. If channels 7, 9, 11, and 13 are used for TV in one locality, wireless microphone systems must be confined to the portion of the spectrum occupied by channels 8, 10, and 12. In the UHF portion of the spectrum in the United States wireless microphones operate near 450 MHz and in the range 947 to 952 MHz. The noise conditions are better in the UHF region because the interference from automobile ignition, fluorescent lights, and other electrical equipment is less. The power radiated by wireless microphone transmitters is limited by the Federal Communications Commission to 50 milliwatts as compared to the 1-watt power of most walkie-talkies. This throws an exceptional burden on the designer to get high quality service with such low power.

A major problem with wireless microphones is

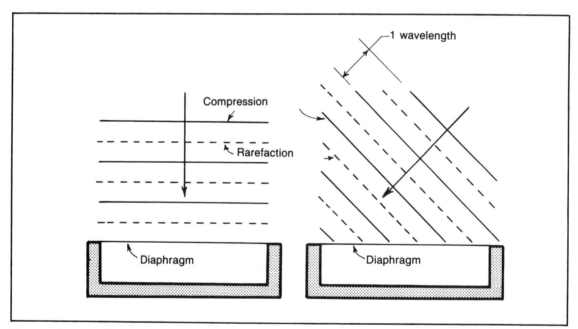

Fig. 7-13. If microphone diaphragms are too large (greater than 1-inch in diameter, for instance) rarefactions and condensations of sound arriving at angles off the perpendicular actuate the diaphragm simultaneously. This results in loss of response and irregularity of response.

so-called drop-outs as the one wearing the microphone transmitter moves about. Standing wave conditions change, resulting in a greatly fluctuating signal at the receiving antenna. Having the performer wear a directional antenna is impractical, therefore greater demands fall on the receiving equipment. Applying the principle of diversity at the receiver has resulted in quite satisfactory operation. This diversity can be obtained by having several receivers whose antennas are physically separated all receiving the same signal with the best signal being selected. Another approach is having a single receiver with several separated antennas. A microprocessor switching system always selects the highest signal (Fig. 7-14).

Figure 7-15 shows the Swintek (Ref.11) Mark Q-ac/db-S, an economical non-diversity wireless microphone system suitable for use in business, school, and church applications. It utilizes the high VHF FM band to reduce interference generated by citizen's band radios, automobiles, fluorescent lights, etc. Signal processing in the form of companding (compression and expansion) is used to increase the dynamic range. The transmitter in the handle of the microphone operates on a standard 9-volt transistor battery. The receiver requires a 14-18 volt power-pak or a standard 110-volt power module.

A highly professional wireless microphone system, widely used in entertainment circles and for film and television production, is shown in Fig. 7-16. The Cetec Vega (Ref.12) Model 77 transmitter weights but 5 ounces and is small enough to fit in a pocket or be taped to the body of a performer. A miniature microphone is commonly used. Compression and limiting is employed to limit peak amplitudes in a gentle way rather than the harsh, simple slipping often used. Crystal frequency-

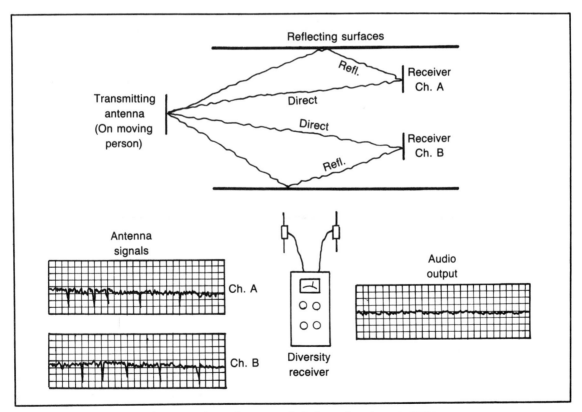

Fig. 7-14. A diversity system improves the performance of wireless microphone systems.

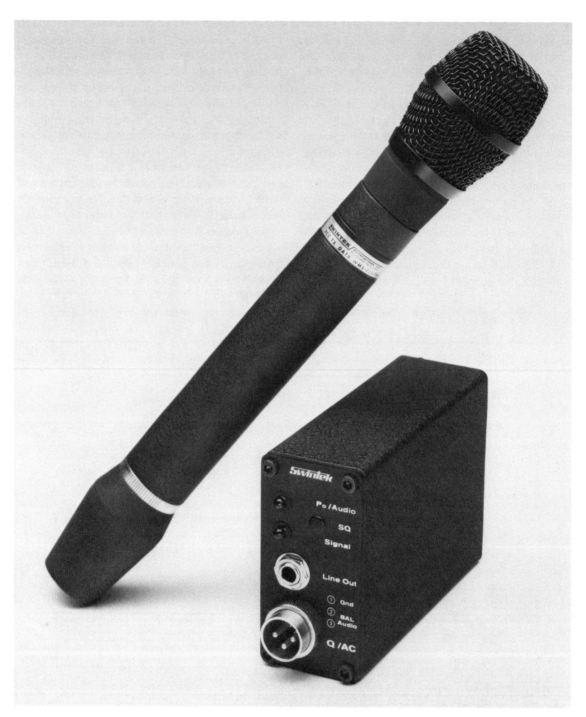

Fig. 7-15. The Swintek Matk Q-ac dB-S wireless microphone system suitable for use in business, school, and church applications. This is a non-diversity system. The transmitter is in the handle of the microphone (courtesy Swintek Enterprises, Inc.).

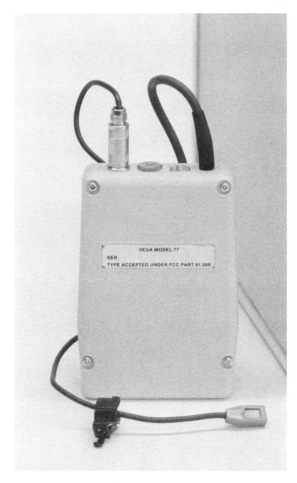

Fig. 7-16. The Cetec Vega Model 77 professional transmitter weighing only 5 ounces (courtesy Cetec Vega).

control provides stable operation.

Four Cetec Vega receivers are described in Fig. 7-17 and three hand-held wireless microphones in Fig. 7-18. The component parts of the Cetec Vega Q system wireless intercommunicating system used widely in television and film production and elsewhere are shown in Fig. 7-19.

7.14 BOUNDARY MICROPHONES

Boundaries have always had their effect, usually harmful, on the signals picked up by microphones. Reflections from floor, wall, tabletop, or other surfaces combining with the sound travelling directly to the microphone have degraded

quality since the first microphone was placed in service. The resulting comb-filter distortions, with their alternating constructive and destructive interference down through the audible spectrum, have long been a problem (Ref.3). Veneklausen applied a fresh approach, that of mounting the microphone in a hole in the tabletop so that the diaphragm was parallel to the surface of the table, causing the reflections from the tabletop to bounce harmlessly away. This principle spawned a host of brackets and "mice" to hold microphones close to the tabletop for voice pickup or close to the floor for distant pickups such as stage plays.

The Pressure Zone Microphone ™ (Ref.4) brought in a new relationship between microphones and reflecting surfaces. Long and Wickersham (Refs. 5,6,7) reasoned that placing the diaphragm of a microphone very close (5 to 10 thousandths of an inch) to a hard, reflecting surface, it could respond only to off-axis random incident sound and would therefore have a flat response to both on- and off-axis sound. This Pressure Zone Microphone, illustrated in Fig. 7-20, yields an omnidirectional pattern and has a frequency response as flat as that of the capsule employed. It also has a good transient response and virtually eliminates phase cancellation. That the idea of the PZM is a good one is borne out by the fact that their use is fast increasing and that other manufacturers now have their version of boundary microphones.

The theory of the Pressure Zone Microphone can be discussed with the aid of Fig. 7-21. In Fig. 7-21A the usual comb filter producing setup is shown. The sound from the source travels directly to the microphone while a second component reflected from some adjacent surface also travels to the microphone. The reflected component will arrive later than the direct because it travels further. There is an acoustical vector combination of the two in the air immediately in front of the microphone diaphragm. At some frequencies the two add in phase and a + 6 dB peak is formed. At a slightly higher frequency the two are 180 degrees out-of-phase, tending to cancel each other. Such peaks and dips occur throughout the audible spectrum, their spacing depending on the magnitude of

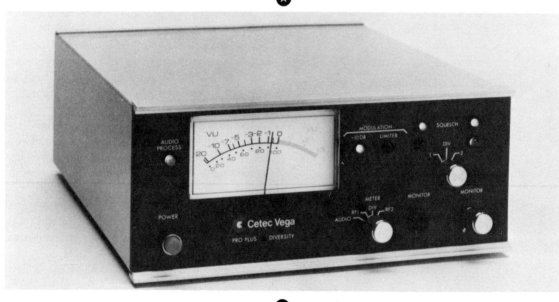

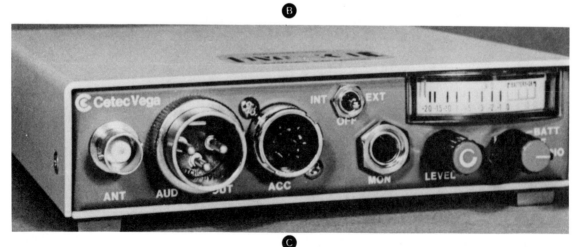

Fig. 7-17. The Cetec Vega Pro wireless microphone receivers: (A) the Model R-31, (B) the Pro Plus ultra low noise Model R-41 and R-42, (C) the Model 66A portable, and (D) Model 67A dual diversity receiver (courtesy Cetec Vega).

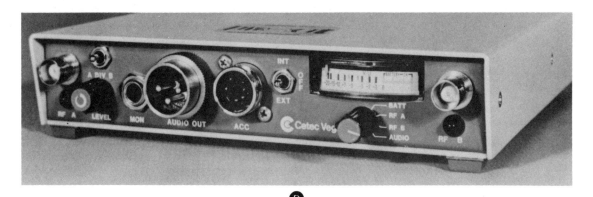

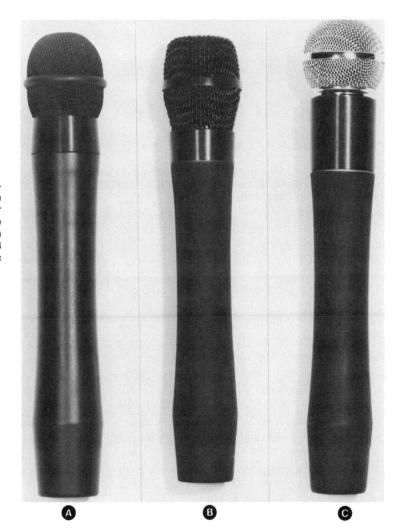

Fig. 7-17. The Cetec Vega Pro wireless microphone receivers: (D) Model 67A dual diversity receiver (courtesy Cetec Vega).

Fig. 7-18. The Cetec Vega hand-held wireless microphones: (A) Model T-83 with AKG 535 condenser element, (B) Model T-82 with Shure SM85 condenser element, and (C) Model T-81 with Shure SM58 dynamic element (courtesy Cetec Vega).

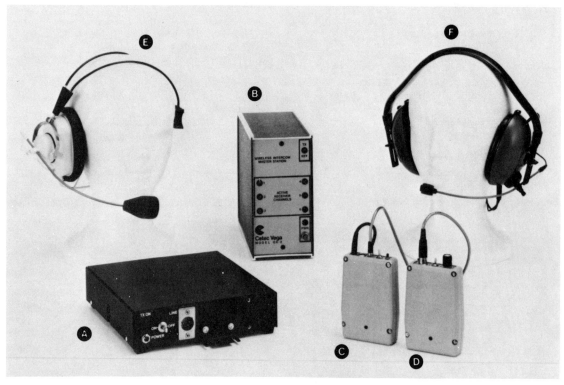

Fig. 7-19. The Cetec Vega professional wireless intercom components: (A) the QT-1 transmitter, (B) the QR-1 receiver, (C) the QX-1 base station, (D) the QX-2 base station, (E) the Model 168 single-muff headset, and (F) the Model 163 double-muff headset (courtesy Cetec Vega).

the delay. For most reflections from lectern tops. tabletops, floor, and nearby wall, these peaks and dips occur within the audible spectrum with a resulting raw edge effect imparted to the signal.

The construction of the PZM is illustrated in Fig. 7-21B. The microphone capsule, an electret condenser, is placed so that its diaphragm is extremely close to the metal plate reflecting surface. This diaphragm is now in the "pressure zone" a layer very close to a reflecting surface in which some interesting things happen. Obviously, the air particle velocity associated with the sound wave must be zero at the surface, as the heavy surface cannot be moved. At this point the kinetic energy of the air particles is changed to potential energy in the form of an increase in sound pressure. Although this pressure zone is a result of and responds to direct and reverberant sound falling on it, the presence of the plate of appreciable size protects

the zone from secondary reflections such as shown in Fig. 7-21A. The reflections of very, very short delay, such as shown in Fig. 7-21B are present, but their effect is moved to ultrasonic regions where they do no harm.

The typical comb-filter response shown in Fig. 7-21C helps us to understand that the very short reflections in the PZMicrophone place its operation in that part of the comb-filter response that is not only flat, but has a +6 dB boost in response. Peaks and dips exist, but they occur at frequencies outside the audible range of interest. For the longer delays, in the order of milliseconds, associated with the usual lectern or tabletop, there is precious little flat portion and many peaks and dips right within the audible region and their effects are readily heard.

There is a loss of pressure build-up in the PZM at low frequencies at which the size of the PZM

116

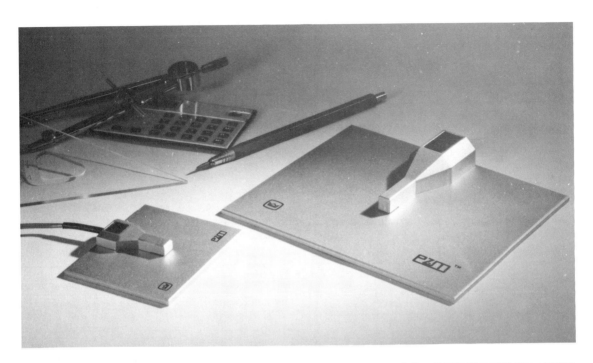

Fig. 7-20. Two models of the Crown Pressure Zone Microphone, one having a base plate 5×6 inches, the other 2-1/2×3 inches. Below are the switchable phantom/battery power supplies required to operate the microphones. The PZM operates in the pressure zone between the condenser microphone capsule diaphragm and the boundary plate, a spacing of only a few thousandths of an inch. This operating principle avoids comb-filter effects from nearby reflecting surfaces, which are a problem for conventional microphones.

reflecting plate is small compared to the wavelength of the sound. For a given plate size, as frequency is reduced, a 6 dB shelf will be found. As frequency is reduced further, eventually the low-frequency cutoff of the capsule will further reduce response. If we assume that the – 6 dB shelf will occur when the plate dimension corresponds to a quarter wavelength of the sound, the frequency of this plate cutoff is 282 divided by the plate edge length in feet. For example, for a 1-foot plate the – 6 dB shelf occurs at 282 Hz. The low frequency response can be further extended by placing the PZM on the floor, a table top, a piano lid, a wall, or a piece of plastic sheet if mounted on a stand.

The + 6 dB boost in the response of the PZM shown in Fig. 7-21C occurs in the pressure zone. The ratio of direct sound to reverberant sound, however, increases only 3 dB. Further data on the Pressure Zone Microphone may be found in Refs. 8, 9, and 10 as well as the Crown literature.

7.15 LAVALIER AND CLIP-ON MICROPHONES

In many difficult sound reinforcement situations, the only way the systems can be made to operate without feedback is to maintain minimum distance between the mouth of the one speaking and the microphone. The lavalier and the clip-on

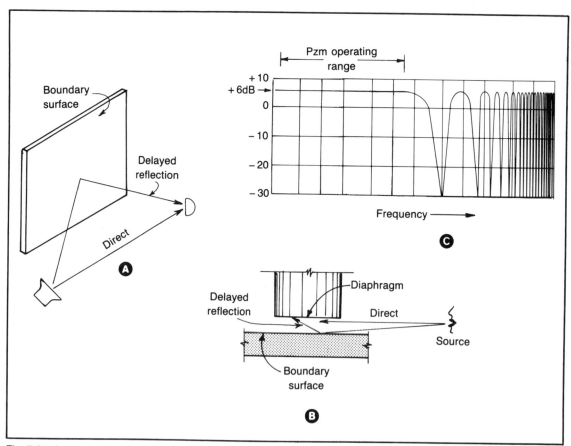

Fig. 7-21. A common problem with conventional microphones is the comb-filter effect resulting from the acoustical combination at the microphone diaphragm of the direct and reflected rays, which is illustrated in (A). In (B) the only such combination in the PZM microphone involve such short delays that the response irregularities are moved into the ultrasonic region. (C) The PZM operating range is on the flat response region, taking advantage of the + 6 dB pressure gain. This + 6 dB is lost at the lower frequencies.

microphones are often used under such conditions. They are also widely used in television conference and interview shows. They are very useful microphones, but they need equalization.

Graph A of Fig. 7-22 is the result of extensive studies in comparing the response of a lavalier microphone in lavalier position with the same microphone directly in front of the mouth of the one speaking. This curve reveals a peak at about 700 Hz attributed to chest resonances. There is also a notable fall off of response at frequencies above 2 kHz due to the directional effects of these frequencies at the mouth. The lavalier or clip-on microphone does not pick up the beamed higher frequencies from the mouth very well. The inverse of curve A shown in curve B is the equalization needed to overcome the deficiencies of the lavalier or clip-on position of the microphone.

Sennheiser built such equalization in its MD 214 lavalier. The Shure Model SM83-CN miniature lavalier also includes such equalization to make its signal sound natural. The response of the Shure microphone is plotted as a broken line (C) in Fig. 7-22. The chest resonance peak is smoothed out by a corresponding dip. The high frequency boosting, however, is less than that required as indicated by (A), probably leaving the rest of the required equalization to the operator at the mixer. These high frequencies are important for understanding speech.

References

1. Ludwig, Travis, 1983. "The Inside Story: A General Microphone Primer," *Sound & Video Contractor*, Vol. 1, No. 1, (Sept), pp 38-40, 44-52.

2. Woram, John M., 1981. "The Mathematics Of The Microphone," *dB The Sound Engineering Magazine*, Vol. 15, No. 6 (June), pp 44-47.

3. Everest, F.Alton, 1981 *The Master Hand-*

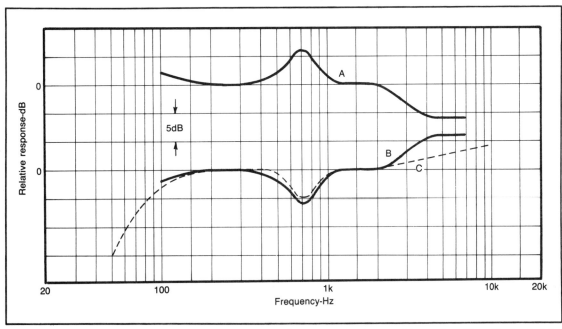

Fig. 7-22. Curve A is a comparison of a lavalier microphone's response in chest position and positioned in front of the mouth of the speaker. In the chest position a prominent peak at about 700 Hz is attributed to chest resonances. The fall off in the highs results from the directivity of high-frequency components emerging from the mouth. The Sennheiser MD214 lavalier microphone incorporates correction for these two effects. Curve B is the converse of A and represents the correction required to compensate for chest resonance and high-frequency fall off. The broken line is the response of the Shure SM83 lavalier microphone which partially corrects for high-frequency fall off.

book of Acoustics. TAB BOOKS, Inc., Blue Ridge Summit, PA 17214, #1296. Chapter 5, "Acoustical Comb Filter Effects."

4. ———,PZMicrophones, PZM, and Pressure Zone Microphones are trademarks of Crown International, Inc., Elkhart, IN 46517.

5. ———,1978. *Tech Topics* Vol. 5, No. 7, Synergetic Audio Concepts, San Juan Capistrano, CA 92693.

6. ———,1979. *Newsletter*, Vol. 7, No. 1, pg 6, Synergetic Audio Concepts, San Juan Capistrano, CA 92693.

7. Long, Edward, 1980. "The Pressure Recording Process," *dB The Sound Engineering Magazine*, Vol. 14, No. 1 (Jan), pp 31-33.

8. Andrews, David M., 1980. "Pressure Zone Microphones ™ - A Practical Application Of The Pressure Zone Recording process™," presented at the 66th convention of the Audio Engr. Society, Los Angeles (May), reprint No. 1647(J-4).

9. Barclay, Clay, 1981. "PZM; Theory and Practice Of a New Microphone Design," *dB The Sound Engr. Magazine*, Vol. 15, No. 6, (June), pp 34-39.

10. Wahrenbrock, Kenneth A., 1984. "The Development Of The Multiboundary Pressure Zone Microphone™," *Tech Topics*, Vol. 11, No. 4, Synergetic Audio Concepts, San Juan Capistrano, CA 92693.

11. Swintek Enterprises, Inc., 1180 Aster Avenue, Unit J, Sunnyvale, CA 94086

12. Cetec Vega, 9900 Baldwin Place, El Monte, CA 91731.

Chapter 8

Microphone Use and Placement

THE READER MUST UNDERSTAND THAT THE use and placement of microphones is a highly personal, subjective, and controversial activity. The problem for the writer is that readers also have their own ideas of what "sounds good." For this reason, the following discussion may seem to follow those avenues, that have some basis in science and engineering. This introduces a problem in that the ear must be the final arbiter in all questions of audio quality. But whose ear? The horns of this dilemma are dulled a bit by the knowledge that there is a growing body of measurement technology (both electronic and psychoacoustic) which correlates well with human reaction and is tending to bring widespread subjective judgements (of experts, at least) together. An example of this is the omnipresence of comb-filter distortions. A recent forward surge in appreciation of the harmful effects of acoustic phase interference (comb filters) is giving a rational basis for understanding such effects rather than considering them as a characteristic of the microphone.

There are a few general suggestions regarding use and placement of microphones which apply to most of the following sections. A good rule to follow is to listen critically in the search for a possible microphone location and place the microphone where the source sounds best to the ear. Another piece of advice is, in any given fixed installation, to try to specialize on a single type of microphone rather than accumulating samples of all available types. This simplifies equalization and allows rapid substitution and switching in emergencies. There are those who would say that it is good advice to specialize in unidirectional microphones as the most generally applicable type.

8.1 BALANCE

There are at least two ways of looking at the meaning of the word *"balance"* in regard to audio signals. The conductor of a vocal and/or instrumental group strives valiantly to give the audience a proper balance of vocal versus accompaniment, violins versus brass, etc. The person at the mixing console may have an entirely different view of balance as he considers the limitations of the recording channel and the final recording medium. The mixer must also make independent judgement on the relative level of organ or piano accompaniment and vocal sound.

Another quite different approach to the subject of balance is that of direct sound versus indirect, the balancing of direct sound into the microphone as compared to reverberation. This view of balance would include comparison of direct sound versus offending noise such as audience noise or noise from an air conditioning grille. A microphone very close to the source may essentially eliminate the audibility of reverberation or noise while a more distant microphone may allow reverberation or noise to dominate.

8.2 USING THE DYNAMIC MICROPHONE

Each type of microphone shares some characteristics with other microphones while differing in other characteristics. The distinctions may be confused as there is such a wide variation within each class of microphone. In spite of this there are certain outstanding characteristics associated with each type of microphone. The dynamic or moving coil microphone, for instance, is robust and forgiving of rough handling and has low handling noise. It also gives less overload distortion and is less susceptible to wind noise and so-called "pops" when the p's and t's are sounded. The dynamic microphone requires no external power supply which may be the determining factor in some applications. It is also cheaper.

8.3 USING THE CONDENSER MICROPHONE

The crowning glory of the condenser or capacitor microphone is its smooth and exceptionally wide frequency response. For this reason (and others) special condenser microphones are standard in acoustical measuring instruments. It was inevitable that studio personnel would try these measuring microphones in studio applications and they found them to offer such advantages that Bruel & Kjaer, the Danish firm specializing in acoustical measuring instruments, has adapted such measuring microphones to studio applications and is now marketing them.

Condenser microphones, in spite of their close tolerances, are surprisingly rugged. They do require an external power supply, but offer in return some 10 or 15 dB higher sensitivity. Condenser microphones are generally in the highest price category. An exception to this is the electret type of self-polarized microphone which offers many of the straight condenser advantages.

8.4 USING THE RIBBON MICROPHONE

With close to a half century behind it, the ribbon microphone has accumulated a host of followers charmed with its ability to make a voice sound better than life and adding a warmth lacking in other microphones. It also has low self noise and low transient distortion. An important characteristic, responsible for its wide use in early motion picture production, is its figure-8 polar pattern which allows discrimination against stage activity noises. It gives full response fore and aft, with deep nulls to port and starboard. The cost of the ribbon microphone is normally between that of the dynamic and the condenser microphones.

8.5 USING THE BOUNDARY MICROPHONE

Any reasonably small microphone may be called a boundary microphone of sorts by placing it close to a boundary such as a floor or tabletop. For example, The Electro-Voice Model RE-15 dynamic super-cardioid can be placed in the E-V Model 411 "Mike Mouse" of acoustically transparent foam material as shown in Fig. 8-1. This mounting places the diaphragm of the RE-15 fairly close to the tabletop for use in conferences, or the floor for stage pickups. Although close to the boundary, the diaphragm is not close enough to avoid comb-filter alterations of the frequency response. A 10 dB dip at about 7 kHz is evidence of this. The manufacturer suggests a felt or carpet under and immediately in front of the microphone to reduce the bounce from the tabletop. Such a mounting for standard microphones adapts them to boundary applications and numerous manufacturers

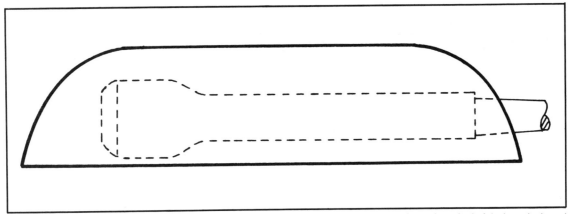

Fig. 8-1. The Electro-Voice Model 411 "Mike Mouse" made of acoustically transparent foam, is typical of devices designed to place a standard microphone as close as physically feasible to the floor or table surface to minimize acoustic phase-cancellation (comb-filter) effects.

offer such mountings for their microphones. Clipping a lavalier microphone to a plate allows an even closer placement of the diaphragm to the boundary surface than that of Fig. 8-1.

The Pressure Zone Microphone™ incorporates the first new microphone principle to be introduced since the cardioid in 1936 and its full utility has yet to be defined (Refs. 1, 2). Its freedom from interference effects due to primary reflections has made it a favorite with many. At first, the use of the PZM™ was envisioned largely on surfaces such as floor and tabletop but many current applications place them on stands or suspended over large musical groups.

An important addition to PZM lore is the recent addition of more reflecting surfaces in the immediate vicinity of the microphone. These are usually plastic sheets. The polar pattern of the bare PZM is in the form of a hemisphere. Placing the PZM at the 90 degree intersection of two plastic sheets reduces the response to a quarter sphere. Placing it at the intersection of three sheets of plastic restricts the response to one-eighth sphere. The size of such sheets determines the low-frequency response of the microphone because the effect of the sheets begins to disappear when the wavelength of the sound approaches the dimensions of the sheets.

For further investigation of the potential of the PZM, References 1 and 2 of this chapter and References 4 to 10 of Chapter 7 are recommended.

8.6 USING THE OMNIDIRECTIONAL MICROPHONE

The omnidirectional microphone is characterized by a sealed chamber behind the diaphragm as shown in Fig. 7-4. The sound pressure acts only on the front of the diaphragm, irrespective of the direction of arrival of the wave. The omnidirectional microphone may be of the dynamic, ribbon, or condenser type. With its omnidirectional polar pattern this microphone cannot discriminate against unwanted sounds such as reverberation, audience noise, or air conditioner noise.

There are advantages. Microphones with the omni pattern generally have smoother frequency response. This may mean less feedback in sound reinforcement situations because such feedback frequencies usually seek out response peaks in the equipment or in the room environment. Microphones with the omni pattern are also generally more free from popping sounds as p's and t's are enunciated, more rugged, and less likely to give spurious signals when handled or subjected to mechanical shock.

8.7 USING THE CARDIOID MICROPHONE

The two nulls of the early bidirectional microphone were often one null too many. Directing one null to fight a noise source often directed the remaining null and the back lobe in ways that caused other problems. The cardioid pattern provided the simplicity associated with a broad acceptance pattern and a broad region of low response in the opposite direction. There are several sound reinforcement systems that direct considerable sound toward the microphone such as the split column system, portable systems, and the use of stage monitors. Using the cardioid microphone in such situations provides enough rejection of direct sound to assure its popularity. The usable gain of sound reinforcement systems of the above types is ordinarily very low and the few decibels of rejection contributed by the cardioid is sometimes the difference between feedback and no feedback. For the central cluster type of sound reinforcement system, in which the cluster is 20 to 40 feet from the microphone, the performance of the omni and the cardioid microphones is about the same and often the omni is preferred for its other advantages. The cardioid microphone usually has poorer frequency

response than the omni and is less rugged. The fact that the cardioid also is more subject to wind noise and pops of t's and p's is less important because built-in filters care for such problems in many versions.

Off-axis coloration is often an important consideration of cardioid microphones as well as others. The response of the microphone on axis may look good. What is its response off axis? Figure 8-2 shows the response of a well respected supercardioid microphone both on axis and at 150 and 180 degrees. Off-axis coloration of sound will be no problem with this microphone because the off-axis response is quite flat.

8.8 USING THE BIDIRECTIONAL MICROPHONE

The bidirectional microphone still has its followers today. It is convenient as a double-sided microphone for interviews. The side nulls still provide protection against noise sources that fall within their angular limits. Not all bidirectional

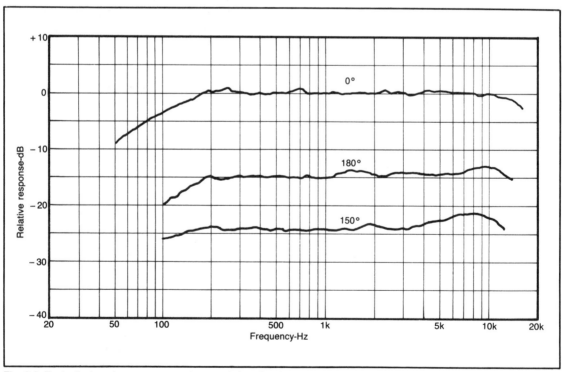

Fig. 8-2. Typical microphone response characteristics showing excellent response off axis. Nonuniform response at 180 and 150 degrees can cause coloration of sound arriving at the microphone at off-axis angles..

microphones are ribbons; some are condensers with acoustical filters and a few bidirectional dynamics are extant. While the off-axis response of most bidirectional microphones is quite flat with frequency, some are afflicted with off-axis response that is not flat.

8.9 A WORD ABOUT MICROPHONE FREQUENCY RESPONSE

The frequency response curves in the microphone catalogs are obtained in anechoic chambers, which are about as different from our practical spaces as can be imagined. However, there is some value in being able to compare microphones on some standard basis and the anechoic measurements serve that purpose. We tend to place greater emphasis on flatness of response than our ears do. The ultimate goal should be to strive for the best sound, not the flattest response. Again, the emphasis must be placed on what it sounds like, not what the meter readings say. There are many situations, such as a church sound reinforcement system, in which flatness of response should be sacrificed for understandability of speech. A 5 dB peak in the speech frequencies may greatly increase intelligibility of speech. Too flat a response, in the low-frequency region in a system used primarily for speech may cause problems of noise and rumble. The classic case of equalization of the lavalier microphone is not so much to make it flatter as to make the sound more intelligible. Close talking certain microphones may increase low-frequency response greatly and this deviation from a flat response may serve a very useful purpose. The genius in departing from the flat condition is to utilize some good effect obtained thereby.

8.10 THE PULPIT/LECTERN MICROPHONE

When two microphones are seen on a lectern or pulpit, the experienced audio person begins to wonder. Are the two microphones there to provide diversity in case one gives up the ghost, the second one available by switching? Does one of the microphones feed one service and the other a second service, two independent channels? Or (gasp, choke, wheeze) are their outputs summed and fed to the same amplifier? When the latter condition exists, our experienced audio person slumps down in the seat with a very pained expression. Why this reaction? Because things are bad enough with a single microphone, why tempt fate with two?

Comb-filter effects are the hazard with two microphones paralleled into a common amplifier. The sound from the person speaking energizes both microphones. If the mouth is exactly (within a small fraction of an inch) the same distance from the two microphones, and the two microphones are properly connected, the two electrical signals will be in phase and a 6 dB increase in level over that of a single microphone will prevail. If he moves a fraction of an inch to the left or right, the path lengths will differ, one signal will be delayed, and at some frequencies there will occur the +6 dB constructive interference, and at other frequencies there will be destructive interference (cancellation, partial or complete). The relatively flat basic response of each microphone is changed to a series of 6 dB peaks interspersed between 30 or 40 dB cancellations down through the spectrum.

Let us take a specific pulpit/lectern setup and study the extent of the comb-filter problem. In Fig. 8-3A a cardioid microphone is placed at a distance of 12-inches from the mouth of the one speaking by means of a flexible gooseneck. The direct sound travels 1-foot while the sound reflected from the surface travels 1.60 + 1.15 = 2.75 feet. The reflected sound arrives (2.75 – 1)/1130 ft/sec - 1.5 milliseconds later than the direct. The delay alone is enough to tell us at which frequencies the peaks and cancellations will occur, but the level of the two components will reveal the height of the peaks and the depth of the dips. Assuming inverse square propagation, the level of the reflection will be 20 log (1.0/2.75) = – 8.8 dB, or 8.8 dB below the direct. A cardioid microphone is indicated and its pattern must also be considered because the reflection comes in at an angle of 80 degrees from the axis, which means that it will be down 7.0 dB below the on-axis signal. The reflected signal is thus 8.8 + 7.0 = 15.8 dB below the direct. In my book (Ref. 3) a graph tells us that, on a calculated basis, the peaks will be + 3 dB high and the cancellations will

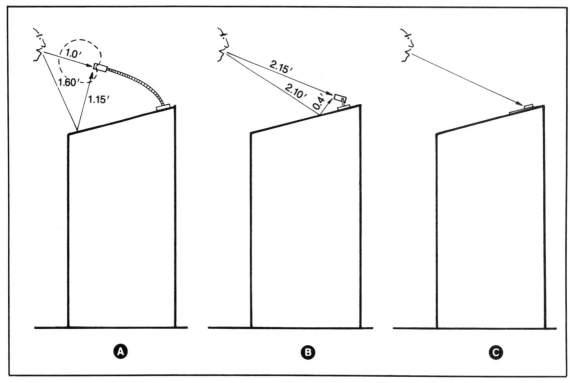

Fig. 8-3. Three possible pulpit/lectern microphone arrangements. (A) The geometry shown results in a ray reflected from the surface which arrives at the microphone diaphragm 1.5 milliseconds later than the direct which causes relatively modest +3 dB peaks and –4 dB dips in the system response. (B) Another arrangement of the same cardioid microphone in which the reflected ray is delayed 0.3 milliseconds which results in +5 dB peaks and – 18 dB dips in the system response. (C) Using a boundary microphone, such as the Pressure Zone Microphone TM, essentially eliminates system response alterations due to acoustic phase cancellation. The greater distance to the microphone tends to be offset by the greater "reach" of the PZM.

be – 4 dB deep. The first dip will occur at 350 hertz and subsequent peaks and dips will be spaced 700 hertz apart. This is shown graphically in Fig. 8-4A. We see, then, that some comb-filter distortion accompanies the setup of Fig. 8-3A.

Next let us use the same cardioid microphone on a short stand as shown in Fig. 8-3B. There is less difference in path length between the direct and the reflected components than in Fig. 8-3A. Without tracing each step in the calculations, the difference in path results in a 0.3 millisecond delay of the reflected component and the difference in level between the two is 8.3 dB. This means that the peaks will be +5.2 dB higher than normal and the dips will be 18 dB below normal. The first dip for a 0.3 millisecond delay will occur at 1.7 kHz and

the peaks and dips will be spaced twice this or 3.4 kHz up through the spectrum. Figure 8-4 shows this comb-filter situation. It is seen that the setup of Fig. 8-3B results in wilder fluctuations in response than that of Fig. 8-3A.

The pulpit/podium microphone setup of Fig. 8-3C shows how comb-filter effects may be essentially eliminated with the PZM microphone. The difference in path length between the direct and the reflected component is now so small as to throw the dips into the ultrasonic region while we still retain the valuable +6 dB remnant (see Fig. 7-21). This +6 dB increases the "reach" of the PZM which tends to offset the greater distance from mouth to microphone in Fig. 8-3C.

Other microphones to be considered for the

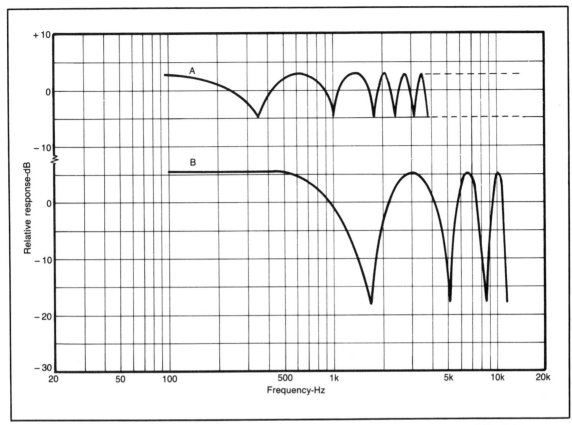

Fig. 8-4. Calculated system response resulting from corresponding pulpit/lectern arrangements of Fig. 8-3.

pulpit/lectern must include the lavalier. Sometimes opposition is encountered with respect to the trailing cord and the neck loop, but the distance from mouth to microphone is reasonably constant and reasonably short. The clip-on microphone is functionally comparable to the lavalier, both requiring external equalization if it is not built in.

8.11 MICROPHONE PLACEMENT—SMALL GROUPS

Let us take the small vocal group to illustrate the basic principles determining microphone placement. First, two vocalists as illustrated in Fig. 8-5. As so eloquently demonstrated by Burroughs (Ref. 4), the 3:1 rule should be considered a minimum in deciding on the geometry of any microphone arrangement. This means that if one of the vocalists is 1 foot from the closest microphone, there should

be at least a 3 foot separation between microphones. The distance between vocalist #1 and microphone #2 then becomes 3.16 feet. The inverse square rule then says that the level of sound from vocalist #1 at microphone #2 would be 20 log (1/3.16) = −10 dB, or 10 dB below that at microphone #1. It has been established that if this 3:1 ratio of distances is maintained the comb-filter wiggles on the combined response are subdued to the point of being generally acceptable to the ear. In our thinking for the future, then, let us associate this 10 dB level difference with the 3:1 distance ratio rule.

In Fig. 8-6 a row of vocalists is considered with a choice of placing the microphones for the vocalists at a distance of 1 foot or 3 feet. Which is best from the viewpoint of the 3:1 distance ratio rule? The 1-foot spacing corresponds to the arrangement of

127

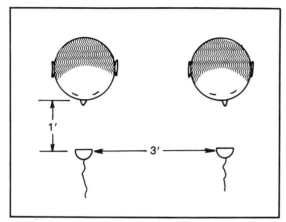

Fig. 8-5. The separation of two adjacent singers should be at least 3-feet if the mouth-to-microphone distance is 1-foot. This is one expression of the 3:1 rule designed to keep comb-filter effects inaudible.

Fig. 8-5 and yields a 10 dB difference in levels as the microphone outputs are combined at the mixer. For a 3-foot microphone distance, the slant distance between vocalist #1 and microphone #2 becomes 4.24 feet. The level at microphone #2 below that of microphone #1 becomes 20 log (3/4.24) = −3 dB. Increasing the microphone distance from 1 foot

to 3 feet results in the level of singer #1 at microphone #2 being 7 dB higher than the minimum 10 dB separation desired. Conclusion: when vocalists are close together, their individual microphones should be close to their mouths to avoid audible comb-filter effects.

8.12 MICROPHONE PLACEMENT —CHOIRS

Condenser microphones have certain advantages in picking up sound from a choir. Their 10 to 15 dB higher level is one advantage and their excellent transient response is another. The electret form of condenser microphone can be slim and therefore unobtrusive. Remote powering is required, but this is a small price to pay for lower noise and other advantages. The most difficult question is how many microphones are required? Rather than making this decision on the basis of what a church down the street does with apparent success, let us consider the factors involved in choir microphone placement.

In Fig. 8-7 a three-row choir is assumed with risers of about 10 inches. Possible microphone positions D and C are discarded for rather obvious

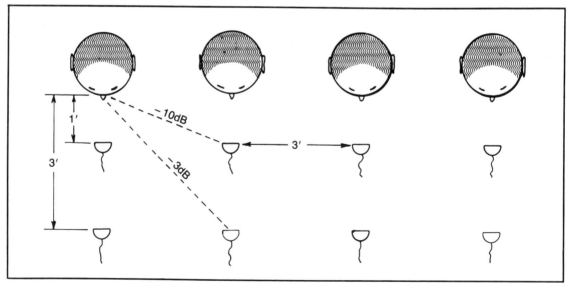

Fig. 8-6. Microphone arrangements for small singing groups should always be done with the 3:1 rule in mind. The 1 foot mouth-to-microphone distance corresponds to the 3:1 rule and results in the voice level of singer A being 10 dB down as it strikes microphone B. If the mouth-to-microphone distance is increased to 3 feet, the delayed signal in microphone B will be only 3 dB down and the comb-filter effects will be much more pronounced.

128

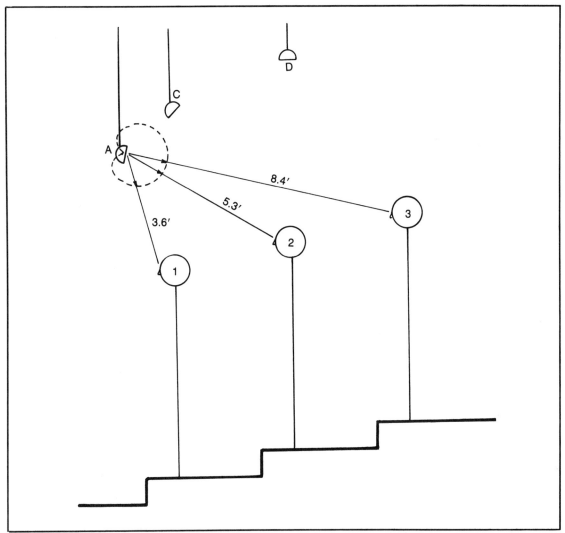

Fig. 8-7. This choir microphone is 1-foot in front of and 3.5-feet above the head of front row singer 1. The cardioid pattern and inverse square divergence "loss" tend to compensate each other resulting in signal levels from singers 1,2,3 being within 3 dB of each other (see Table 8-1).

reasons and position A selected for our analysis. A cardioid condenser microphone is selected and positioned about one-foot in front of the front row and 3-1/2 feet above the heads of those in the front row. The slant distances to the three sources then become 3.6, 5.3, and 8.4 feet. These values are entered in Table 8-1 just to keep our data organized. Aiming the cardioid pattern at singer #3 in the back row gives angles of 17 and 60 degrees for singers #2 and #1, which, in turn, give cardioid response values of −1 and −5 dB for singers #2 and #1. The inverse square law states that singer #2 is 4 dB and singer #1 7.4 dB higher than #3 because they are closer. The important point to observe here is that the cardioid pattern response and the inverse square "loss" are opposite to each other, that one tends to compensate for the other. The last column of Table 8-1 shows that the levels of the three singers at the microphone are within 3 dB of each other (assuming, of course, that the

Table 8-1. Choir Microphone Placement.

Singer	Slant distance feet	Mic angle degrees	Cardioid Mic response dB	Level difference (Inverse square)	Relative level of singer's voice at Mic A dB
3	8.4	0	0	0	0
2	5.3	17	−1	+4	+3
1	3.6	60	−5	+7.4	+2.4

level of each singer is the same). We conclude that placing the microphone at A was a happy selection and we shall remember that placing the cardioid microphone 1 foot in front of and 3.5 feet above the front row was a good compromise between cardioid pattern and distance to the singers.

We still have not answered the question of how many microphones are required so we turn to Fig. 8-8 and consider a small choir of three rows of eight singers in each row. Singers #1, #2, and #3 are still lined up in front of microphone A as in Fig. 8-7. Our problem now is to see what happens if a second microphone is placed at B. First we examine how microphone A works out for singers #4, #5, and #6 and accumulate the data in Table 8-2. The horizontal distances to these three microphones turns out to be 9.0, 6.0, and 4.2 feet. The corresponding vertical distances to these same three microphones turns out to be 2.1, 2.9, and 3.5 feet. The triangles on the left of Fig. 8-8 must be solved

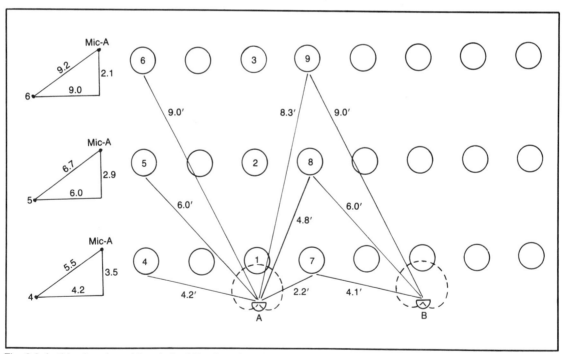

Fig. 8-8. In this plan view of the choir of Fig. 8-7 microphone B has been added and it introduces comb-filter problems. Signals from singers 7,8,9 arrive at the two microphones at comparable amplitudes but at different times. Although this, or similar, microphone arrangements are in common use, the use of the second microphone introduces serious response irregularities.

130

Table 8-2. Choir Level Comparison.

Mic to singer	Mic angle degrees	Cardioid mic response dB	Mic to singer slant distance feet	Level diff- (Inverse square) dB	Relative level of singer's voice at Mic A dB
6	25	−1	9.2	0	−1
5	31	−1.5	6.7	+2.8*	+1.3
4	75	−2.5	5.5	+4.5	−3.0
* 20 log (9.2/6.7)					

for the slant heights which are found to be 9.2, 6.7, and 5.5 feet. The level differences due to inverse square divergence of the sound, figured with respect to the more distant singer #6, are found to be 2.8 and 4.5 dB. Combined with the cardioid pattern response we find that even for the edge singers the level differences are within 3 dB. So far, so good.

Now let us place a second microphone symmetrically at B and explore the effects on singers #7, #8, and #9. In Table 8-3 we see that the actual distance ratios for these three singers are 1.1:, 1.2:, and 1.3:1 instead of the desired 3:1. This means that the signals from singers #7, #8, and #9 are nearly equal in microphones A and B. As the outputs of both microphones are combined in the mixing console, serious comb-filter variations in response are assured. Such is the sad effect of adding the second microphone. There are other sad effects in trying to cover this choir with a single microphone as other calculations involving inverse square and cardioid pattern will disclose. This is

the dilemma: using a single microphone and not picking up the more distant singers very well or using the second microphone and seriously coloring and sound from the two rows between the microphones. Any symmetrical arrangement of two microphones will have this same problem. Take your pick, but it emphasizes the wisdom of using a single microphone whenever possible. The use of PZM microphones will not eliminate this problem.

8.13 THE HAND-HELD MICROPHONE

Hand-held microphones have become a part of the personality and performance of vocalists, along with a few bad microphone habits. With little hope of changing the situation we shall consider what is preferred from the standpoint of quality of the pickup, although quality may not be in top priority in this setting.

The usual working distance is anything from minus-two inches (inside the mouth) to six or eight inches in front of the mouth. Usually the axis of the

Table 8-3. Choir 3-to-1 Rule.

Slant Distance to				
Singer	Mic A ft	Mic B ft	Actual ratio	Desired minimum ratio
9	8.6	9.2	1.1 to 1	3 to 1
8	5.6	6.7	1.2 to 1	3 to 1
7	4.1	5.4	1.3 to 1	3 to 1

microphone is pointed toward the mouth, which tends to place both the fist and the microphone in front of the face. Another disadvantage of this position is that breath noises, heavy sibilants, and pops of p's and t's are accented. It is suggested that placing the axis of the microphone vertically takes care of these problems and yet provides adequate pickup of the voice at close range.

If floor monitors are used, or if there are other sources of direct loudspeaker sound at the microphone position, the cardioid pattern may be indicated. The omnidirectional microphone handles breath pops better and may be preferred in some instances. Either can serve well if used within their capabilities. The proximity effect of close use must be considered and adequate shock mounting may be indicated to minimize handling noises.

8.14 MICROPHONE PLACEMENT—MUSICAL INSTRUMENTS

In the placement of microphones for pickup of the sounds of musical instruments we are treading upon ground that is considered sacred by those active in the field. By the very nature of the task, subjectivity reigns supreme although a number of studies have been made of the directional characteristics of various instruments. The trade journals are a prolific source of opinions and data and are recommended for those responsible for microphone placement for instruments (Ref. 5, 6, 7, 8). An exhaustive treatment of solo versus musical groups, classical versus contemporary musical forms, and the best position for the microphone for the piano and other musical instruments is far beyond the space requirements of this book as well as the expertise of the author. There is one rule that applies in most cases: place the microphone where your ear tells you that the instrument or the group sounds best.

8.15 PRESENCE EQUALIZATION AND THE MICROPHONE

Anticipating Chapter 18 which treats equalization more completely, it is well to mention presence equalization again with respect to microphone selec-

tion and use. Presence equalization is the boosting of response at the speech frequencies between 2 and 4 kHz in order to allow speech to "cut through" background music or interfering noise of one kind or another. Boosting frequencies in this range contributes to the clarity of the voice, be it narrator or vocalist. For this very practical goal the ephemeral ideal of flatness of response is abandoned.

There are two ways of obtaining presence equalization. One method is to buy microphones with such equalization built in. This is a worthy approach if the use of such microphones is dedicated to an unchanging situation. However, if the microphone is to have general use, such equalization will degrade signals in other uses. The other approach depends upon the experience and training of the one on the mixing console as well as the resources of the console itself. Equalization filters with octave spacings are too course to be of much use for presence equalization. The flexible parametric equalizers are especially useful as they allow adjustment of frequency, amplitude, and shape of curve.

8.16 THE PHASE/POLARITY CONTROVERSY

When a pair of leads is reversed on a microphone or loudspeaker there is no question that a 180-degree phase shift has taken place. What was positive is now negative and vice versa. But this phase shift is true for all frequencies in the audible spectrum and beyond. The name that should be given to this action is "a reversal of polarity", not "a reversal of phase". Phase, used in its true sense, varies with frequency while polarity does not.

This switching of leads on a microphone, for instance, is trivial only in its simplicity, not in its significance. If several microphones are used for a recording they must have the same polarity. For a given positive pressure wavefront striking the several microphones the output voltages must be in the same direction lest serious consequences, especially at the low frequencies, result. The manufacturers give adequate warning on this point. For example, Electro-Voice microphone specifications read, "positive pressure on generating element causes positive voltage on red cable lead." If this information is not in the catalog, it probably will be on the technical data sheet for that microphone. Adhering to a standard is important so that microphones from different manufacturers can be used together harmoniously.

In three-pin microphone connectors of the XL-type, it is generally agreed that pin 1 should be connected to shield and/or ground. There is less agreement on the other two pins. The Europeans seem to prefer pin-2 high and pin-3 low. The Japanese seem to have adopted the reverse, pin-3 high, pin-2 low. The Americans seem not to have yet made up their collective minds, but pin-3 high is becoming widely used in studio activities (Ref. 9). One thing is certain, within a given activity it is imperative that all microphones, cables, and equipment be so connected that a positive going acoustical pulse will give a voltage response *in the same direction* for all microphone signals. Otherwise, as mentioned, serious loss of low frequency response will be experienced.

8.17 NOISE CANCELLATION

A little trick that may save the day in an emergency is the way to utilize polarity reversal between two microphones to achieve a desired end. Let us say you wish to announce at a sporting event and the crowd noise is so high as to drown out the commentary. Two identical microphones can be taped together so that the heads are within a few inches of each other or the handles taped together so that the heads are in opposite directions. They are then connected in parallel, but with the leads of one of them reversed. Noise coming from the crowd strikes both microphones, tending to be cancelled. The announcer speaking close to one of the microphones comes through with minor effect on the voice. Utilizing similar principles, AKG offers their Model D-58E noise cancelling dynamic microphone, for example.

8.18 MICROPHONES FOR VIDEO RECORDING

When microphones are used to pick up the sound associated with motion pictures, camera noise is a problem. Every resource is exhausted to keep this noise from interfering with the desired sound, such as camera "blimps", highly directive microphones, and maintaining maximum separation of microphone and noise. There is much activity of an amateur and semi-professional level with video cameras recording on videocassette recorders or other video recording equipment. The microphones for this service have less camera noise to contend with, but hum pickup, sensitivity to shock and vibration, sensitivity to wind noise, and maximum working distance are vital characteristics to be studied. The omni microphone is best with regard to low hum and sensitivity to shock, but the cardioid has a working distance 1.7 times as great.

References

1. Barker, Steve, 1981. "Pressure Zone Microphones," *Recording Engineer/Producer*, Vol 12, No 1 (Feb), pp 80-85.

2. Anthony, Bob, 1982. "Pressure Zone Microphones," *Studio Sound*, Vol 24, No 9 (Sept), pp 54-60.

3. Everest, F. Alton, 1981. *Master Handbook of Acoustics*, TAB BOOKS Inc. #1296, Blue Ridge Summit, PA 17214.

4. Burroughs, Lou, 1974. Microphones: *Design And Application*, Sagamore Publishing Co., Plainview, NY 61803.

5. Lamm, Michael E. and John C. Lehman, 1983. "Realistic Stereo Miking For Classical Recording," *Recording Engineer/Producer*, Vol 14, No 4 (Aug), pp 98-109.

6. Bartlett, Bruce, 1982. "Microphone Techniques For Predictable Tonal Balance Control," *Recording Engineer/Producer*, Vol 13, No 2 (Apr), pp 60-69

7. Carr, Robert, 1982. "Recording The Horn Section," *Recording Engineer/Producer*, Vol 13, No 5 (Oct), pp 73-83.

8. ———, 1981. "Recording Acoustic Guitar," *Recording Engineer/Producer*, Vol 12, No 5 (Oct), pp 112-122.

9. Butt, Peter, 1979. "A Fuss About Plus: Preservation of Audio Signal Polarity of the Recording Signal Chain," *Recording Engineer/Producer*, Vol 10, No 6 (Dec), pp 66-71.

Chapter 9

Loudspeakers

L OUDSPEAKERS HAVE COME A LONG WAY since grandfather put the earphone to his crystal set in a teacup in the 1920s. The old Magnavox loudspeaker was little more than an earphone connected to a horn. The coming of the dynamic loudspeaker was a major step forward. A baffle board or a box-without-a-back improved its performance, but the tuned reflex cabinet came much later. The dynamic loudspeaker gave quite good on-axis response, perhaps 100 Hz to 10 kHz, but the actual power radiated goes done as the frequency is increased. The diminished power at higher frequencies is concentrated in every tightening beams. To counteract this is multi-way loudspeaker involving several different transducers, each suitable for its own band, was a step toward total power response, uniform with frequency.

In the late 1960s and early 1970s directional control of radiated loudspeaker energy became a major concern and much development activity was directed toward this end. The impetus for this development was the need for ever larger sound reinforcement systems in auditoriums, concert halls, and sports arenas. In this field transducers were also developed, that were efficient for low-, mid-, and high-frequency use. Today the development work continues to deepen our understanding of just what goes on in a loudspeaker and to relate such findings to the way our ears perceive distortions of many kinds.

9.1 THE DYNAMIC CONE-TYPE LOUDSPEAKER

The loudspeaker is an electro-acoustic transducer, radiating acoustic power into the air with a waveform which follows closely that of the electrical waveform driving it. There is the direct radiator having a diaphragm coupled directly to the air and the radiator, which utilizes a horn to couple it to the air. The direct, dynamic, cone-type loudspeaker will be treated in this section. It is very important because of its widespread use, which is a result of its simplicity, compactness, relatively uniform frequency response, and modest cost. Because of practical limits on any single type of

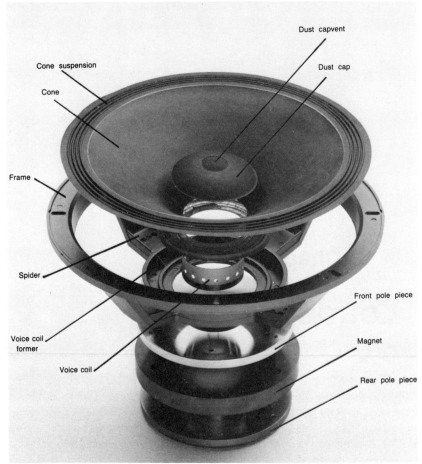

Fig. 9-1. Cut-away view of the construction of a modern cone-type dynamic loudspeaker (courtesy Altec Corporation).

Dust capvent

Dust cap

Cone suspension

Cone

Frame

Spider

Front pole piece

Voice coil former

Magnet

Voice coil

Rear pole piece

transducer, to achieve uniform response over the entire audible spectrum requires a combination of several types of radiators.

Figure 9-1 shows a sectionalized cone-type loudspeaker. The cone, the actual radiating element, must have the right combination of lightness and stiffness. Felted paper is often used in the construction of cones but other hi-tech materials are constantly being experimented with. The voice coil is cemented to the cone, driving the cone in a piston-like motion. The voice coil moves in a strong magnetic field produced by a permanent magnet structure. It is important that the travel of the coil/diaphragm structure does not take the voice

coil out of the intense magnetic field or distortion results.

Little acoustical radiation will take place from a cone type loudspeaker suspended all alone in the air. As the cone moves outward, the air immediately in front of it is compressed and the tendency is for this compressed air to rush in to fill the rarefaction created by the same action at the rear of the diaphragm. Only at high frequencies at which the physical size of the loudspeaker is great in terms of wavelength of the sound will there be appreciable radiation. Placing the same loudspeaker in a large baffle will improve low frequency response because the distance from one face of the loudspeaker to the other is greatly increased by the baffle. It can be said that, without the baffle, the loudspeaker unit is not "loaded" for the low frequencies, i.e., its radiation resistance would be low.

9.2 HIGH FREQUENCY HORNS

Think of the cheerleader's megaphone as a transformer that better matches the voice to the air medium. The better the acoustical impedance match attained, the better is the voice energy carried to the crowd in the grandstand. It is a matter of efficiency in energy transfer The efficiency of dynamic cone-type loudspeakers is not very high. The efficiency of horns can be as high as 25 percent because of the ability of the horn to achieve a good impedance match between the driver and the surrounding air. Amplifier power is expensive and the use of horns is one way to transfer a maximum portion of electrical power to acoustical power. A horn loads a driver by controlling the column of air, by gradually increasing the width of this air column. A properly designed horn presents a resistive load to the driver, which means power transfer. Reactive components of the load im-

pedance lead to out-of-phase current flow, which does not represent real power at all. The magnitude of this all-important resistive component of the load impedance is controlled by the design of the horn. A conical horn shape provides little load at low frequencies. An exponential shape loads the driver down to a certain cutoff frequency.

In 1921, at the inauguration of President Harding, early horns made by the Western Electric Company proved their worth. Audio power in electrical form was scarce because of the limitations of the primitive vaccum-tube amplifiers available. Long exponential horns at the Harding inaugural at Arlington, Virginia, made it possible to cover 125,000 people with only 40 watts of amplifier power. In your mind's eye, imagine the amplifier power and the loudspeaker stacks a modern jam session for 125,000 people would use. Of course, the sound level would be somewhat higher than for Harding's inaugural!

Horns have another important role to play besides properly loading the drivers. Horns make possible the directional control of the acoustical energy. This is another way overall efficiency is improved, by confining the precious acoustical energy

Fig. 9-2. Altec multicellular and radial (sectoral) horns. Such horns have seen wide usage in large sound reinforcement installations (courtesy Altec Corporation).

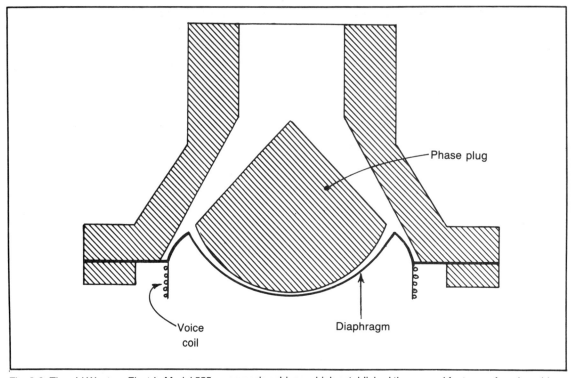

Fig. 9-3. The old Western Electric Model 555 compression driver, which established the general features of modern drivers such as the first use of the phase plug.

to the desired areas instead of wasting it by radiating it where the people are not. Muticellular and radial (sectoral) horns, such as illustrated in Fig. 9-2, have been the basis of a new industry, that of well-designed and effective sound reinforcement systems for large spaces such as auditoriums, concert halls, and sports pavilions. Even though multicellular and radial horns have been the basis of sound reinforcement system design for many years, and are still serving an important function, they are expensive to manufacture and they have certain faults in pattern control. A new development on the horizon is the constant directivity type of horn.

9.3 COMPRESSION DRIVERS

The "loudspeakers" to drive horns are especially designed for the service. Although many refinements have been added in recent years, the basic construction of the so-called compression driver is well illustrated by the Western Electric 555 driver of Fig. 9-3. designed by Wente and Thuras in the late 1920s (Ref. 1). This was the first driver to use a phase plug. The rigid dome-shaped diaphragm of 0.002-inch aluminum was a distinct departure from the flat diaphragms prevalent at that time. The compliant edge was such as to allow large excursions necessary for low-frequency radiation. The purpose of the "phase plug" was to increase the radiation resistance. Note how the curvature of the diaphragm and the phase plug and the throat itself are such as to provide close to exponential increase in cross-sectional area as the main part of the throat is entered. The frequency response with a large horn was essentially flat from 600 Hz to 7 kHz in those early days, and since has been extended to 50 Hz to 10 kHz in subsequent models. With only 10-watts input to this driver attached to a large horn, 3-watts of acoustical energy was delivered,an efficiency of 33 percent!

Fig. 9-4. The Emilar EC320A high-frequency compression driver. Each diaphragm is individually spun from aluminum and heat treated. The phasing plug, of classical slotted construction, is cast from a nonresonant, nonmetallic material (courtesy Emilar).

Typical modern day drivers are illustrated in Figs. 9-4 and 9-5. Although built on the general pattern of the historic W.E. 555, these drivers incorprate many refinements made possible by modern developments and materials. Their performance must be evaluated with specific horns attached.

Fig. 9-5. A group of mid/high frequency compression drivers offered by Altec. These drivers incorporate high performance ferrite magnetic structures and radial phase plugs (courtesy Altec Corporation).

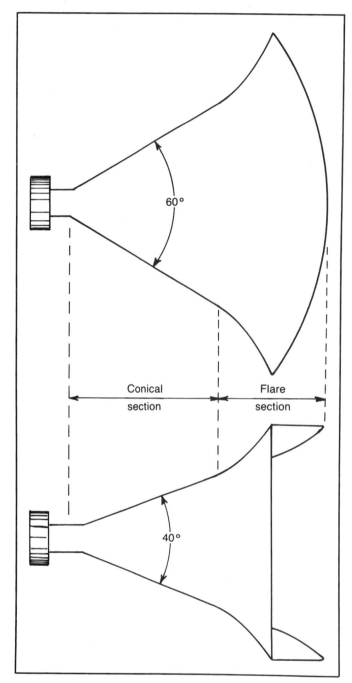

Fig. 9-6. One type of constant directivity horn showing the merging of a conical section into a flare section.

9.4 CONSTANT DIRECTIVITY HORNS

This type of horn has been given different names by different manufacturers. Electro-Voice (Ref. 2) has adopted the name "constant directivity" and we shall favor that name because it was E-V who first introduced their line of "White Horns" having constant directivity. Soon after

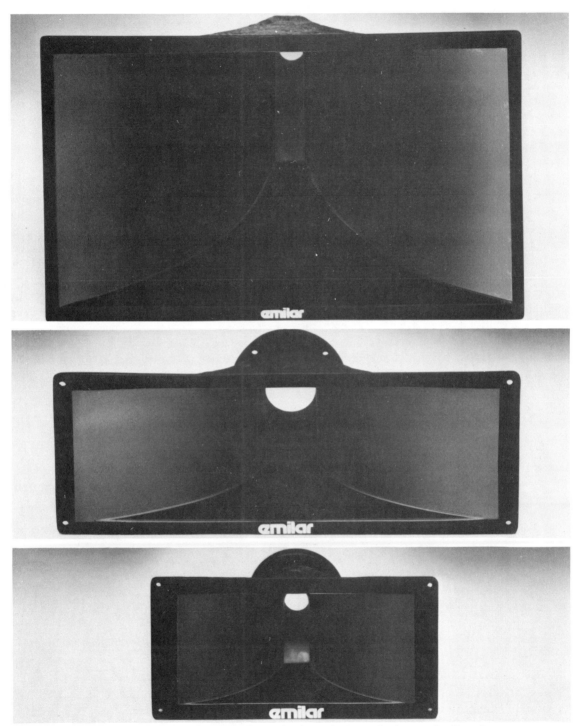

Fig. 9-7. The family of Emilar Uniform Directivity Dispersion horns feature a flat front and uniform frequency response on and off axis (courtesy Emilar).

Altec (Ref.3) released their line of "Mantaray" horns. Emilar (Ref. 4) offers their "uniform directivity" horns, Renkus-Heinz their "constant beamwidth" horns, and Community their "pattern control" horns.

All of these horns feature a departure from exponential shape to achieve desirable directional properties. An exponential throat expansion is followed by a smooth transistion into a straight-sided conical shape. The conical shape works into a flare section, which gives good horizontal directivity control without the mid-frequency beaming characteristic of most early horns. Figure 9-6 shows the two-thirds of the horn length devoted to the conical shape and the outer third the flare section. This describes briefly the E-V White Horn shape.

The Altec Mantaray horns are characterized by large vertical mouth dimensions and narrow-angled sidewalls to which are added a flare section. Good directivity control is thus achieved in both the horizontal and the vertical directions. This control holds down to about 800 Hz and extends up to about 20 kHz. The horns of other manufacturers (Figs. 9-7, 9-8, 9-9, and 9-10) offer various combinations of driver loading compromises and irregularities in beaming. Suffice it to say that a new era in horn design has arrived, which gives the designer far better possibilities in the control of the distribution of sound energy over the audience area.

9.5 LOW FREQUENCY HORNS

For adequate-low frequency radiation of sound energy from a cone-type loudspeaker, proper loading must be achieved. This is more difficult at low frequencies because of the very long wavelengths involved and the great physical size required. One way to obtain a large horn to aid low-frequency radiation is to fold the horn such as the Fig. 9-11. Klipsch has utilized this idea by using the intersection of corner walls and floor for a virtual extension of a properly placed and shaped loudspeaker cabinet.

In addition to loading the loudspeaker unit for

Fig. 9-8. A series of compact Pattern Control horns designed for use in two- and three-way cabinet systems and for very compact cluster designs (courtesy Community Light & Sound, Inc.).

Fig. 9-9. The Community series of ''White'' horns designed for Constant Directivity. These horns join an exponentially flared throat section to a straight-sided conical section. The outer third of the horns have an additional flare section of double the conical angle (courtesy Community Light & Sound, Inc.).

good output, there is the problem of directivity control. Just what is feasible in directivity control in a unit of reasonable size is illustrated in Fig. 9-12

picturing the Community VB664 unit (Ref. 5). This unit gives a beamwidth of about 160 degrees at 100 Hz and 80 degrees at 300 Hz, which can work well

Fig. 9-10. The Altec Mantaray R Constant Directivity Horns are so-called because of their elongated throats and wedge-shaped bodies. These horns are capable of projecting broad band sound into highly selective areas (courtesy Altec Corporation).

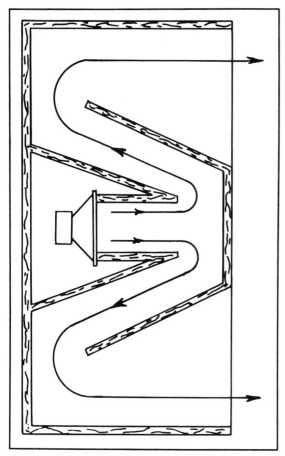

Fig. 9-11. Cone-type loudspeakers may be loaded by folded horn sections of approximate exponential form. Good low-frequency radiation can be obtained thereby.

with high-frequency horn patterns.

9.6 THE BOX AND THE LOUDSPEAKER

In the early loudspeakers used in theaters the low-frequency cone-type dynamic radiators were mounted in boxes without backs. This allowed a considerable fraction of the sound energy to be radiated into the rear stage area to cause problems as it bounced around behind the screen. Simply closing up the back of the box in those early days caused problems associated with box resonances. Advances in understanding of what happens to sound in cavities led to what is called the reflex loudspeaker or the vented or ported type of

enclosure. There is a 180 degree difference in phase between the sound radiated from the rear of the diaphragm and sound radiated from the front. If there were just some way to make the backwave add in phase with the front wave, all that backwave energy could be conserved. By the use of a carefully designed port, such as shown in Fig. 9-13, this can be done. Many advantages accrue with this mode of operation. An octave or so can be added to the low-frequency response of a loudspeaker. This is achieved with less cone excursion than a sealed or open back enclosure would provide. Further, it reduces harmonic distortion and virtually eliminates the old problem of having the voice coil/cone striking the structure on great excursions.

It is amazing what a simple hole in the loudspeaker box can do, but that hole must be just right to realize the above advantages. In the design of such a system, an enclosure volume and port opening are chosen so that the enclosure resonates at the same frequency as the loudspeaker alone in free air. This reverses the phase of the backwave at the port so that sound radiated from the port is

Fig. 9-12. The Community VB664 dual-driver vented bass horn employing 15-inch drivers. These are designed for radiation of sound energy from 45 to 1,000 Hz. Above 100 Hz excellent pattern control is achieved (courtesy Community Light & Sound, Inc.).

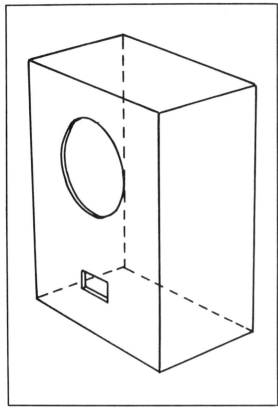

Fig. 9-13. The simplest form of vented or ported enclosures for extended low-frequency response. The backwave from the cone is 180 degrees out-of-phase with the frontwave. The port is adjusted so that the backwave is radiated from the front with the same phase as the frontwave.

in phase with that radiated from the front of the loudspeaker diaphragm. The close coupling of the enclosure to the speaker, where both are tuned to the same frequency, results in two damped resonant peaks, one on either side of the frequency of the original peak. By this method, substantial radiation from the loudspeaker is achieved below its free-air resonance frequency (Ref. 6).

9.7 INTEGRATED LOUDSPEAKER SYSTEMS

It is common practice to cover the audible band with a loudspeaker system incorporating several transducers, each assigned the task of radiating sound energy in that portion of the band for which it is adapted. This leads to what are called two-way,

three-way, or even four-way systems. Most of the larger sound reinforcement systems of the past were two-way, but as quality demands increase, this is rapidly changing to three-way. In sound reinforcement the various radiators are assembled into a cluster and their cross-over points, aiming, and relative levels are adjusted by the sound contractor on very much a custom basis.

Integrated systems are used as monitors in the control/mixing room, as consumer loudspeakers, and for a host of other playback systems of a modest size. Occasionally the integrated system in a single box is used for the smaller sound reinforcement installations, but the rigidity of their angular and power handling capability limits them in such service. A selection of such multiway systems-in-a-box is illustrated in Figs. 9-14, 9-15, and 9-16.

9.8 CROSSOVER SYSTEMS

When a tweeter is used to radiate the high end of the band, a midrange loudspeaker to radiate midfrequencies, and a woofer for the low frequencies, crossover networks of some sort are necessary to divide the spectrum and to send the several portions of spectral audio energy to their intended radiators. Networks for this purpose may be designed to operate either at low or high level. By this it is meant that the network can be placed either before or after the power amplifier. If it is placed before the power amplifier, it follows that a separate power amplifier is needed for each radiator. If placed after the power amplifier, the filter (network) components must be capable of carrying relatively heavy currents.

The very simplest high-level two-way network is illustrated in Fig. 9-17A. It is composed of a single inductor and a single capacitor. The values of these components determine the crossover frequency. For 8-ohm loudspeakers, a 40-microfarad capacitor and a 2.5-millihenry inductor give a crossover frequency of 500 Hz. This means that the response of the high-pass section involving the capacitor and the low-pass section involving the inductor are equal and down 3 dB at 500 Hz. At 500 Hz audio energy (or power) is radiated equally from

Fig. 9-14. (A) The Community four-way loudspeaker system which features a special midrange 6-1/2-inch cone transducer loaded by a 4-inch throat horn which contributes to natural musical sound.

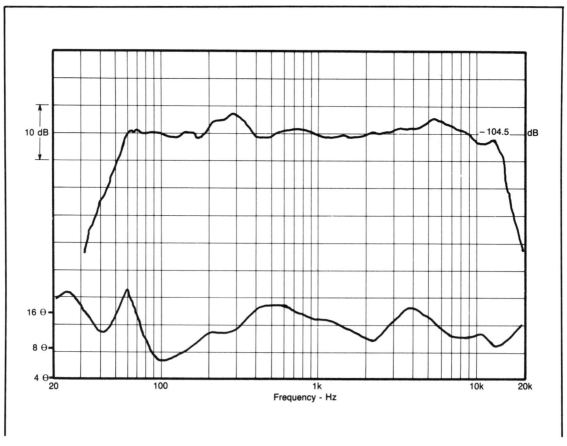

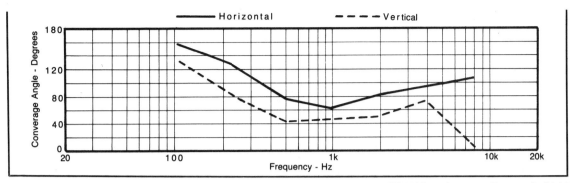

Fig. 9-14. (B) Response, impedance, and coverage angle versus frequency for the RS440 horn (courtesy Community Light & Sound, Inc.).

both sections and doubling the power at 500 Hz means the overall response is increased 3 dB, giving flat overall response. The calculated response of the two sections is shown in Fig. 9-17B.

The 6 dB per octave roll-off of each section is considered a slow roll-off. The slower this roll-off the wider the shared band of frequencies radiated from both loudspeakers. For instance, energy at 300 Hz is radiated by both sections and their amplitudes are only slightly over 4 dB apart. At any point in the listening field of this loudspeaker at 300 Hz signal from one transducer combines with that of the other transducer and if one is delayed with respect to the other, comb-filter distortion results. The narrower this confused crossover region, the less troublesome such distortion.

Such simple approaches to crossovers have their problems (Ref. 7). The responses of Fig. 9-17B, as mentioned, are calculated ones and the loudspeaker impedance of 8-ohms is assumed to be a pure resistance of fixed value. This is not very descriptive of actual loudspeaker impedances. Changes in resistance and the existence of reactive components in the loudspeaker in the response curves and odd sounding signals.

More complex, second order and higher, networks may be employed to achieve steeper roll-off and thus to narrow the range of frequencies radiated by two transducers. For the high-level system, more complicated networks become bulky and expensive. The crossover network placed in the low level part of the system (Fig. 9-18 and Ref. 8) makes much more sense. Typical commercially

Fig. 9-15. The Community RS320 compact three way system, top, and the VB990 auxiliary woofer, bottom (courtesy Community Light & Sound, Inc.).

Fig. 9-16. (A) The Electro-Voice Interface:B Series III high-fidelity loudspeaker system, and (B) the Interface:C Series II system, (C) with grille. The exceptional bass response of the C Series II unit is only 3 dB down at 30 Hz and it can deliver a sound-pressure level of 93 dB, 1-meter, 1-watt. The specially designed midrange transducer uses the same optimally vented technology used for woofers. An exceptionally low crossover, 400 Hz, is made possible by the midrange design. An acoustical lens gives wide dispersion of highs from the dome type tweeter (courtesy Electro-Voice, Inc.).

B

149

Ⓒ

Fig. 9-16. Continued from page 148.

150

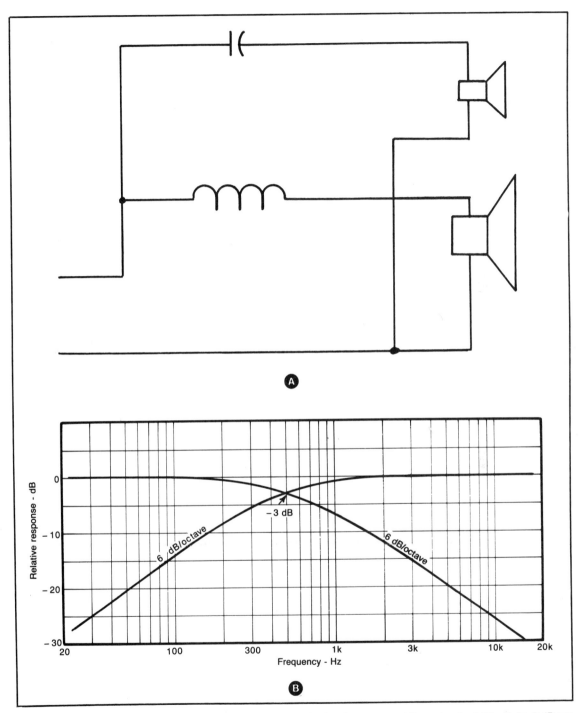

Fig. 9-17. (A) A simple, high-level dividing network. (B) The calculated response of the network of (A) with its 6 dB per octave roll-off assumes loudspeaker resistance of 8-ohms pure resistance. Reactive components of real life loudspeakers cause irregularities in such curves.

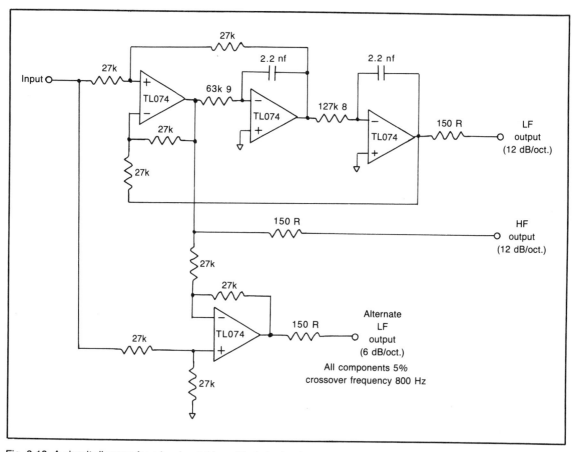

Fig. 9-18. A circuit diagram for a low-level, biamplified electronic crossover system. The roll-off rate is 12 dB per octave with this circuit. The roll-off rate of the alternate low-frequency output is 6 dB per octave. (After Winer, Ref. 8.)

available electronic crossovers such as that offered by Furman Sound (Ref. 9) are shown in Fig. 9-19. While the electronic, low-level network, has many advantages, a separate amplifier is required for each division of the spectrum; two amplifiers for two-way (biamplification), three amplifiers for three-way, etc. This does allow independent equalization and level control for each section.

9.9 TIME DOMAIN RESPONSE

The phrase, "time-aligned," is a trademark of E.M. Long Associates (Ref. 10) but the process is also called "time coherent" and "phased array" by various manufacturers. In basic terms, such alignment in the time domain of the sound coming from

a loudspeaker assures that the phase (time) relationship between the fundamental and overtones of a complex, transient acoustical signal at the listener's ears matches that of the electrical sign applied to the input. In other words, this is an attempt to make the loudspeaker the truly "transparent" device we have always hoped for. It can be said, with little fear of contradiction, that this utopia has not yet arrive, although significant steps are being made in that happy direction.

A gross time problem is associated with the simple geometrical fact that three transducers in a three-way integrated system are separated and not at the same spot. As shown in Fig. 9-20 the distance from the acoustical centers of each transducer and the listening ear differ and differences in distance translate into differences in time (phase). In all that is said on this subject, this simple fact must not be forgotten. In an attempt to bring the acoustical centers of the various transducers of a loudspeaker system into physical alignment a stepped facing has been tried. Reflections and diffusion traceable to these steps in the loudspeaker facing have created other problems.

The act of alignment of a loudspeaker in the time domain then involves the following steps: (1)

Fig. 9-19. Three electronic crossovers offered by Furman Sound. (Top) The TX-3 three-way mono or two-way stereo unit. (Center) The TX-4 three-way stereo or five-way mono unit. (Bottom) The TX-5 four-way stereo unit. Two Butterworth filters give 12 dB per octave slopes (courtesy, Furman Sound, Inc.).

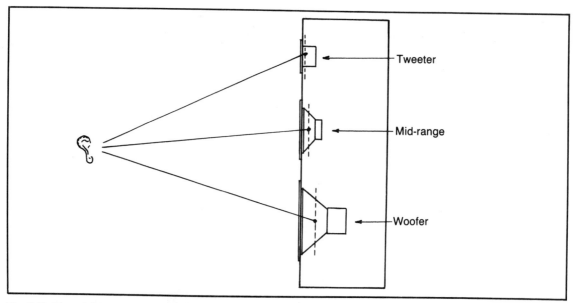

Fig. 9-20. Time delays are phase shifts. Any multi-way loudspeaker introduces phase shifts due to the difference in path lengths of the several transducers to the hearer's ear. This can be corrected only for one listening position. Other phase shifts are introduced within the transducers. Such shifts can be compensated by electrical networks, possibly incorporated with the high-level dividing network.

physical alignment of the acoustical center of each transducer for one listening position, (2) consideration of the response of each transducer and its cut-off points, and (3) design of dividing networks with built-in time delay to compensate for delays found in (1) and (2).

There can be little question on the improvement in sound of a loudspeaker system that has this sort of attention to compensate for its built-in delays. The question is, what magnitude of delay is the ear capable of hearing? Blauert and Laws have made a careful study of this (Ref. 11). It has been found that many of the top-grade monitor loudspeakers fall within the Blauert and Laws criteria, that is, they produce delays that are inaudible according to the experiments of Blauert and Laws.

9.10 LINE ARRAYS

A column loudspeaker is a line array. Placing a number of cone-type dynamic loudspeaker units close together in a straight line constitutes a line array (Fig. 9-21). Placing this array in a vertical

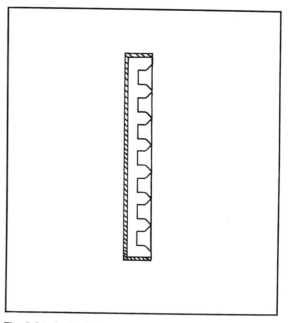

Fig. 9-21. A simple line radiator. In uncorrected form this type of radiator has the disadvantage of excessive changes in directional pattern with frequency. In spite of its serious deficiencies, it is widely used, especially in older systems installed in the 1960s.

position it is found that the horizontal pattern is essentially the same as that for just one of the loudspeakers. The vertical pattern, however, is found to be a much sharper beam due to the interaction of patterns of the several loudspeakers. If a single loudspeaker has a vertical pattern of 120 degrees, stacking a second loudspeaker above the first and driving them with the same signal reduces the vertical pattern to 60 degrees and the on-axis level is increased 6 dB. Each time the number of speakers is doubled, the vertical angle is halved. In the early 1960s column loudspeakers became very popular because of their pattern control and their low price. During these early days columns proliferated in auditoriums, schools, and churches. The fact that they are already installed and provide a service of sorts results in a reluctance to shell out money to bring the system up to date and improve the quality a very great amount. The very common split loudspeaker system with a column on each side of the platform is a scourge on the race, but is very well entrenched in inertia.

The line source tends to become increasingly directional as the frequency is increased, which means that the vertical beamwidth changes with frequency. At high voice frequencies the beam may be so narrow that only a slice of the audience is covered. What is needed is to make the acoustical length of the column change with frequency. It should be half as long acoustically at 4 kHz as at 2 kHz. The center unit should be the only one allowed to reproduce the full width of the spectrum. This column shortening can be done electrically or acoustically. Figure 9-22 is an example of electrical tapering so that the top and bottom units radiate less high frequency energy than the center ones, those second from the end radiating somewhat more high frequency energy, those third from the ends even more and, as mentioned, the center unit radiates the full spectrum. The interaction of the inductor and the resistance of the loudspeaker of the inductor and the resistance of the loudspeaker is such as to form a low-pass filter, the higher the frequency, the more of the applied voltage that appears across the inductor rather than the loudspeaker.

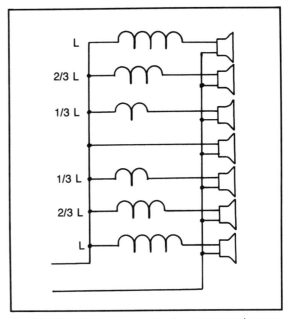

Fig. 9-22. Electrical compensation is a step toward correction of the deficiencies of the column loudspeaker. With inductors arranged as shown, the high-frequency response of the end units is greatly restricted, with the units second from the end restricted less, and in the units on either side of center still less. The center unit radiates the full band.

An example of acoustical tapering is shown in Fig. 9-23. It is widely appreciated that glass fiber absorbs high-frequency sound well, but that low-frequency sound tends to pass on through, depending upon the thickness. By tapering the thickness of the glass fiber, the radiation of high frequency energy is reduced depending upon the thickness of the glass fiber.

Two modern line array loudspeakers of the tapered variety are shown in Fig. 9-24. The unit in Fig. 9-24A, the Electro-Voice Model LR4B, is shown in cutaway form in Fig. 9-25. The central unit is a high quality horn which maintains the horizontal pattern at 120 degrees above 3,500 Hz. A special crossover network adjusts the acoustical length of the array by reducing the high-frequency response of the outer loudspeakers as shown in Fig. 9-26. The angular placement of the two outer loudspeakers is designed to control beaming and has the same general effect as the earlier curved array. The polar patterns of the E-V Model LR4B

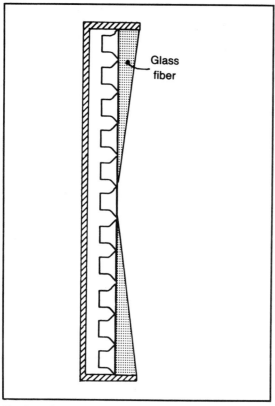

Glass
fiber

Fig. 9-23. Compensation of line arrays by means of absorbent material such as glass fiber. The variable thickness of the glass fiber introduces a tapered amount of high-frequency loss which tends toward keeping the array the same acoustical length in terms of wavelength.

line array are shown in Fig. 9-27. Even though these horizontal and vertical patterns are made much smoother by the use of octave bands of noise in the measurement procedure, the resulting relative constancy of pattern throughout the audible range is a major improvement over the traditional uncorrected column. These corrected units are ideal for those sound reinforcement applications in which cost rules out the use of the full multiway cluster.

Still another method of line array design to stabilize the directional properties with frequency is illustrated in Fig. 9-28. This is called the dual tapered array proposed by Benson (Ref., 12). It is a linear broadside array of identical dynamic cone loudspeakers which are electrically filtered so that the acoustical array is a constant number of

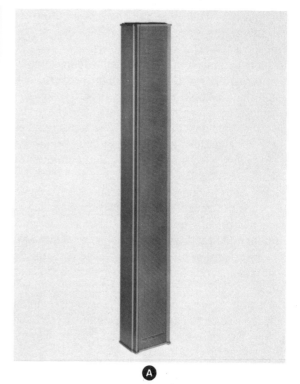

A

B

Fig. 9-24. Modern, corrected line array units offered by Electro-Voice: (A) model LR4B, (B) LRSA (courtesy Electro-Voice, Inc.).

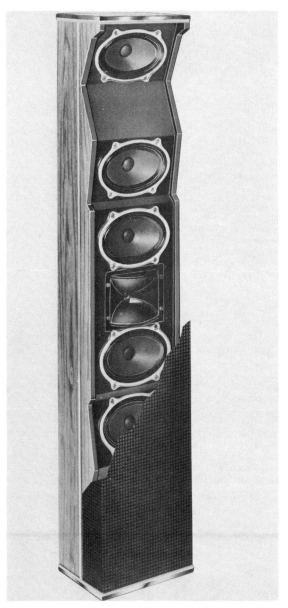

Fig. 9-25. A cut-away view of Electro-Voice Model LR4B line array. Note the high quality horn in the center and the canted units which simulate a curved front to the line array (courtesy, Electro-Voice, Inc.).

wavelengths long at different frequencies which holds the beamwidth constant. Further information on improved line arrays may be found in References 13 and 14.

9.11 STAGE MONITORS

Performers, chiefly in musical groups, need to hear themselves in order to carry out their own performance successfully. Hearing oneself with the sound of drums and amplified instruments nearby requires outside help. Stage monitors, such as shown in Fig. 9-29, are used for this purpose and are usually placed at the edge of the stage and aimed up at the performer. Placing a loudspeaker so that it is aimed up at the performer with a handheld microphone obviously creates the potential for feedback. The use of such stage monitors requires delicate control of their level.

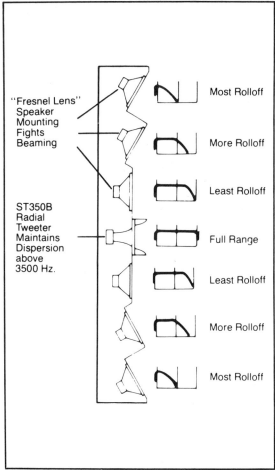

Fig. 9-26. An illustration of the tapered frequency responses of the various units in the array. These are accomplished by electrical networks (courtesy Electro-Voice, Inc.).

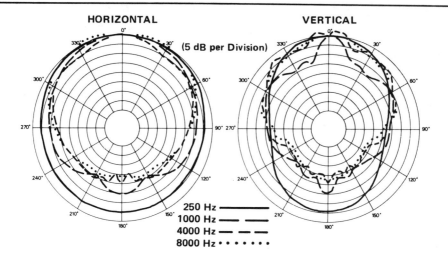

HORIZONTAL   VERTICAL

(5 dB per Division)

250 Hz ———
1000 Hz — —
4000 Hz — — —
8000 Hz • • • • •

Polar Response (1/3 octave pink noise
4 volts/10 feet)

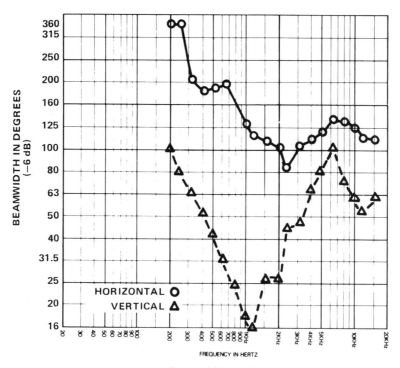

Beamwidth vs Frequency
Whole Space (anechoic)

158

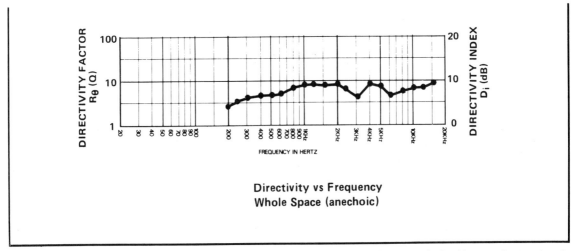

Directivity vs Frequency
Whole Space (anechoic)

Fig. 9-27. Directional patterns for the Electro-Voice LR4B line array. Note that these were obtained by use of octave bands of noise, which tends to smooth out the smaller lobes. The excellent pattern control that units of this type offer suggests their use in sound-reinforcement installations too small for the cluster approach (courtesy Electro-Voice, Inc.).

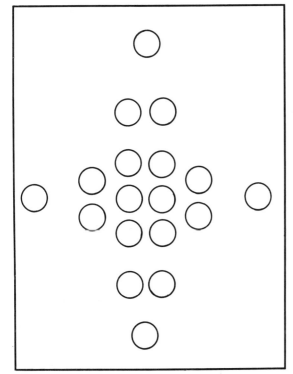

Fig. 9-28. The dual tapered array suggested by Benson (Ref. 12). These identical radiators are electrically filtered similar to Fig. 9-22, the outside units at the top, bottom, and sides having their highs rolled off most, the next four pairs less so, and the inside group of six radiating the full band.

Fig. 9-29. Stage monitors enable the performer to hear himself or herself above the blast of loudspeakers behind (courtesy Electro-Voice, Inc.).

159

References

1. Wente, E.C. and A.L. Thuras, "A High-Efficiency Receiver For a Horn Type Loudspeaker of Large Power Capacity, Sound Reinforcement, and Anthology, Document D81," *Audio Engineering Society.*

2. Electro-Voice, Inc., 600 Cecil St., Buchanan, MI49107.

3. Altec Corporation, P.O. Box 26105, Oklahoma, OK 73126.

4. Emilar, 1365 N. McCan St., Anaheim, CA 92806.

5. Community Light & Sound, Inc., 333 East Fifth St., Chester, PA 19013.

6. Thiele, A.N., 1971. Loudspeakers in Vented Boxes, *Jour. Audio Engr. Soc.:*

    Part I-Vol 19, No 5 (May) pp 382-391

    Part II-Vol 19, No 6 (June) pp 471-483.

7. Small, Richard H., 1971. Constant-Voltage Crossover Network Design, Jour. Audio Engr. Soc., Vol 19, No 1 p 12.

8. Winer, Ethan, 1982. "Spectrum Analyzer and Equalizer Design." *Recording Engr./Prod.,* Vol 13, No 1 (Feb) pp 44-54.

9. Furman Sound, Inc., 30 Rich St., Greenbrae, CA 94904.

10. Long, Edward M., 1976. "A Time-Align Technique For Loudspeaker System Design," Presented at the 54th convention of the Audio Engr. Soc., Los Angeles, (May). Preprint #1131(M-8).

11. Blauert, J. and P. Laws, 1978. "Group Delay Distortion in Electro-Acoustical Systems," *J. Acous. Soc. Am.,* Vol 63, No 5 (May) pp 1478-1483.

12. Benson, J.E., 1976. "Electrically Tapered Loudspeaker Systems," Proc. of IEEE International Conf. on Acoustics, Speech, and Signal Processing.

13. Augspurger, G.L. and James S. Brawley 1983. "An Improved Colinear Array," Presented at the 74th convention of the Audio Engr. Soc., New York (Oct), Preprint #2047(D-6).

14. Klepper, David L. and Douglas W. Steele, 1963. "Directional Characteristics From A Line Source Array," *Jor. Audio Engr. Soc.,* Vol 11, No 3 pg 198.

Chapter 10

Lively Lessons in
Loudspeaker Care and Feeding

(or Feedback From The Front Lines)

MURPHY'S LAW STATES THAT ANYTHING that can happen will happen. When things happen in low-level audio circuits a simple "p-f-f-f-t" followed by a dead silence and a small puff of smoke tell us that "there goes a capacitor!" or a resistor or a transistor, or . . ... In the high level world where loudspeakers live and move and have their being things happen on a bigger scale. This illustrated guide points out certain precautions which should be observed when working with power amplifiers and loudspeakers, especially the larger variety.

The original cartoons were drawn by Barry McKinnon of DSE Production Equipment and Ser-

vices, Ltd., of Calgary, Alberta, Canada. These were published by Cetec. The people at Altec saw them and published them in 1983 as Applications Note #10 after Larry Lutz, then an Altec employee, enlarged the original version slightly and oversaw the redrawing of the sketches. Ted Uzzle, Manager, Market Development, at Altec also did a version keyed to motion picture theater sound, which was published in Boxoffice Magazine. Barry, you really have communicated the essence of loudspeaker care and feeding. Thanks to you and to Altec for permission to perpetuate these little gems in this context.

Fig. 10-1. **Connecting a Speaker** to an amplifier that is already turned on is very hazardous to both loudspeaker and amplifier. This is true whether or not the amplifier is being driven by a signal.

Fig. 10-2. **Avoid Feedback** like the plague. High-frequency compression drivers can very quickly be brought down in flames by the excess power of sustained feedback.

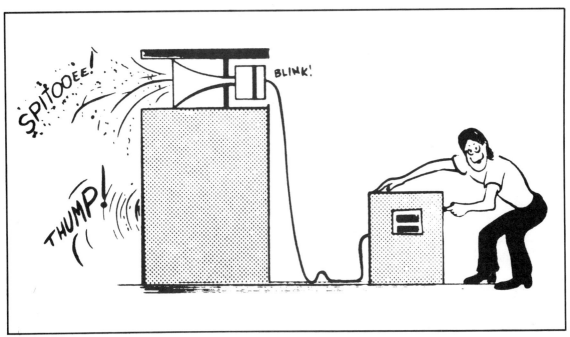

Fig. 10-3. **A Dc Blocking Capacitor** should always be used on high-frequency compression drivers when biamplification is used. This protects them from turn-on transients and spurious low-frequency signals.

Fig. 10-4. **Low-level Electronics** (mixer, graphic equalizer, signal processor) should always be turned on before the power amplifiers are turned on.

Fig. 10-5. **Foreign Objects** such as dust, dirt, popcorn, spiderwebs, dead mice, etc. should be kept out of the throat of the high-frequency horns. They increase the load on the driver and significantly reduce high-frequency output.

Fig. 10-6. **Ground Loops** should be avoided. Ground loops and high power amplifiers may be fatal to loudspeakers. Do not make connections to equipment with levels up or power amplifiers turned on. Use connectors that make the ground connection first such as the XLR type. Keep cables in good repair.

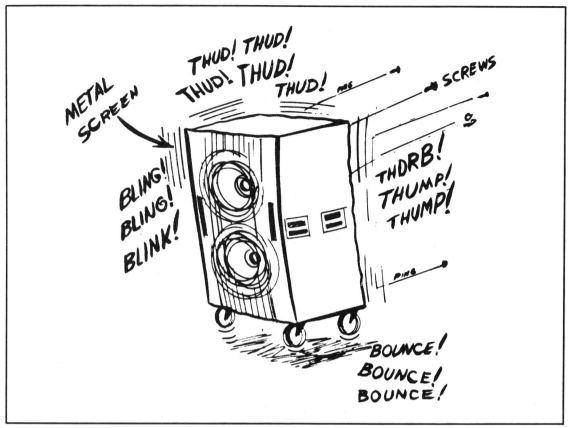

Fig. 10-7. **Excessive Low Frequency** signals should be avoided or severe cone damage can result. Use high-pass filters, 40-60 Hz, 18 dB/octave.

Fig. 10-8. **Clipping** in power amplifiers can reduce both amplifier and loudspeaker life expectancy.

Fig. 10-9. **A Heavy Grille** should be used on stage monitors to prevent performer puncturation.

Fig. 10-10. **Runaways** of heavy loudspeaker cabinets and amplifier racks with casters can be avoided on ramps by thinking about it in advance and using a rapelling rope.

Fig. 10-11. **Solid Support** for heavy equipment is always a good idea.

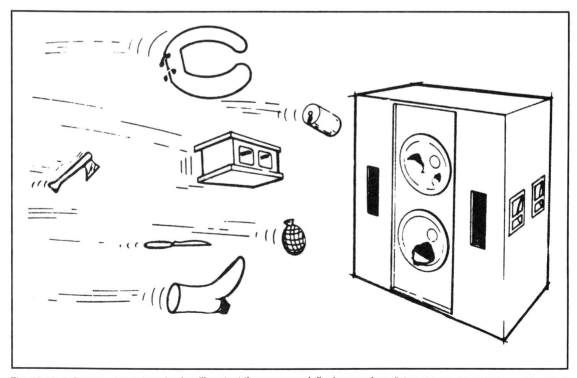

Fig. 10-12. **A Screen** of metal or plastic will protect those exposed diaphragms from flying objects, identified or unidentified.

Fig. 10-13. **Electronic Protection** at the outputs of all power amplifiers protects against the application of dc voltage to loudspeakers. Failure of output transistors can plop the full power supply voltage across your woofer or tweeter voice coil. The typical power supply for 200 watts per channel can deliver a lot of current and it can do it fast. A fastblow fuse takes a half second to open the circuit, yet loudspeakers are designed to respond to transients of a millisecond or less. This means potential voice coil or other damage before the fuse blows.

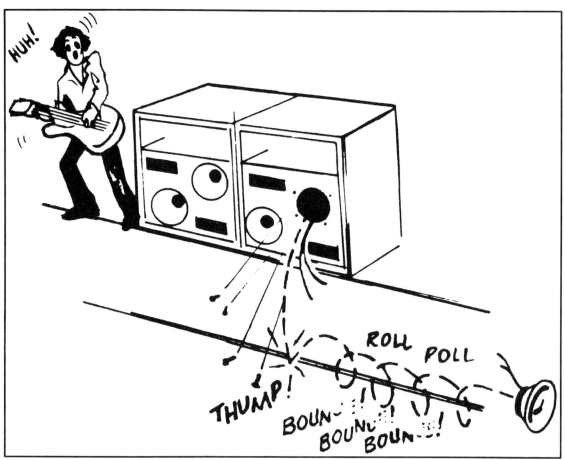

Fig. 10-14. **Mounting Bolts** clamping loudspeakers to cabinets should be checked for tightness regularly.

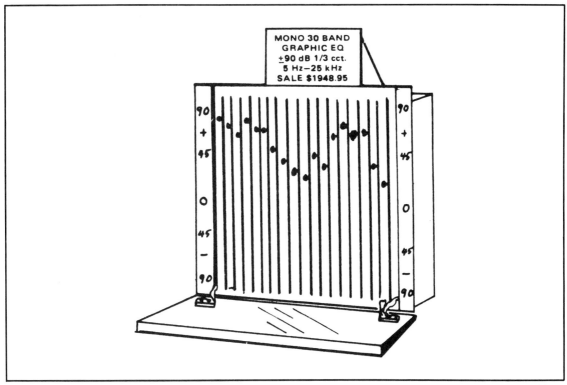

Fig. 10-15. **Excessive Equalization** can present demands that most loudspeakers and amplifiers cannot handle without damage. Increasing bass response by EQ boosting can easily lead to overload.

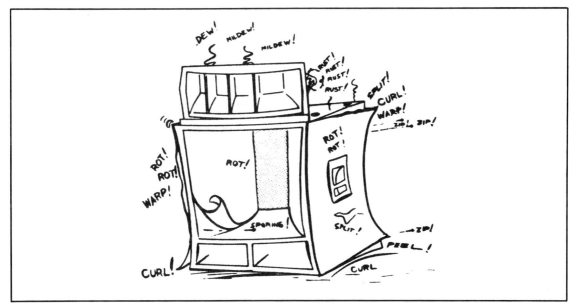

Fig. 10-16. **Speaker Storage** should be in protected spaces having reasonable ranges of temperature and humidity.

169

Fig. 10-17. **Outdoor Venues** should always be approached with a generous supply of plastic sheeting, plastic trash bags, etc. to be used in case of rain. Having such protection practically guarantees it will not rain. Even a small amount of rain or water can damage the bass speaker cone and cause rusting of the internal surface of the drivers.

Fig. 10-18. **Horns Need Protection** when packing for a road show. Multicellular, radial, sectoral, and fiberglass horns should be transported in sturdy packing boxes. A hard cover should be placed over the face of the bass boxes.

Fig. 10-19. **Speaker Stacks** are heavy and if they are supported by scaffolding, make sure the planking is equal to the job.

Fig. 10-20. **Proper Grounding** of electronic musical instruments and electronic gear saves lives. Be alert. It is not always apparent whether the performer acts that way all the time or whether he is being fried by connecting 110 volts to ground through his body.

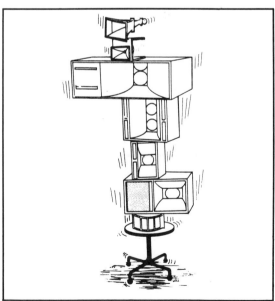

Fig. 10-21. **Loudspeaker Stacking** presents remarkable opportunities for creative expression, but it is suggested that physical laws such as gravity should be observed in the process.

Chapter 11

The Mixing Console

THE MIXING CONSOLE, AT LEAST IN ITS LARger form, is one of the most impressive machines the electronics industry has to offer. Hundreds of knobs, beautiful colors, trembling meter needles indicating that something is going on inside the breast of this mighty beast, such things catch the attention of the potential recording client like nothing else. More important than studio acoustics, the determining question is often, "How many tracks?."

Mixing consoles are not restricted to the recording studio. They have been found to be extremely useful, yea absolutely necessary, in radio and television broadcasting studios, in traveling musical presentations, as adjuncts to the sound reinforcement installations in school, church, and auditorium. As the sophistication of audio activities grows, so grows the necessity for controlling multiple microphones, multiple recording channels, numerous types of signal processing. The mixing console seems to be here to stay and we must not be deterred by its apparent complexity. It must be considered as a creative tool.

What does one call the person operating the mixing console? A four-year stint at the university may yield a bachelor's degree in engineering; the holder is then called an engineer. It is also what the Southern Pacific Railroad calls those driving their huge diesel-electric locomotives. In the recording studio the person in charge of the console and the recording process is also called an engineer, even though his background is music with a dabbling in electronics. Confusion reigns, in general, but within each field the meaning of the term seems to be reasonably clear.

11.1 WHAT DOES A MIXING CONSOLE DO?

First of all, the console provides *amplification*. It takes the weak microphone signals and amplifies them to intermediate levels suitable for controlling actions and sends them on to outboard power amplifiers driving loudspeakers. Such amplifiers in the console provide needed isolation between circuits and needed recovery from losses in dividing networks and attenuators.

The console also provides *equalization* to smooth out irregularities in response, to achieve dramatic effects, and to discriminate against noise. Equalizers are more often the key to a salable product than a key to "true" response.

The console provides for *channel routing*, i.e., the means for the operator to send the signal from a given microphone or channel to a network which sums it with signals from other channels.

The console has provision for *aural monitoring*. It is necessary for the operator to hear the sounds he or she is dealing with. This gives the basis for judgment on equalization or quality of performance.

Level control is a vital function of the console. Rows of VU meters, strings of light-emitting diodes (LEDs), or simple peak indicators tell the operator whether the signals in each and every channel are within operating limits.

Mixing is, by its very name, a basic function of the console. The signals from the various channels must be combined into the proper mono or stereo form. Externally generated signals such as reverberation must also be combined with selected channels at appropriate levels.

Faders are resistive level controls on each input, output, and cue channel.

Reverberation (Often incorrectly called "echo") of an artificial type is generated in an outboard device but is controllable at the console. At some stage the signal is sent to the reverberator and returns from the reverberator for combining with the original signal in the proper proportions.

It is necessary to provide certain performers with signals related to their own performance. This is often done with headphones. The signal sent is called *foldback* and the console usually has provision for a special mix for this.

The operator communicates verbally with those in the studio by means of the *talkback* facility. Sometimes recorded sections are played back to the studio through the talkback system. The latter requires much higher quality of the system than the former which is for speech only.

The console provides *panpot* control so that signals coming to the board from the various chan-nels can be sent to the left or right stereo channel or any position in between.

The above are the more obvious functions of the mixing console, but there may be other less obvious ones. For instance, there is probably a jackfield for routing of circuits in non-normal ways, test tones for checking quality of channels, etc., etc.

11.2 OUTBOARD EQUIPMENT

The mixing console is the control center involving much more than microphones connected to the input. It also controls the routing, level control, and functioning of pieces of heavier equipment located in the same room or at a distance. The sound monitor loudspeakers, of course, are located near the console in a position favorable to the operator. Both multitrack and mastering recorders are probably also near at hand. The power amplifiers to drive the sound monitor loudspeakers or the playback loudspeakers in the studio need not be close to the console. In fact, there are advantages to removing from the control area the heat they generate and the noise of their cooling fans.

Signal processing equipment, aside from the equalizers, which are part of the mixer, may be mounted near the console for convenience. The many types of signal processing equipment include limiters, compressors, companders as well as effects devices depending upon digital delay for their functioning such as flanging. Noise reduction equipment is usually located near the board because it is silent in operation. The reverberator, however, may not be so quite and it is usually located well down the hall. An important device at the operator's elbow is the SMPTE time code controller which allows rapid and accurate finding of takes on magnetic tape.

11.3 GENERAL FEATURES OF MIXING CONSOLES

One item of great interest to the potential purchaser of a mixing console is whether it fits into the professional or the semi-professional category. Price may automatically determine the category of interest. The different standards in what constitutes "zero level" on the meters is a distinction that was described back in Section 4.6, especially Fig. 4-3, discussing the pitfalls of zero levels. The semi-pro approach can provide excellent service, but the buyer must be aware of the trade-offs.

An important feature of a console is whether or not transformers are used on the inputs. Poor transformers can create distortion and roll-off the high frequencies. Good transformers can perform quite well with modest levels of distortion and roll-off. Transformers are fast being supplanted by electronic circuitry that offers high common-mode rejection, excellent stability, and low noise. The advantage of transformers is that true isolation of one circuit from another can be achieved but similar isolation, without the disadvantages, can now be obtained with electronic design.

Mixing consoles differ greatly in the flexibility and characteristics of the equalizers provided. Most consoles are used with outboard graphic equalizers leaving rather modest requirements for the board equalizers. For this reason the simpler type of equalizer often serves well. But there is a wide difference between the different types. The parametric equalizer is the more flexible. With it the frequency at which the boost or dip is to act is adjustable (in common with other simpler types), the amount of the boost or dip is adjustable (also in common with others), but also the width of the boost or dip curve is adjustable. The number of parametric sections available in each channel determines the fineness of the adjustments possible.

Mixing consoles vary greatly in the type of metering. Some use the standard VU meters. In Europe another type of meter called the peak-program meter (PPM) is widely used. There is no question that knowledge of the program peaks is valuable to the operator who is charged with the responsibility of avoiding overdriving the recording medium. However, peak information is easily and cheaply provided by LEDs and this form of metering is widely used in the less expensive mixers. By having a fast attack and a slow recovery designed into them, the LED level indicator gives true peak information with recovery slow enough for the eye to follow with minimum fatigue.

11.4 A TYPICAL INTERMEDIATE MIXER

Figure 11-1 shows a famous and widely used mixer that is about as simple as they come, the Shure Model 267 (Ref. 1). This mixer and its predecessor the Model 67 are often seen in the most sophisticated installations in which they are used as outboard expansion mixer of related sounds, which are then fed into a single channel on the big board. In spite of its low price and simplicity, it is a thoroughly professional device, capable of doing the simple task well. Not only that, it can be operated on batteries if desired. Three 9-volt alkaline batteries will provide 20 hours of continuous service.

The microphone and keyboard mixers shown in Fig. 11-2 offered by Furman (Ref. 13) represent another common type of utility mixer that is not of the console form. The Model MM-4 is a 4-input, 4-output mono mixer and the MM-8 is for stereo use. Such mixers fill an important niche for concert and recording sub-mixing, multi-keyboard mixing, audio dubbing for video production, compact sound reinforcement mixers for small church and auditorium systems, and other uses in broadcast and commercial sound. An effects send and receive loop is included with send level controls as well as a switchable low cut (100 Hz, 6 dB/octave) filter for each channel.

Taking the Shure Model 267 mixer as one extreme, there are numerous other mixers in the six figure range, which constitute the other extreme. These highly professional mixers are the foundation of the recording industry today in the larger studios. On the assumption that most of the readers of this book are more closely aligned with lower budget installations, the Bimix (Ref.2) console of Fig. 11-3 will be given close scrutiny. The three types of modules, the input/output (I/O), the stereo mix module, and the communications module will be studied in detail as the function of each and every knob, button, and switch is listed.

The I/O module is shown in Fig. 11-4. The stereo mix module in Fig. 11-5, and the communications module in Fig. 11-6. These terms may vary from manufacturer to manufacturer. The functional

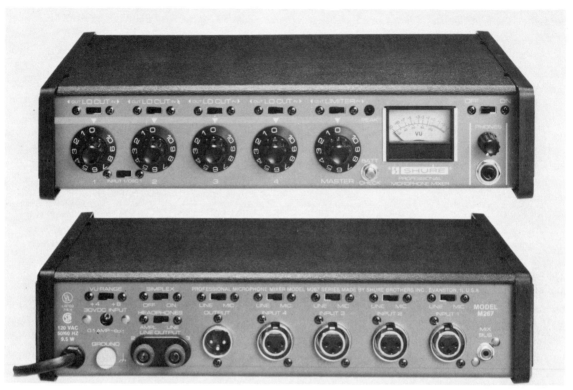

Fig. 11-1. The Shure Model 267 compact, lightweight professional microphone mixer combining professional features and low cost. This mixer is widely used outboard to expand mixing capabilities of large mixing consoles as well as a mixer for modest recording activities (courtesy Shure Brothers, Inc.).

Fig. 11-2. The Furman microphone and keyboard mixers, Model MM-4 (mono) and Model MM-8 (stereo) (courtesy Furman Sound, Inc.).

Fig. 11-3. The Bimix modular mixing console from Biamp Systems, Inc., offering great flexibility for live performance, studio and broadcast applications. As a result of its modular construction, this mixer may be used in any combination of 1 to 24 outs and from 8 to 40 inputs. To examine the function of every control on the three basic modules of this mixer see Figs. 11-4, 11-5, and 11-6 (courtesy Biamp Systems, Inc.).

layout will be different in the different boards. However, the tasks to be accomplished must be quite similar in different boards so this Bimix console can serve to show us how one manufacturer met the challenges.

11.5 POWERED MIXERS

For certain types of service it is convenient to have the power amplifier combined with the mixer. A traveling singing group, for instance, desiring to control its own sound reinforcement wherever it goes, would find it most convenient to be able to reduce the number of pieces of equipment with such a combination. Mounting the power amplifier and the mixer together also makes sense from the cost standpoint as well as the simplification of hookup by relatively inexperienced persons.

The Biamp (Ref.2) Model 829 8-channel powered mixer shown in Fig. 11-7(A) delivers 500-watts into a 2-ohm load in single channel opera-

tion or 300 watts when both channels are driven at rated total harmonic distortion of 0.25 percent. Automatic limiting is included in soft-clipping form to minimize the harsh distortion of amplifier clipping. Another more compact powered mixer by Biamp is their Model 619 6-channel mono mixer shown in Fig. 11-7(B). The power amplifier of this mixer delivers 350 watts into 2-ohms.

The Neptune (Ref. 3) approach to powered mixers is exemplified by the 8-channel Model 811P of Fig. 11-8(A) and the 6-channel 60 Series in a portable case of Fig. 11-8(B). The Model 811P mixer includes a power amplifier capable of delivering 80-watts rms into 8-ohms or 125-watts rms into 4-ohms. The TOA (Ref. 4) Model 106 powered mixer is shown in Fig. 11-9.

11.6 PERSONAL MULTITRACK RECORDERS

When Teac Corporation of America introduced their Tascam Portastudio® during the late 1970s

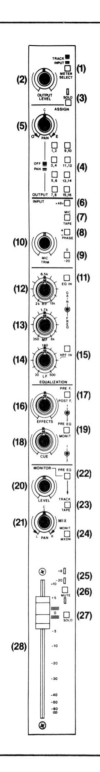

Fig. 11-4. Input/output module. (1) Meter Select Switch: selects (output) or channel (input). (2) Output Level: Sets output level for track output (1-16), (Efx 1-2), (Cue 1-2). (3) Solo: Sends output signal to solo buss, and turns on solo LED. (4) The switches select desired outputs. (5) The pan control pans the channel signal odd-even, between the output selected. (6) Phantom Power (+48 V) Select Switch: Each input channel phantom power has a slow on/off to protect quality microphones and to reduce noise. (7) Mic-Tape Select Switch: Selects either mic input or tape input (tape trim on rear panel). (8) Phase Switch: reverses mic input polarity. (9) Input Attenuator Switch: Attenuates microphone balanced input before the amplifier by 20 dB. (10) Mic-Line Trim Control: Adjusts the input amplifier gain to match input levels. This control should be set so that all input faders have the same sensitivity. (11) EQ In-Out Switch: Bypasses EQ in the down position for comparison and dry record playback. (12) High-Frequency Controls: Top, +/-18 dB range, center detent. Bottom, 2 kHz to 15 kHz true shelving. (13) Mid-Frequency Controls: Top, +/-12 dB range, center detent. Bottom, 350 Hz to 6 kHz peaking. (14) Low-Frequency Channels: Top, +/-18 dB range, center detent. Bottom, 30 Hz to 500 Hz true shelving. (15) High-Pass Filter Switch: 18 dB/octave roll off of low frequencies, -18dB at 30 Hz. (16) Effects Send 1-2 Controls: Sends the channel signals to their respective master effects. Separate controls for separate effects mixes. (17) Effects Pre-Post Select Switch: This switch routes pre or post fader signal to the effects level controls. (18) Cue Send 1-2 Controls: The low-level controls send channel signal to the respective cue mixers 1 and 2. These mixes can be used for separate musician headphone mixer, off the monitor send, or stage monitors off the channel output (pre-fader, pre-EQ). (19) Pre EQ-Monitor Select Switch: This switch selects pre EQ pre fader (stage) mix, or monitor (recording) mix for the cue send controls. (20) Monitor Level Control: Sets output level from monitor. (21) Monitor Pan Control: Pans monitor L-R in stereo to mix module stereo fader. (22) Pre EQ - Track Selector Switch: Up (stage mix) selects channel pre fader, pre EQ to monitor level. Down (track-tape) selects output off track tape switch to monitor level. (23) Track Tape Selector Switch: Up (Track) selects track output from module to monitor level. Down (Tape) selects tape input from module to monitor level. (24) Monitor Mixdown Selector Switch: Up (Monitor) stereo channel monitor. Down (Mixdn) selects channel output and, with mic/tape switch pressed, sends multitrack tape outputs directly to pan and mix outputs. (25) Channel LED Indicators: (monitors, channel input, output, patch, and EQ). +8 LED Red stays on when channel reaches +80 dB. -20 dB LED Green stays on when channel reaches -70 dB. Flashes on -20 dB peaks. (26) Mute Switch: Turns off channel and effects sends, but not monitor, solo, cue or track output. (27) Channel Solo: Sends channel signal to solo buss and turns on solo LED. (28) 100mm Fader: Retrofittable with Penny & Giles 3210.

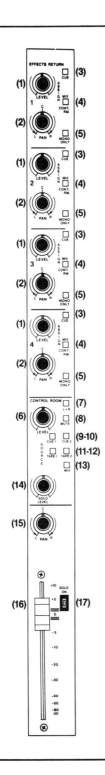

Fig. 11-5. Stereo Mix Module. (1) Input Level Control (1-4): Control input level. (2) Return Stereo Pan Control: Pan returns signal in L-R Mix, L-R Control Room, or Cue 1-2. (3) Cue Select Switch: Assigns pan control to (CUE 1 Left) - (CUE 2 Right). This allows effects return signals or aux. signals to be sent to musicians headphones during recording, independent of recording. If the cue sends are used for live sound monitors this can then be used as an effects or aux. return for them. (4) Mix-Control Room Select Switch: Up position—Effect Return Pan is assigned to L-R mix. Down position—Effect Return Pan is assigned to Control Room L-R and not the L-R Mix, so that the effect can be adjusted before it is sent to the Mix. (5) Mono Only Select Switch: This switch removes the effect return from CUE, Mix, or Control Room and sends the effect signal directly to the MONO Sum Buss only.

Stereo Control Room Monitor. (6) Control Room Level Left And Right: This stereo control sets the output signal level for the control room monitor speakers. (7) Switch L + R: This switch changes the stereo control room signal to two equal Mono signals so you can preview a Mono Mix. (8) Mute Switch: This switch attenuates the control room signal 20 dB for phone calls, etc., and mic adjustments. (9-10) Cue Select Switches: These switches send the Cue 1 and/or Cue 2 outputs to the Control Room Monitors. This is handy when setting up the musician's headphone mixes and effects returns. (11-12) Tape 1 - Tape 2 Select Switches: Tape 1—2 Track return 1 Left and Right (stereo), Tape 2—2 Track return 2 Left and Right (stereo). These switches allow stereo monitoring the 2 track returns in the control room monitors. (13) Mix Select Switch: This switches the stereo mix signal to the control room monitors. (14) Master Solo Level Control: Level control for the solo mix. (15) Mix Pan Control (Mix Balance): This pan control follows the stereo mix fader and pans the mix left and right. (16) Stereo Mix Fader: (Retrofittable with Penny & Giles 3212). (17) Solo on LED: When this LED is off, the control room speakers, headphones, and headset are monitoring the stereo signal selected by the control room source switches (usually the mix). Pressing any solo switch will light the LED. When this LED is on the sum of all the solo switches pressed will be heard on the control room speakers, the headphones, and the headset. No control room controls or solo controls affect the mix, this is a monitoring system only.

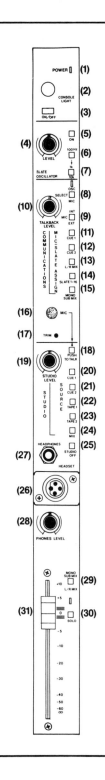

Fig. 11-6. Communications Module. (1) Console Power On Indicator. (2) Console Lamp Connector: Standard B.N.C. (3) Console Lamp Switch.

Slate Oscillator. (4) Oscillator Level Control: Also controls level of external click. (5) Oscillator On-Off Switch: Frequency selector switches. (6) Up—100 Hz, Down—1 kHz. (7) Down—10 kHz.

Talkback—Communications. (8) Oscillator—Microphone Selector Switch: Selects either oscillator—click in or microphone signals to be sent to assign switches. For external click in (external click track generator). Select oscillator with oscillator switch off, the oscillator level will control click in. (9) Internal-External Microphone Selector Switch: This switch selects internal chassis mounted microphone, or external headset microphone. (10) Talkback Level Control: Adjust level of internal and external headset microphone. (11-12) Cue 1—Cue 2 Assign Switches: Sends selected talkback signal to Cue 1 buss or Cue 2 buss. Normally internal or external mic or click to musicians' headphones for recording. Normally headset microphone for live sound when Cue 1-2 are used as stage monitors. (13) Left-Right Mix Select Switch: Sends selected talkback signal to Left-Right Mix recording—set levels with oscillator—stereo slate—track notes (microphone). Live sound—House paging (headset microphone). (14) Slate 1-16 Select: Sends selected talkback signal to multitrack outputs (slate tone). (15) Mono Submix Select: Sends selected talkback signal to mono mix fader. (16) Internal microphone. (17) Internal Microphone Trim: Screwdriver adjustment.

Stereo Studio Playback and Communications System. (This system is separate from recording or live sound mixes and does not affect those mixes. It is designed to control the studio monitor speakers or an auxiliary headphone system.) (18) Push-To-Talk Switch (momentary): This switch sends the talkback microphone (internal or external) to the studio outputs left and right. It also attenuates the control room level by 20 dB to prevent feedback. (19) Stereo Studio Playback: Communications level control. (20-21) Cue Source Switches: These switches send the Cue 1 and/or Cue 2 outputs to the studio monitors. (22-23) Tape 1-Tape 2 Stereo 2-Track Return Selector Switch: These switches select the 2-track returns 1 or 2 left and right and send them to the studio monitors for playback without affecting your mix settings. (24) Mix Select Switch: Sends L-R mix signal to studio monitors. (25) Studio Off Switch: Turns off studio monitors. (26) Headset Connector (4 way): For use with stereo or mono headsets with low impedance microphone. (27) Stereo Headphone Connector: For use with headphones 8-ohms to 600-ohms, 8-watts rms maximum power. (28) Stereo Headphones and Headset Level Control. (29) Mono Mix—L/R Mono Mix Selector Switch:up—the mono mix will be the sum of all track outputs plus mono effects returns. The track outputs are now submasters for the mono mix. DOWN—the mono mix is now the sum of the stereo mix. (30) Mono Mix Solo Switch. (31) Mono Mix Fader.

Fig. 11-7. Biamp powered mixers: (A) Model 829, (B) Model 619 for rack mounting or portable use (courtesy Biamp Systems, Inc.).

A

B

Fig. 11-8. Neptune powered mixers: (A) the 8-channel Model 811P, (B) the 6-channel 60 Series in portable case (courtesy Neptune Electronics, Inc.).

they really tapped a market among musicians, songwriters, and aspiring recording artists (Ref. 11). Here was a miniature recording studio complete with mixer and 4-track cassette recorder in a compact case and for an affordable price. Numerous manufacturers jumped on the bandwagon to meet the ever-growing need. A selection of nine personal multitrack recorders available today are described in Table 11-1 and in Figs. 11-10 and 11-11. It should be noted that these units embrace quite sophisticated features such as noise reduction, pitch control, sync recording, and equalization. As for price, all the units listed are in the budget range except the Akai 12-channel micro

Fig. 11-9. TOA Model 106 6-channel powered mixer (courtesy TOA Electronics, Inc.).

Table 11-1. Personal Multitrack Recorders.

Manufacturer	Model Number	Number of Tracks	Noise Reduction	Tape Speed (ips)	Pitch Control %	Number of Tracks Sync Record	Mic Connector	Equalization Controls	EQ Type	Effect Sends Per Channel	Meters
AKAI	MG 1212	12	dbx	3-3/4 7-1/2	± 12	12	XLR	12 HF, MF, LF	Parametric	2	14 LED
ARIA	Studiotrack	4	Aria NR	3-3/4	± 10	4	1/4″	- - -	- - -	- - -	4 VU
CUTEC	MR402	4	- - -	3-3/4	± 10	4	1/4″	- - -	- - -	- - -	4 VU
CLARION	XD-5	4	Dolby B	3-3/4	± 10	4	1/4″	- - -	- - -	- - -	4 LED
FOSTEX	X-15	4	Dolby B	1-7/8	± 15	2	1/4″	2 HF, LF	Shelf	-	2 LED
FOSTEX	250 AV	4	Dolby C	1-7/8	± 10	4	1/4″	4 HF, LF	Shelf	1	4 VU
TASCAM	234	4	dbx	3-3/4	± 12	4	1/4″	- - -	- - -	- - -	4 VU
TASCAM	244	4	dbx	3-3/4	± 15	4	1/4″	4 HF, LF	Parametric	1	4 VU
YAMAHA	MT44-MM30-RB30	4	Dolby B Dolby C	1-7/8	± 10	4	1/4″	4 tone controls	Shelf	1	6 LED

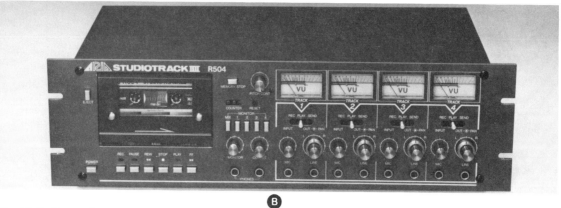

Fig. 11-10. Personal multitrack recorders: (A) Akai MG1212, (B) Aria Studiotrack, (C) Cutec MR 402, (D) Clarion XD-5 (Refs. 6 through 9).

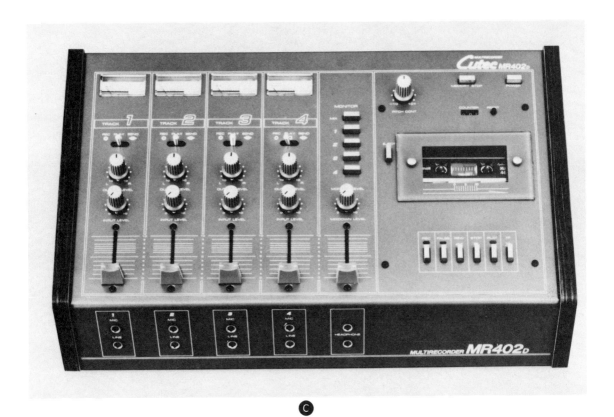

C

D

Fig. 11-10. Continued from page 184.

studio system, which is considerably higher priced as would be expected.

11.7 AUTOMATION

The digital revolution is making itself felt in the field of mixing consoles. As time goes on, the very expensive automated features available today will be more generally available at lower prices. With automation comes the luxury of a mixer that "remembers" fader settings so that an exact mix is immediately available for playback with no hands touching the faders. Equalizer and other settings on each channel can also be recorded for later re-

Fig. 11-11. Personal multitrack recorders: (A) Fostex X-15, (B) Fostex 250AV, (C) Tascam 234, (D) Tascam 244, (E) Yamaha MT44-MM30-RB30 (Refs. 10, 11, and 12).

B

C

D

E

Fig. 11-11. Continued from page 187.

call. Automation does not change the basic ingredient of the mixer operation, the skill of the operator, it only makes it possible for that operator to concentrate on the creative side of the job.

References

1. Shure Brothers, Inc., 222 Hartrey Avenue, Evanston, IL 60204.

2. Biamp Systems, Inc., P.O. Box 728, Beaverton, OR 97075.

3. Neptune Electronics, Inc., 934 N.E. 25th Avenue, Portland, OR 97232.

4. TOA Electronics, Inc., 480 Carlton Court, South San Francisco, CA 94080.

5. Petersen, George, "1984. Multitrack Cassette Recorders," Mix, *The Recording Industry Magazine*, Vol 8, No 7 (July), pp 14-22.

6. The Akai MG1212 micro studio system is distributed by International Music Corporation, 1316 E. Lancaster, Ft. Worth, TX 76102.

7. The Arai Studiotrack IIII is distributed by the Aria Music U.S.A., Inc., 1201 John Reed Court, City of Industry, CA 91745.

8. The Cutec MR402 mixer/recorder is distributed by Dauphin Company, P.O. Box 5137, Springfield, IL 62705.

9. The Clarion XD-5 mixer/recorder is distributed by Kamen Music Distributors, P.O. Box 507, Bloomfield, CT 06002.

10. The Fostex X-15 and 250 mixer/recorders are distributed by Fostex Corporation of America, 15431 Blackburn Ave., Norwalk, CA 90650.

11. The Tascam 234 and 244 mixer/recorders are distributed by Teac Corporation of America, 7733 Telegraph Road, Montebello, CA 90640.

12. The Yamaha MT44/MM30/RB30 mixer/recorders are distributed by Yamaha International Corp., P.O. Box 6600, Buena Park, CA 90622.

13. Furman Sound, Inc., 30 Rich Street, Greenbrae, CA 94904.

Chapter 12

Power Amplifiers

MODERN POWER AMPLIFIERS HAVE COME A long way since the days of vacuum tubes. High power ratings are now possible in reasonably sized packages as a result of solid-state devices. The performance specifications of amplifiers are far better than the loudspeakers they drive. Although the appearance of the numerous power amplifiers may be similar, there are differences in their performance, which may have great influence on their long range service. They are similar only in the fact that they take a 1-volt signal representing little power at the input and convert it to considerable power at the output, power sufficient to drive loudspeakers to high acoustical output levels.

12.1 POWER RATINGS OF AMPLIFIERS

Rating an amplifier brings into focus the great difference between the sine-wave signal, easily obtained in the laboratory, and the voice or music signal the amplifier is called upon to reproduce. Unfortunately, there is no standard voice or music signal available for rating amplifiers. For this reason, it is common to see an amplifier rating that says something like, "250 watts rms into an 8-ohm load." the rms refers to the effective value of the sine-wave signal used in the measurement. Voice and music signals have high peaks as compared to their effective value and amplifier headroom must be reserved to care for these peaks. Far less power will be radiated with voice or music signals than the rms sine rating would indicate.

Power amplifiers drive loudspeaker loads and the impedance of loudspeakers is anything but what the simple "8-ohms" would infer. This would appear to indicate that the loudspeaker impedance is a pure resistance, which is far from the truth. When a graph of loudspeaker impedance variations with frequency is shown it is the vector impedance composed of the resistive and reactive components. Heyser has discussed this in a very important article (Ref. 1), which is highly recommended. Amplifiers vary greatly in the way they handle reactive loads and it must be remembered that the rating is for a pure resistance load.

Frequency response at low amplifier power levels may be quite different from that at high power levels. This is the result of the amplifier's inability to switch power rapidly at the higher audio frequencies. For this reason special equalization may be necessary to maintain flat response at higher frequencies for power levels to be employed.

12.2 HEATSINKING

No one worries about the efficiency of a power amplifier because power from the ac outlet is so cheap. However, it is instructive to give it some thought from the standpoint of heat, which must be carried away from the amplifier. One famous amplifier (Crown Model D-150A, Fig. 12-1) under certain conditions takes 250 watts from the power lines as it delivers 160 watts to the load. Thus 64% of the power into the amplifier is delivered to the load as the amplifier delivers full output. The 250

– 160 = 90 watts of power is dissipated in the amplifier and must be carried off to prevent an unwarranted increase in operating temperature. Just sitting there and delivering no output, this amplifier takes in 30 watts, which amounts to an efficiency of zero % and all 30 watts must be radiated as heat.

The power not delivered to the load must be dissipated to the surrounding air in some way. Such power is spread throughout the amplifier by conduction through the metal chassis, panel. etc. Heatsinks, usually in the form of finned metal radiators, add to this transfer of heat from the metal to the air. Passive systems depend on convection to achieve this transfer. These may be bulkier, but they are cheaper, quieter, and have no mechanical problems. Active systems rely on fans to keep temperatures under control. Although smaller and less bulky, such fans require maintenance and they make noise.

Fig. 12-1. (A) The Crown Model D-150A Series II power amplifier delivers 125 watts (FTC) per channel minimum (both channels operating) into a 4-ohm load over a bandwidth of 1 Hz to 20 kHz with a total harmonic distortion of 0.1 percent. (B) The Crown Model DC-300A Series II power amplifier. This is the current improved model of the DC-300 amplifier, which has become something of a standard in professional circles around the world. It is rated (EIA) at 300-watts rms stereo at less than 1 percent distortion over a frequency range of 20 Hz to 10 kHz within 1 dB. (C) The Crown Delta Omega 2000 monaural power amplifier which is rated at 2000 watts rms into 2.2-ohms, 10 to 500 Hz, with a 50 Hz, 50% duty cycle tone burst. This amplifier controls the inertia of the loudspeaker voice-coil assembly by sensing the back emf generated in that coil. Compensation for nonlinearities reduces loudspeaker distortion and improves sound quality (courtesy Crown International, Inc.).

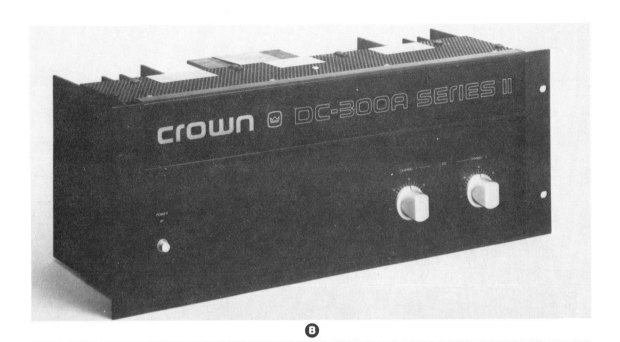

B

C

12.3 POWER SUPPLIES

Two power amplifiers are required for stereo and in multi-way sound reinforcement systems, using low-level crossovers, separate power amplifiers are used for woofer, midrange, and tweeter. When several power amplifiers are employed in one system or the other, should they all be driven by a common power supply or should there be a power supply for each amplifier? Many factors go into such a decision. We can at least say this, that if one power supply is to serve more than one amplifier, its regulation must be very good. That is, if one channel is called on to handle a surge of power, the voltage should not be pulled down appreciably or the functioning of the other amplifier will be impaired.

It is always desirable to have separate function indicators so that a blown fuse or opened circuit breaker can be located immediately.

12.4 INDICATOR LIGHTS

In addition to the power supply fuse/breaker indicator mentioned, lights are required to convey information on the functioning of the amplifier. A clipping indicator is very valuable. When clipping takes place in a power amplifier, strong high-frequency harmonics are generated that can overload and burn out the tweeter. Tweeters are designed to handle only the reduced high-frequency energy present in normal voice and music signals and are, for this reason, vulnerable to such unnatural overload. Input metering is often supplied in power amplifiers. This can also be helpful in avoiding clipping. Headroom indicators give an indication of how close one is operating to clipping or other form of overload.

Some amplifiers have metering calibrated in watts to indicate the power being supplied to the loudspeakers. These are often simple indicators of voltage across the load and are calibrated in watts. As the load usually has strong reactive components, such indicators may not be accurate in terms of resistive watts or true power.

12.5 RELIABILITY

Power amplifier failure can cause failure in other parts of the sound system and is, for this reason, doubly important to avoid. Manufacturers vary greatly in their testing procedures. It is probably too much to expect a manufacturer to "burn in" every amplifier he sends out, but the better ones will approach this ideal. What the warranty covers is important to the purchaser, but even more important is the ease of obtaining replacement parts in case of failure. How long will you be shut down in waiting for such a part? Are service and repair facilities available locally?

12.6 UNDERSTANDING THE SPECIFICATIONS

Taking the Crown Model D-150A Series II once more as our model (Fig. 12-1A) let us scan through the specifications of this power amplifier.

Output power may be specified in several ways. The Federal Trade Commission has issued a set of standards for consumer advertising. The Electronics Industries Association (EIA) has issued specifications that are commonly used in the design of amplifiers for commercial and professional applications. In Table 12-1 the output power of the Model D-150A Series II amplifier is listed by Crown International in both standards. The total harmonic distortion is found by this procedure: a pure sine wave is put in the front end and the voltage across a pure resistance of the rated value on the output is analyzed with a harmonic analyzer. The fundamental and harmonics are isolated and measured. The rms value of all the significant harmonics is first found by squaring the value of each, adding them together, and then taking the square root of the total. This gives the root-mean-square value of harmonics. Dividing this by the value of the fundamental and multiplying by 100 gives the percentage total harmonic distortion. In practice, another method is frequently used which rejects the fundamental with a special notch-filter circuit. The harmonics that remain are measured with an rms voltmeter. Expressing this reading as a percentage of the fundamental gives the total harmonic distortion directly.

The *frequency response* of the Crown D-150A Series II amplifier is listed as ± 0.1 dB dc—20 kHz at 1-watt into 8-ohms or ± 1 dB dc—100 kHz. Do

Table 12-1. Power Rating of Crown D-150A Series II Power Amplifier.

Federal Trade Commission Standard Specifications (for consumer advertising)	Electronics Industries Association (EIA) Specifications (more commonly used for professional and commercial amplifier design)
Output Power (4 ohms): 125 watts per channel minimum rms (both channels operating) into a 4 ohm load over a bandwidth of 1 Hz-20 kHz at a rated rms sum total harmonic distortion of 0.1% of the fundamental output voltage. **Output Power (8 ohms):** 80 watts per channel minimum rms (both channels operating) into an 8 ohm load over a bandwidth of 1 Hz-20 kHz at a rated rms sum total harmonic distortion of 0.05% of the fundamental output voltage. **Output Power (8 ohms):** 250 watts minimum rms into a 8 ohm load over a bandwidth of 1 Hz-20 kHz at a rated rms sum total harmonic distortion of 0.1% of the fundamental Output voltage (mono). **Output Power (16 ohms):** 160 watts minimum rms into a 16 ohm over a bandwidth of 1 Hz-20 kHz at a rated rms sum total harmonic distortion of 0.05% of the fundamental output voltage (mono).	**Output Power (4 ohms):** 140 watts rms at less than 1% distortion ±1 dB over a frequency range of 20 Hz-20 kHz (stereo). **Output Power (8 ohms):** 95 watts rms at less than 1% distortion ±1 dB over a frequency range of 20 Hz-20 kHz (stereo). 280 watts rms at less than 1% distortion ±1 dB over a frequency range of 20 Hz-20 kHz (mono). **Output Power (16 ohms):** 55 watts rms at less than 1% distortion ±1 dB over a frequency range of 20 Hz- 20 kHz (stereo). 190 watts rms at less than 1% distortion ±1 dB over a frequency range of 20 Hz-20 kHz (mono).

not expect to get this extremely flat response at 160 or 250 watts. The power bandwidth is quite another thing as mentioned previously.

Harmonic distortion is stated to be less than 0.001% from 20 to 400 Hz and increases linearly to 0.05% at 20 kHz at 80 watts rms per channel into 8-ohms. The distortion figures are excellent.

"I.M. distortion" means intermodulation distortion. These measurements are made with a high audio frequency and a low audio frequency mixed together. If there is any non-linearity present, the low will modulate the high and upper and lower sidebands will be created. With a filter, the sideband frequency is selected as a measure of the non-linearity prevailing in the amplifier. This will not necessarily be the same as the total harmonic distortion above, but each approach to distortion adds to our overall understanding of performance. For this amplifier the I.M. distortion is given as less than 0.05% from 0.01-watt to 0.25-watt and less than 0.01% from 0.25-watt to 80-watts into 8-ohms per channel.

Slewing rate is a measure of the rate at which the output signal can change. It is given as 6-volts per microsecond for this amplifier.

Damping factor is a measure of the ability of the amplifier to interact with the loudspeaker diaphragm in a way to control the excess inertia of the voice coil. As the voice coil moves in the magnetic field, a back emf is generated. If the impedance looking back into the amplifier is zero (the ideal case) this zero impedance would act as a sort of electronic brake on the voice coil. As the ratio of the loudspeaker impedance to amplifier output impedance increases, the damping factor increases and greater is the control over the inertia of the voice coil/diaphragm combination. For this Crown D-150A Series II amplifier, the damping factor is greater than 400, dc to 400 Hz, into 8-ohms, which is good.

Output impedance of the amplifier, mentioned above, is listed for this amplifier as less than 15 milliohms in series with less than 3 microhenries. We can calculate what the impedance is looking back into the amplifier at any particular frequency. At 400 Hz this impedance turns out to be 0.168-ohm and it is predominately inductive. This is to be compared to the 8-ohm load as far as the damping factor is concerned.

Load impedance for this amplifier is listed as 4- to 16-ohms (see Table 12-1) but the amplifier will safely drive any load including completely reactive loads with stability.

Voltage gain is listed as 20.6 ± 2% or 26.3 dB ± 0.2 dB at maximum gain.

Inut sensitivity is given as 1.19-volts ± 2% for 80-watts into 8-ohms.

Output signal is unbalanced, dual channel.

Hum and noise for a band 20 Hz to 20 kHz is 110 dB below rated output.

Phase response is +0, −15 degrees, dc to 15 kHz at 1-watt.

Input impedance is 25-kohms ± 30%

Many other bits of information are given on this amplifier such as output protection, dc output offset voltage, power requirements, etc., but this is enough to show the great detail a responsible manufacturer is willing to reveal about his product.

Two other Crown power amplifiers are shown in Fig. 12-1 and are briefly described in the captions.

12.7 OTHER POWER AMPLIFIERS

Many manufacturers other than Crown offer

power amplifiers at the professional level. Typical of these are the Altec Lansing Models 1268, 1269, and 1270 shown in Fig. 12-2. These are two-channel amplifiers with power output ratings of 100, 200, and 400 watts, respectively, per channel into 4-ohms. In bridging (mono) mode the power output into 8-ohms is 200, 400, and 800 watts with less than 0.05% total harmonic distortion, 20 Hz to 20 kHz. These direct-coupled amplifiers are protected by advanced computer circuitry. Input and output circuits are continually monitored and compared. Any peak/error causes the appropriate peak/error indicator to illuminate. Output anomalies detected include excessive voltage, excessive load current, excessive slew rate, and any other significant differences between channel input and output signal.

12.8 REDUNDANCY

If several power amplifiers of the same type are used in a given installation, there is a certain comfort in knowing that in an emergency amplifiers may be shifted around to maintain service. The maintenance problem is also simplified. The modular concept is coming into rather wide use and it will be discussed here by considering the products of two prominent manufacturers, Altec Corporation and Spectra-Sonics.

The Altec Lansing modular system (they call it the "incremental" system) is built around their Model 2275 and Model 2276 amplifiers (Figs. 12-3

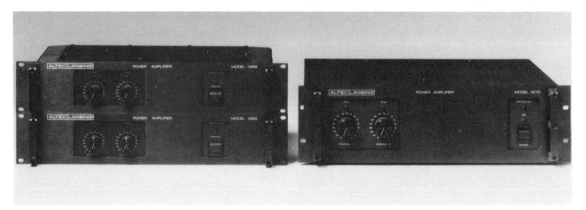

Fig. 12-2. Altec Lansing dual channel power amplifier family, Models 1268 (upper left), 1269 (lower left), and 1270 (right) designed to deliver 100-, 200-, and 400-watts per channel into 4-ohms. These amplifiers deliver twice the power when operated in the bridged (mono) mode (courtesy Altec Corporation).

Fig. 12-3. The Altec Lansing incremental power amplifier system with the 75 watt Model 2275 amplifier (left) and the 150 watt Model 2276 amplifier (right). The Model 2200 mainframe, occupying only seven inches of rack space, can accommodate power supply, blower, input/output termination buses and can be configured to bi-amplified or tri-amplified systems (courtesy Altec Corporation).

and 12-4). The 2275 is capable of delivering 75 watts into a 16-ohm load and the 2276 delivers 150 watts to an 8-ohm load. With various connections, multiples of this amplifier can deliver up to 600 watts.

The Altec Model 2200 mainframe (visible without cover in Fig. 12-3 and with cover in Fig. 12-4) will hold eight of the 2276 or four of the 2275 power amplifier modules. This mainframe has the slots to receive the amplifier cards, a power supply, blower,

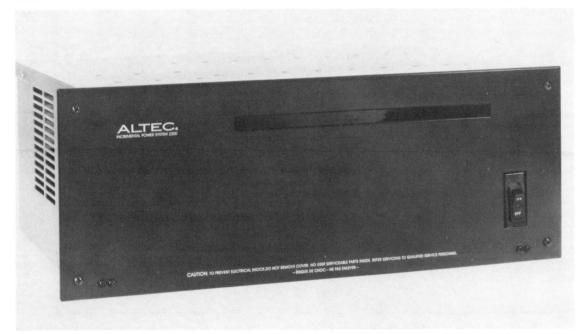

Fig. 12-4. The Altec Lansing Model 2200 mainframe used with their incremental power amplifier system (courtesy Altec Corporation).

and input and output termination buses. It requires only a 7-inch space in a standard rack.

The Altec Model 2275 and the 2276 power amplifier modules can be used in various modes. For example, they can be used independently as single units working into their own loads. They may also be paralleled for multiples of 75 or 150 watts, the maximum power for either module is 600 watts. They may also be used in what is called the bridged mode in which the inputs of two amplifiers are driven out-of-phase and the load connected to the two hot terminals at the output. This gives a balanced 70-volt loudspeaker line.

A typical two- or three-way loudspeaker system utilizing the Altec lansing incremental plan is shown in Fig. 12-5. Complete flexibility is realized in such a system. For example, level control between the

long throw and the short throw horns is achieved and complete control to match high-, mid-, and low-frequency units is present. The advantages of redundancy are fully realized as well as the ease of slipping in another amplifier card trouble arise in one of them. There is another advantage of the multi-way approach over the high level crossover approach. If an amplifier goes out in the system of Fig. 12-5, the system continues to work. In the conventional system with the power confined to a single hefty amplifier, if amplifier failure comes, the system is dead and, perhaps, some loudspeaker units are brought down at the same time.

The Spectra-Sonics system, introduced before the Altec system, was influential in the drift toward two- and three-way sound-reinforcement systems. The Spectra-Sonics Model 701 amplifier shown in

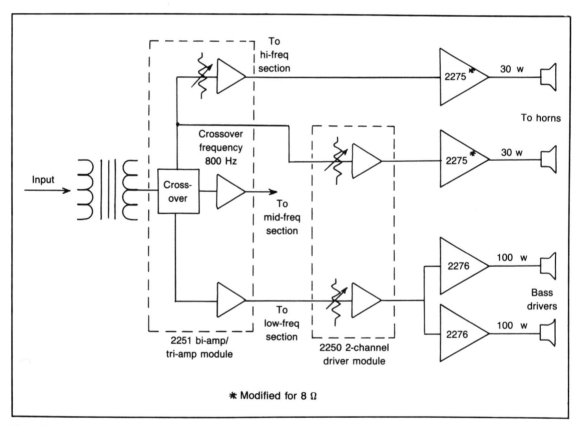

Fig. 12-5. A typical two- or three-way loudspeaker system utilizing the Altec Lansing incremental plan. The advantages of redundancy are achieved as well as an extreme flexibility in adjustment of the low-, mid-, and high-frequency sections (courtesy Altec Corporation).

198

Fig. 12-6. The Spectra Sonics modular power amplifier, Model 701, delivers 80 watts into a load of 2 ohms. This amplifier has a remarkable 1000% peak overload capacity. It is designed to fit into the 202 PC card holder frame of Fig. 12-7 (courtesy Spectra Sonics).

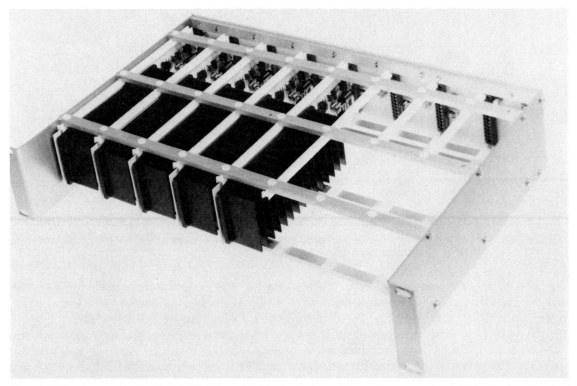

Fig. 12-7. The Spectra Sonics Model 202 PC card holder for their modular system occupying 3-1/2 inches in a standard rack. It will accept one Model 505 crossover filter and between six and nine Model 701 power amplifier cards. This card holder is available pre-wired for full frequency, bi-amplified, tri-amplified, or custom configurations (courtesy Spectra Sonics).

199

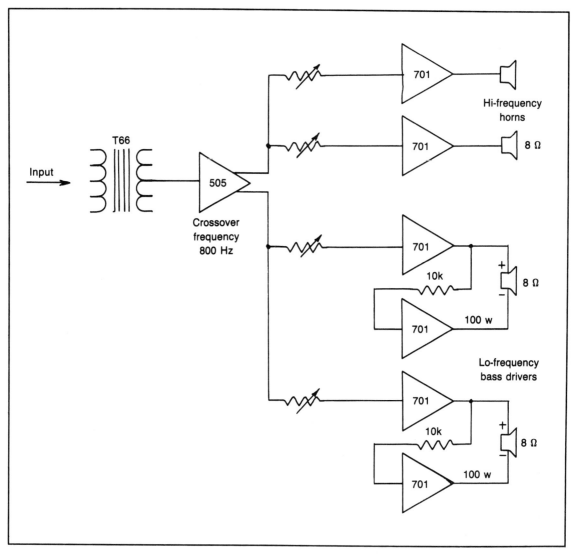

Fig. 12-8. The Spectra Sonics modular system configured for a typical two-way auditorium sound-reinforcement system. Flexibility and redundancy characterize this modular system.

Fig. 12-6 delivers 80 watts into a load of 2 ohms and has the unusual characteristic of delivering power on the basis of load impedance. For instance, the 701 will deliver 15 watts into 16 ohms. If two 701s are bridged into an 8-ohm load they will deliver 120-watts rms, a 4-fold or 6 dB increase. Doesn't a doubling of power give a 3 dB increase? Yes, that law is still with us. What happens here is that each amplifier operating in parallel is work-

ing into half the load impedance. In this way 3 dB is picked up by operating into 4-ohm loads and another 3 dB by having two amplifiers.

Another interesting feature of the Spectra-Sonics system is that tremendous peak overload capacity is built into each amplifier, up to 1000 percent. This means that rated power output can be delivered on either a sine wave or program signal basis.

In Fig. 12-7 the 202PC rack mount card holder is shown. It occupies only a panel height of 3-1/2 inches in the rack. It will hold a 505 crossover card and six to nine 701 amplifier units. In Fig. 12-8 is shown the circuit diagram for a typical two-way sound-reinforcement system using the Spectra Sonics system.

References

1. Heyser, Richard C., 1984. "Speaker Impedance, More Complex than One Number," *AUDIO*, Vol 68, No 6 (June) pp 42-46.

Chapter 13

Reverberation Devices

MULTITRACK RECORDING HAS REQUIRED acoustically dead spaces to achieve the necessary track separation. Naturally, this results in "dry" recordings, recordings with little or no reverberation. This situation has given rise to a new industry to design and build artificial reverberation machines so that reverberation can be put back into the recordings. Philosophers will have fun trying to figure out the ultimate purpose and significance of such tail-chasing activity.

In concert halls, the sound of classical music and the sound of the hall in which it is played are very much intertwined. Much effort has gone into the search for the reasons why some halls are "good" and others are "bad," but the best orchestras can be made to sound bad in some halls. In recording a symphony orchestra in a concert hall, great effort is expended in microphone placement, not only to cover the orchestra properly, but to get just the right proportion of reverberation from the hall, so that, in the finished recording, the orchestra sounds "natural," i.e., like it does in that hall.

Adding reverberation to the signal at hand in the recording studio or control room may be guided by such sophisticated goals. Maybe the operator just wants to make it sound "different," which often means "more salable." Whatever the guiding principle, early workers in the field arranged tape recorders with multiple heads to simulate the reverberation effects of large spaces. This set off an avalanche of artificial reverberation machines involving acoustical delay tubes, springs, plates, and now digital devices. The more typical of these devices will be considered in this section with emphasis on the types in wide use in the field.

On many consoles and in the literature the word "echo" is used instead of "reverberation." Echo is more properly associated with discrete packets of delayed energy, not the smooth decay of multitudinous reflections which tell us so much about the hall in which the music was played. Although it is admittedly a losing battle, I shall stick to the reverberation term because it is so much closer to what is happening.

13.1 THE SPATIAL IMAGE

Listening to a recording of an orchestra playing one can form a quite good picture of the hall in which the music is played. At least this is true if it is a "natural" recording as contrasted to a multitrack job built up piece by piece under conditions which minimize room effects. The size of the concert hall, its liveness are intuitively perceived. What is there about reverberation which conveys such information?

In Fig. 13-1 the amplitude of reflected sound at a given seat is plotted against time. Zero time is the time of arrival of the sound at this seat over the most direct path. Some time after the arrival of the direct sound, early reflections, possibly single reflections from the side walls, begin to arrive. After these secondary reflections, those undergoing more than one reflection, begin to arrive. The density of reflections then becomes so great that one can only note the shape of their decay envelope. Because amplitude has been plotted, this decay will take on an exponential form. If reflection level in decibels (log amplitude) had been plotted, this exponential decay would have been a straight line. In fact, Fig. 13-1 depicts the beginning of the reverberatory decay from which the reverberation time can be found by noting the ime required for a 60 dB decay. But we are more interested, for the moment, in the first few reflections.

Many concert halls have been studied in an attempt to identify the physical factors associated with those halls which have been universally judged excellent by experts. One factor so identified is what has been termed the "initial time delay gap." This is the time between the arrival of the direct sound and the early reflections as shown in Fig. 13-1. In the best halls it was found that this gap was of the order of 20 milliseconds. If this gap is filled with a confusion of reflections from close surfaces, music quality is affected adversely. This gap contributes to the impression of the size of the hall. We see, then, that reverberation has form and character and conclude that artificial reverberation devices must simulate this form and character if accurate impressions are to be given.

13.2 REVERBERATION CHAMBERS

A very natural approach to artificial reverbera-

Fig. 13-1. The significant descriptors of reverberation are (a) the arrival time of the direct signal at time = 0, (b) the initial time delay gap of at least 20 milliseconds, (c) the arrival of early reflections, typically from hall sidewalls, and finally (d) the avalanche of closely packed later reflections, which constitute the exponential reverberatory decay of the room.

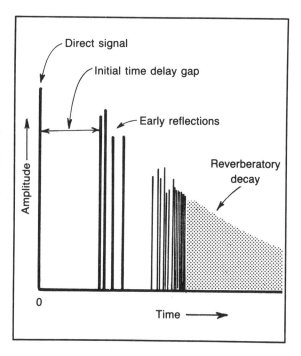

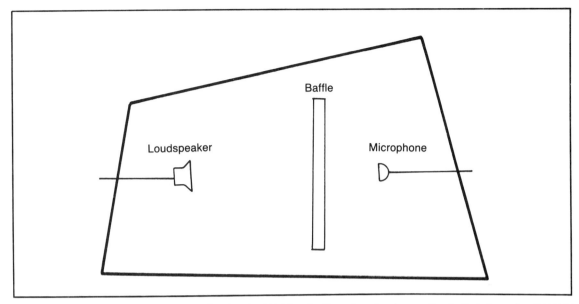

Fig. 13-2. The reverberation chamber of earlier days had highly reflective splayed surfaces with a baffle between loudspeaker and microphone. The high cost of such chambers limited their use and their small size made them subject to modal resonance problems.

tion is to use the reverberation produced in a special room. In the early days these rooms were built with splayed surfaces so that no two walls were parallel. As shown in Fig. 13-2, a baffle was commonly used between the loudspeaker and the microphone to force multiple reflections. The room surfaces were made hard and reflective to achieve the desired long reverberation times in relatively small rooms.

The disadvantages were many. Such rooms, especially built to minimize interfering noises, were very expensive. Cost usually kept the size down and thus these rooms were subject to colorations of the sound resulting from poor distribution of modal frequencies. They were also very inflexible; adjustment of reverberation time was limited or non-existent. As soon as effective artificial reverberation devices were available, chambers became of historical interest only.

The many attempts to use an empty room, a back hall, or stairwall as a reverberation chamber were only partially successful. In addition to inflexibility and colorations due to poor modal distribution, such makeshift arrangements invariably suffered from intrusion of interfering noises.

13.3 PLATE REVERBERATORS

One thing about the reverberation chamber, it did operate in three dimensions like the hall it emulates. The plate reverberator operates in only two dimensions, like a room without height (shades of flatland!). The EMT 140-TS reverberation plate was the standard of the recording industry around the world for a long time and is still in use in many places. In this device a special steel plate, suspended in a frame, was made to vibrate transversely (bending waves) by a transducer. Vibration pickups served as receiving transducers as shown in Fig. 13-3. Reverberation time was adjustable from 1- to 4-seconds by a special damping plate whose distance to the main plate was adjustable. Another plate type reverberator utilized a special foil as the medium, bringing in certain improvements, especially in compactness.

13.4 SPRING REVERBERATORS

A very early type of artificial reverberation de-

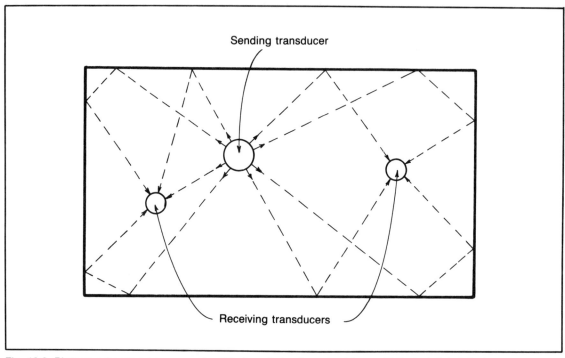

Fig. 13-3. Plate reverberators have served well but are being forced out by sophisticated digital devices.

vice depended on sound traveling in a wire. This wire is formed into a spring to get significant length within a reasonable space. A sending transducer is affixed to one end of the spring (Fig. 13-4) and a receiving transducer to the other end. Sound traveling longitudinally down the spring is reflected from any discontinuity. In Fig. 13-4 such a discontinuity has been purposely added in the middle where two springs are joined together. Multiple reflections are sketched assuming only three reflecting points, the two ends and the discontinuity in the middle. In commercial spring reverberators, a greater density of reflections is obtained by using several springs and by dents and etching of the surface of the spring.

The spring reverberator, a one dimensional device, is the most widely used today because it is inexpensive, compact, and gives a reasonable facsimile of natural reverberation. A typical contemporary spring reverberator, the N.E.I. (Ref.1) Model 351, is shown in Fig. 13-5. This unit is built around the Accutronics type 9 "reverb tank." One

special feature is the proprietary switchable SAR™, signal activated reverberation, which minimizes spring slap and rumble. A five-band equalizer allows shaping of the reverberation characteristic. The N.E.I. Model 351 reverberation system is especially adaptable to guitars and other instruments.

Another form of commercial reverberator is exemplified by the Furman (Ref.2) Model RV-1 (mono) and Model RV-2 (stereo) shown in Fig. 13-6. This unit is built around a shock mounted 16-inch, triple spring assembly by Accutronics. A sophisticated tone control allows adjustment of the midrange (160-1400 Hz) by a quasi-parametric circuit plus 10 dB of boost or cut treble shelving beginning at 2.5 kHz. A fast-attack peak limiter provides protection from "pops and boings" arising from overdriving the input transducer of the spring. The decay time is fixed at 1.8 milliseconds with 30 to 40 milliseconds of initial delay to simulate the initial time delay gap. The RV-1 and RV-2 units are said to be adaptable both to studio and road use.

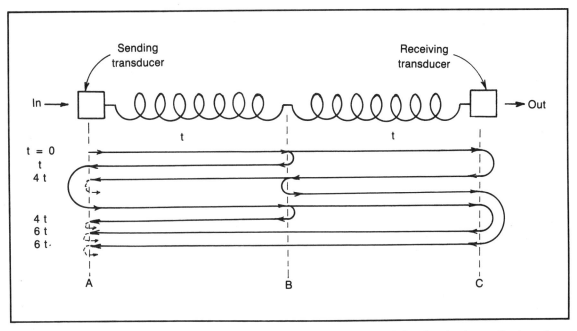

Fig. 13-4. In the spring reverberator the electrical signal is changed to mechanical vibrations by the sending transducer and back to electrical form by the receiving transducer. The received signal is not only a discrete signal delayed by the spring transit time, but also a torrent of lesser reflections from every discontinuity along the spring.

13.5 THE DIGITAL REVERBERATOR

What is it we ask an artificial reverberator to do? Well, first we require a stream of "reflections" of the input signal. We then ask that these reflections be spread out in time according to a certain desired pattern. The rate of decay and decay shape are then of primary interest. This sounds like the sort of thing a computer can do well.

The digital approach to artificial reverberation

differs from all those described above. By the use of programmable read-only memories (PROMs) the amplitude and time patterns of reflections can be made to conform to any concert hall or other space desired. Touch one button and the characteristics of your favorite concert hall shape your signal. Touch another and the bright, tight characteristic of a reverberator plate adds body to brass and drums. Still another characteristic gives warmth to

Fig. 13-5. The N.E.I. Model 351 spring reverberator. It incorporates circuitry to minimize slap and rumble, common faults when the sending transducer is overloaded. The five-band equalizer allows shaping of the reverberation characteristic (courtesy Neptune Electronics, Inc.).

Fig. 13-6. The Furman Model RV-1 (mono) and RV-2 (stereo) reverberation system. A quasi-parametric midrange equalizer adjusts frequencies in the range 160 - 1400 Hz. Treble shelving starts at 2.5 kHz. A fast-attack peak limiter minimizes overdrive "pops and boings" (courtesy Furman Sound, Inc.).

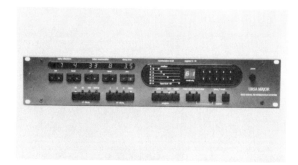

Fig. 13-7. Amplitude and time patterns of artificial reverberators are easily controlled by programmable read only memories (PROM) in digital reverberators such as the Ursa Major 8 × 32. Four pre-set programs allow simulation of two concert halls of different sizes and characteristics and fast and slow mechanical plate effects. Each program can be fine tuned by adjustment of seven reverberation parameters. Nonvolatile storage for 64 setting combinations is available (courtesy Ursa Major, Inc.).

voice signals. In the Ursa Major (Ref.3) 8 × 32 digital reverberator pictured in Fig. 13-7, typical of others, four pre-set programs create the spatial effects desired. Then, microprocessor-based controls allow adjustment of key reverberation parameters, which may be stored in nonvolatile memory. Decay times as long as 20 seconds are available. There is little question but what this is the approach to artificial reverberation of the future.

References

1. Neptune Electronics, Inc., 934 N.E. 25th Avenue, Portland, OR 97232

2. Furman Sound, Inc., 30 Rich Street, Greenbrae, CA 94904

3. Ursa Major, Inc., Box 18, Belmont, MA 02178

Chapter 14

Audio Signal Processing

ANY RECORDING/PLAYBACK COULD BE CONsidered as "processing" of audio signals, but this not the meaning behind this chapter title. Audio signal processing in this chapter has to do with alterations in the signal with a view of making the signal better serve some particular function. The producer of rock and roll music may have as his goal in signal processing the production of some new distortion that gives a distinctive sound, which is considered salable. Another person might introduce signal changes with the goal of improving the clarity of the music or voice. Another goal might be simply the improvement of the signal/noise ratio. In general, processing is for the purpose of improving the practical usefulness of the signal.

Limiters and compressors are covered in this chapter as well as other closely allied devices. Other forms of audio signal processing such as spectral shaping (equalizing) and noise reduction are important enough to demand separate chapters.

14.1 DYNAMIC RANGE CONSIDERATIONS

There are certain limitations in our recording and playback of audio signals. Noise establishes a lower limit of sound level, which can serve a useful purpose. Signals covered by noise are of little use to anyone. The equal loudness contours which we have studied in Fig. 5-6 have something to say about limitations of the human hearing mechanism. There is a lower threshold of hearing below which signals would be swamped by the noise of molecular motion in the air. As sound pressure levels are increased, a threshold of pain is eventually reached in the region of 130 dB. Obviously, sounds louder than this not only hurt, they damage ears. We see, then, that there are all sorts of practical limitations in the usable range of sound levels in our world.

Let us consider some of these sound ranges with the help of Fig. 14-1. Here is a scale of sound pressure levels ranging from zero, which is the

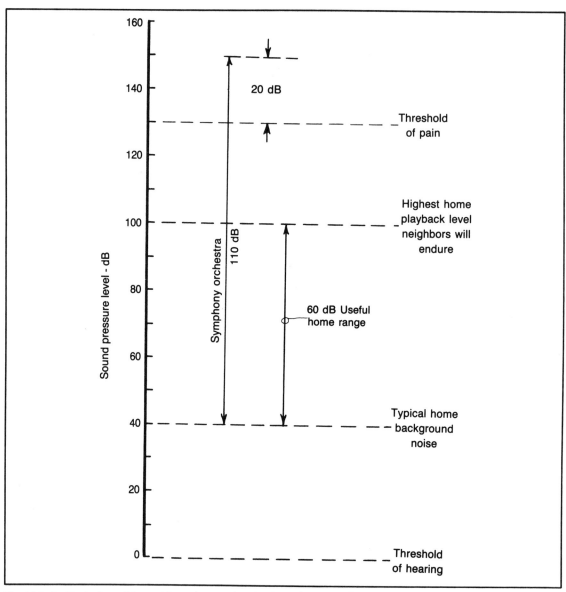

Fig. 14-1. An illustration of the problem of squeezing the dynamic range of a symphonic orchestra (as much as 110 dB) between the home background noise level (typically 40 dB) and the highest level the neighbors will stand (say, 100 dB).

threshold of hearing, to some arbitrary level such as 160 dB. If we are listening to records in our home, the background noise prevailing establishes a lower level below which musical sounds cannot be perceived. If the object of our aural enjoyment is the sound of a symphony orchestra we hope to hear the full range of its sound from the whisper of the piccolo to the full crashing of the percussions. It has been established that this range of sound pressure levels might be something like 110 dB. If it were possible to reproduce this full range in the living room we would want the piccolo to be audible above the ambient background noise in the room. This would mean that the crashing of the percussions would reach the 150 dB sound pressure level which is something like the blastoff of a space shuttle rocket. Of course, we have not yet seen the loudspeaker which would do this! But here is the problem: we are interested in listening to this orchestra but in this living room there is the 40 dB lower limit established by the ambient environmental noise over which one has little control and the upper limit established by the tolerance of the neighbors. We must somehow squeeze the 110 dB range of the orchestra into the 30 or 40 dB range of the living room.

There are limitations built into all the possible communication channels between the orchestra and the living room. FM radio might handle a range of 50 dB. Disc recordings have a top dynamic range of something like 60 dB and compact discs about 90 dB. But, everywhere we turn we encounter limitations in the dynamic range of sound intensities that can be handled.

What can be done, for instance, toward squeezing the symphony orchestra into a disc recording? One approach would be a sound mixer with a knowledge of music sufficient for him to follow the score and move the fader down in anticipation of the fff portions and move it up for the ppp portions.

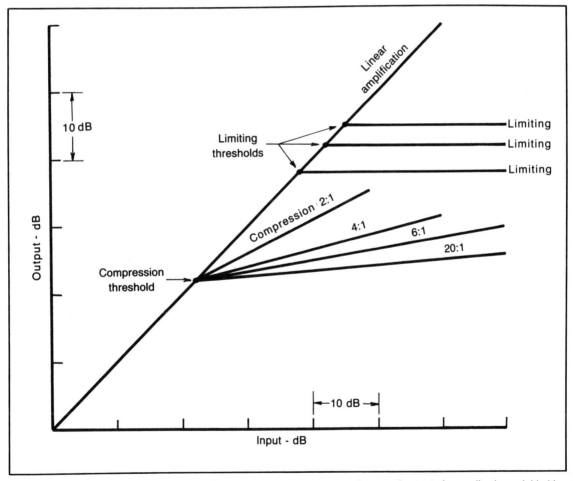

Fig. 14-2. The inclined straight line represents a linear relationship between input and output of an audio channel. Limiting action allows no change in output above some input threshold. Compression allows some change in output above compression threshold.

The conductor of the orchestra would cringe at the idea of giving over this important part of his job to the man on the board, but this operation has to be done either manually or automatically. Ah! Automatically! This brings us to limiters and compressors.

14.2 THE LIMITER

We consider the limiter first because of the simplicity of its basic function—prevention of overdriving or overload. In the radio broadcast station this would be avoiding overmodulation of the carrier, a subject of interest to the FCC. In cutting a master disc recording it would be avoiding overcutting from one groove to another. There is less need for limiting in tape recording because the tape itself has a sort of limiter in the form of tape saturation.

In Fig. 14-2, upper part, limiting action is illustrated. The straight line between input and output represents linear amplification. The horizontal limiting line means that no matter how much the input is increased above limiting threshold, there is no increase in output. By adjustment of the threshold, the point at which limiting action takes place is controlled.

Figure 14-2 is a picture of system gain changes, not of operating line of instantaneous voltage changes. In other words, the flat limiting region does not mean that the peaks are clipped, but rather that above the limiting threshold the gain of the system remains constant.

14.3 THE COMPRESSOR

The action of the compressor is illustrated in the lower part of Fig. 14-2. At a compression ratio of 2:1 an increase of input signal above the threshold of 10 dB would result in only a 5 dB increase in output. For a ratio of 4:1, the same 10 dB increase in input would result in only a 2.5 dB increase in output. It is apparent that a 20:1 ratio is essentially a limiting action. A ratio of 1.5:1 or 2:1 yields what is called in the trade a "soft" compression action that is usually inaudible.

The heart of the compressor is a voltage-controlled amplifier in the main signal line. The voltage to control this amplifier is obtained from a so-called side chain which samples the input voltage and from it shapes a control voltage, which in turn controls the gain of the voltage-controlled amplifier.

In Fig. 14-2 all of the compression ratio curves extend from a single threshold point. This threshold, however, is usually adjustable as shown in Fig. 14-3. Compression and limiting action are usually used together. It is common to set the limiting action about 8 dB above the compression threshold.

Limiting is used most often to control the occasional short lived peaks. The information that these peaks contribute to the signal is small compared to the distortion they cause if not removed. If the signal does not have such peaks, limiting should not be used.

Compression is used to minimize the change in level resulting from a vocalist or instrumentalist changing distance to the microphone. It is also used to equalize the changes in level between different ranges of an instrument. For example, some bass guitar strings are louder than others; horns are louder in some registers than others. The average level of the signal can be increased by the use of compression. If two persons are talking and one is louder than the other, compression could be used to help equalize the two.

14.4 ATTACK AND RELEASE TIMES

The speed of the compressor and limiter action is very important with respect to sound quality. Speed requirements also change for different types of program material and are influenced by what the operator needs to do. Most compressor/limiter devices have attack and release time adjustment controls.

The loudness of sound as perceived by the ear is proportional to the rms value of the signal and, for this reason, short duration peaks have little effect on the loudness of the program. If these short duration peaks were allowed to trigger gain reduction, the dynamics of the program would be adversely affected. To avoid this, the attack time is set so that the signal must exceed the threshold

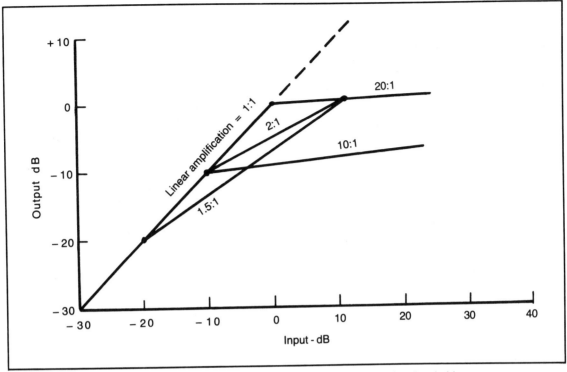

Fig. 14-3. It is common to set the limiting threshold about 8 dB above compression threshold.

level long enough to result in an increase in average level so that gain reduction will not decrease the overall level. If the release time is set too short (that is, if full gain is restored each time the signal falls below the threshold) audible faults are produced in the form of "breathing," "thumps," and "pumping." These are caused by the increase in background noise as gain is increased. Another effect of very short release times is that the automatic gain action tries to follow low-frequency program content and serious distortion is produced.

A very fast attack time tends to give a "gritty" edge to the sound. Extremely fast attack times cannot be tolerated in broadcast, pulse code modulation digital recorders, and disk cutters.

Limiters and compressors have adjustments of threshold, attack time, release time, compression ratio, and gain. Suffice it to say that anyone not having a thorough knowledge of what each knob does can produce some weird sounds and degrade the signal greatly.

14.5 THE EXPANDER

If a compressor limits the dynamic range of a signal to squeeze the signal into the limitations of a communication channel, it may be desirable at a later stage to restore the dynamic range to its original value. This requires an expander with a characteristic the opposite to that of the compressor. Expanders are sometimes used in playback situations to recover the dynamic restrictions of the channel.

14.6 THE NOISE GATE

The Kepex noise gate put out by Allison Research, Inc., will illustrate the functioning of a noise gate, although many compressor/limiters have the noise gate feature. Referring to Fig. 14-4 the desired signal extends from A to B but in-between this burst of program material and the next one there is much noise and reverberation, which we wish to get rid of. Whenever the program exceeds the threshold the amplifier has unity gain. As soon as the program drops below the threshold at B, the amplifier gain is reduced as much as 60 dB, which essentially eliminates the bothersome noise and reverberation that otherwise would be very noticeable during quiet periods.

14.7 SIBILANT CONTROL

When the program material has excessive sibilants in a voice a so-called "de-esser" is employed to correct them. This is often a feature of the compressor/limiter device. It is simple in mode of operation. A filter is inserted in the compressor circuit in such a way that the high-frequency energy associated with sibilants triggers compression. In this way gain is reduced only at the frequencies giving trouble.

14.8 TYPICAL SOUND PROCESSING EQUIPMENT

The Biamp (Ref. 1) limiter/compressor/noise gate is shown in Fig. 14-5 in both the stereo (upper) and quad (lower) forms. The two-and four-independent channels feature front panel threshold control and switchable selection for limiting or noise gate. Each channel has an LED indicator to show limiting or signal through the noise gate. This device can drastically reduce microphone rumble and

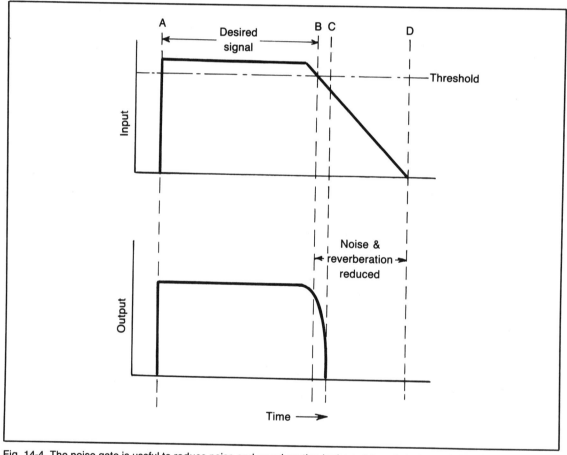

Fig. 14-4. The noise gate is useful to reduce noise and reverberation in the quiet spots between bursts of desired signal. The threshold may be adjusted to introduce as much as 60 dB attenuation during quiet spots by means of a voltage controlled amplifier.

Fig. 14-5. The Biamp limiter/compressor/noise gate is shown in two- and four-channel form. Attack and release times are adjustable (courtesy Biamp Systems, Inc.).

low-level background noise. If several keyboards are connected, only the one being used is "on," the others are "off" reducing hum and noise. Individual screwdriver controls adjust attack and release time in the range 0.15-1.5 seconds.

The Compellor ™ from Aphex Systems, Ltd., (Ref. 2) is shown in Fig. 14-6. It is a stereo audio compressor, leveler, and peak limiter simultaneously. As a leveler it maintains output level within 1-dB for a 20-dB change in input level and its action is slow enough to have minimal effect on program transients or short term program dynamics. Compression is accomplished over a 20-dB range of input levels with the ratio varying from 1.1-1 to 20:1. The peak limiter holds an absolute ceiling 12-dB above the nominal 0VU level.

The input control adjusts the amount of processing desired. There is a control to adjust the balance between compression and leveling. Once these are properly set, the rest is automatic.

The Model LC-3 limiter/compressor offered by Furman Sound (Ref. 3) is illustrated in Fig. 14-7. In addition to input and output level controls, it features separate controls for attack time (100 microseconds to 5 milliseconds), release time (50 milliseconds to 1.1 seconds), and compression ratio (2:1-50:1). Gain reduction is displayed by an LED style meter. LEDs also provide for overload and power-on indication. Front panel pushbuttons select between normal compression, "de-essing," and "side-chain" modes. The latter two functions allow for the gain controlling signal to be processed

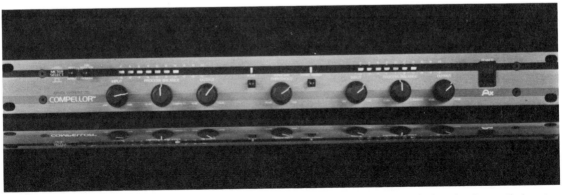

Fig. 14-6. The Aphex Compellor™ which is a stereo audio compressor, leveler, and peak limiter simultaneously (courtesy Aphex Systems, Ltd.).

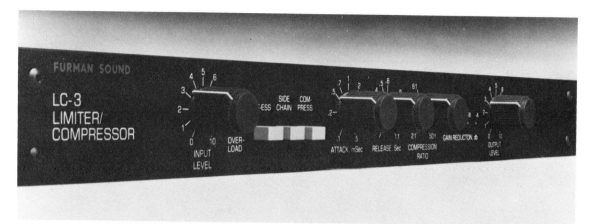

Fig. 14-7. The Furman Model LC-3 limiter/compressor. Attack and release times and compression ratios are adjustable. A "de-essing" feature is also included (courtesy Furman Sound, Inc.).

through either an internal high-pass filter, which passes only sibilance frequencies, or through any external equalizer or other device. The user thus may elect to compress only in a restricted frequency range. The side-chain input may also be used alone to allow a completely unrelated signal to control gain for special effects. Low noise, low distortion, and modest cost are also features of the LC-3.

Furman Sound also offers the Model QN-4 quad noise gate as shown in Fig. 14-8. This four channel noise gate works on the principle that noise (and leakage from one instrument to another) is most noticeable when no signal is present. By turning channels off when no signal is present, such noise and leakage are greatly reduced. Each channel has two controls: one to adjust the level below

which muting begins (the "threshold"), the other to control the rate at which the channel turns off. The latter, called "fade time," is continuously variable from five milliseconds to over five seconds. Each channel is also provided with an LED "channel on" indicator. Advanced variable pulse-width modulation technology to achieve muting action is said to result in favorable signal/noise and distortion specifications.

The Orban (Ref. 4) Model 424A compressor/limiter/de-esser shown in Fig. 14-9 is different from other such devices in several ways. For example, to improve ease of operation the attack time, release time, and compression ratio controls are purposely made interactive with each other and with the threshold of limiting. Slower attack times

Fig. 14-8. The Furman Model QN-4, a 4-channel noise gate that reduces noise when no signal is present. Muting level and "fade time" are adjustable (courtesy Furman Sound, Inc.).

216

Fig. 14-9. The Orban Model 424A compressor/limiter/de-esser. In this unit the attack time, release time, and compression ratio are purposely made interactive because these parameters are interrelated. This results in improved program control (courtesy Orban Associates, Inc.).

permit more overshoots, so the threshold of limiting is automatically lowered to compensate. Other unusual features are the use of feedback control, an averaging detector, and a conventional "hard knee" static compression curve. Feedback in the control loop is said to result in improved sound quality. The effect of the type of detector selected is essentially irrelevant in the face of major attack time adjustments. The "hard knee" compression better serves in making a wide dynamic range vocal cut through a heavy instrumental backing. In the 424A, attack and release time controls merely scale the processes faster or slower without giving up the advantages of program control. The de-ess function is essentially independent of the compression/limiting action.

The Orban (Ref. 4) Model 536A dynamic sibilance controller, pictured in Fig. 14-10, provides two channels of de-essing effective over a 15 dB input range. The balanced active input may be strapped for +4dBm (professional) or –10dBm (semi-professional) use. The 536A threshold control establishes the amount of sibilant energy as a certain fraction of the non-sibilant speech energy, even if the input changes as much as 15 dB. A dual LED display indicates the amount of de-essing occurring ("Normal," "Heavy"). An overload indicator warns of clipping anywhere in the circuit. Using the 536A on voice mixed with other sounds may be unsuccessful as it operates on high-frequency sounds whether or not of sibilant origin. The 424A would be more suitable for this task.

The dbx (Ref. 5) Model 165A shown in Fig. 14-11 is their top-of-the-line compressor/limiter. This single-channel unit is strappable for stereo operation and offers a choice of manual or automatic attack and release rates. In manual mode, attack and release rates allow the 165A to be used as peak, average, or rms-detecting limiting. The dbx Over Easy ® circuit design ("soft knee" as opposed to "hard knee") is said to provide inaudible transition into compression, even at high compression ratios. The reasons given for the use of an rms detector in the 165A are: (a) it simulates the reaction of the human ear, providing "natural" compression, and (b) it accurately correlates to thermal energy developed in loudspeakers, providing optimum driver protection. Feed forward gain control allows infinity:1 compression ratios without gain instability. The input-output capability is +24 dbm.

References

1. Biamp Systems, Inc., 11000 SW 11th Street, Beaverton, OR 97005

Fig. 14-10. The Orban Model 536A dynamic sibilance controller. Two channels of de-essing, effective over a 15 dB input range, are provided (courtesy Orban Associates, Inc.).

Fig. 14-11. The dbx Model 165A compressor/limiter, a single channel unit strappable for stereo operation. A choice of manual or automatic attack and release control is given. The "soft-knee" transition into compression is utilized (courtesy dbx, Incorporated).

2. Aphex Systems, Ltd., 13340 Saticoy Street, North Hollywood, CA 91605

3. Furman Sound, Inc., 30 Rich Street, Greenbrae, CA 94904

4. Orban Associates, Inc., 645 Bryant Street, San Francisco, CA 94107

5. dbx, Incorporated, Professional Products Division, 71 Chapel Street, Newton, MA 02195

Chapter 15

Time Delay

I T TAKES TIME FOR SOUND TO TRAVEL FROM one point to another. The speed of sound in air (1,130 ft/sec) is a snail's pace compared to the speed of light (186,000 mi/sec). The sound engineer deals in both of these categories of speed. In a sound reinforcement system in a large auditorium, for instance, the signals the sound operator sends to the loudspeaker cluster travels at close to the speed of light as electrical signals in the conductors. Once the sound is radiated from the loudspeaker one must fall back on sound's snail pace speed. One does not have to worry about the time it takes an electrical signal to travel from the power amplifiers to the loudspeakers; little accuracy is sacrificed to call it zero. The sound in air, however, is so slow that delays are created that can cause major headaches.

If sound travels 1,130 ft/sec it follows that sound travels 1.13 feet in a thousandth of a second (or one millisecond). That is a handy figure to remember: 1.13 ft/ms because the time frame in auditorium acoustics is best expressed in

milliseconds. A convenient scale for finding the transit time of sound over various distances, or the number of feet to give a certain delay, is shown in Fig. 15-1.

15.1 ECHO AUDIBILITY

The sad fact is that echoes are produced if sound amplitude and delay are above certain critical levels. The word "echo" implies that ears are involved and ears mean that we step over into the field of psychoacoustics. To answer the question, "How much must a sound be delayed to be audible as an echo?", one must know something about level of the original sound as well as the level of the delayed sound. Level is all tied up with delay, the two must be considered together to reap useful answers.

In Fig. 15-2, two heavy curves labelled RT60 = 1.1 and RT60 = 0.5 seconds were obtained by presenting direct and delayed samples of speech to panels of carefully selected observers and asking

219

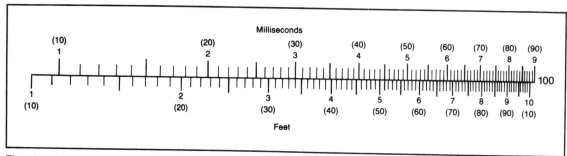

Fig. 15-1. A convenient graphical method of showing the relationship of sound transit time (milliseconds) and the path length (feet).

them to say when they were disturbed by the echoes (Ref.1). These heavy lines represent 20 percent of the observers being disturbed. This percentage is selected because the threshold of echo onset is so erratic and ill defined. These curves separate the disturbance-free area below from the echo disturbance area above. If a certain direct sound from a loudspeaker in an auditorium and a reflection of it from a wall are measured, both in relative level and delay, plotting this point on this graph and assuming the room reverberation time corresponds to one curve or the other, it can be determined whether such a reflection will or will not be perceived as a discrete echo.

Let us examine these curves closely. An exponential reverberatory decay will be a straight line on this plot. The broken lines are for such reverberatory decays at these two reverberation

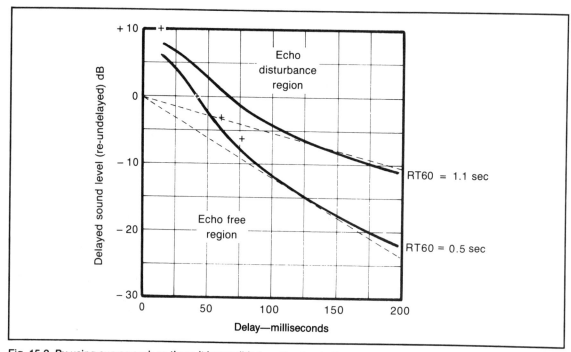

Fig. 15-2. By using curves such as these it is possible to estimate whether or not echoes will be disturbing from a knowledge of delayed sound level and amount of delay. The solid curves, obtained by psychoacoustical techniques (Ref.1), may be approximated by actual reverberation decay (broken lines) for delays greater than 100 milliseconds.

times. They are easily obtained from a simple ratio. If the decay is 60 dB (by definition) for a reverberation time of 1.1 second, what will be the decay in 200 ms (0.2 second)? This gives 10.9-and 24-dB intersections at the 200-ms delay for reverberation times of 1.1 and 0.5 second. We know there is zero decay at zero time so drawing lines between the two points gives the straight line reverberatory decay. The interesting thing is that beyond 100 ms or so the reverberatory decay lines and the psychoacoustically determined curves practically coincide. Therefore, if we have an auditorium with a reverberation time of 1.8 seconds, we can approximate the psychoacoustical curves for that reverberation time be applying this ratio.

Below about 100 ms there is a significant deviation from the reverberation lines. This is the Haas effect (Ref.2). This is an excellent time to review Section 5.8 and restudy Fig. 5-9. The four small "x" marks in Fig. 15-2 are taken from Haas' paper and they seem to be "in the ballpark" in spite of somewhat different conditions. Haas' reverberation is indeterminate because he worked on the roof of a building. This ties the work of Nickson, et al with Haas and for the shorter delays we will do well to go back to Fig. 5-9.

Figure 15-2 shows criteria curves, one might say, by which physical measurements of level, delay, and reverberation time can be used to get answers (echoes? no echoes?) of a subjective kind. For this reason these curves are of very great value to sound operators needing to know whether a certain combination of geometry and equipment will produce echoes.

15.2 DELAYS IN SOUND REINFORCEMENT

A rather common example will illustrate the relationship of space and time delay of signals and how problems can be corrected. In Fig. 15-3 a sound reinforcement cluster is 60 ft from a certain seat under the balcony. The distributed system to cover the seats in the shadow of the cluster places one loudspeaker only nine ft from this seat. The sound emanates from both the cluster and this closer loudspeaker essentially simultaneously because the speed of electrical signals in the wires is close to the speed of light. The airborne signals will not arrive at the same time because one travels only nine feet and the other 60 feet, or a difference of 51 feet. Reference to Fig. 15-1 tells us that 51 feet corresponds to a delay of 45 milliseconds. The Haas cure of Fig. 5-9 is reproduced in the lower part of Fig. 15-3. This 45 millisecond delay is seen to be well outside the fusion zone indicating that discrete echoes would result.

If the signal fed to the under-balcony loudspeakers is delayed 30 milliseconds, the person sitting in this seat would hear a perfect fusion of the two, the illusion that the sound is coming from the podium would prevail, and good intelligibility would be experienced. This simple application of a delay device before the power amplifiers feeding the under-balcony loudspeakers solves what otherwise is a very exasperating problem.

Another possible sound reinforcement situation is illustrated in Fig. 15-4. This is a distributed system in which the need for delay devices is very uncertain. A person at A receives direct sound from the first loudspeaker and fringe sound from B loudspeaker and relatively little from C and D. There would be very little delay between A and B, hence the possibility of needing delay in such a system is remote.

In Fig. 15-5, however, the separation of the two sets of loudspeakers (assuming two on the opposite wall) in this case could very well be sufficient to cause an echo effect for people in the rear of the room.

15.3 DELAY DEVICES

Through the years there have been many types of delay devices developed and used. An electrical delay line composed of inductances and capacitances in a ladder configuration is possible, but the wide bandwidth necessary would make it very bulky and expensive. Various acoustical delays in pipes and mechanical delays in rods with transducers at each end have been used but they are not suited for our use. (The spring reverberator

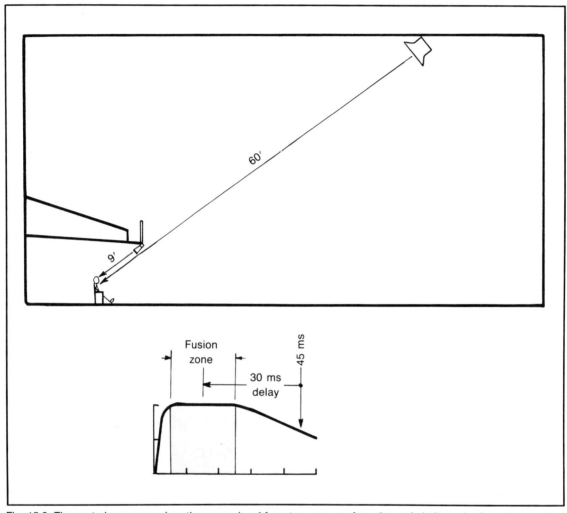

Fig. 15-3. The seated person receives the same signal from two sources, from the underbalcony loudspeaker nine feet away and the main cluster 60 feet away. The main cluster sound arrives later by the time it takes sound to travel 60 − 9 = 51 ft, or 45 ms, which is outside the Haas fusion zone. By delaying the underbalcony loudspeaker signal 30 ms, the two will be perceived as coming from a single source, the podium.

is a delay device of this type but its delay is short because of the high sound speed in steel). Adjustable delays have been satisfactorily obtained from tape machines with multiple heads, but the wear of the tape and upkeep is a grave problem.

Electronic delay devices are the answer because they are compact and dependable. They are of two types, analog and digital. The analog delay is based on charge transfer devices. The digital delay "line" changes the analog signal to digital form, which is then delayed by shift registers and then translated back into analog form. These are by far the most satisfactory, reasonable in cost, and stable in operation.

The Fostex (Ref.3) Model 3050 digital delay, shown in Fig. 15-6 is able to give a straight delay suitable for use in sound-reinforcement applications, but also has the capability of modulation to generate many musical and sound effects. It is capable of giving that simulation of the initial time

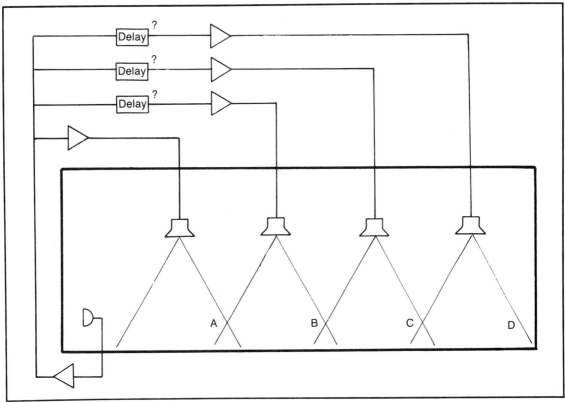

Fig. 15-4. A distributed loudspeaker system in which the need for delay devices is questionable. A person at A, for example, receives sound from both A and B but they are probably close enough in time of arrival to fall within the fusion zone.

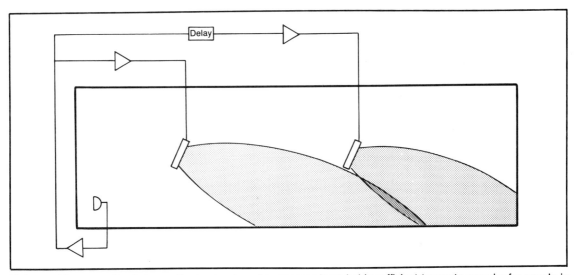

Fig. 15-5. The separation between the two loudspeaker sources is probably sufficient to create an echo for people in certain seats.

Fig. 15-6. The Fostex Model 3050 digital delay device capable of giving delays from 0.27 to 137 ms, selectable in ten steps and continuously adjustable over a ×1/2 to ×2 range. This expands the range to 0.13 to 270 ms (courtesy Fostex Corporation of America).

delay gap in artificial reverberation, which contributes much to its naturalness. It can be used for vocal doubling to make a solo voice sound like a chorus, for phasing/flanging to add depth to sounds, etc. Its delay range is 0.27 to 137 milliseconds selectable in ten steps. The delay can be continuously varied from 1/2 to ×2, which expands the usable delay range up to 270 milliseconds or shrink it down to 0.13 milliseconds. There is a built-in oscillator that can modulate the amount of delay from one to 30 times per second.

The Eventide (Ref.4) Model JJ193 digital delay line, manufactured by a pioneer in the delay field, is shown in Fig. 15-7. This is a device of the type preferred by sound reinforcement designers for permanent installations. While it is capable of signal doubling, realistic echo effects, and pre-reverberation delay for making plate and spring reverberation more natural, it is especially adaptable to the permanent installation mentioned above. This delay line features random-access memories for versatility and reliability and CMOS logic system. It has four outputs and one input and

is available in 510 millisecond, 1.022 second, and 2.046 second versions. The electrical specifications include a frequency response of 50 Hz to 11 kHz within 1/2 dB, a dynamic range of 90 dB from clipping to noise floor, and distortion of 0.15 percent. Six LED indicators show input-level relative to clipping point.

References

1. Nickson, A.F., R.W. Muncey, and P. Dubout, 1954. "The Acceptability of Artificial Echoes With Reverberant Speech and Music," *Acustica*, Vol 4 pp 515-518.

2. Haas, Helmut, 1972. The Influence of a Single Echo on the Audibility of Speech, *Jour. Audio Engr. Soc.*, Vol 20, No 2 (Mar) pp 146-159. This is an English translation of the original Haas paper in Acustica, Vol 1,No 2 (1951).

3. Fostex Corporation of America, 15431 Blackburn Avenue, Norwalk, CA 90650.

4. Eventide, Inc., One Alsan Way, Little Ferry, NJ 07643.

Fig. 15-7. The Eventide Model JJ193 digital delay line features random access memories for versatility and reliability. Available in 510 ms, 1.022 second, and 2.046 second versions. Delay is variable in 2 ms steps by setting DIP switches (courtesy Eventide, Inc.).

224

Chapter 16

Noise Reduction

THE SERENITY OF OUR NEIGHBORHOOD WAS broken the other morning by an ear-splitting, screaming, penetrating noise. Investigation revealed a gardener down the block with a back-pack gasoline-engine-driven blower and a blower nozzle in his hand. He industriously blew grass cuttings, leaves, and a cloud of dust all around the premises until finally he either deposited them in the street, on the neighbor's lawn, or simply lost them. After an uneasy truce with power lawnmowers, Japanese motorcycles, and impromptu ball games in the street, a new challenge to surburban peace and quiet has arrived.

Each new step forward in 20th century mechanization brings its own brand of environmental noise. For example, a noise source that has escaped attention has been pointed out by Coddington (Ref.1). This is the noise put out by Cathode-ray-tube circuits in television receivers, computer displays, etc. In analyzing environmental noise, the levels in the octave band centered on 16 kHz are usually in the region of 10 to 20 dB. I have measured levels of 75 dB at the housing of our television set and 70 dB at my computer monitor. This sound is at the horizontal scanning frequency which is 15,734 Hz in the NTSC standard. Sound pressure levels of the order of 50 dB are common at listener or operator positions. The "high" in high fidelity has to do with 16 kHz commonly taken as the upper limit of hearing in humans. There is a great mystery as to why "golden ears" have not been offended by such an assault on their admittedly keen senses. At the same time we now understand why dogs and cats may be uncomfortable when the family TV is turned on!

This chapter goes beyond the noise reduction devices used in the recording studio to include environmental noises of acoustical origin and the interference from radio frequency and power sources as well. Noise is everywhere and it requires knowledge as well as diligence to combat it. There is acoustical noise from without trying to get into our microphones, there is electrical interference trying to spoil our weak signals. There is tape hiss associated with magnetic recording media and digitizing noise to degrade digital signals. Noise is the Yin which stands against the Yang of audio signals, always, everywhere.

16.1 AIRBORNE ACOUSTICAL NOISE

Walls are erected to protect us, among other things, from the onslaught of environmental noise. Walls (along with ceilings and floors) help us to provide reasonable quietness for recording or listening to desired sounds. This brings us to a definition of noise as nothing more or less than what is undesirable in a given situation. One person's noise may quite well be another person's highly desirable signal.

It is well for us to consider the basic principles of physics that enable us to protect ourselves from environmental noises. The first such principle is that heavy walls keep out noise better that light walls, which, of course, everyone knows. Not everyone know, however, how heavy walls are figured and how heavy a wall must be to accomplish a certain amount of isolation from undesired noises. The "Mass Law" of Fig. 16-1 relates surface density of walls to transmission loss, or the number of decibels of loss a sound incurs in traveling through the barrier. This transmission loss is very much frequency dependent. Surface density is nothing more than the weight of the barrier associated with a square foot of surface. For example, a single layer

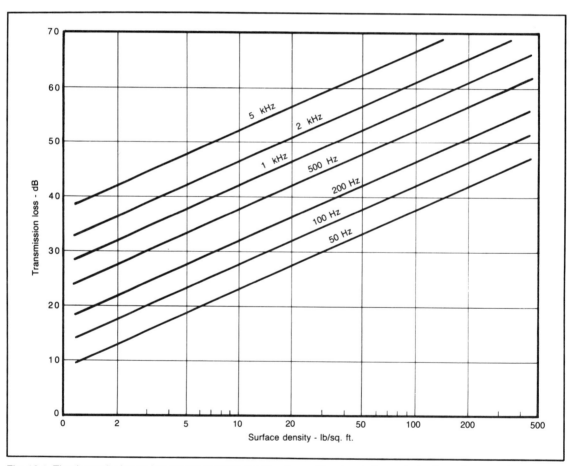

Fig. 16-1. The theoretical mass law relating surface density of sound barriers to transmission loss. For example: an 8-inch wall of concrete blocks has a surface density of 34 lbs/sq ft. At 500 Hz this wall offers a transmission loss of 45 dB.

of 5/8-inch gypsum board on each side of simple 2×4 studs works out to be about 6 lbs to each square foot of wall surface, thus the surface density is 6 lbs/sq ft.

Entering Fig. 16-1 at this surface density of 6 lbs/sq ft we see that at 50 Hz this wall offers only about 20 dB transmission loss, but at 5 kHz the transmission loss is almost 50 dB. Transmission loss is easily obtained for high frequencies, but far more difficult to obtain for low frequencies. There is a compensating factor in human hearing. Back in Chapter 5 we learned (Fig. 5-6) that the ear is less sensitive to low-frequency sound. This tends to make up for the relative transparency of barriers to low-frequency sound.

The mass law curves of Fig. 16-1 provide an excellent starting point in rough appraisals of the effectiveness of walls but it is of theoretical origin, not practical. It neglects the ever-present resonances at low frequencies and the coincidence effects at higher frequencies. Such effects tend to make real life transmission loss measurements depart somewhat from the pure mass law values. In one sense this complicates the application of this sort of data to practical problems.

To rate a given barrier with a single number the concept of Sound Transmission Class (STC) has been adopted. A standardized transmission loss versus frequency shape has been adopted and this is fitted to graphs of actual transmission loss measurements on a given barrier and from the fit between the two a single STC value is deduced to represent that particular barrier. One might look on the STC rating of a partition as a sort of average transmission loss in dB descriptive of that partition.

In Fig. 16-2 we see an adaptation of the mass law called the empirical mass law (Ref. 2). Here all the mass law information is concentrated in the STC ratings and plotted against frequency.

Table 16-1 lists common frame constructions and their STC ratings. Some rather uncommon, but easily attained, frame constructions which yield much higher STCs are also included. These may be compared to the 8-inch concrete block wall in their ability to stop sound.

The wall constructions of Table 16-1 are represented in Fig. 16-2 by plotting their STC values. Wall A and the concrete block wall G fall close to the empirical mass law curve, which means that their performance can be generally attributed to the brute force effect of their mass. All of the other walls are above the empirical mass curve which means that something new has been added to their brute force mass effect. The E wall is a double wall and the C wall utilizes staggered studs, both of which tend to isolate one wall diaphragm from the other except around the periphery. The same is true for Walls F, D, and B with the added layers adding mass. The lesson to learn from this is that much better wall performance than pure mass is readily available in quite practical constructions.

Space will not allow further examples, but some general principles can be considered. One can expect another 3 to 6 dB of transmission loss by adding fiberglass to the air space between the two leaves of a partition. Gypsum board can be installed by either screws or nails or mounted on resilient channels. If such channels are used on one side of a partition, another 5 or 6 dB of transmission loss may be added. It is always advantageous to make one side of the partition different than the other as this makes them resonate at different frequencies. Making a room airtight is helpful as slight cracks can pass an amazing amount of sound. A nonhardening sealant should be used in sealing around the periphery of all partitions.

Doors are notoriously weak in guarding against noise intrusion. Household doors are of little value in this sense and for isolation against noise solid core doors are a minimum step. Studios commonly employ sound locks to overcome the poor sealing characteristic of even good doors. With a sound lock, several doors open into this corridor so that two doors are in series between any two sound-sensitive areas or between each sound-sensitive area and the noise environment outside.

Observation windows have caused many headaches, both in regard to their design and their poor performance. Measurements have recently been made that answer many of the questions answered before by blind experimentation (Ref. 3).

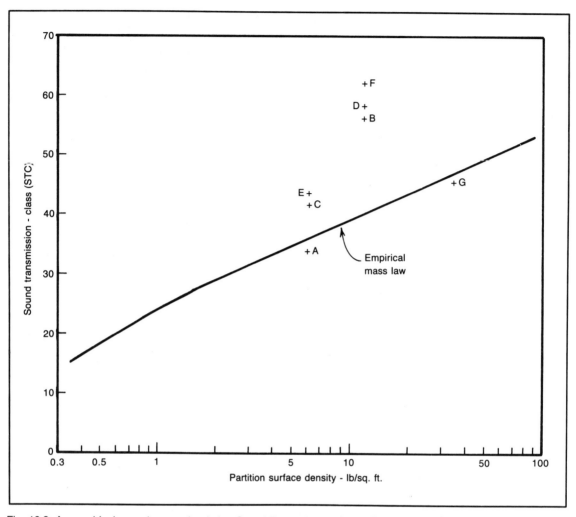

Fig. 16-2. An empirical mass law graph relating Sound Transmission Class (STC) ratings and barrier surface density. The letter identifications on the plotted points refer to Table 16-1.

The overall results of these measurements point to the following generalizations. (1) Use large inter-pane spacing; 3 dB gain in transmission loss for each doubling of spacing. (2) Use heavy glass, 6 dB in transmission loss for each doubling of surface mass. (3) Use glass of different thickness on the two sides; this staggers the coincidence dips. (4) Use thick absorbent on the edges of the interpane cavity to control interpane modal resonances. (5) For very high transmission loss windows laminated glass is recommended. (6) Inclining one or both glass panes is not justified by any of the measurements although

it may be helpful in controlling light reflections or other things.

16.2 STRUCTURE-BORNE ACOUSTICAL NOISE

To those who might be a bit skeptical of the importance of noise traveling through the structure, try to recall the sound of heel taps on stairways or the floor above. Solid materials transmit sound more efficiently than air does. The combination of airborne and structure-borne sound is often a diffi-cult problem to overcome. For instance, a large wall acting as a diaphragm can be excited by airborne sound falling on it and then it transmits the sound throughout the structure, possibly exciting a distant wall, which efficiently radiates the sound back into the air in a different room.

Recording studios are often built on a room-within-a-room basis. One way of doing this would be to first pour a 4-inch concrete floor "floated" on springs or rubber "hockey pucks" to isolate it from the main structure. The walls, possibly one of those listed in Table 16-1, are then built on this floating slab. The double gypsum board ceiling is then suspended by wires from the main structure, but with a vibration isolator in each wire. This provides adequate sound isolation for most requirements.

If the sound-sensitive space under consideration is in a building occupied by others on the floor above, interest focuses on the nature of the floor-ceiling structure above. If this is a frame structure, it is probably made of 2 × 10 joists with a wood floor with a ceiling below of a single layer of gypsum board. The overall rating of this will probably be of the order of STC 30. What can be done to

Table 16-1. Ratings of Typical Wall Constructions.

Identification	Side-A Facing	Construction	Side-B Facing	STC Rating
A	1 layer 5/8" gypsum board	2 × 4 plate 2 × 4 studs 16" o.c.	1 layer 5/8" gypsum board	34
B	2 layers 5/8" gypsum board	2 × 4 plate 2 × studs 16" o.c.	2 layers 5/8" gypsum board	56
C	1 layer 5/8" gypsum board	2 × 6 plate 2 × 4 studs staggered	1 layer 5/8" gypsum board	42
D	2 Layers 5/8" gypsum board	2 × 6 plate 2 × 4 studs staggered	2 layers 5/8" 1 layer 1/2" gypsum board	58
E	1 layer 5/8" gypsum board	two 2 × 4 plates spaced 1" 2 × 4 studs 16" o.c.	1 layer 5/8" gypsum board	45
F	2 layers 5/8" gypsum board	Two 3-5/8" steel runners spaced 1", 3-5/8" steel studs 24" o.c.	2 layers 5/8" gypsum board	62
G	Sealed with latex paint	8" light weight concrete block 34 lbs/ft²	Sealed with latex paint	46

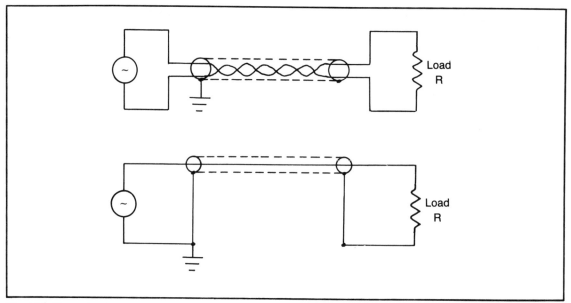

Fig. 16-3. Illustrating balanced (above) and unbalanced (below) transmission lines. The twisted pair tends to cancel out interference penetrating the shield.

"beef up" this floor-ceiling situation to protect the people downstairs? The greatest single gain would be to make sure carpet covers the entire sensitive area upstairs. Another possibility would be to pour 1-1/2 inch of lightweight concrete (not on the carpet!) on 1/2-inch of sound deadening board over 5/8-inch plywood. On the ceiling below the 5/8-inch gypsum board is supported on resilient channels spaced 24-inches and 3-inches of mineral wool or fiberglass placed above the gypsum board before it is too late. This may increase the rating of the floor-ceiling structure from STC 30 to STC 57, which shows what care and proper action can do.

16.3 ELECTRICAL NOISE REDUCTION

Electrical noises are everywhere. AM and FM broadcasting, television, police and scores of different commercial communication channels, and now we have Citizens Band radiations, which are probably harder to control than all of the others put together.

In addition to radio-frequency signals swirling about our heads (silently, until our audio systems are turned on or the fillings in our teeth rectify

them!) there are the power lines and their leads into every home and business structure. Aside from our main topic, we also learn that there are even problems underground as ground currents eat our water pipes by electrolytic action. As our standard of living rises, so do the hums, buzzes, snaps, pops, and crackles of electrical interference in our audio systems. Eliminating such disturbances requires all the knowledge and sophistication required in the design and operation of the audio systems in the first place. All we can do here is offer possible approaches to some of the problems.

In Fig. 16-3 the balanced and unbalanced transmission line cases are illustrated. The higher impedance of the unbalanced system makes it more susceptible to pickup of interference. With the balanced devices, the twisted pair tends to cancel out interference penetrating the shield.

This is illustrated more fully in Fig. 16-4. In both the balanced and the unbalanced cases let us take the instantaneous signal voltage to be 2-volts (Ref. 4). In the balanced system this voltage is obtained from a center-tapped transformer with the center tap grounded. This can be viewed as +1 volts on one lead and -1 volt on the other. The ex-

230

ternal electrostatic field represented by the wiggly lines induces 2-volts in both the balanced and the unbalanced lines. In the unbalanced line the 2-volts of interference is added to the 2-volts of signal to give 4-volts of noisy combination. At the receiving end of the balanced line we then find $+2 + 1 = 3$ volts on one side of the line and $+2 - 1 = +1$ volt on the other. The difference voltage of $+3 - 1 = 2$ volts appears across the load resistance. This is the original signal, the induced voltages have cancelled out. The balanced line achieves its advantage from the differential type of operation. This is known as common-mode rejection because voltages common to both wires are basically rejected. Shielding this balanced line and employing the twisted pair brings further protection from interference.

One form of ground loop is illustrated in Fig. 16-5. The utility transformer belonging to the power company and probably on a nearby pole has a secondary probably connected in a wye with the center grounded to a waterpipe or other ground near the switchbox. In Fig. 16-5 a simple center-tapped secondary serves our purpose. Two conve-

nience outlets, #1 and #2, are fed from this branch. The resistors represent the resistance of the conductors from which one can never escape. Even if the resistance is very low, an ac voltage drop resulting from load current being drawn means that all of the ground connections are at different potentials. For example, a load current of 10-amperes results in an ac voltage drop of 1-volt even if the resistance is only 0.1-ohm.

One piece of equipment plugged into outlet #1 will have a ground at a different potential from another piece of equipment plugged into outlet #2. This could be a possible source of hum appearing in the signal circuits.

Another form of loop responsible for electromagnetic and other forms of interference is illustrated in Fig. 16-6. If the two pieces of equipment are physically separated and plugged into different outlets, the virtual loop antenna is formed, which picks up interference quite efficiently inducing currents in these various ground connections separated by lead resistance. In this way rf voltages can float around in surprising places to be picked up on sensitive circuits and injected

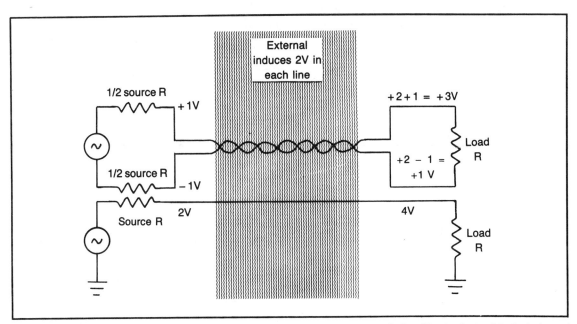

Fig. 16-4. An external field inducing 2-volts in the unbalanced line adds to the 2-volt signal for 4-volts total. In the balanced line only the difference voltage of 2-volts original signal appears across the load resistance.

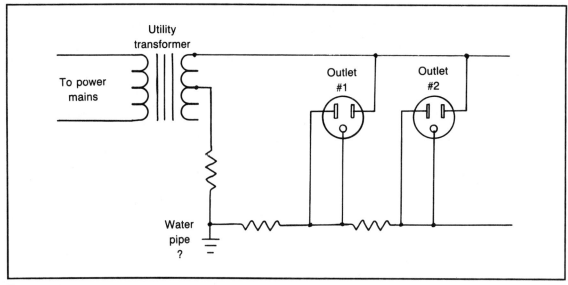

Fig. 16-5. One piece of audio equipment plugged into power outlet #1 and another plugged into outlet #2 will have their grounds at different potential because of the voltage drop in common line resistance.

into the signal. Sometimes such problems can be cured by the use of an isolation transformer to feed power to one element of the offending circuit.

One of the situations most susceptible to hum, noise, and shock problems is that associated with electrical instruments in musical groups and in recording situations. High-impedance equipment is common, yet there is the necessity of feeding clean signals from these instruments into consoles without hum and noise. In Fig. 16-7 is a circuit diagram for a direct box (Ref. 4) which takes an unbalanced high impedance signal in, putting it through a transformer, and sending it on its way as a balanced, low-impedance circuit. The high-

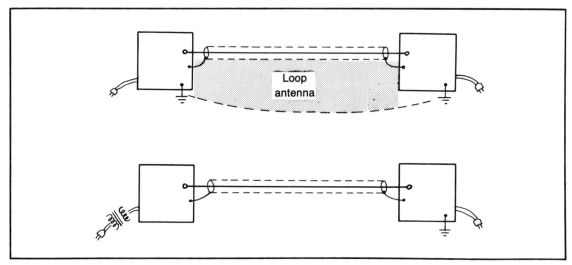

Fig. 16-6. Physically separated pieces of audio equipment plugged into different outlets may form a loop antenna by virtue of the ground path. Such an antenna can pick up radio frequency energy, which then finds its way to sensitive circuits.

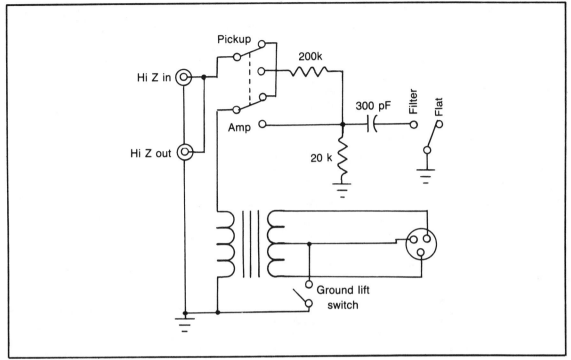

Fig. 16-7. Circuit for a direct box for use with electrical musical instruments which can take an unbalanced, high-impedance signal in, put it through a transformer and send it to a console as a balanced, low-impedance circuit.

impedance out-jack would normally feed into an on-stage monitor. The pickup-amplifier switch changes the gain to accommodate both high-output amplifiers and relatively low-output pickups or preamps. The filter switch allows a selection of flat response or one with rolled off highs. Opening the ground lift switch allows complete isolation of the input and output circuits but it can be closed if this yields the lowest hum level.

There are those who say that even loudspeaker leads should be shielded (Ref. 5). Often it is preferable to ground the shield at one end only to avoid ground loops. In existing cases in which troublesome rf is picked up on loudspeaker leads that are not shielded, and shielding them is impractical, bypass condensers may be the answer. A capacitor of 0.02 μF across the loudspeaker terminals may provide an effective short for the rf without appreciably affecting the audio. Radio-frequency fields can cause problems in audio circuits only through (a) being picked up on some sort of

"antenna," (b) applied to some sort of nonlinearity which rectifies the rf, and (b) an amplifier that builds this rectified signal up to bothersome proportions. The loudspeaker leads can provide the antenna, feeding rf into the rear end of the amplifier where it finds one end of a feedback loop which carries it back into earlier circuitry. To eliminate such a problem as this, an rf choke in the loudspeaker leads right up against the amplifier terminals may be the answer. Such a choke can easily be made by wrapping about 25 turns of the loudspeaker leads around a 4-inch by 1/2-inch ferrite rod. These ferrite rods are the type used in portable radio antennas. Such chokes should prevent rf being fed back into the amplifier.

16.4 NOISE REDUCTION SYSTEMS

When FM broadcasting was inaugerated in the late 1940s an important technique was used called *preemphasis* and *deemphasis*. Adopting this standard has done much to reduce the noise in FM broadcasting. As the signal is broadcast, the treble frequencies are boosted and in the receiver the treble frequencies are brought back to their normal position and the net result is a decrease in noise. The reason for this is that the background noise remained fixed as the highs were boosted in the first operation. But at the receiver, as the highs are brought back down, the high frequency noise, including the objectional hiss, is reduced.

Because the hiss type of noise is so readily perceived, there have been many efforts to achieve a simple sort of noise reduction. One method the hi-fi listener often uses is simply to turn back the treble tone control. This reduces high-frequency response to everything, signal and noise together, yet the compromise between signal fidelity and lowering of noise is always there in this procedure. Attempts to build automatic systems that sense the

high-frequency noise and use it to adjust treble response have not proved successful.

If the signal can be processed before the noise or hiss is added, then a complementary processing at playback can restore the response and reduce noise picked up in intermediary steps. This is really the preemphasis and deemphasis used in FM radio, tape recording, and the production of phonograph records.

16.5 COMPANDING NOISE REDUCTION

The companding approach to noise reduction has been with us a long time. The name is formed from "compressing" and "expanding," a two stage process. Figure 16-8 illustrates the compression stage as the output signal increases more slowly as the input drive is increased. In expansion, the out-

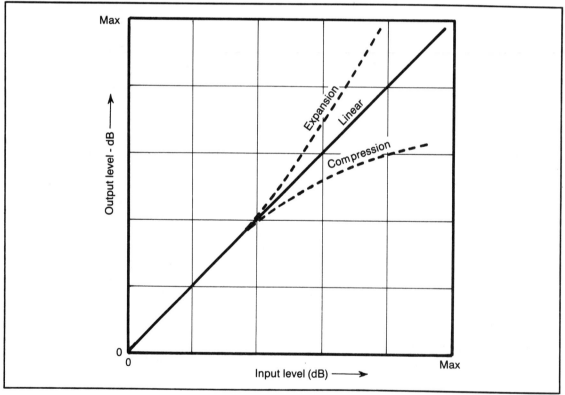

Fig. 16-8. Illustrating the companding approach to noise reduction. If a signal is expanded before tape hiss is introduced, a reduction in noise is realized upon compressing the signal. This system is subject to noise modulation and certain forms of transient distortion.

234

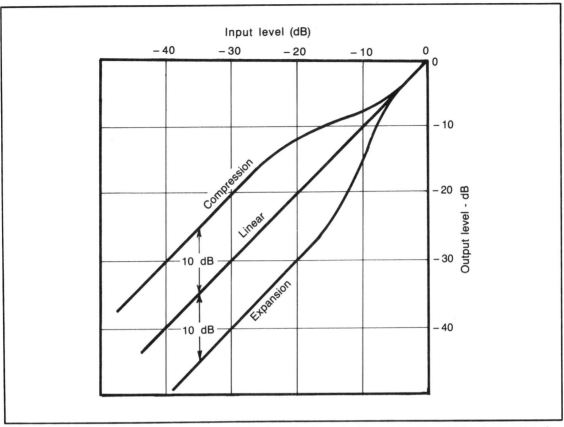

Fig. 16-9. The input-output characteristics of the Dolby Type A noise reduction system. After dividing the band into four parts, each is processed separately in an optimum manner as compression and expansion are applied to low-level signals.

put increases relatively faster than the input. Properly balanced, the expansion can restore any previous compression. If the expansion is applied to the signal before the stage at which the hiss is introduced (for example before the signal is recorded on tape), then when restored in compression an improvement in signal to noise ratio is obtained. The system is, unfortunately, subject to "noise modulation." If a drum is struck regularly, the hiss level can change audibly resulting in a disturbing effect. The system is also subject to some forms of transient distortion and other problems.

16.6 DOLBY NOISE REDUCTION

The Dolby Type A noise reduction system is designed for the most sophisticated, professional

use. The audible frequency range is broken down into four bands and each band is processed separately and in an optimum manner. This reduces the chances of noise modulation being a problem. The input-output characteristics of this system is shown in Fig. 16-9. This compression and expansion is limited to low-level signals. Type A Dolby is applicable for the professional high-speed tape recorders, magnetic film, and professional video tape recorders.

The slower tape recorders on which so much of this world's business is done are better served in regard to noise reduction by use of the Dolby Type B system. Unlike the four fixed bands of the A system, the B system has a single processing band. It is capable of providing 3 dB noise reduction at 600 Hz, 8 dB at 2 kHz, and 10 dB at 4 kHz.

The type B system works only on the lower-level signals, like the A system, but over a narrower frequency region. The Dolby B system is an encode-decode system also like the A type. To avoid detrimental effects, the equalization is dynamically controlled by the frequency and levels of the incoming signal. The incoming signal is split into two paths, one of which receives no dynamic processing and the other in which all low-level signals above 2 kHz are processed. A variable bandwidth filter shown in Fig. 16-10 is involved in the processing. In playback a mirror image reciprocal characteristic restores flat response. This signal is then treated as shown in Fig. 16-11. This low-level processing of signals involves a separate signal path but provides excellent tracking as well as reduced noise.

Figure 16-12 illustrates what happens in the Dolby B system. The high-level signals throughout the process remain unchanged. The low-level components, however, are boosted before the hiss noise of the tape system is added. Later, when the low-level signals are restored to their proper level, the hiss noise is reduced at the same time.

16.7 THE DBX NOISE REDUCTION SYSTEM

The dbx (Ref. 6) noise reduction system is a switchable record or playback unit. During recording it is a compressor and during playback it is an expander. It is a full-frequency range compander whose operation is shown in Fig. 16-13. It is designed to keep the lowest-level signal above the background noise and to keep the highest-level signal below the level of distortion or tape saturation. Preemphasis is applied in the recording process, and deemphasis in the playback mode. The dbx system is widely used in professional recording studios.

The dbx Model 150 Type 1 noise reduction system is designed for use with high quality tape recorders of the semi-professional kind operating

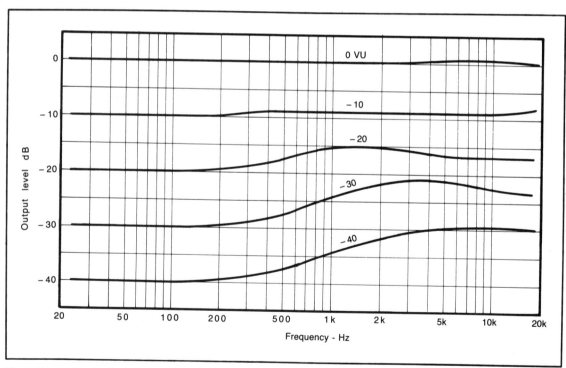

Fig. 16-10. The Dolby Type B system has a single processing band. The processing of lower level signals is dynamically controlled by frequency and level. The variable bandwidth illustrated here is involved in the processing.

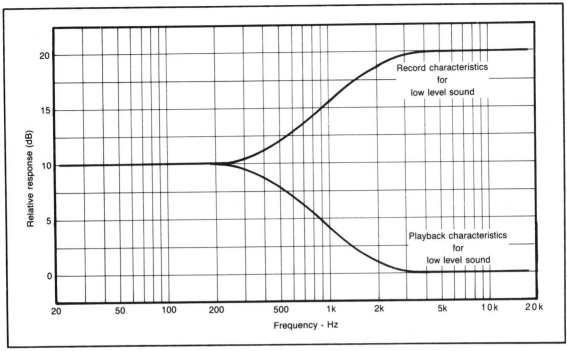

Fig. 16-11. The record-playback characteristics for low-level signals in the Dolby Type B system.

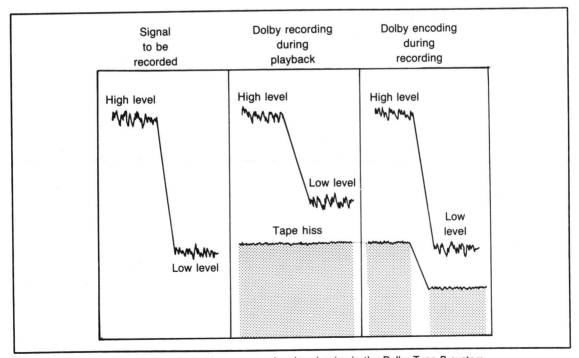

Fig. 16-12. An overall illustration of what happens to signal and noise in the Dolby Type B system.

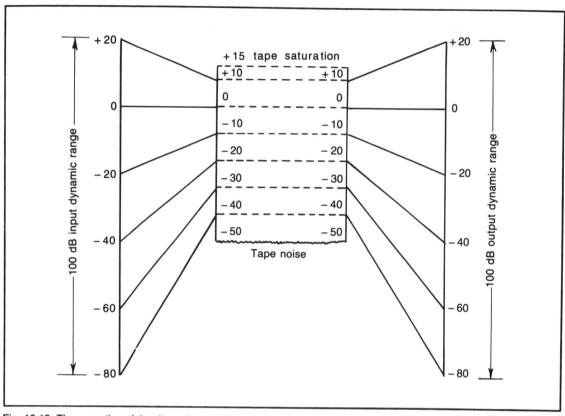

Fig. 16-13. The operation of the dbx noise reduction system. It is a full frequency compressor during recording and an expander during playback. Preemphasis is applied during recording and deemphasis during playback.

Fig. 16-14. The dbx Type 1 (A) Model 150 for semi-professional tape recorders and (B) Model 180 for professional tape recorders. A lower noise floor and wider dynamic range is claimed for the dbx system than that of 16-bit PCM digital audio systems (courtesy dbx Inc.).

at low level (nominally -10 dBV) and high impedance. It increases their dynamic range by 40 dB (30 dB of noise reduction and 10 dB increase in headroom). The compression-expansion ratios are 2:1:2. The Model 150 two channel unit is shown in Fig. 16-14(A).

The dbx Model 180 Type 1 noise reduction system is designed for use with professional quality tape recorders operated at high (nominally $+4$ dBV) signal levels and high speeds. Like the Model 150, dynamic range is increased by 40 dB (30 dB of noise reduction and 10 dB increase in headroom) and the compression-expansion ratios are 2:1:2. The Model 180 is shown in Fig. 16-14(B).

References

1. Coddington, R.H., 1984. "Putting a Finger on Acoustic Pollution," Letter to the editor, *db The Sound Engineering Magazine,* Vol 18, No 4 (May), pp 2,4.

2. Jones, Robert E., 1978. "How To Design Walls For Desired STC Ratings," *Sound and Vibration,* Vol 12, No 8 (Aug), pp 14-17.

3. Everest, F. Alton, 1984. Glass in the Studio, *db The Sound Engineering Magazine:* Part I, Vol 18, No 3 (April), pp 28-33, Part II Vol 18, No 4 (May 1984), pp 41-44.

4. Beard, Dale, 1982. "Technique For Hum and Noise Reduction," *db The Sound Engineering Magazine,* Vol 16, No 9 (Sept), pp 47-51.

5. Hearle, John M., 1976. "RF Interference," *Jay's Jargon* #12 (4 May), J.W. Davis & Co., P.O. Box 35313, Dallas, TX 75235.

6. dbx Inc., Professional Products Division, 71 Chapel Street, Newton, MA 02195.

Chapter 17

Room Acoustics

T HE WRITER ON ACOUSTICAL SUBJECTS HAS two general courses open, that of making things so simple everyone understands or going for accuracy and mathematical detail. While everyone "understands" in the first approach, really no one does and the false security engendered by a little knowledge can lead the reader into practical problems. On the other hand, treating the subject fully limits the readership drastically and the practical person is left with no helping hand. It is the author's goal to avoid both extremes, giving maximum practical application to the average audio person having extensive background in electronics, music, and/or audio equipment operation, installation, or even design, but possibly little background in the physics of sound. The intangible nature of sound waves casts over the subject an air of mystery, which we shall do our utmost to dispel.

17.1 ACOUSTICS OF SMALL ROOMS

The category of small rooms covers acoustics of home listening rooms, small recording studios, control rooms, sound monitoring and control rooms associated with large sound-reinforcement installations, classrooms, etc. In Chapter 1 the general characteristics of sound waves were introduced. The fact is that sound waves behave quite differently outdoors, as compared to indoors. Outdoors a ray of sound going out from a source may be completely unimpeded while indoors walls, floor and ceiling are changing the direction of sound rays by reflection at every turn. What is received at any given point is the net summation of these many components. The small room is a special case of indoor sound.

The dimensions of a room in term of the wavelength of the sound being considered is the "open sesame" to understanding the sometimes inexplicable conditions observed in small rooms. Visible light covers one octave of the electromagnetic spectrum. Audible sound (20 Hz to 20 kHz) covers ten octaves. When we try to "illuminate" our room with 20 Hz sound (having a wavelength of 56.5 ft as shown in Fig. 1-3) a very special condition ex-

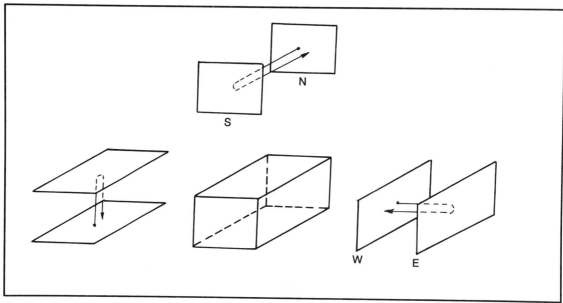

Fig. 17-1. Sketch of a rectangular room showing the three families of axial modes associated with the three pairs of parallel wall surfaces.

ists because the longest dimension of the room's less than this. As frequency is increased from 20 Hz the various pairs of surfaces of the assumed rectangular room come into resonance as shown in Fig. 17-1. These are called normal modes, resulting kin sound-pressure distributions akin to those of Figs. 1-7 and 1-8. We are now operating "inside the organ pipe," as it were. Whenever the space under consideration is a fraction of a wavelength or a small number of wavelengths in length, width, and/or height, small-room rules must apply because the sound-pressure distribution is dominated by the natural resonances of the room. At his point a review of the simple calculations leading up to the diagram of Fig. 1-9 is in order.

17.2 MODAL FREQUENCIES OF SMALL ROOMS

Equation 1-2 in Chapter 1 told us that the frequency at which any two parallel surfaces of a room come into resonance many be readily calculated by dividing the speed of sound by twice the separation of the two surfaces. Let us take a room of 16-feet × 20-feet × 12-feet dimensions for an example. The modal frequency associated with the

N and S end walls of Fig. 17-2 separated by 20 ft = 1130 ft/sec / 2 × 20 ft = 28 Hz approximately. At this frequency these two walls act like an organ pipe closed at both ends. The sound pressure is a maximum at the surfaces of the N and S walls and zero along a line bisecting the room east and west. an attempt to make this sound distribution understandable, read Fig. 17-2(A) as having a pile of sound at the N and S ends of the room but none across the center. If one were to go into this room with a sound-level meter while the room is energized at 28 Hz, maximum pressure could be read anywhere on the end wall surfaces and the vertical zero-pressure plane across the center of the room could be verified.

Next, we consider the E and W walls as a resonant system. These resonate at 1130 ft/sec /2 × 16 = 35 Hz approximately. The sound pressure is a maximum all over the E and W wall surfaces and the vertical zero-pressure plane runs down the center of the room at right angles to that for the N and S walls. This is illustrated in Fig. 17-2(B).

The floor/ceiling combination resonates at 1130 ft/sec 2 × 12 = 47 Hz. Here again maximum pressure is found all over the floor and ceiling sur-

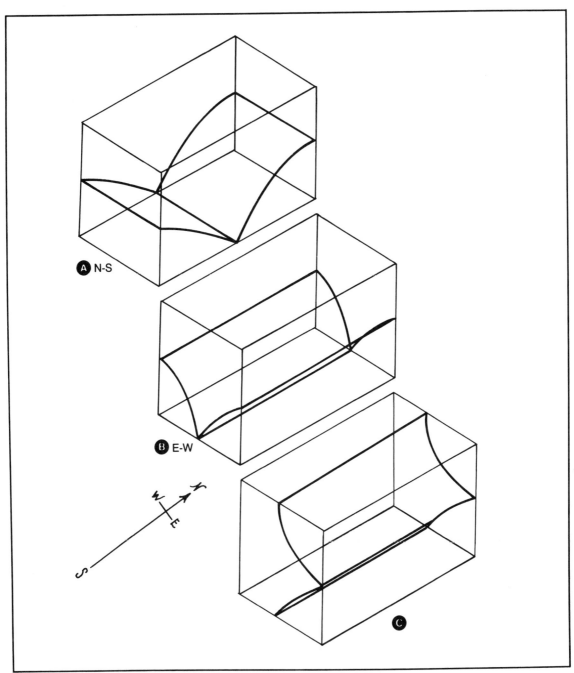

Fig. 17-2. The distribution of axial mode sound pressure in a 20-foot by 16-foot by 12-foot room. (A) The north and south end walls separated 20 feet resonate at 28 Hz. For this mode maximum pressure exists near the surfaces of the north and south walls and has a vertical zero plane in the middle of the room. (B) The east and west walls, separated 16 feet, resonate at 35 Hz with maximum sound pressure near east and west walls and a vertical zero plane along a lengthwise line in the middle of the room. (C) The ceiling and floor planes, separated 12 feet, resonate at 47 Hz. Maximum sound pressures for this mode are found near the floor and ceiling surfaces. A horizontal zero pressure plane exists at a 6 foot height.

faces. The horizontal zero plane is at a 6 ft height as shown in Fig. 17-2(C).

The lowest axial modal frequencies, which we have just studied, are a bit messy to visualize but now let us consider what happens in normal audio operation in this room. (A) The signal now which energizes the modes of the room is either music or speech which chases up and down the spectrum at various amplitudes. (B) Each of the three axial modes spring to life as components in the signal excite them but multiples of each are also just as active, so instead of just three resonances at 28, 35, and 47 Hz we have 2×28, 3×28, 4×28—as well as 2×35, 3×35, 4×35 . . . .and 2×47, 3×47, 4×47. At each of these axial frequencies the signal sound pressure in the room will be boosted. (C) We have considered only the axial modes, each of which involves only two room surfaces. There are also tangential modes, which act in a similar way but involve four room surfaces, and the oblique family of modes, which involve all six room surfaces on one round trip. These are treated in some detail in References 1, 2, and 3 (especially 2 and 3) and will not be further treated here. The point is that when all these modal frequencies work together in a small room, the picture is far too complex to hope to visualize. Their composite action, however, is relatively simple to understand and use.

That which makes a room sound like a room (as contrasted to outdoors) is the horde of resonances, each giving its individual boost to the signal sound pressure in the room. To make the room sound right these modal frequencies must be distributed in such a way that there are no great stretches of the spectrum without such resonances and there are no "piles" of resonances, one on top of the other, which would give an unusual accentuation (or color) to the sound at that frequency.

17.3 FACTORS IN THE ACOUSTICAL DESIGN OF A SMALL ROOM

Acknowledging the degrading effects of too high background noise level, happy is the audio room designer who has something to say about the location of the room in advance. Only by such ad-

vance planning can the effects of environmental noise be minimized. What is the traffic noise situation? The neighbor's air conditioner noise? Footstep noises overhead or on nearby stairs? Elevator noises? All such possible contributors to the general environmental noise, external to the sound sensitive space should be analyzed carefully in advance. Internal noise sources may be dominated by the HVAC (heating, ventilating, air conditioning) equipment serving the sensitive area. The less expensive HVAC installations usually come with small ducts and high air velocities which cause hiss at the grilles. The complete survey of external noise exposure gives data upon which wall construction can be based. The only solution to HVAC noise is to locate the machinery on a separate foundation at some distance and then to make sure the ducts attenuate the noise sufficiently. This is a very truncated approach to the noise problem.

The next question to be addressed is that of size of the room. It must be understood that if the room is too small there is no way satisfactory sound conditions can be realized. The physics of sound dictate that in a very small room the modal resonances will be too few and separations too great. Experience has shown that rooms having volumes less than 1,500 cu ft will have insurmountable sound colorations built-in, which either cannot be corrected or corrected at great expense. The days of the "speech booth" of telephone booth size are gone, the victim of high fidelity requirements.

After the size of the room is established, attention then must be focused on the shape of the room. Splayed walls give the visual impression popularly associated with a well-designed room. Such splaying of walls is usually quite expensive and often quite unnecessary. Opposite walls that are not parallel do eliminate the possibility of flutter echo but carefully placed patches of absorbent do it just as well. One thing is certain, canting walls will never eliminate modal resonances. The most they will do is distort the sound field and shift modal frequencies slightly, but all the modal problems remain. The most important aspect of room design with the goal of distributing modal frequencies favorably is adjusting the proportions of a rectangular room.

The positive value of this can be illustrated by the most negative case imaginable, that of the cubical room. With such a room the N-S, E-W, and vertical axial modes will fall on the identical frequency and the trains of multiple frequencies will also be coincident. Room response at these frequencies will be abnormally high and the gaps between will be normally great resulting in very irregular room response. Proper proportioning of length, width, and height of the room will distribute modal frequencies evenly.

As a guide to selecting room proportions, see Fig. 17-3. In this graph the ratio of length is plotted against width for a height of unity. Values of ratios of length and width for unity height that fall within the shaded area are deemed acceptable,

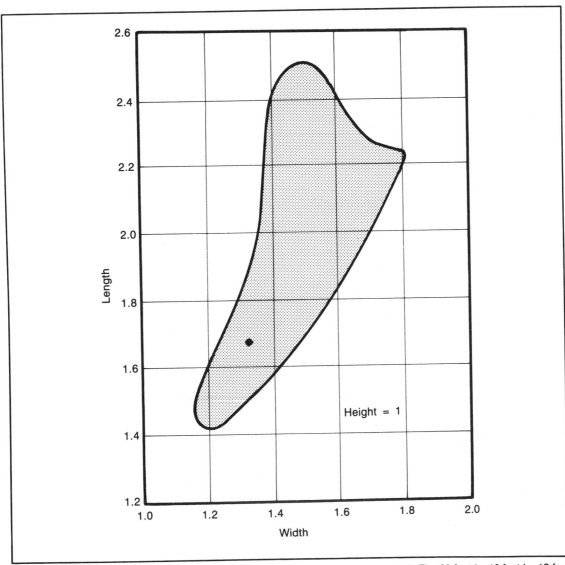

Fig. 17-3. The area of favorable room dimension ratios proposed by R.H. Bolt in 1946. The 20-foot by 16-foot by 12-foot room used as an example has proportions of 1.67 × 1.33 × 1.0. The black spot locates this set of ratios as having a favorable distribution of modal frequencies.

those falling outside the shaded area are considered unacceptable. Are the proportions of the 120-foot × 16-foot × 12-foot room of the previous example satisfactory? Taking the 12-foot height as unity, the width ratio is 16/12 = 1.33 and the length ratio is 20/12 = 1.67. Plotting these coordinates on Fig. 17-3 shows that this room is well proportioned with respect to distribution of modal frequencies. The shaded area of Fig. 17-3 shows that this room is well proportioned with respect to distribution of modal frequencies. The shaded area of Fig. 17-3 is called the "Bolt area" after R.H. Bolt who proposed it many years ago. It is not foolproof, but it is an excellent initial indication of how certain room proportions may work out. It does not guarantee freedom from pileups, it only reduces their number.

Calculations of at least the axial modes on any room proportions being seriously considered should be made according to detailed instructions in Refs. 1, 2, and 3.

17.4 ACOUSTICAL TREATMENT

The concept of reverberation time (the time required for sound to decay 60 dB) has a somewhat questionable application in small rooms. The hallowed formulas for reverberation time are based on statistical ideas that tend to average out modal irregularities. This is acceptable for large rooms, but for rooms having dimensions comparable to the wavelength of the sound in them the application of these formulas is questionable. However, we need some place to start. How much absorption is needed? One approach is to assume brazenly that the Sabine equation can be used in small rooms such as the one under consideration. This is the Sabine equation:

$$RT60 = 0.049 \ V \ / \ U \qquad \textbf{Eq. 17-1}$$

in which RT60 = reverberation time in seconds

V = volume of room in cubic feet

U = total absorption units in sabins

The total absorption units of the room must be found by adding the absorption of the various materials. For example, a 2 inch thickness of fiberglass has an absorption coefficient of 1.0 at 500 Hz. An area of 100 square feet of this material would have a total absorption of (100)(1.0) = 100 sabins, or absorption units. Applying this material in a room of 1,500 cubic feet volume gives a reverberation time of:

$$RT60 = (0.049) \ (1,500) \ / \ 100$$

$$= 0.7 \ second$$

Which is a bit high for a small room, but 200 sq ft of the same material would bring the RT60 down to half this amount.

It is impractical in this context to go into room treatment in greater detail because the task is quite detailed. For instance, we need to examine the change of reverberation time with frequency. This means absorption coefficients for many materials are needed for many frequencies. If the walls are plaster or gypsum board, their low-frequency absorption must be considered, as well as the high-frequency absorption of carpet, etc. This illustrates how inapplicable statistically derived formulas can at least give us a starting point in acoustically treating a small room. References 1, 2, and 3 treat the subject in detail.

17.5 ACOUSTICS OF LARGE SPACES

For large spaces, modal frequency problems tend to disintegrate. true, they are present, but the greater dimensions smooth out their effect. If two opposing walls are 100 feet apart, the lowest axial frequency becomes 1,130 ft/sec / (2) (100) = 5.65 Hz, which is subaudible. Something unmentioned above is the fact that each of these modal frequencies has a finite bandwidth having a width in Hz of approximately 2.2 / RT60. For a reasonable reverberation time of 1.5 seconds for a large auditorium, the bandwidth of the modes would be about 1.5 Hz. For the audible frequencies in a large space we see that there are so many modal frequencies that their spacing and bandwidth assure continuous and smooth room response.

17.6 CONCERT HALLS

Halls used exclusively for musical performances have very special acoustical requirements. Conductors, in general, have great antipathy toward sound reinforcement. They are often willing to allow sound reinforcement for spoken parts and sometimes even for soloists, but for orchestras and large choral groups there is preference for hall acoustics that do not need reinforcement. The only reason sound reinforcement can be avoided is that the source power is great. A full symphony orchestra can put out as much as 70 acoustic watts on peaks. At 1% efficiency this is the equivalent of 7000 electrical watts being fed to a loudspeaker cluster!

The shape of the concert hall becomes all important. The Boston Symphony Hall has been called a "shoebox" because of its rectangular shape but, along with numerous European halls of the same shape, its acoustics have been highly praised. The importance of reflected energy from the side walls is generally recognized and compromising hall shape to accommodate more paying customers usually deteriorates side wall reflections. What has been recognized as associated with excellent acoustics is the presence of an "initial time delay gap" of about 20 milliseconds. This is the time delay between the arrival of the direct sound at a given seat in the audience area and the arrival of reflections (from side walls or other surfaces). See Fig. 13-1.

17.7 MULTIPURPOSE AUDITORIUMS

When more than one purpose is to be served by a given space, acoustical compromises result. For example, a given space is to accommodate speech presentations and musical programs. The recommended reverberation time of the space must favor one or the other or rest on the misty flats in-between, which is not optimum for either. An auditorium having a volume of 250,000 cubic feet should have a reverberation time of one second or less for speech, but about 1.6 seconds as a concert hall. Organ music thrives on long reverberation time and sounds good even in European cathedrals having reverberation times as much as 6 or 7 seconds. Speech under such conditions is completely unintelligible. With an RT60 of 1.6 seconds, speech intelligibility is substantially less than at one second. Reverberation time, of course, is only one factor in judging hall quality but the element of compromise pervades all multipurpose spaces.

Churches are usually very much multipurpose in that speech and music must both be accommodated. The music director quite naturally presses for conditions that will make the organ, choral, and instrumental music sound best. The preacher likes the fan-shaped audience area as it brings the audience closer and tends toward better and more intimate communication. But this fan shape tends to dissipate the energy output of the choir, lowering average sound levels over the audience. In the average church, as plans for a new building are being formulated, nice thick carpets and pews, upholstered seats and backs, appeal to the building committee. Usually such amenities mean that the resulting reverberation time is too low even for a reasonable compromise between speech and music. The fan-shaped space usually results in an almost perfectly semicircular rear wall which creates echo problems on stage and at front seats. But with too much absorbence already on the floor and the pews, adding absorption to this wall to control echoes further degrades the reverberation time for music (this will not hurt speech, the lower the RT60 for speech the better).

The range of multipurpose rooms seems to grow continually. There are even special names for some of them (e.g., cafetorium). A gymnasium is built first with the understanding that it will also serve temporarily as an auditorium. This poses some interesting sound-reinforcement problems. Where will the audience be seated next time? Where can the cluster be placed to serve both sports and the auditorium use? Where will the movable stage be placed for Tuesday night?

17.8 ACOUSTICAL EVALUATION OF LARGE AND SMALL SPACES

The microprocessor revolution has descended with a vengeance on equipment for evaluation of acoustical quality of large and small spaces. In the old days reverberation measurements satisfied even the specialists. Not so today. Impulse measurements are still valuable for detecting echo hazards but modern instruments go beyond that. Time-delay spectrometry can not only select out one particular reflection but can instantly give its frequency response. Computers with special software can compute and display fast Fourier and other transforms as easily as reading a voltmeter. Computer programs are available that can aid in solving auditorium design problems, which, until recently, were quite intractable.

References

1. Everest, F. Alton, 1979. *How To Build A Small Budget Recording Studio From Scratch . . . With 12 Tested Designs,* TAB BOOKS, Inc, Blue Ridge Summit, PA 17214. TAB #1166. Chapters pertinent to this chapter: "My studio—How Big and What Shape?" (Chap 1), "Elements Common To All Studios" (Chap 2).

2. Everest, F. Alton, 1981. *The Master Handbook of Acoustics,* TAB BOOKS, Tab #1296. Pertinent chapters: "Sound Indoors—a' la mode" (Chap 6), "Reverberation" (Chap 8), "Absorption of sound" (Chap 10), "Diffusion of Sound" (Chap 11), "Setting up The Home Listening Room" (Chap 13), "Building a Studio" (Chap 14), and "The Control Room" (Chap 16).

3. Everest, F. Alton, 1984. *Acoustic Techniques For Home and Studio,* TAB BOOKS TAB #1696. Pertinent chapters: "Standing Waves in Listening Rooms and Small Studios" (Chap 6), "Acoustical Materials and Structures" (Chap 9), "Acoustical Design of Studios" (Chap 11), "Acoustical Design of a Control Room" (Chap 12), "Tuning The Listening Room" (Chap 14), and "Evaluating Studio Acoustics" (Chap 15).

Chapter 18

Equalizing the System

EQUALIZATION IS THAT PROCEDURE BY which undesired shape of frequency response or irregularities in it can be corrected. There is no question about the need for equalization in the average system but there are serious misgivings as to how equalization is often applied. The most serious problem is lack of knowledge as to the effect of applying too much equalization in the wrong place. In low-level circuits unrestrained use of equalization may damage only the sound quality. In high-level circuits, such as power amplifiers driving tweeters and woofers in the loudspeaker interface, incorrect equalization can result in damage to or even destruction of transducers (Ref. 1).

18.1 THE TONE CONTROL

The simple tone control, which was introduced in audio antiquity, is one of the simplest forms of equalization. It is found on almost every consumer type radio receiver, amplifier, and on many cassette and tape decks. It is there to make the signal sound better. It is adjusted to suit the ear. Typical re- sponse curves of the simple tone control are shown in Fig. 18-1. The high-frequency knob applies boost or cut to a range of frequencies above some nonstandard frequency. Record scratch and other high-frequency noises can be reduced by cutting highs, but the high-frequency components of the signal are reduced at the same time. Rumble, wow, flutter, hum may be reduced by cutting low frequencies but in so doing signal components are also lost. However, the enjoyment of the program may be considerably improved by reduction of the noise even though the signal is degraded. The tone control is truly an unsophisticated device designed for use by those who are unsophisticated in their audio needs and requirements.

18.2 BANDWIDTH AND Q

Before diving into some of the more fascinating forms of equalization it is desirable to define a few terms that will be usable later in comparing one device with another and in fitting the equalizer to the specific need. Bandwidth is defined in Fig. 18-2. It

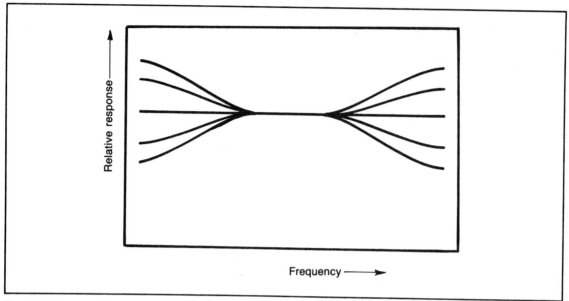

Fig. 18-1. The equalizing range of the typical, simple tone control. This type of equalizer in hi-fi installations is adjusted "by ear."

is measured at the half power (– 3 dB points) as far as peaks or boosts are concerned. There are problems, however, with trying to apply this same rule to the cut curve. In the case of the cut equalization curve the bandwidth is measured at – 3 dB from the horizontal axis.

The ear is approximately logarithmic in its response and it is well to remember this as the effects of equalization are pondered. For example, at 100 Hz a filter having a bandwidth of 50 Hz affects almost an octave. This same filter of 50 Hz bandwidth at 10,000 Hz, however, is only one-half of one percent of 10,000 Hz. This 50 Hz filter would have a major effect on the sound at 100 Hz, but probably no audible effect at all at 10,000 Hz.

To take into account such effects, the concept of Q is employed. With reference to the boost curve of Fig. 18-2, Q is defined as the ratio of center frequency to bandwidth. In the example of the previous paragraph, the 50 Hz bandwidth at 100 Hz would represent a Q of 100/50 = 2, which is in the range familiar in equalizing circuits. At 10,000 Hz, however, Q = 10,000/50 = 200 which is a very high Q. High Qs mean low circuit losses. High Qs also are the cause of "ringing" in electrical

circuits. Applying a square wave to a high Q circuit can result in ringing as shown in Fig. 18-3. The very steep wavefront "kicks" the circuit hard enough to make it ring at its natural frequency. Such ringing effects can be quite audible and are considered very undesirable in audio circuits.

18.3 OCTAVE LANGUAGE

Literature dealing with equalizers uses the word "octave" with reckless abandon. It is helpful not only to understand the basic meaning of the word but to know enough about it to be able to find the edges of bands, width of bands, etc. Basically, an octave is any 2:1 ratio of frequencies. Going from 20 Hz to 40 Hz is one octave; so is going from 10,000 to 20,000 Hz. The 20 Hz - 20,000 Hz band covers 10 octaves.

Octaves cover a constant percentage of the frequency band and the ear works, more or less, on a constant percentage basis. This is in contrast to bands of fixed width, which would change on a percentage basis with frequency. The real time analyzer to which we shall refer in coming sections utilizes constant percentage bandwidths as do the

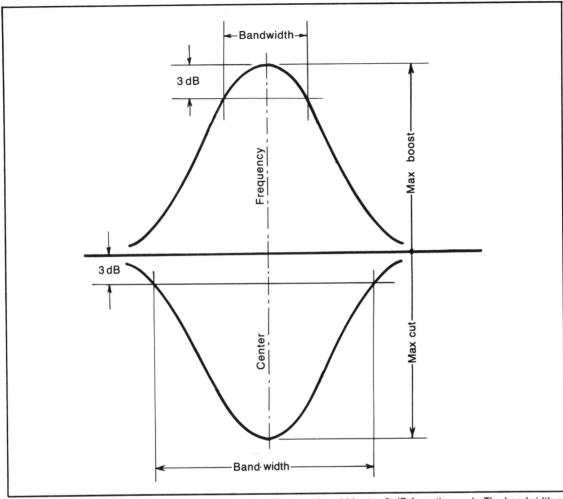

Fig. 18-2. The bandwidth of boost-equalizer filters is defined as the width at −3 dB from the peak. The bandwidth of the cut equalizer filter is defined as the width 3 dB below the horizontal axis.

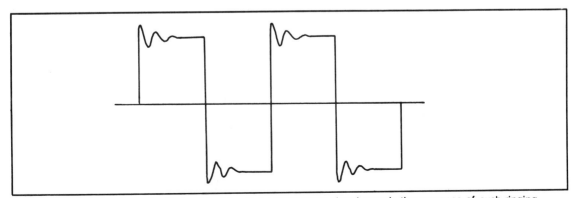

Fig. 18-3. High Q, low loss circuits tend to "ring." A square-wave signal reveals the presence of such ringing.

graphic equalizers. This adapts them better to the workings of human hearing. The critical bands of the ear-brain mechanism are approximated by 1/3 octaves. This, at least partially, accounts for the popularity of 1/3 octave analyzers and equalizers.

Octave equalizers are relatively coarse in their frequency adjustments. Half octave, one-third octave, one-sixth octave equalizers are progressively narrower in their operating range.

Octave bands are described mathematically by the expression:

HF edge/LF edge = 2 to the nth power **Eq. 18-1**

in which

> HF edge = high-frequency edge of the band under consideration
>
> LF edge = low-frequency edge of the band under consideration
>
> n = number of octaves

For example, how many octaves are there in the frequency range 100 - 1,000 Hz? Substituting in Eq. 18-1:

$$1,000 / 100 = \text{2 to the nth power.}$$
$$10 = \text{2 to the nth power}$$

taking logarithms of both sides,

$$\log 10 = n \log 2$$
$$1 = 0.301\ n$$
$$n = 3.32$$

That is, there are 3.32 octaves between 100 and 1,000 Hz.

Another example: What is the upper edge of an octave band centered on 1,000 Hz? We have the band center, but not the edges. However, we do know that the edges are a half octave above and a half octave below the center frequency of 1,000 Hz, so the key is to treat this as two half octave problems as follows:

$$\text{HF edge} / 1,000 = \text{2 to the 1/2 power} = \sqrt{2}$$
$$\text{HF edge} = (1,000)\ (1.414)$$
$$\text{HF edge} = 1,414\ \text{Hz}$$

The lower edge of the octave band centered on 1,000 Hz is then found from:

$$1,000 / \text{LF edge} = \text{2 to the 1/2 power} = \sqrt{2}$$
$$\text{LF edge} = 1,000 / 1.414$$
$$\text{LF edge} = 707\ \text{Hz}.$$

This square root of 2 pops up all the time in dealing with center frequencies of octaves. In dealing with center frequencies of 1/3 octave bands the factor is 2 to the 1/6 power or 1.1225. The upper edges of bands will always be the center frequency times this factor and the lower edges the center frequency divided by this factor. With the information of Table 18-1 you are able to calculate the upper and lower edges of octaves and 1/2, 1/3, 1/6. and 1/12th octave bands at any center frequency.

18.4 CONSTANT Q AND VARIABLE Q FILTERS

When considering the purchase of a given equalizer, the specifications may or may not state whether the filters are based on the constant Q or the variable Q system. Both are widely used, and each has its strong points as well as limitations. The constant Q approach is illustrated in Fig. 18-4. Note that the boost curves have different shapes than the cut curves. The cut curves are sharper. The variable Q type of filter, illustrated in Fig. 18-5, have the same shape in both boost and cut modes. Such curves are called "reciprocal" because of this similarity. Even if the manufacturer may not mention whether the filters in a given equalizer are constant or variable Q, the typical curves invariably shown will reveal this. If the boost and cut curves are reciprocal, the variable Q approach is used. If the cut curves are sharper than the boost curves, the constant Q approach is followed. In fact, some equalizers have a switch that changes from constant to variable Q when thrown. As we shall see later, there are certain equalization tasks that are better

Table 18-1. Calculation of Band-Edge Frequencies.

Band	Low Frequency edge	High Frequency edge
Octave	(Center freq) (1.414)	(Center freq)/1.414
1/2 Octave	(Center freq) (1.189)	(Center freq)/1.189
1/3 Octave	(Center freq) (1.122)	(Center freq)/1.122
1/6 Octave	(Center freq) (1.059)	(Center freq)/1.059
1.12 Octave	(Center freq) (1.029)	(Center freq)/1.029

served by narrow cut curves.

18.5 SHELVING

A high-frequency shelving characteristic of a filter (equalizer) would provide a uniform boost or cut above a certain frequency, called the "turnover" frequency as shown in Fig. 18-6. Similarly, a low-frequency shelving would yield a uniform boost

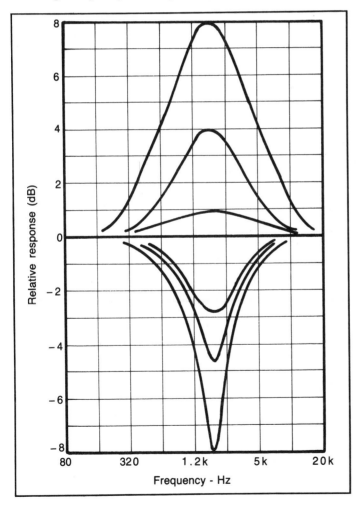

Fig. 18-4. In constant Q equalizers the boost- and cut-filter curves are of different shapes. The cut-curves are sharper than the boost.

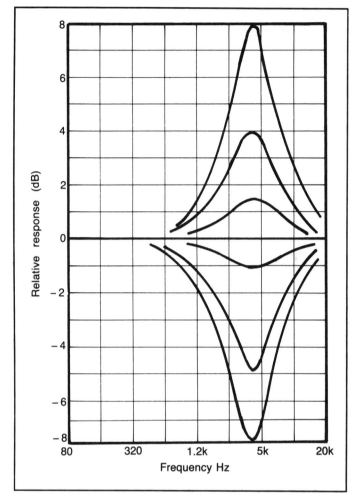

Fig. 18-5. In variable Q equalizers the boost- and cut-filter curves are of the same shape.

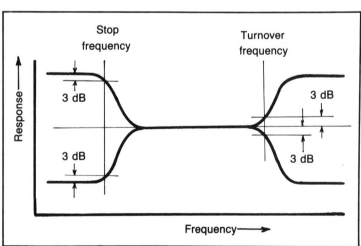

Fig. 18-6. Definition of terms for shelving filters (equalizers). The turnover frequency is that frequency at which the curves are 3 dB from the horizontal axis. The stop frequency is that frequency at which the curves are within 3 dB of their final value.

or cut below a certain turnover frequency. The frequency at which the shelving curves are within 3 dB of their ultimate value is called the "stop" frequency.

Such shelving adjustments are similar to the elementary tone control arrangement of Fig. 18-1, but offer more flexibility to the user. They are of value in correcting roll-offs at the extremes of the audio band. There are other less likely uses such as correcting for mismatching of driver levels in packaged-type loudspeaker systems.

18.6 BAND-LIMITING FILTERS

The shelving type equalizer gives flat response to extremely-low and extremely-high frequencies. There may be spurious out-of-band signals that can cause problems. Because of this band-limiting filters are employed to control these subaudible or ultrasonic signals.

Typical characteristics of band-limiting filters are shown in Fig. 18-7. These are adjustable in frequency in the UREI Model 539. The low-frequency-cut curve is shown at 3 dB down at 250 Hz which is the extreme adjustment. The low-frequency-cut curve may also be adjusted to 3 dB down at 20 Hz, which would be off the graph. Similarly, the high-frequency-cut curve is shown 3 dB down at 3.5 kHz, its low extreme, and is adjustable continuously to 20 kHz. The slopes are 12 dB/octave but the high-frequency-cut curve may be switched to 6 dB per octave if desired.

These band-limiting filters follow the good engineering principle of limiting the band to the frequency range desired and reducing out-of-band response as insurance against problems. Certainly there are plenty of problems within the desired band to engage our attention without asking for problems elsewhere.

18.7 GRAPHIC EQUALIZERS

By examining a number of graphic equalizers on the market, the wide range of their characteristics may be explored. The Model 537 1/3 octave graphic equalizer engineered by UREI and distributed by JBL Incorporated (Ref. 2) is pictured in Fig. 18-8. This equalizer incorporates 27 adjustable slide-type controls offering 12 dB boost and 12 dB cut. The term "graphic" in describing such equalizers comes from the fact that a plot of the equalization curve is visually available at a glance by the settings of these sliders. The 537 has extremely low noise (110 dB) resulting from the use

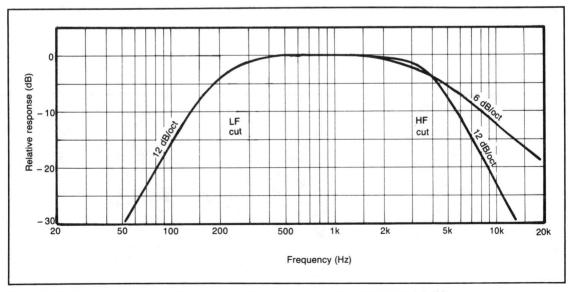

Fig. 18-7. Typical characteristics of band limiting filters, in this case the U.R.E.I. Model 539.

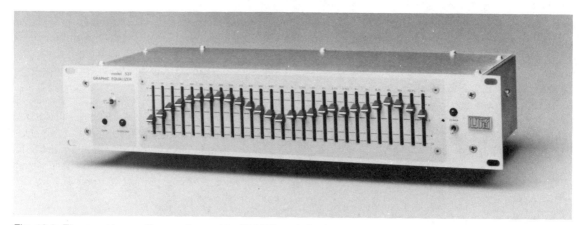

Fig. 18-8. The graphic equalizer engineered by U.R.E.I. and distributed by JBL, the Model 537. This unit provides 12 dB boost and cut in 27 bands 1/3 octave wide. Discrete inductors are used instead of electronic simulated inductors to lower the noise floor (courtesy JBL Incorporated).

of discrete inductors instead of electronically simulated inductors (gyrators) often employed. The UREI reputation for well engineered products attaches itself to the 537.

The Fostex (Ref. 3) Model 3030 incorporates two 10-band octave equalizers for stereo or other use. Figure 18-9 shows the simplicity of the layout. There is a master input level control with three LED indicators; normal level illuminates the green one, when any signal is present the "present" light is lit, and a red LED indicates the level "limit." The range of cut and boost equalization available is indicated in Fig. 18-10 (A). In Fig. 18-10 (B) is illustrated the wide range of uses of the Fostex 3030

and other equalizers. This equalizer is designed especially for the musician, but surely it is not limited to this field.

The Neptune (Ref. 4) Model 2711 1/3 octave equalizer is shown in Fig. 18-11. This equalizer features balanced and unbalanced inputs and outputs and gain control with LED peak indicator. The 27 slide controls each offer 12 dB of boost and cut. The gain control has a center detent at the unity gain position.

The Furman SG-10 equalizer, shown in Fig. 18-12 (A), has 10 bands 2/3 octave wide (Ref. 5). An interesting feature in this equalizer is the flexibility to sweep the center frequency of each band

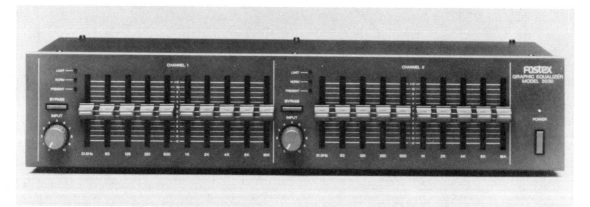

Fig. 18-9. The Fostex Model 3030 graphic equalizer. Two 10-band octave equalizer sections are provided having the characteristics pictured in Fig. 18-10(A) (courtesy Fostex Corporation of America).

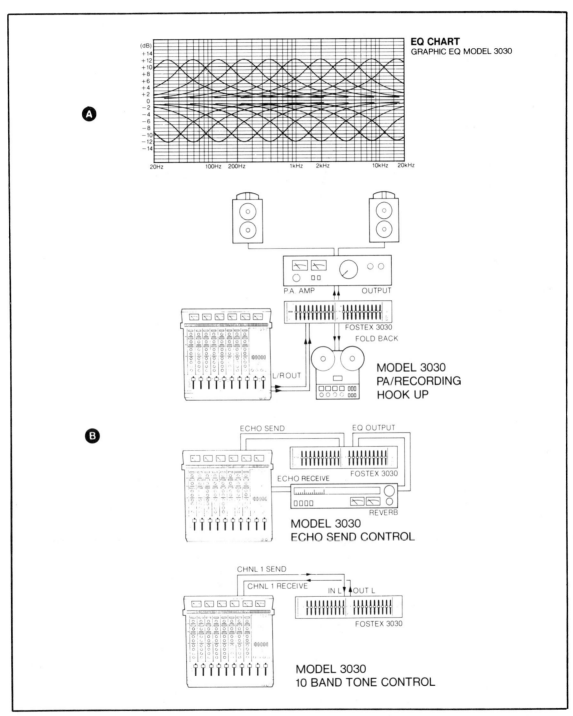

Fig. 18-10. The (A) characteristics and (B) the wide range of uses of two channel equalizers such as the Fostex Model 3030 graphic equalizer (courtesy Fostex Corporation of America).

Fig. 18-11. The NEI Model 2711 equalizer offering 12 dB boost and cut in 27 1/3-octave bands (courtesy Neptune Electronics, Inc.).

over a four-octave range. In this way the SG-10 bridges the gap between the graphic equalizer and the parametric equalizer soon to be studied. The SG-10 also has a stereo-mono switch by which the 10-band mono sweep graphic equalizer may be adapted to stereo 5-band operation. This equalizer has features of interest to the musician as it can be used as an integral instrument preamplifier, a "splitter" and/or a "direct box." Overload indicators for each channel are also included. The ranges of the five bands are as follows:

Band 1	16 - 250 Hz
Band 2	32 - 500 Hz
Band 3	125 - 2,000 Hz
Band 4	500 - 8,000 Hz
Band 5	1,000 - 16,000 Hz

A low-cut, band-limiting filter, 3 dB down at 80 Hz, is also included. Equalization range is plus or minus 15 dB and the Q is 1.5 for all ranges. As the Q is constant, the cut curves are sharper than the boost curves as shown in Fig. 18-4.

In summary it can be said that graphic equalizers of octave width are useful only for tonal balance with the ear as the indicating instrument. Graphic equalizers are almost always fixed frequency (the Furman SG-10 is an exception) and almost always constant Q. The separate filter sections are also usually connected in parallel, which brings with it certain interaction when adjacent controls are being adjusted. However, the low cost of this type of graphic equalizer assures wide use and, as stated above, they are quite satisfactory for tonal balance.

18.8 PARAMETRIC EQUALIZERS

Parametric equalizers are so-called because

Fig. 18-12. The Furman equalizers: (A) Model SG-10 sweep graphic equalizer which allows sweeping the center frequency of each band over a 4-octave range, bridging the gap between graphic and parametric equalizers. The 10-band mono function may be switched to two 5-band equalizers for stereo use. (B) the PG-6 two channel parametric equalizer and (C) the PG-3 single channel parametric (courtesy Furman Sound, Inc.).

Fig. 18-13. The Orban true parametric equalizer, the Model 622. This stereo model has four parametric sections in each channel. The peak boost is 16 dB and the maximum cut is minus infinity. The Q is adjustable from 0.29 to 3.2. See Fig. 18-14 for filter shapes (courtesy Orban Associates, Inc.).

they offer adjustments of all three basic parameters: boost/cut setting, Q or sharpness of cut or boost, and center frequency. This makes them extremely flexible and desirable for many functions. With a parametric equalizer it is possible to apply a broad boost to improve tonal quality or to reduce a hum with a very narrow notch.

The versatility of the parametric equalizer is illustrated by the Orban Model 622 true parametric equalizer shown in Fig. 18-13 (Ref. 6). This is a stereo model having four sections in each channel. The four sections cover the following ranges: 20-500 Hz, 68-1700 Hz, 240-5850 Hz, and 800-20,000 Hz. Note the generous overlap of ranges. The peak boost is 16 dB and the maximum cut is theoretically minus infinity but practically 40 dB is achieved. The Q is adjustable from 0.29 to 3.2. The curves of Fig. 18-14 illustrate the very wide adjustments possible

in boost/cut and Q.

The adjustment of a single parameter, such as center frequency, does not affect the other two parameters. The "quasi-parametric" equalizer, such as the Orban 672A, does permit some interaction. For example, changing frequency changes Q to some extent. Allowing such interaction has little disadvantage in some types of service and allows considerable reduction in cost.

The Furman (Ref. 5) parametric equalizers are shown in Figs. 18-12 (B) and (C). The equalizer in Fig. 18-12 (B) is the stereo form containing two units identical to (C). These equalizers have preamplifiers for musical instruments built into them. Three bands are included in each channel: a bass range of 25-500 Hz, a midrange of 150-2,500 Hz, and a treble range of 600-10,000 Hz. A boost of 20 dB is available as well as a theoretically in-

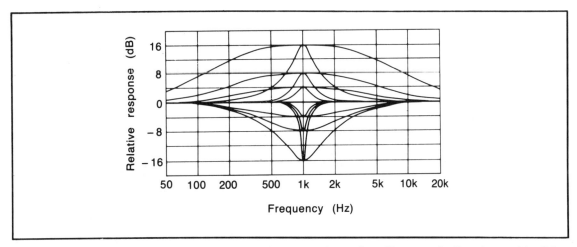

Fig. 18-14. The wide range of adjustments available in the parametric equalizer. Shown are the filter shapes of the Orban Model 622 parametric equalizer (courtesy Orban Associates, Inc.).

259

Fig. 18-15. The NEI Model 342 two-channel parametric equalizer. Four equalizing sections are in each channel with adjustable Q, level, and frequency in each section (courtesy Neptune Electronics, Inc.).

finite cut. This equalizer is also of the constant-Q type. Balanced inputs and outputs are available as options.

The Neptune (Ref. 4) Model 342 dual channel parametric equalizer is illustrated in Fig. 18-15. This equalizer offers four equalization sections in each channel with Q (bandwidth), level, and frequency controls in each section. EQ in/out switching and LED peak indicators are also included in each section. Specifications of the Model 341 (single channel) and the 342 include noise: – 80dBV, bandwidth: 0.1-3.5 octaves, and total harmonic distortion: 0.01%.

18.9 EQUALIZING THE
SOUND REINFORCEMENT SYSTEM

In equalizing a sound reinforcement system or a sophisticated listening facility such as a monitoring/control room, one is faced with the basic and difficult realities of linking electronic amplifying and processing gear, electro-acoustic transducers,

and the acoustics of the space in which they are expected to perform. Taming of electronic equipment is probably at a more advanced stage than taming transducers and space acoustics. It seems that anything having to do with acoustics, whether the acoustics of the space or the transducers that interface that space, is more difficult to manage than signals flowing in electronic circuits.

Current practice in equalizing sound-reinforcement systems is to use equalizers which have only cut facilities, no boost. While it is agreed that certain broadband adjustments may be desirable to flatten the overall curve, when it comes to improving the gain before feedback, the cut-only filters are most satisfactory. A typical equalizer for this purpose used widely in professional systems is the U.R.E.I. (Ref. 7) Model 539 room equalization filter set is shown in Fig. 18-16. This equalizer provides 27 filters centered on standard ISO 1/3 octave frequencies from 40 Hz to 16 kHz. Each filter provides 0 to 15 dB attenuation in a stepless con-

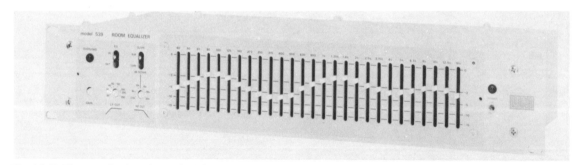

Fig. 18-16. The equalization of sound reinforcing systems is best accomplished with cut-only type filters. The widely used U.R.E.I. Model 539 is of this type. Up to 15 dB attenuation is available in 27 1/3-octave filters having center frequencies from 40 Hz to 16 kHz (courtesy JBL Incorporated).

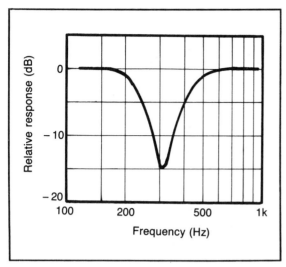

Fig. 18-17. Typical shape of the filter attenuation curve of the U.R.E.I. Model 539.

trol and has the typical shape shown in Fig. 18-17.

In addition to the 27 filters spaced 1/3 octave the Model 539 has band-limiting filters. The low-cut filter is continuously adjustable from 20 Hz to 250 Hz and has a slope of 12 dB/octave. The high-cut filter is adjustable from 3.5 to 20 kHz and slopes of 6 or 12 dB/octave are selectable. The 27 band-reject filters are active, minimum phase LC networks, whose skirts properly combine for minimum ripple and phase shift when used in combination.

The usual procedure for equalizing a sound-reinforcement system would be to connect the equalizing filters before the electronic crossover in the low-level portion of the circuit as shown in Fig. 18-18. The podium microphone is normally the one used in the process. The gain of the system is increased until feedback occurs. It is often helpful to measure the feedback frequency as an aid to deter-

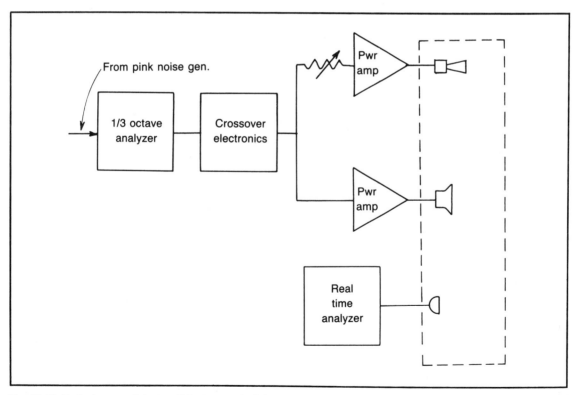

Fig. 18-18. Typical approach to equalizing a sound reinforcement installation. A pink noise signal is fed to the loudspeaker through the 1/3-octave cut-only equalizer, low-level crossover network, and power amplifiers. A measuring microphone (optional: the installation microphone) picks up the radiated acoustical signal and passes it to the real-time analyzer which displays the response in each 1/3-octave band. The equalizer is then adjusted to give the desired system response.

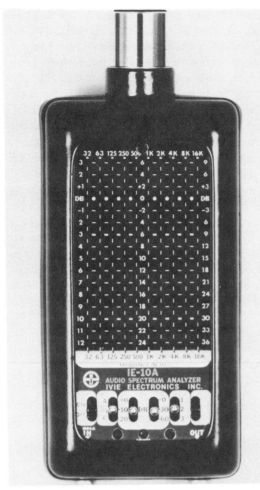

Fig. 18-19. The Ivie Model IE-10A handheld octave spectrum analyzer is a useful device to explore system response at various positions in the room. Local anomalies may be identified in this way.

mining which band-reject filter should be introduced. The attenuation in the band containing the feedback frequency is adjusted the minimum amount to stop the feedback. The system gain is then increased until feedback again occurs at some other frequency and the process is repeated until little further system gain is attainable. An improvement of four or five dB in overall system gain achieved this way seems like a small improvement but it often is the difference between good quality sound and poor. The farther from the room regeneration (feedback) point the system can be operated the better, because sound quality suffers if the system must be operated near feedback to achieve sufficient gain.

18.10 THE REAL TIME ANALYZER

Some sort of indicator is required to display the overall system response as adjustments in equalization are made to achieve the desired response. The real time analyzer is the device to use to give rapid and accurate indications of system response. The Ivie (Ref. 8) Model IE-10A real time analyzer is typical of handheld and extremely portable units, which are useful for observing the system response at various points in the room (Fig. 18-19). It is deficient for 1/3 octave adjustments, however, because it is an octave analyzer. Figure 18-20 shows a typical 1/3 octave real time analyzer, the Neptune (Ref. 4) Model 2709B to which the podium microphone can be attached for the equalization procedure.

If pink noise drives the system, as indicated in

Fig. 18-20. The NEI Model 2709B real time analyzer useful in system response measurements such as in Fig. 18-18. The response in each of 27 1/3-octave bands is displayed as an LED bar chart (courtesy Neptune Electronics, Inc.).

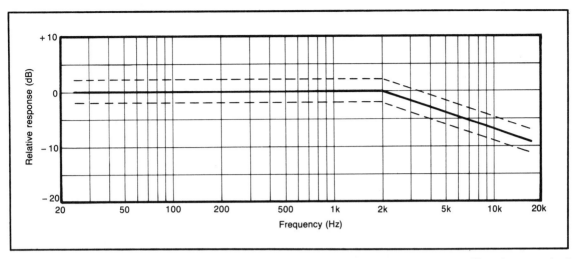

Fig. 18-21. A curve of this general shape is the goal in equalizing a sound-reinforcement system. There is no standard agreement on just where the high-frequency break should begin, but all agree on the desirability of reducing high-frequency response.

Fig. 18-18, a flat real-time analyzer response indicates a flat overall system response. But do we want a flat response for best sound in an auditorium? Based on experience, a curve having the general shape of Fig. 18-21 gives the best balanced sound. There is no hard and fast agreement on the frequency at which the break should take place. Some say 1 kHz, some 2 kHz, and some even higher but there is better agreement that the rolloff should be at a rate of about 3 dB/octave.

References

1. Ampel, Frederick J., 1984. *Dimensions in Equalization* (Editorial). The following articles are in *Sound & Video Contractor,* Vol 2, No 2 (15 Feb), pages 23-57:

Cabot, Richard, "Everything You Always Wanted to Know About EQ;" Uzzle, Ted, "Room and Regenerative Effects;" Bohm, Dennis A., "A New Generation of Filters;" Orban, Robert, "Choosing Equalizers;" Wahl, Juergen, "Tailoring The Response;" Kelly, Jack, "Design and Application;" Belville, Michael, "And Now For Something Completely Different;" Spectra Sonics, "Measuring Performance."

2. JBL Incorporated, 8500 Balboa Blvd., Northridge, CA 91329

3. Fostex Corporation of America, 15431 Blackburn Ave., Norwalk, CA 90650

4. Neptune Electronics, Inc., 934 N.E. 25th Avenue, Portland, OR 97232

5. Furman Sound, Inc., 30 Rich St., Greenbrae, CA 94904

6. Orban Associates, Inc., 645 Bryant St., San Francisco, CA 94107

7. The U.R.E.I. products are handled by JBL Incorporated, Reference 2

8. Ivie Electronics Incorporated, 1366 West Center, Orem, Utah 84057

Chapter 19

Automatic Microphone Mixers

SINCE THE FIRST MULTIPLE MICROPHONE setup there have been problems associated with human limitations in mixing the signals in the different channels.Sometimes things happen so fast that it is difficult to give each channel the attention it deserves. Sometimes there are just too many channels for two hands. (Old timers may remember "Neutrodyne Newt The Three-Armed Wonder," and tuning three dials simultaneously in the early neutrodyne radio receiver). In sound-reinforcement systems having multiple microphones either one or more skilled operators are required or some automatic system that can either replace the operator entirely or make his task an easier one.

19.1 THE NEED FOR AUTOMATIC MIXING

Consider the Podunk Town Council. The mayor sits facing the council members and the secretary sits at a separate desk to the mayor's left. The mayor has a microphone, the secretary has her own microphone, and each of the six council members has an individual microphone. If all these microphones are open at the same time in this reverberant room the system howls or at least there is a great reduction of usable gain. Realizing this dilemma, the local sound contractor who installed the system said there must be a mixing desk and an operator. One is installed and the sound contractor is engaged to operate during biweekly council meetings. He really has problems. Occasionally excitement reigns and everyone talks at once and when this happens the system howls and the mixer receives scowls from everybody. Trying to open used and close unused channels is possible only during the more quiet and orderly times.

19.2 THE PROBLEM OF TOO MANY OPEN MICROPHONES

Let us take a certain sound-reinforcement system with a single open microphone. By increasing the gain the feedback threshold is determined. If a second open microphone is introduced it also picks up loudspeaker sound and contributes to feedback as much as the first microphone. This results

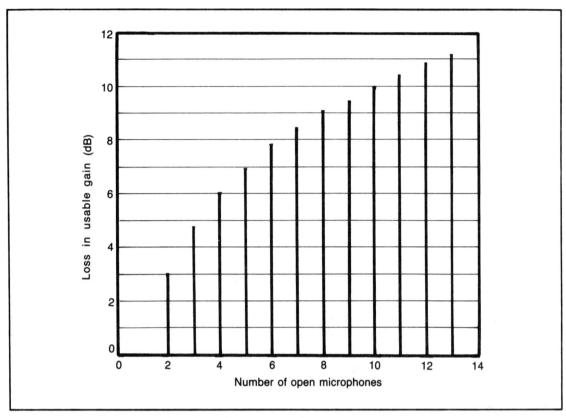

Fig. 19-1. If more than one microphone is used in a sound-reinforcement system, the usable gain is reduced. Each time the number of microphones is doubled, another 3 dB of usable gain is lost as shown in this graph. Feedback howling is the price paid for too little usable gain.

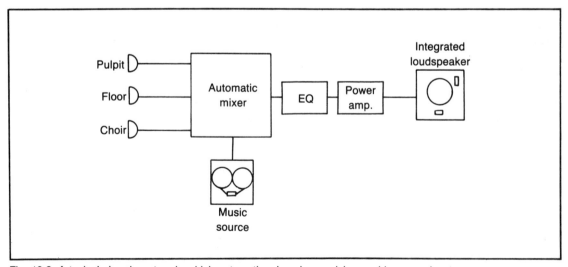

Fig. 19-2. A typical church system in which automatic microphone mixing could prove advantageous.

in degradation of the feedback howling situation. It is found that the system gain must be reduced 3 dB if the second open microphone is introduced. If a total of four microphones are open in this system, the gain must be reduced 6 dB. Each doubling of the number of open microphones results in a further 3 dB reduction of system gain to prevent feedback. The rule may be expressed this way: Usable gain reduction = 10 log (NOM) where NOM = the number of open microphones. This is graphed in Fig. 19-1.

With the usable system gain dependent upon the number of open microphones, technical people naturally turned to means of automatically turning off microphones not in use at the moment. Simple voice-operated switching devices were introduced about a decade ago and they worked—after a fashion. What is needed in addition to turning off unused microphones is an automatic adjustment of gain to conform to the number of microphones in action. These two functions are basic to the more advanced automatic microphone mixers available today and, in addition, each has its own set of special features. Typical arrangements of automatic microphone mixing are shown in Figs. 19-2 and 19-3. Although automatic microphone mixers are manufactured by JBL, Industrial Research Products, Edcore, and probably by others, we shall study in more detail only the two manufactured by Altec Corporation and Shure Brothers (Refs. 1 and 2)

19.3 THE ALTEC LANSING SYSTEM

In 1975 Dugan described an automatic microphone mixer (Ref. 3) that used analog computer circuits to achieve constant gain and minimum feedback hazard as multiple microphones were switched on and off. The early automatic microphone mixer introduced by Altec Corporation in 1976 was based on Dugan's design. This system has been improved and the latest Altec Lansing devices, the Model 1674 (4-channel) and the 1678 (8-channel), are shown in Fig. 19-4. The 8-channel unit may be linked up in multiple to provide up to 80 channels.

The analog computer circuits in the Altec Lansing mixer provide automatic mixing following this basic rule: Each individual input channel is attenuated by an amount, in dB, equal to the difference, in dB, between that channel's level and the sum of all channel levels. What does this mean? If only one microphone is used, all the other channels are effectively turned off. If the microphones of channels 1 and 2 are in use, they are each attenuated 3 dB and all other channels are effectively off. After at-

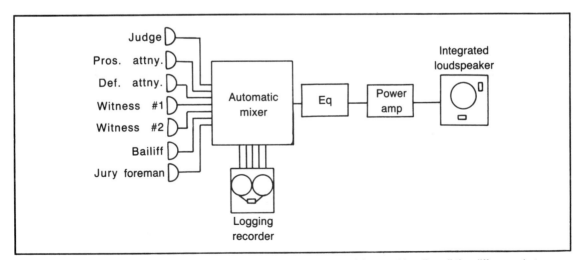

Fig. 19-3. A typical courtroom system in which automatic microphone mixing could well spell the difference between a successful sound system and failure.

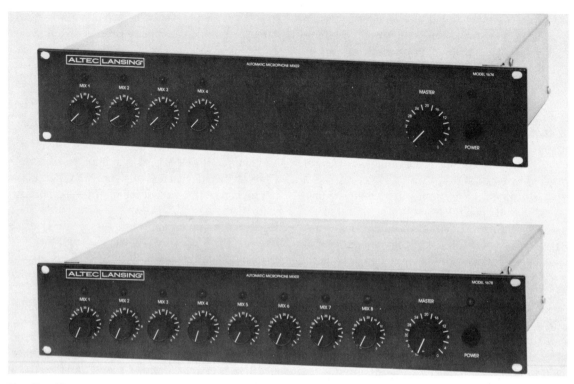

Fig. 19-4. The Altec-Lansing Model 1674 (above) and Model 1678 (below) automatic microphone mixers. The 8-channel unit may be linked up in multiple to control up to 80 microphones (courtesy Altec Corporation).

tenuation, channels 1 and 2 are mixed together, routed to the main mixer output. These two microphone levels, each attenuated 3 dB, mix back together to produce a signal level that is exactly equal to the level of either microphone before attenuation. Thus, the final level is the same as if only a single microphone had been in operation. The name "gain-sharing" is given to this operation.

In addition to the automatic functions, there are manual volume controls in each channel that allow the operator to adjust the input channel level before any automatic mixing takes place. This allows compensation for weak- and strong-voiced talkers.

This mixer is also able to distinguish between coherent and noncoherent signals and to make them appropriate adjustment to care for them. A single talker positioned between two microphones would introduce a coherent signal into both channels. A distant slammed door would do the same thing. Noncoherent signals would be the opposite, quite

different in waveshape, phase, etc. When two non-coherent signals are mixed together, the resultant signal is 3 dB higher. When two coherent signals are mixed together, the resultant signal is 6 dB higher. It would be possible for a coherent signal to throw the system into feedback because of this extra 3 dB. The Altec Lansing 1674 and 1678 mixers automatically compensate for the difference between coherent and noncoherent signals.

Other features of the Altec Lansing 1674 and 1678 include phantom power for microphones, switchable microphone gain of either – 60 dB or – 74 dB to accommodate different types of microphones. On the rear panel of each input unit are line outputs for routing signals to external devices and a TTL (transistor-transistor-logic) terminal for control of recorders or loudspeaker muting. The loudspeaker muting feature can be very helpful in rooms with a low ceiling and loudspeakers mounted therein. If a loudspeaker is close to a microphone

268

problems could ensue and by means of this muting circuit the close loudspeaker could be turned off while that microphone is open.

19.4 THE SHURE SYSTEM

Shure Brothers have approached the problems of automatic microphone mixing from the true systems standpoint involving everything from specially designed microphones to the output terminals. Ordinary microphones cannot be used with the Shure Automatic Microphone System without sacrificing most of the automatic features. Coming on the scene late, Shure had the advantage of studying the products already on the market and noting their strong and weak points. The system has two basic parts, the mixer and the microphone. The microphone comes in three basic forms to meet the divergent needs.

Two models of the Shure Automatic Microphone System are available, the Model AMS 4000 (4 channel) unit and the AMS 8000 (8 channel), which is shown in Fig. 19-5. These are identical except for the number of channels.

The three microphones designed into this system are shown in Fig. 19-6. The AMS22 low profile microphone, for use on the table top, is shown in A. The AMS 26 microphone, for gooseneck or stand use, is shown in B and C. The Model AMS28 lavalier microphone is shown in D.

The Shure Automatic Microphone System operates on principles quite different from other automatic systems. For one thing, there are no threshold controls, the mixer controls are conventional in their function. There is no scanning and averaging of input levels. The microphones may operate in quite different acoustical environments while connected to the same mixer. The secret of control lies in the construction of the microphones.

Figure 19-7 illustrates the uniqueness of the AMS microphones in that they "look" not only forward, but backward as well. The forward part responds to the desired signal, the rearward part "reads" environmental noise. This is accomplished by incorporating two separate and distinct capsules in each microphone. Special circuits compare the ambient noise level of the rearward facing capsule with the signal level from the front facing capsule and turns on the channel only when the difference

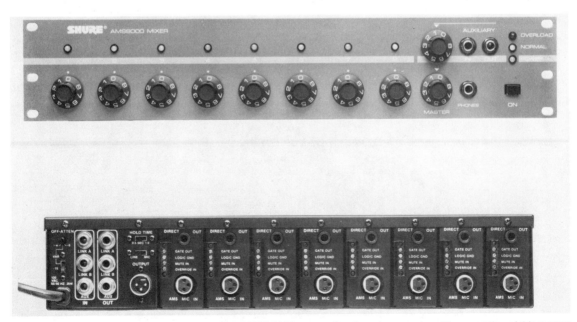

Fig. 19-5. Front and rear views of the Shure Model AMS 8000 automatic microphone system. The operation of this system is closely tied to the special microphones which must be used (courtesy Shure Brothers Incorporated).

Fig. 19-6. Microphones which are a part of the Shure AMS 8000 automatic system: (A) the AMS 26 low-profile microphone for table top use, (B)&(C) the AMS 26 for gooseneck or stand use, and (D) the AMS 28 lavalier (courtesy Shure Brothers Incorporated).

270

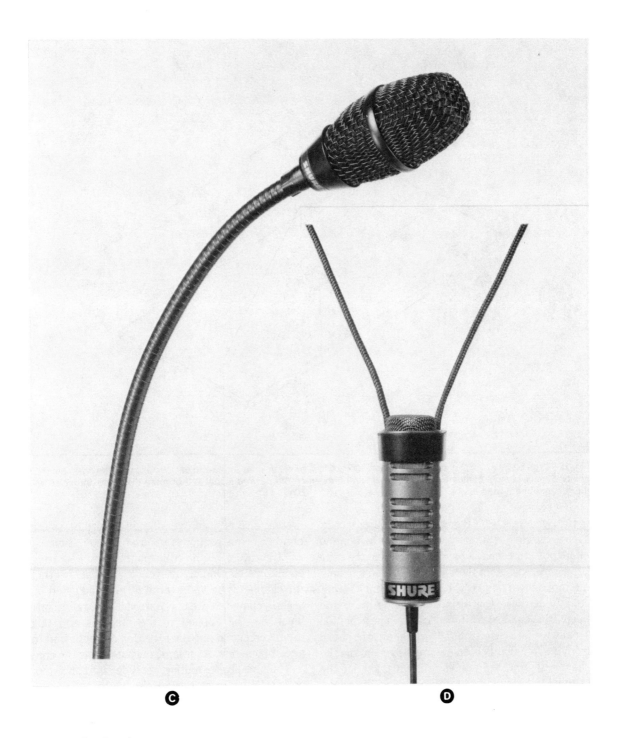

C   D

Fig. 19-6. Continued.

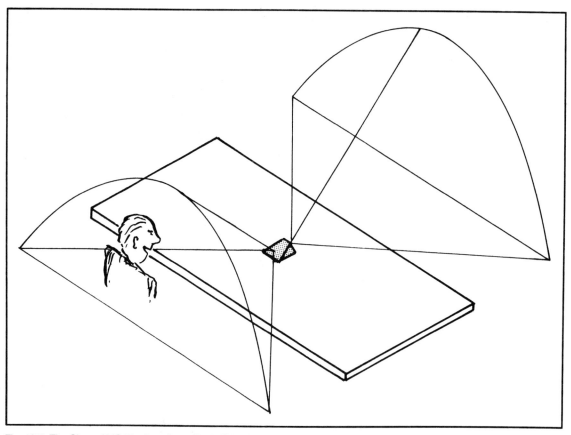

Fig. 19-7. The Shure AMS 22 microphone "looks" forward toward the desired sound and backward toward the environmental noise. Special circuits compare the two signals and only when the desired signal is 9 or more dB above the noise will that channel be turned on.

in the two levels is 9 dB or greater. In other words, the rearward-looking microphone sets the floating or adaptive threshold for each channel and the computer senses whether the sounds are present in both microphones. If equal levels are present the circuitry "decides" that it is background noise and keeps the channel switched off. When a person speaks within this front 120 degree angle, the signal from the frontward capsule is much greater and the channel is switched on. The time it takes for the channel to be switched on is about 4 milliseconds. When the person stops talking, the channel remains open for 0.5 to 1 second (user adjustable) and then begins a slow fade off. This slow fade eliminates chopping syllables and switching transients. The

system also adjusts overall gain according to the number of microphones open at any one time.

Indicators on the front panel show operating conditions continually. A yellow LED shows that the channel is on and overall level is indicated by green-yellow-red LEDs. External signals at line level may be applied to the mix bus and this premixed signal may be recorded or connected to a telephone line. Four logic outputs allow the control of loudspeaker muting, recorder start and stop, or meet other customer needs.

The Model AMS880 video-switching panel makes possible the turning on and off video cameras according to which channels are turned off. This allows automatic switching of cameras to follow the persons talking.

It can be said that automatic microphone mixing has come of age. Further improvements undoubtedly will be forthcoming, but equipment is available today for satisfactory automatic microphone mixing to replace the operator in the simpler systems or to augment his efficiency in the more sophisticated systems.

References

1. Altec Corporation, 10500 West Reno, P.O. Box 26105, Oklahoma City, Oklahoma 73126

2. Shure Brothers Incorporated, 222 Hartrey Avenue, Evanston, IL 60204

3. Dugan, Dan, 1975. Automatic Microphone Mixing, *Jour. Audio Engr. Soc.*, Vol 23, No 6 (July/August), pp 442-449.

Chapter 20

Foldback for Platform and Choir

DISCRIMINATION IS BEING OPPOSED ON EV-ery hand, so why should it be allowed to flourish in sound-reinforcing systems? Especially when the ones being discriminating against are the dignitaries seated on the platform! These august persons may include the chief speaker of the occasion whose opening lines should certainly bear some relationship to introductory remarks, visitors whom we wish to impress, and various other important persons on display. Surely these people should hear what is spoken from the podium as clearly as an average person in the audience. But such is often not the case. The worst seats in the house are often those on the platform behind the podium. The speech they hear is often confused and garbled, reaching them only after one or more bounces from rear and side walls.

In churches the members of the choir are often seated where intelligibility of speech from the sound system is poor. This is more true of choirs located behind, or to the side of the pulpit than choirs in a balcony loft to the rear of the audience

and in the beam of the main loudspeaker cluster. Instrumental musical groups or performers on platform or stage are frequently in positions off the axis of the main loudspeaker cluster and, as a result, are poorly served by the house system. The purpose of this chapter is to encourage the concept that such persons in roles supportive of the program are entitled to good listening conditions. Nor is it only a matter of fairness. Missing a cue or not catching a "punch line" can be a major obstacle to smooth and effective communication.

20.1 THE HOWLBACK PROBLEM

Foldback and howlback have both phonetic and acoustical associations. Foldback, as used in sound reinforcement, is the term applied to the special provisions for sound coverage for those behind the pulpit or podium, or otherwise out of the coverage of the main system. Special loudspeakers to cover those discriminated against by the main house system have the problem of being close to the microphone, thus rendering the foldback system especially prone to howlback. The problem of providing these key people with good sound then resolves itself into a problem of obtaining enough gain from these supplemental loudspeakers to do any good before breaking into oscillation. Thus foldback and howlback go hand in hand and solving one without exciting the other becomes the challenge of this chapter.

20.2 DISTRIBUTED CEILING LOUDSPEAKERS

The physical arrangement of sanctuaries and auditoriums vary widely and, as a result, so do their adaptability to certain approaches to solving the foldback problem. The greater the physical and

acoustical separation between foldback loudspeakers and pulpit or podium microphones the better. Shown in Fig. 20-1 are plan and elevation views of the front end of a church sanctuary seating about 400. The platform to audience left is used by an orchestra, that to the right by the choir. Several chairs are behind the pulpit. Mounting foldback loudspeakers in the low ceiling to cover the platform area seemed the best approach to the sound contractor. In Fig. 20-1, FB-1 loudspeakers covers the area occupied by the orchestra, FB-3 covers the choir area, and FB-2 handles the seats behind the pulpit. These foldback loudspeakers are high quality coaxial units, i.e., a small directive loudspeaker for the high frequencies is mounted on

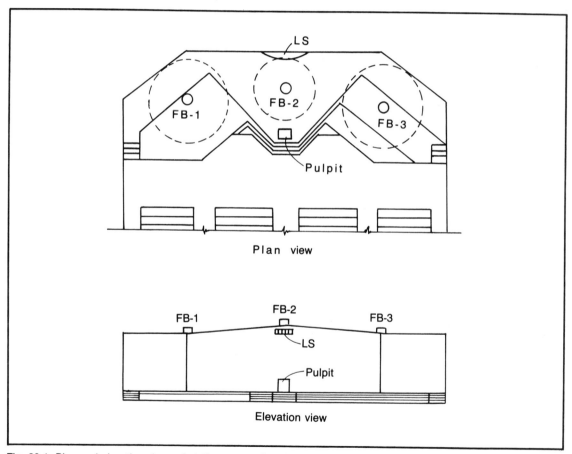

Fig. 20-1. Plan and elevation views of platform area of a church sanctuary seating about 400. Three coaxial foldback loudspeakers are flush mounted in the ceiling in boxes of appropriate volume. FB-1 covers the orchestra area, FB-3 the choir area, and FB-2 the seats behind the pulpit. The loudspeaker cluster for the house system is located at LS.

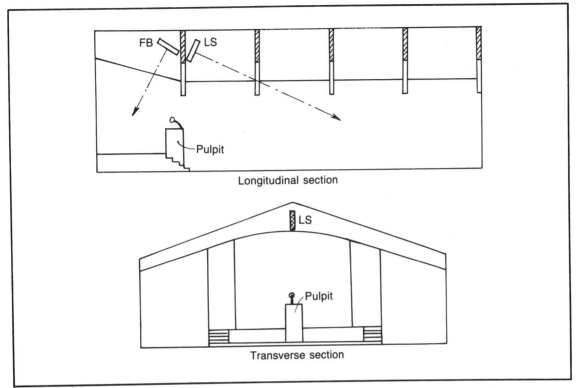

Fig. 20-2. In this small church both audience and choir are served by column loudspeakers. The foldback loudspeaker level may be reduced because of its proximity to choir personnel, thus reducing its tendency toward feedback. Directivity of column loudspeakers in the vertical plane is of help in this arrangement.

the axis of the larger bass unit. Each loudspeaker is backed by a glass fiber filled box of appropriate volume.

20.3 DISTRIBUTED LOW LEVEL LOUDSPEAKERS

In high vaulted stage area and in churches having high ceilings the foldback loudspeaker placement depicted in Fig. 20-1 is impractical. If the distributed approach is used, the loudspeakers must be located nearer the floor plane. If there are permanent seats, small loudspeakers may possibly be mounted on seat backs, one to every three seats. For the more open stage areas floor monitors such as shown in Fig. 9-29 may be used. The way these floor monitors are usually used with contemporary music groups the level is anything but low because of the very high level of the loudspeakers situated

near instrumentalists or solo singer. For this reason such floor monitors are capable of quite good quality and are built to handle very appreciable power levels.

20.4 SINGLE POINT LOUDSPEAKERS

Using distributed loudspeakers for foldback can create howlback problems difficult to overcome. While subject to some hazards, a single loudspeaker having more directional characteristics is often the better solution. Horns are especially directive and useful, but their low-frequency deficiencies yield poor overall quality, although they are not too bad for speech alone. Much depends on the physical layout of the particular auditorium. Figure 20-2 shows longitudinal and transverse sections of a rather typical small church, which utilizes laminated roof beams. Two column loudspeakers

277

are employed, one of the better tapered type serving the audience and a second ordinary one covering the small choir area behind the pulpit P. Because of the proximity of the microphone on the pulpit and the small choir area to be covered, a relatively low level on the foldback loudspeaker must be used.

Another example of the use of a single point loudspeaker for choir foldback is shown in Fig. 20-3. A single column unit has been mounted

behind the edge of the proscenium arch. In this position it is hidden from the view of the audience. Careful aiming and level control are required to avoid howlback problems.

20.5 FOLDBACK WITH REVERSE-POLARITY LOUDSPEAKERS

If more that a single transducer is used in an integrated (cabinet type) loudspeaker or in a clus-

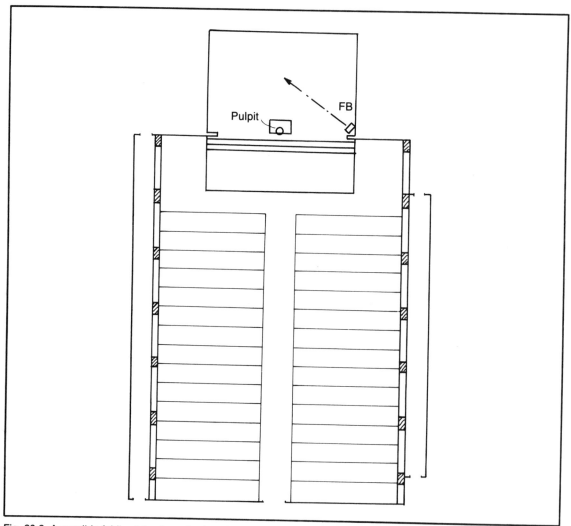

Fig. 20-3. A possible foldback loudspeaker location in a typical church. The foldback loudspeaker FB is hidden from the audience by mounting it behind the edge of the proscenium arch. Careful location, aiming, and level control are required to avoid feedback.

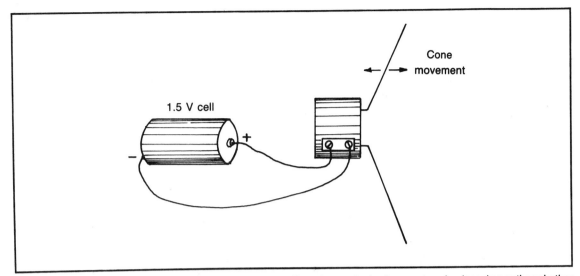

Fig. 20-4. A single flashlight cell may be connected momentarily to the terminals of a cone type loudspeaker, noting whether the cone movement is outward or inward. The battery polarity required in a similar test on a second loudspeaker to give the same cone movement determines how the two should be connected for same-polarity operation (both cones moving together) or reverse-polarity operation (cones moving in opposition). Two identical loudspeakers from the same manufacturer would be expected to be identical in the polarity marking of the terminals. This test should not be used on compression drivers.

ter, it is imperative that the polarity of the individual units be correct. By this is meant that when a positive gong electrical signal is applied to the different component transducers, the motion of the diaphragms of all units must be the same. For instance if, with the positive going electrical signal mentioned above, some of the diaphragms moved outward and some moved inward, serious audio distortions would result. The aim is to have all diaphragms moving in unison. Diaphragms will move together in unison if they are connected with the proper polarity. In the past (and in some areas at present) this condition has been described as "being in phase." This is a misnomer. True, reversing the terminals will introduce a 180 degree phase shift, but phase is frequency dependent, polarity is not. Polarity is the proper term to apply to what we will be doing to connections to loudspeaker terminals.

The polarity of various loudspeaker units may be determined by applying a given pulse to the units and noting whether the resulting acoustical pulse is positive or negative going. This requires not only a pulse source, but also a microphone-amplifier-

cathode-ray oscilloscope combination to observe the acoustical pulse resulting from the electrical pulse excitation. With cone-type loudspeakers it is safe to connect a single 1.5 volt cell momentarily to the loudspeaker terminals and observing which way the cone moves as shown in Fig. 20-4. As the circuit is briefly completed, note which way the cone moves. Mark the loudspeaker terminals plus and minus to correspond to the cell poles to which they were connected. Now, the same test can be applied to a second loudspeaker. This time mark the terminals plus and minus to obtain the same cone movement. When the two loudspeakers are connected together to be driven by the same amplifier the usual rule is that they must have the same polarity or some weird effects result.

It may be something of a surprise to the sound operator to be told that reverse polarity connection of loudspeakers might have a useful result. The benefit stems from the unusual polar patterns obtainable from a pair of identical loudspeakers so connected in the "wrong" way as in Fig. 20-5. Some beautiful nulls are developed, and pointing a null toward the sound system microphone means that his pair can radiate substantial amounts of audio power, even when located quite close to the microphone, without causing howlback.

Figure 20-6 illustrates the directional characteristics of a pair of identical loudspeakers, placed back-to-back, radiating a white noise signal (Ref.1). The interesting thing here is that, at 90 degrees off axis, the radiation from one loudspeaker tends to cancel that from the other. This polar response is taken in the horizontal plane, but nulls are just as deep in a plane passing between the loudspeakers perpendicular to their axes. Thus the nulls exist not only in the horizontal plane but above and below as well. If the microphone is located in this null it will receive a relatively small amount of signal from the loudspeaker. The effect is not perfect, but with white noise the signal radiated in the direction of the null is about 20 dB below that radiated at 0 and 180 degrees.

The degrees of cancellation varies with frequency, the higher the frequency the greater the cancellation and the deeper the null. With the loudspeakers back-to-back as shown in Fig. 20-6, the pure tone nulls are about 18 dB at 100 Hz, about

30 dB down at 1,000 Hz, and about 35 dB down at 10,000 Hz. White noise, which is something of a mixture of all audible frequency components, yields a null depth of about 20 dB as mentioned above.

What happens if the loudspeakers are arranged so that they are close together, but with axes at 120 degrees instead of 180 degrees? The polar pattern for white noise for this condition is shown in Fig. 20-7. The null toward which the loudspeakers are somewhat inclined tends to fill in, but the rear null is sharp and deep.

If the two loudspeakers are back-to-back but separated, the beam gets narrower as the separation increases, but the nulls are still alive and well and pointing in the same direction. The white noise directional pattern for a three-foot separation of loudspeakers is shown in Fig. 20-8.

20.6 APPLYING THE REVERSE POLARITY IDEA

These beautiful directional patterns can be put to good use to combat the oft met problem of moun-

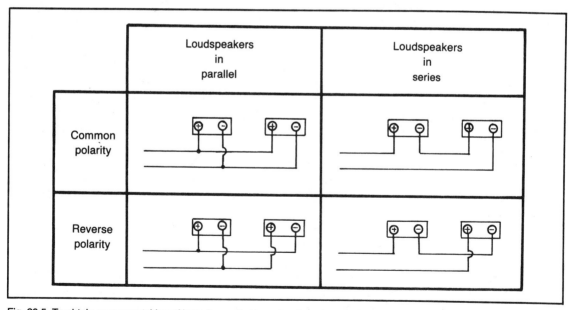

Fig. 20-5. To obtain proper matching of impedances between loudspeakers and amplifier, parallel connection of loudspeakers is sometimes used, sometimes series, sometimes a combination. The same-polarity and reverse-polarity connections are shown for both the series and parallel condition.

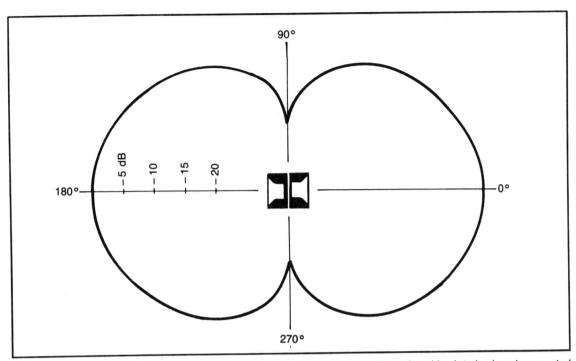

Fig. 20-6. Directional pattern in the horizontal plane of two identical loudspeakers placed back to back and connected with reverse polarity. The signal used: white noise. Nulls approximately 20 dB deep are created by partial cancellation. When used in a foldback system, directing the null toward the house system microphone helps to control feedback (see Ref. 1).

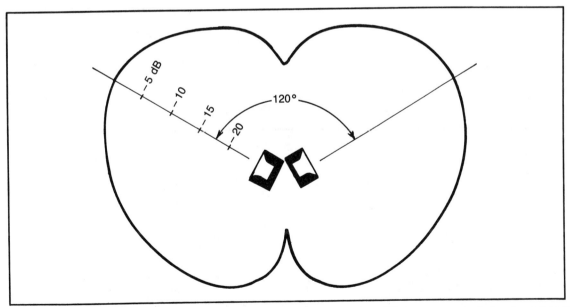

Fig. 20-7. By directing the axes of two identical, reverse-polarity loudspeakers 120 degrees apart, shallow forward and deep rearward nulls are formed (see Ref. 1).

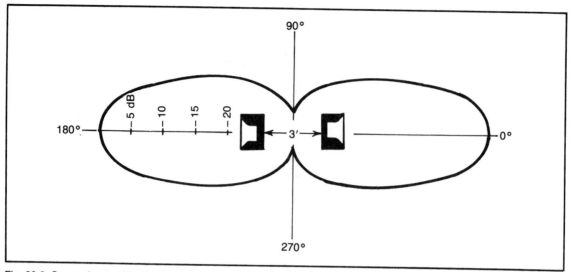

Fig. 20-8. Separating two identical loudspeakers, connected in reverse polarity, by three feet narrows the beam and yields deep nulls (see Ref. 1).

ting foldback loudspeakers near the microphone in use. Three examples are given in Fig. 20-9. The divided choir (A) can very well be served by a pair of back to back loudspeakers mounted coaxially. The problem is one of living with loudspeakers in this location. There are some excellent bookshelf loudspeakers on the market today which are small and uniform in response. Perhaps a pair of these could be mounted above the floor. Suspending them at a considerable distance above the floor is another

possibility, but esthetic senses may be violated by mounting in such a visually critical spot.

A choir arranged in a single group immediately behind the pulpit may be served by a pair of loudspeakers set at an angle to each other, as shown in Fig. 20-9(B). This arrangement directs the sharpest null toward the microphone. Choir members are, however, seated in the shallower null opposite the microphone. These persons should hear sound levels comparable to those heard by

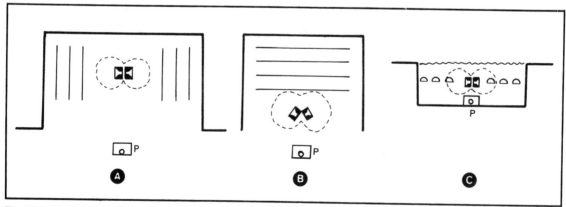

Fig. 20-9. Examples of the use for foldback of two loudspeakers connected in reverse polarity. (A) Back-to-back identical loudspeakers for divided choir. The house system microphone is located at the pulpit P. (B) Angled reverse polarity loudspeakers provide sound to choir area behind the pulpit P. (C) Back-to-back reverse polarity pair of loudspeakers to provide sound coverage for dignitaries seated on platform behind the podium P.

choir members near the lend of the rows because they are closer to the loudspeaker. It is also possible that those exactly on the line of symmetry, with one ear on each side of this line, may hear the voice from the pulpit as multiple voices speaking in unison due to reflections from walls (Ref.2), but the effect is not seriously disturbing.

For the typical school auditorium platform arrangement, with podium and a row or two of seats behind it, a possible location for the reverse polarity foldback loudspeaker pair is directly behind the podium, as shown in Fig. 20-9(C).

All of these foldback loudspeaker pairs connected with reverse polarity should have their volume controlled by someone receiving output from them. The house sound operator has no way of judging proper levels in the foldback area unless he is in it. The range of such a volume control should be limited so that, if turned full on by an inexperienced person, it cannot throw the system into a howlback condition.

Loudspeakers for reverse polarity use, or any other foldback use for that matter, should be of high quality. Irregularities in response limit the range of usable gain before howlback. Further, those involved in the program are as much entitled to hearing natural, understandable speech as those seated in the audience area.

20.7 MICROPHONES IN THE FOLDBACK AREA

When choir or orchestra areas are served with separate foldback sound reinforcement, what happens when they perform? They often need microphones for adequate pickup of their musical numbers and such microphones are invariably in the beam of the foldback loudspeakers. Normally, they do not need sound reinforcement to hear themselves, only to hear the talker at pulpit or podium. Switching the foldback system off during musical numbers is the logical action for the sound operator. This situation is similar to the common radio studio or recording studio problem. If the operator in the control room opens his microphone to talk to those in the studio over the talkback loudspeaker, howlback results unless open microphones in the studio are switched off. It is commonly arranged so that this is done automatically as the control operator operates his "push to talk" button or switch. Likewise, when choir or orchestra microphones are switched on, the foldback system should be disabled automatically.

20.8 DESIGNING THE FOLDBACK SYSTEM

Although it seems simple and of secondary importance, the foldback sound-reinforcement system should not be attempted by amateurs. It can be more difficult to design, set up, and operate effectively than the house system. The services of a qualified sound contractor should be sought, preferably at the time the main house system is being designed originally or an improvement program is being considered.

References

1. Jones, Edward S., 1971. "Providing Foldback With Out-Of-Phase Loudspeakers," *Jour. Audio Engr. Soc.*, Vol 19, No 4 (April) pp 306-309. Figures 20-7, 20-8, and 20-11 are adapted from the Journal of the Audio Engineering Society, copyright 1971, with the permission of the author and AES.

2. Draper, Melvin S., 1970. "A Sound Reinforcement System For Multiple Conference Rooms," *Jour. Audio Engr. Soc.*, Vol 18, No 2 (April) p 184.

Chapter 21

Magnetic Tape Recording

W HY TREAT ANALOG MAGNETIC TAPE RE-
cording when digital is just around the corner? Everyone said television was just around the
corner in the 1940s but it really did not become a
commercial success until the 1950s. There is no denying the great advantages digital recording will
bring. The handwriting is on the wall. Digital is the
system of the future and we are all impatient for
it to dominate the recording scene. But the fact is,
it does not yet dominate, analog recording does.
With analog magnetic tape recorders everywhere
carrying the bulk of the recording load, this chapter
must concentrate on them with no apology. They
have served long and well and it will be a decade
or more before digital crowds out analog in all the
many fields in which magnetic recorders serve us
today.

The signal to noise ratio possible with digital
recorders exceeds that possible with analog

magnetic tape recorders, but not by all that much
if compared to top flight recorders handled with an
expert touch. What will really be a big step forward
is the ability to rerecord as many generations as
necessary with NO deterioration in quality. The ar-
chival as well as the commercial possibilities are
staggering. With large scale integrated circuits the
cost of digital will probably be lower than analog
eventually. The digital editing problems of the present will all be solved in time. With our eyes glanc-
ing ahead to digital we focus our main attention on
getting the best performance possible out of the
analog magnetic tape recorders carrying the load
today.

21.1 REVIEW OF PRINCIPLES

The principles on which magnetic recording
rests have been known for decades, but it was not
until World War II that practical applications were

Some of the material of this chapter is taken from the booklet, "Recording Basics" published by 3M Company, 3M Center,
Saint Paul, Minnesota 55101. My thanks to 3M for permission to reproduce certain figures and to adapt some of the sections of this book.

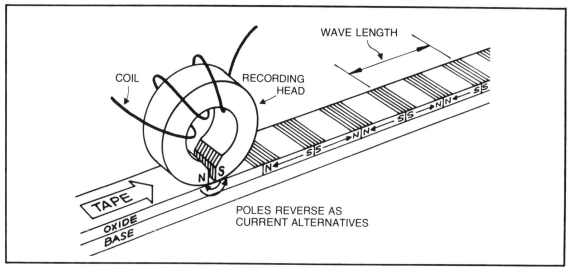

Fig. 21-1. As the tape passes the recording head of a magnetic tape recorder, an alternating current in the head magnetizes the tape with alternating polarity.

actually made. Wire recorders were in extensive use during the war, recording many types of radio traffic. Crude tape recorders, using metallic tapes, were constructed and used in limited, special applications. But, it was not until acetate and then polyester backings were developed, coated with special metallic oxides, that magnetic recording came into real prominence.

The high signal-to-noise ratio of tape and its ability to be erased and re-used, added impetus to its rapid adoption as the favored way to make sound recordings.

At the heart of every tape recorder is an electromagnet called a magnetic head. The head is actually a coil of fine wire wound on an iron core whose poles are brought closely together to form an extremely narrow gap. The fringing flux of this gap magnetizes the metallic-oxide coating of the tape as it passes the head as shown in Figs. 21-1 and 21-2. Some recorders use a single head for both recording and playback and a second erase head upstream from the first. Many machines have three heads, each performing a specific function. Ideally, individual heads are assigned the erase, record, and playback functions arranged as shown in Fig. 21-3. Often the term "head" is used to describe the pole surfaces. These are highly polished areas of the

head that come in intimate contact with the oxide surface of the tape. Great care must be exercised not to scratch the head surfaces.

The signals from the microphone, amplified and fed to the magnetic record head, appear as pulses of magnetic flux, which magnetize the oxide on the tape. As the tape passes the head at a uniform rate, a magnetic replica of the microphone signal is fixed on the oxide coating. In playback, the tape is moved at the same speed over the playback head and the magnetic field of the tape

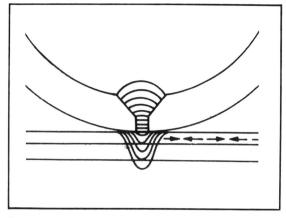

Fig. 21-2. It is the fringing magnetic flux of the recording head that is effective in magnetizing the tape.

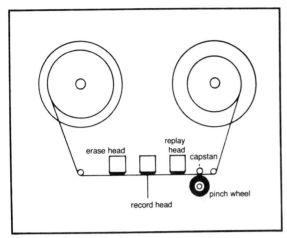

Fig. 21-3. Typical arrangement of the erase, record, and play heads of the typical magnetic tape recorder.

coating induces a voltage in the coil of the playback head. This voltage is a near replica of the microphone signal and may then be amplified to drive a loudspeaker, which reproduces the microphone signal.

The magnetic medium of the tape is affected by nonlinearities which, if not corrected, cause severe distortions. By applying a high-frequency bias signal to the record head along with the microphone signal, the nonlinearity is corrected. The frequency of this bias signal is of the order of 100 kHz, far outside the range of the human ear. The bias performs two important functions during recording: (1) it reduces distortion, and (2) it maximizes the audio signal recorded, increasing the signal-to-noise ratio. Because proper biasing is necessary to achieve optimum performance, some attention to matching tape and bias must be given. Although each type of tape has an optimum bias, an exact biasing level is rarely a precise point. It is normally a compromise point at which characteristics that are themselves opposed achieve the best possible tradeoff of characteristics that are desirable.

A remarkable feature of magnetic recording is the ease with which a recorded tape can be erased and reused. Demagnetizing is automatically done in the erase head whenever the machine is in the record mode. The erase head is located ahead of the record and playback heads as shown in Fig. 21-3. In the record mode it is fed an ultrasonic alternating current which causes rapidly rising and falling magnetic fields at the poles. As the tape passes through this field it is demagnetized and essentially all traces of any recording already on the tape is erased.

21.2 RECORDING FORMATS

A great advantage of magnetic tape over disc recording is the ability to provide discrete sound channels, that is, channels that are spatially and electrically independent. Discrete channeling permits the precise placement of sound (musicians, speakers, special effects) to provide a spatial location very similar to the one originally recorded.

Tape recorders and tape decks are available in a number of head arrangements. It is the head arrangement (not the tape) that governs the format of recordings that can be made. These include full and half-track mono, two-track stereo, four track stereo, and quadrasonic stereo. Some machines permit monophonic recording on each of four tracks.

Considering open reel magnetic recorders, the early ones were full-track. The magnetic head covered the entire width of the quarter-inch wide tape. Full-track recorders are still used in applications where extensive tape editing is necessary. The full-track mono format is illustrated in Fig. 21-4(A).

With advances in head design it became possible to achieve a doubling of recording time by reducing the width of the recording to slightly less than half that of the tape. The tape was recorded in one direction; reels were interchanged and a second recording was made in the opposite direction. Each reel thus held twice the amount of recorded information. This also ended the necessity of rewinding at the end of play. This half-track mono format is shown in Fig. 21-4(B).

Early two-channel stereo recording utilized this half-track format by the design of an in-line head which played both tracks simultaneously. Discrete two-channel stereo had arrived! Gone was the economy in recording time; half-track stereo of that

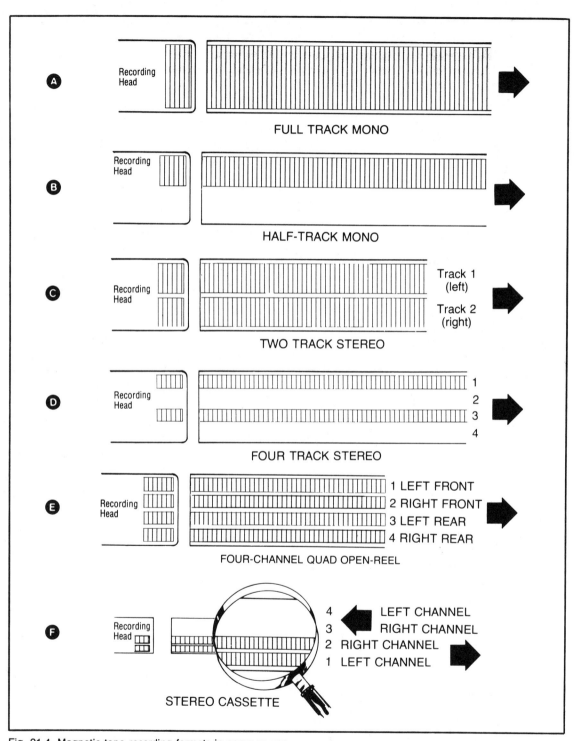

Fig. 21-4. Magnetic tape recording formats in common use.

day was a play-and-rewind affair. But, the half-track format provided the perfect synchronization and isolation necessary for lifelike three dimensional sound. Stereo was here to stay, and today's professionals still use this format, which is pictured in Fig. 21-4(C).

The same demand for economy soon brought the four-track format. Head design, however, had not yet progressed to the point that would permit adjacent channel assignments, and channel separation brought the 1-3, 4-2 format for left and right channels as shown in Fig. 21-4(D), the four track stereo.

While it can be seen that a full track mono recording will play back perfectly on a four track stereo machine, a four track stereo tape cannot be played back on a full track head. In this case the head would see all the information on the tape. This would include tracks 1 and 3 as well as the backward program on tracks 4 and 2.

If a half track mono tape is played on a four-track stereo machine, the program will play through the left channel. The volume control on the right channel should be turned down to silence the second track of the tape, which will be playing backward. However, a four-track stereo tape cannot be played on a half track head as the head would be seeing the left channel of the desired program and also the right channel of the second program playing backward.

Great economies in tape costs and library space can be had when recording lectures or other monophonic material by single track employment of a four-track stereo recorder. Many recorders have individual switches for left and right channels. The four-channel quad open reel format is shown inn Fig. 21-4(E).

In the mid 1960s the compact cassette recorder came on the scene. It began as a half track monophonic medium, but soon followed with cassette stereo. Putting four tracks on a ribbon of tape only 150 mils (1/7-inch) wide was indeed an engineering feat. But the fact that stereo pairs could be placed on adjacent rather than alternate tracks was even more important. With this adjacent track configuration a mono tape will play back on both

channels of a stereo machine and a stereo tape will present both channels of information to a mono head. The content of both left and right channels will be heard combined on the one loudspeaker. Unlike the open reel, the cassette is truly mono/stereo compatible. The stereo cassette format is shown in Fig. 21-4(F).

The eight track stereo cartridge has had its day as a favorite medium for prerecorded music in two channel stereo. The eight tracks are used in pairs as the two poles of a movable magnetic head are switched automatically across the width of the quarter-inch tape. The shifting positions of the two-channel head assembly are illustrated in Fig. 21-5(A). Discrete four-channel sound of quadraphonic-8 cartridges is obtained through the use of four-channel head with two positions as shown in Fig. 21-5(B).

The voltage induced in the playback head is directly proportional to the width of the track. This width varies widely between the full track on quarter-inch tape and a single track of cassette tape. The lower voltage induced in the cassette playback head means that the signal-to-noise ratio is reduced just that much. There is a price to pay for narrower tracks.

21.3 MAGNETIC LEVELS ON TAPE

The level of a signal recorded on tape is not measured in dB or VU. These units refer to voltage or power levels. Signals stored on tape are in the form of changing magnetic flux levels and such signals in magnetic form must be described in magnetic terms. When the signal on the tape in the form of magnetic flux is moved past the coil of wire of the playback head a voltage is induced. The unit of "moving flux," the Weber, is defined as the amount of magnetism on the tape that will induce 1-volt in a single-turn coil during one second. This definition results in a unit, the *Weber*, that is too large. One thousandth of a millionth of a Weber, called the nanoWeber, is about the right size.

Moving from the single-turn coil to the practical domain, the actual voltage induced in a playback head depends not only on the changing

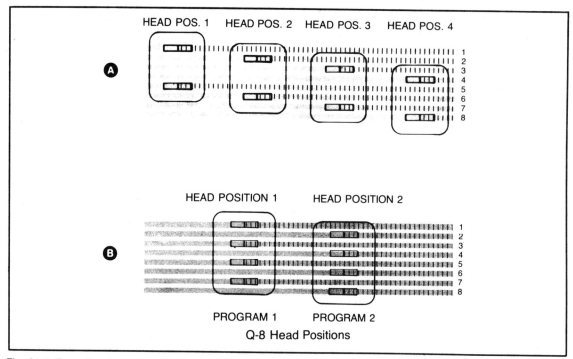

Fig. 21-5. Recording format for the 8-track cartridge, (A) stereo, (B) quadraphonic.

magnetic flux stored on the tape, but also on the tape speed, the track width, and the design of the head. The manufacturer of the tape machine, fortunately, takes into consideration these factors.

There are three commonly used reference flux levels for open reel tape recorders: 185, 250, and 320 nanoWebers per meter of track width (a meter is about 500 times wider than most tracks). The 185 nWb/m record level was formerly the standard and is still used on most consumer equipment. The coming of higher output tapes brought in 250 nWb/m as the normally used level. The 320 nWb/m level is used in Europe.

If a tape recorder is adjusted for the standard 250 nWb/m level it means that a signal of zero level will magnetize the tape to the standard level. It makes no difference what electrical level is required to achieve that zero level. The manufacturer of semiprofessional machines (0 reading = − 10 dBV) and the manufacturer of fully professional machines (0 reading = + 2 dBV) as explained back in Fig.

4-3, have adjusted their machines so that a calibration tone recorded at zero level on one machine will play back at zero level on the other machine. This follows as long as all adhere to the 250 nWb/m standard.

21.4 USING THE TAPE RECORDER

Modern stereo tape recorders and tape decks are actually two machines in one. They share many of their components, such as motors and controls, as they operate to record and play twin programs physically synchronized by their placement on the tape.

Quality depends upon the constancy of the tape speed. The higher the basic tape speed the better the high-frequency response. Tape speeds in common use for open reel machines are 3-3/4 inches-per-second (ips) and 7-1/2 ips. Professional mastering machines use the 15 ips speed and occasionally 30 ips. A speed of 1-7/8 ips is useful for recording speeches or for logging functions where quality is

secondary. The 1-7/8 ips is the standard for cassette recorders.

The dynamic range of the human ear approaches 120 dB, which is about double that of the best magnetic tape recorder. The dynamic range of sounds to be recorded, such as an orchestra, requires some manual compression by the mixer. The low-level sounds must be boosted to avoid losing them in the noise. The high-level sounds must be cut down to avoid magnetic saturation of the tape and electrical overloading, which lead to distortion. The accepted procedure is to record sounds so that the peaks just touch the red area of the meter above 0dB or 0VU. Headroom sufficient to care for peaks the meter cannot follow is usually built into the machine. The operator finds it an advantage if the meters to be followed are genuine VU meters having the standard ballistics.

21.5 TYPICAL RECORDERS

Of the host of magnetic recorders on the market today, some selection must be exercised to fit into the confines of this chapter. The line offered by Fostex Corporation of America (Ref.1) covering 2-, 4-, 8-, and 16-track configurations has been selected as typical of the semiprofessional level. Consumer recorders much cheaper, simpler, and less reliable are available. Professional recorders much more expensive, more sophisticated, and of sturdier construction are also available to round out the full spectrum.

The Fostex A-2 two-track mastering recorder/reproducer is shown in Fig. 21-6. The transport mechanism was specifically developed for multitrack operation and utilizes three dc motors. A servo circuit on the capstan motor minimizes speed variations. The transport commands are logic controlled by integrated circuits with full motion sensing in all modes to minimize tape stretch and breakage. The bottom panel flips down to give easy access to the calibration controls. The record/play electronics are on plug-in cards and the transport electronics on a hinged printed-circuit board. The reels accommodated are 7-inch. The VU meters are switchable to indicate saturation or alignment levels and output send levels. A pitch control allows plus and minus 10 percent speed change for stretching or compression of program tape lengths, for effects, or for matching pitch between machines. Three heads allow off-the-tape monitoring. Sync playback mode on both channels is incorporated. Standard speeds are 7-1/2 and 15 ips with 3-3/4 and 7-1/2 ips combination offered as an option. The line input and output levels are – 10 dBV and the machine is calibrated at 250 nWb/m tape flux.

The Fostex A-4 four-track recorder/reproducer is shown in Fig. 21-7. This multitrack machine bears much resemblance to the A-2 in regard to transport and general design. Fully compatible four-track format allows the playback of stereo tapes. Sync/reproduce is equalized in playback mode for greater accuracy and fidelity. Like the A-2, an LED tape counter with return-to-zero memory for fast, easy tape checks is provided. Edit mode allows spooling off unwanted tape easily. Slight reduction in specifications from the A-2 include: frequency response 40 Hz-20 kHz to 40 Hz-18 kHz and signal-to-noise ratio from 65 to 63 dB weighted at both 7-1/2 and 15 ips. Interestingly, crosstalk is listed at 50 dB for both machines.

The Fostex A-8 eight-track recorder/reproducer utilizes quarter-inch tape and still lists crosstalk between channels at 45 dB at 1 kHz. This machine (Fig. 21-8) is of interest to the growing number of musicians, songwriters, A-V professionals and remote recordists. Dolby C™ noise reduction is built in and is defeatable for alignment. A group selector allows recording on tracks 1 through 4 or 5 through 8 simultaneously. Punching in or out is provided through record track buttons. Unlike the A-2 and A-4, the A-8 is a two-head machine, erase and record/play. Frequency response is listed at 45 Hz-kHz, signal-to-noise ratio of 73 dB.

The Fostex B-16 sports 16 tracks and 16 channels, but the tape width is now 1/2 inch. This machine, shown in Fig. 21-9, utilizes three dc motors, two direct drive reel motors and a servo-controlled capstan motor, and operates at 15 ips with a plus or minus 15% variable speed feature. A photo sen-

Fig. 21-6. The Fostex A-2 mastering record/reproducer (courtesy Fostex Corporation of America).

Fig. 21-7. The Fostex A-4 four-track recorder/reproducer (courtesy Fostex Corporation of America).

Fig. 21-8. The Fostex A-8 eight-track recorder/reproducer (courtesy Fostex Corporation of America).

Fig. 21-9. The Fostex B-16 sixteen-track, half-inch tape recorder/reproducer (courtesy Fostex Corporation of America).

sor detects end of tape and automatically disengages the reel motors. This is the only one of the Fostex machines described that has hubs to accommodate the 10-1/2 inch NAB reels. Crosstalk is listed at 55 dB.

21.6 SPLICING AND EDITING

For many owners of open reel machines the ultimate in misfortune is to have the tape break in use. This happened frequently with the old acetate base tape but is less likely to happen with the new polyester base tape. Splicing, however, is a positive sort of exercise that should be mastered by anyone

working around magnetic tape recorders. Besides repairing breaks, splicing allows deleting unwanted portions of tape, and ordering what is left in the proper sequence and timing.

A good splice requires little technique and little equipment. You can be in business with a pair of scissors (demagnetized, however) and a roll of splicing tape. A splicing block makes the job much easier by holding the ends while the splice is made. If a block is used, normal procedure would call for splicing tape narrower than the magnetic tape. Using scissors, the splicing tape is usually wider than the magnetic tape. Do not try to economize on the splicing tape, it is a very sophisticated product. A good splicing tape will have a high shear adhesion (resistance to creeping) and high adhesion (resistance to peel-back). A good splicing tape does not ooze at the splice.

The angle at which the splice is made is important. Butt-splicing is used only when close editing, say on single words, is necessary. A 45-degree angle is right for most splices.

The following steps to a good splice are designed to coordinate with Fig. 21-10.

(1) Place tapes within splicing block guide channel, backing side up. Overlap ends.

(2) Hold magnetic tape firmly in channel with finger and make cut with a sharp, demagnetized razor blade.

(3) Pull out approximately 1-inch of splicing tape and draw downward against cutting blade of dispenser.

(4) Keep tape ends butter together and lay

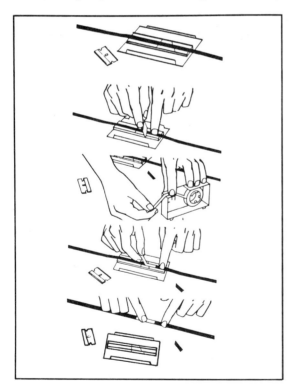

Fig. 21-10. Proper technique in the splicing of tape.

splicing tape carefully on top, inside the channel. Press down lightly to adhere tape to full length of splice.

(5) Remove spliced tape from channel and rub splicing tape firmly with fingernail to remove all air bubbles.

21.7 MAINTENANCE OF TAPE RECORDERS

Regular preventive maintenance makes the difference between good and excellent recordings. Dust and contamination pose a greater hazard to good recordings than does normal wear and tear in the machine. The tape path should be wiped clean regularly and the equipment should be covered while idle.

Cleaning of the heads, rollers, and pressure pads requires some precautions. The problem is to remove accumulations of oxide debris or lint without scratching the surfaces of the heads. Cleaning should be done with a cotton swab, preferably the type that has a paper, rather than a wooden handle. The head surfaces should never be touched with a metal object and even the wooden swab handle is suspect. A standard head cleaner should be used as a solvent; denatured alcohol if cleaner is not available.

Demagnetizing of heads and tape guides is done with a degausser with a piece of electrical tape over its pole piece to avoid scratching the head surface. If the demagnetizer is close to the head as the ac energizing current is switched off, the heads will be magnetized to an extent dependent upon the point on the ac cycle when the switch was opened. The proper procedure is to place the energized demagnetizer against the head and slowly withdraw it, turning it off when the distance is two feet or so. In this way the head is magnetized, first one way and then the other with the ac magnetic flux, and as the demagentizer is withdrawn the alternating magnetic flux gets lower and lower until the magnetization of the head is neutralized.

Magnetic tape should not be subjected to extremely high temperatures such as those occurring in an automobile standing in full sunlight for long periods. At high temperatures, "print through" of recorded material from one layer to another is aggravated. For tape stored for long periods of time, a rewinding operation every six months tends to control print-through.

21.8 ALIGNMENT OF RECORDERS

Test tapes are available at several levels of sophistication. It is strongly urged that one of these be on hand for alignment (calibration) of even the simplest recording operation. Such a tape, and the instruction booklet accompanying it, will greatly simplify head alignment, level adjustment, and frequency response. Most machines have adjustments for record level, playback level, bias current, record equalization and playback equalization. The test tape will assist greatly in adjusting most of these variables. Test tapes are recorded full track.

For the bias current adjustment, a particular brand of tape to be used is threaded on the machine. If 15 ips tape speed is to be used, feed a 1-kHz tone into the machine at zero level. If 7.5 ips tape speed is to be used, feed 500 Hz into the machine at zero level. The machine is then set for record mode and the output in reproduce mode. The amount of bias current affects the signal-to-noise ratio, distortion, signal output level, and frequency response. As bias is increased to a certain point, all of these factors improve. Increasing bias past this point, however, low-frequency response, signal-to-noise ratio, and distortion continue to improve, but high-frequency response starts to fall. As bias is further increased, signal-to-noise ratio and distortion improve but low- and high-frequency response deteriorate. The best bias setting is that which gives peak output of signals in the 500 - 1,000 Hz range. The usual procedure is to increase the bias control by turning it clockwise until the output rises to a peak. Bias is then increased further until output level falls 1 dB. This procedure may be slightly different for best results on some tapes.

References

1. Fostex Corporation of America, 15431 Blackburn Avenue, Norwalk, CA 90650

Chapter 22

Packaged Sound Amplifying Systems

T HE BASIC PROBLEMS ASSOCIATED WITH sound-reinforcement systems, discussed in detail in Chapter 6, are numerous and aggravating. For a permanent installation these problems are struggled with in the design stage and worked out in the installation stage. Some of the problems may even have no economical solution, such as acoustical problems of the space, and must be endured through the years. Now when we come to a temporary installation in a room with unknown acoustical properties, anything can happen.

Portable, packaged sound-amplifying systems are subject to all the problems of the permanent installation, and perhaps a few more. However, there is no denying the great attraction of this type of equipment. A school, church, or other institution having many rooms with no permanent sound-reinforcing equipment in them may understandably look with great favor to a system that can be moved about to meet the current pressures. A traveling lecturer may want to maintain control of sound amplification in his or her appearances and elect to have a personal system to guarantee a minimum

success at least. This need for small, portable systems has been met by a number of suppliers. Typical examples of such systems are described in this chapter.

22.1 THE PORTABLE SYSTEM

A typical portable system is shown in Fig. 22-1. This is the Model CA-130 "Amplicolumn" offered by Paso Sound Products, Inc., (Ref. 1). All of the electronics are housed in the base of the loudspeaker column. With microphone extension cords, the sound radiating column can be placed at a distance, but the volume control is then also at a distance. With experience in using this equipment, rather standard semi-fixed setting of volume control would be expected with occasional feedback howling during the process of adjustment.

The CA-130 system is contained in a custom designed carrying case. The microphone is a unidirectional dynamic unit. The integrated circuit solid-state amplifier is rated at 30 watts. Beside the microphone, there is an auxiliary input so that other

299

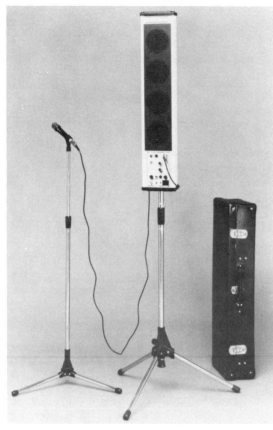

Fig. 22-1. The Pasco Model CA-130 "Amplicolumn" portable sound system. All of the pieces fit into the single case. The amplifier has a power of 30 watts and may be powered from the ac mains or by 10 "D" sized batteries (courtesy Paso Sound Products, Inc.).

signals, such as from a tape recorder, could be fed into the amplifier. An output is available for recording the program and another that could feed an extension column. There are four loudspeakers in the column. The power source is either 117 volts ac or 10 size "D" batteries. The CA-130 is claimed to have power to cover 20,000 sq. ft.

22.2 PORTABLE LECTERNS

The Model TA-8 portable sound lectern of Fig. 22-2 is also offered by Paso Sound Products, Inc., (Ref. 1). This unit is housed in a single case which separates diagonally into a lectern half housing the

amplifier and controls and a loudspeaker half of which can be located at some distance from the microphone on the lectern. Legs are available that can be screwed on the bottom of the lectern to bring it to satisfactory height when only a table top is available.

This unit also employs a unidirectional dynamic microphone and solid-state amplifier. The loudspeaker is a dual unit. The TA-8 operates on 10 standard "D" size batteries or ac with an optional adapter. The amplifier is rated at 40 watts. Controls include volume, tone, and speech filter. There are two microphone inputs as well as a third auxiliary input. Outputs include one for tape recording and another for an external loudspeaker. The unit weighs 25 lbs.

22.3 THE COLUMN LECTERN

In Fig. 22-3 is shown the Model L-271 "Sound Column Lectern" manufactured by Paso Sound Products (Ref. 1). This unit is technically quite different from the previous two units because the microphone, amplifier, and loudspeaker are all mounted together in the same housing. This presents a challenge to the manufacturer in that the

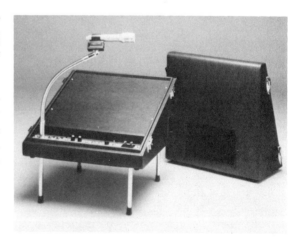

Fig. 22-2. The Paso Model TA-8 portable sound lectern. The loudspeakers are in one half and the amplifier and controls in the other. The amplifier is rated at 40 watts and is powered with 10 "D" cells or by optional ac adapter (courtesy Paso Sound Products, Inc.).

Fig. 22-3. The Paso Model L-271 sound column lectern which has an amplifier rated at 40 watts, powered by 117 volts ac or 10 "D" cells. The lectern face is illuminated with a recessed fluorescent lamp (courtesy Paso Sound Products, Inc.).

possibility of feedback is greatly increased. For one thing, the microphone is close to the loudspeaker. In addition to feedback due to acoustical linkage of output to input, there is the mechanical coupling in which vibrations of the loudspeaker can be fed back to the microphone. Every precaution must be taken, such as resilient mountings, to minimize mechanical coupling. There is nothing that can be done to offset the proximity of loudspeaker and microphone except employ a cardioid microphone. Fortunately, the radiation pattern inherent in the column is in the right direction to help some, and the lectern facing offers some shielding. Optimizing all the variables yields a very convenient lectern/column system with a reasonably workable usable gain.

The Model L-271 has a power output of 40 watts and is powered by 117 volts ac or 10 size "D" batteries. The overall weight is 55 lbs. It has two low-impedance microphone inputs (50-250 ohms) plus one auxiliary input. An output provision for an 8/16-ohm external loudspeaker is provided and another output for tape recorder. The lectern face is illuminated with a recessed fluorescent lamp.

22.4 THE LECTERN WITH BUILT-IN LOUDSPEAKERS

Figure 22-4 illustrates the "Master of Ceremonies" lectern sound system offered by Frazier, Incorporated (Ref. 2). A floor pedestal is also available for use when the lectern must be supported independently. A specially engineered cardioid microphone is used to reduce feedback tendencies. The loudspeaker system includes a 5-1/2 inch woofer with a 3-inch by 7-inch compression horn tweeter. Frequency response is said to be 90 Hz to 17 kHz. A 10-watt amplifier having less than 3 percent distortion is used. An input jack for auxiliary microphone and an output jack for tape recording are also included. The weight of the lectern alone (without the pedestal) is 61 lbs.

22.5 OTHER SYSTEMS

There are many other types of packaged sound systems. The powered megaphones (bullhorns) are an example. A wireless link is often incorporated between the microphone and the packaged system such as the column with amplifier in it. Packaged systems that can convert any van or automobile into a mobile announcing unit are available.

Traveling contemporary music groups often have their own sound-reinforcement system so large that the word "portable" scarcely fits. Their demand for extremely high sound levels covering large seating areas require one or more sixteen wheel trucks to transport all the equipment needed. This is a subject outside the scope of this book; nor does the term "packaged" describe them.

Fig. 22-4. The Frazier "Master of Ceremonies" lectern with and without pedestal. A 10-watt amplifier drives a two-way loudspeaker. A specially engineered cardioid microphone is used to reduce feedback tendencies.

References

1. Paso Sound Products, Inc., 14 First Street, Pelham, NY 10803.

2. Frazier, Incorporated, 1930 Valley View Lane, Dallas, TX 75234.

Chapter 23

Digital Audio

THE 1980S ARE DESTINED TO BE KNOWN AS the decade in which digital audio comes to full fruition. The digital delay line, which appeared in the 1970s, foreshadowed what was coming. The next application of digital techniques in audio was in artificial reverberation devices. Then followed digital recording and reproducing systems. High cost and lack of standardization, understandably, dominate this early period.

It is clear that digital is the way of the future. It is also clear that the audio engineers and technicians who intend to be viable and contributing members of the audio community in the future must become informed in digital techniques. This book might be considered to be hanging for dear life onto the coattails of a vanishing technique, that of analog recording. It has a purpose to be served during the extended transition period, but possibly its greatest contribution would be to convince current analogites that they must become digitites or risk obsolescence.

This is a book on analog sound systems, but in this chapter we are looking into the future. A new language is required of all who would hope to understand current digital literature. The audio journals and magazines are dominated by digital papers that are unintelligible unless one knows the meaning of such words and phrases as quantization error, discrete time sampling, Nyquist rate, PCM, floating point converters, delta modulation, binary digits, and deconvolution. Nor can all these be treated in this brief space. In this chapter all we can hope to do is to treat a few of the very basic concepts of digital audio and these in a relatively superficial way. The reader is urged to follow the writings of Dr. Barry Blesser in the current literature (Refs. 1 and 2) and other writers attempting to raise the digital literacy of audio workers.

23.1 CONCEPT OF STORAGE

Analog recorders store information on discs in the form of wiggles in grooves and on tape in the form of magnetic flux variations on tape. Digital information can also be stored on discs such as the compact disc, in random-access memory, and on magnetic media such as floppy disks, hard disks, etc.

There are advantages and disadvantages of both analog and digital in regard to storage. The big difference is that analog signals have been aptly described as fragile while digital pulses are robust. Everything can happen to analog signals in the line of distortions and degradation of signal-to-noise ratio in multiple generations, but digital can be copied as many times as desired with no degradation of quality. This represents the introduction of something new and different in recording techniques.

23.2 CONCEPT OF QUANTIZATION

An analog signal is a continuum. That is, if it has a peak value of 1 volt all voltages from zero to 1 volt are represented. A signal voltage of 0.8765 volt is different from 0.8766 volt. Borrowing Blesser's illustration of analog signals, we take a jar of water holding 0.8765 quarts. Evaporation takes some, and pouring the water from one jar to another always leaves some on the surfaces. The signal is degraded at each move.

We take a second jar which has a capacity of 1,000 marbles. Our signal is represented by 163 marbles. These can be poured from one jar to another without loss. The "water signal" really carried more information because of its continuous nature, but its fragility is evident. Each marble is a discrete element; there are no fractional marbles. The fractional parts are discarded and they constitute what is called the "quantization error." This error is present in going from analog to digital form, but nothing is lost in going from digital to analog form.

This quantization error is the only limit to the dynamic range of digital systems. It is the "noise" of the system. Later the relationship of the precision of the digital system to dynamic range will be discussed.

23.3 THE BINARY NUMBER SYSTEM

Having lived in Hong Kong several years, I became fascinated with the Chinese abacus and studied it with the aid of a thick book written by a Hong Kong University professor. The proficiency of Chinese clerks in carrying out complex arithmetical computations at lighting speed must be seen to be believed. I shall never forget the hilarity of two teen-age Chinese boys at the sight of a *kwai lo* (foreign devil) using an abacus as I verified the total of a purchase in a store. The abacus caused me to reflect on the decimal system I had taken for granted all my life. On each wooden rod of the abacus are two beads above the bar and five beads below. The two above each have a value of 5 and the five beads below the bar each have a value of 1. My abacus has eleven sets of these beads in the frame, which gives it the capacity of eleven digits. A decimal point is established somewhere on the bar between any two sets of beads. Moving beads toward the dividing bar establishes the initial value of that digit, e.g., moving one upper bead (5s) toward the bar and four lower beads (1s) toward the bar would establish the digit 9. On each rod any number from 1 to 10 can be set. It is a place system, similar to any decimal number. For instance, the number 125 can be represented by 1 hundred, 2 tens, and 5 units. Each digit place has a value of ten and each place is ten times greater than the one before. This is the basis of the decimal system. Moving into digital audio it is necessary to make the acquaintance of another numbering system, the binary.

In the binary system there are only two values for each place and each place has a value twice the preceding one. Really, the only reason the binary system is used is that there is a cheap and available electronic device, the flip-flop, which speaks binary. It says "on" and "off."

The 163 marbles in the jar can be represented as 11010011 in which each 1 is "on" and each 0 is "off." Transforming the decimal 163 to the binary form is illustrated in Table 23-1(A). Division of 163 by 2 gives 81 with one left over. Dividing 81 by 2 gives 40 with 1 left over. Dividing 40 by 2 gives 20 with 0 left over and so on down the column with 1 left over at the end, the remainders building the digital form. This gives the binary representation of 163 as 11010011. There are eight

Table 23-1. Binary and Decimal Numbers.

A

```
2 |163
2 | 81    1
2 | 40    11
2 | 20    011
2 | 10    0011
2 |  5    10011
2 |  2    010011
2 |  1    1010011
  |  0    1101001
```

B

Decimal number	Binary number
0	0
1	1
2	10
3	11
4	100
5	101
6	110
7	111
8	1000
9	1001
10	1010
50	110010
100	1100100
125	11111101

binary digits in this number (or "word") occupying eight places, or eight bits (bit is a contraction of binary digit). The range of binary numbers is determined by the number of binary digits, or bits, and we must remember that it requires one flip-flop for each bit. The binary number 11010011 requires eight flip-flops. In Table 23-1(B) examples of other binary numbers are shown.

23.4 DYNAMIC RANGE

Dynamic range is directly related to the range of binary digits (bits), as follows:

Number of binary digits	Dynamic range
4	24 dB
8	48 dB
12	72 dB
16	96 dB

There are approximate figures computed on the basis 6 x (bits), but they do show how dynamic range is directly a function of the binary range employed. This is because the quantization error, dependent on the binary range, establishes the noise level.

23.5 DIGITIZING THE SIGNAL

Our audio music or speech signal must be converted to a sequence of voltages taken at specific intervals by a sampling process. Only the voltages at these specific sampling times are utilized, all those analog values in-between are discarded. This process may be compared to the motion picture. Still pictures are taken at 1/24th second intervals, yet they still give us a good feeling of continuous motion when projected at 24 frames per second.

The process of obtaining this sequence of numbers to represent our analog audio signal is illustrated in Fig. 23-1. The sine wave of Fig. 23-1(A) represents the audio signal to be digitized. The series of equally spaced pulses of Fig. 23-1(B) are multiplied by the sine signal. Multiplying a pulse by the value of the sine signal prevailing at the instant of the pulse gives a spike having a certain voltage amplitude which appears in Fig. 23-1(C). In-between the spike and the next one, there is nothing. The multiplication process is highly

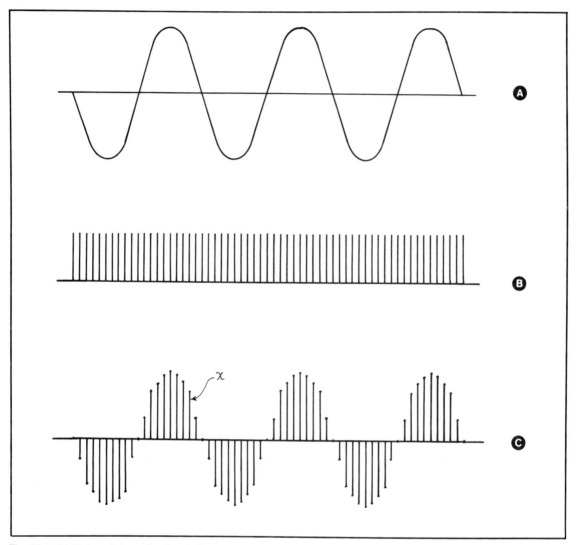

Fig. 23-1. Digitizing of an audio signal. (A) A sine wave to be digitized. (B) The digitizing pulses that are multiplied by the sine wave of (A) to obtain the digitized signal (C). The multiplication process is highly nonlinear, which means that this is essentially a modulation process.

nonlinear. For this reason this digitizing process can be considered a modulation process with upper and lower sidebands.

23.6 QUANTIZING THE SIGNAL

Every pulse of the digitized signal of Fig. 23-1(C) must now be measured, or quantized. Let us focus attention on the single pulse marked "x" in Fig. 23-1(C) which, by a flash of omniscience, we know has a peak of 0.86743 volt. Our task is now to measure this voltage as all the other pulses must also be measured. We cannot come close to realizing the 5-digit precision of 0.86742 volt unless our quantizer has at least 5 digits. The required precision of our measuring voltmeter is determined by the length of the data word in bits (binary digits). The quantizing portion of the analog to digital converter must have sufficient bits to provide the desired precision. A 2-bit quantizer would be able to distinguish between four increments on the voltage scale, an 8-bit quantizer 256 increments, and a 16-bit quantizer would distinguish between 65,536 increments. The number of bits determines the resolution of the quantizer as well as the noise level.

23.7 SPECIFICATIONS OF A DIGITAL SYSTEM

Digitizing and quantizing determine the specifications of a digital audio system. The sampled audio visual cannot contain frequency components greater than half the sampling rate or problems result. Put another way, the sampling (digitizing) frequency must be at least twice as high as the highest audio frequency component of interest. If the signal is sampled at a 40 kHz rate, there must not be any energy in the sampled audio signal higher than 20 kHz or they will be *aliased,* that is, new frequencies will be generated that fall within the desired band below 20 kHz. This requires an anti-aliasing filter which limits the audio range to less than 20 kHz. This low-pass filter is generally a part of the analog to digital converter. Sampling rates of 44.1 and 48 kHz have been widely used.

Quantizing the sampled signal with a word length of 16-bits has yielded excellent quality and signal-to-noise ratio. Quantization noise associated

with 16-bits is determined by the ratio of the number of increments to that uncertain last digit. In a 16-bit quantizer there are 2 to the 16th power increments or 65,536. If we give a value of 0.5 to that last digit, the signal-to-noise ratio, or dynamic range, is $20 \log (65,536/0.5) = 102$ dB. The signal-to-noise ratio is commonly estimated as (6) (number of bits) = (6) (16) = 96 dB. A new era in audio system dynamic range has arrived.

23.8 DIGITAL SYSTEMS

Now that the two independent processes of digitizing and quantizing have been considered in a very sketchy fashion, we can proceed in our mind's eye to put pieces of equipment together to make a digital recording and reproducing system. A block diagram of a basic system is shown in Fig. 23-2. The analog input is fed to an analog to digital (A/D) converter (which also includes the anti-aliasing filter) and thence to a digital processing operation and from there to a storage medium. The reproducing system takes the signal from storage and applies it to a digital to analog (D/A) converter, from which our analog signal is reclaimed in all its pristine glory.

That sounds rather easy, but there are pitfalls along the way. The analog input, as mentioned above, must go through a low-pass filter of very

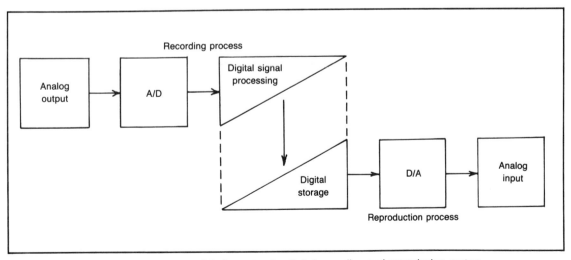

Fig. 23-2. A Block diagram of the essential elements of a digital recording and reproducing system.

critical characteristics. The most critical unit of the digital chain is the digital to analog converter. There are serious accuracy problems in building a 16-bit digital to analog converter. The stringent requirements in handling small signals strain the technology available.

References

1. Blesser, Barry, 1978. "Digitation of Audio: A Comprehensive Examination of Theory, Implementation, and Current Practice," *Jour. Audio Engr. Soc.*, Vol 26, No 10 (Oct), pp 739-771.

2. Blesser, Barry, 1980. "An Introduction To Digital Audio," This is a continuing series of articles which started in *dB The Sound Engineering Magazine*, Vol 14, No 7 (July), pp 22-25 and was still running as a feature department at the end of 1984. These articles are highly recommended.

Glossary

acoustic response—Response of a reproducing system including power amplifier, loudspeaker, and room acoustics.

ambience—Spatially diffused reverberant sound in an enclosure which gives the impression of size and degree of liveness of the enclosure.

analog—Analog techniques are based on representing signals with proportional electrical voltages or currents. An ordinary amplifier is an analog device, as is a voltmeter. (See digital.)

anechoic room—Literally, a room without echoes. A room whose boundaries absorb the incident sound, thereby affording essentially free-field conditions.

assignment—(See delegation.)

attack time—In signal processing devices actuated by signal level (e.g., compressors and expanders), the attack time describes how fast the resulting effect takes place when the signal level is suddenly increased.

attenuator—An adjustable resistance element in electronic circuits for varying the signal level.

baffle—Portable sound barrier used in recording studios to provide some degree of acoustical separation between instruments or performers. Also called *screen*. The term is also used for the loudspeaker mounting board which affects its radiation efficiency.

bass—The energy of sound in the lower frequency range of the human ear.

biamplifier—In the biamplifier loudspeaker system separate power amplifiers are used for the high- and low-frequency radiators. The dividing network is at low level before the power amplifiers. (See dividing network; triamplifier.)

bias—In magnetic tape recording the signal to be recorded is mixed with a high-frequency (60-100 kHz) bias current to reduce distortion in the magnetization process of the tape.

board—A synonym for the control-bearing desktop of an audio control console. (See desk; console.)

buffer—An amplifier used for isolating one circuit from another to avoid interaction.

bus—A term designating major electronic circuits to which many other circuits may be connected, usually at high level such as output bus. Synonymous with *line*.

cardioid—Microphone directivity pattern having a shape like a heart.

coloration—When an acoustic or electrical signal is changed by some external effect, it can be said to be *colored*. For example, room acoustics can color a sound emitted in the room. Derived from light terminology; when the spectrum of white light is affected by an outside agent such as a glass filter, the light becomes colored.

comb filter—A filter having a series of passbands and stopbands distributed uniformly down through the audible spectrum like the teeth of a comb.

compressor—An electronic signal processing device for reducing the dynamic range of a signal. When the dynamic range of the sound source (a symphony orchestra may have a dynamic range of about 70b dB) exceeds that of the recording system, it is necessary to employ either manual or electronic compression. (see also expander.)

console—In audio systems the console is the operational control center which houses the faders, level indicators, control circuits, equalizers, and switches required to function conveniently and efficiently. (See also desk; board.)

critical bands—In human hearing, only those components of noise within a narrow band will mask a given tone. This is called a critical band. The critical bandwidth of the ear varies with frequency, but is approximately 1/3 octave in width.

critical distance—In an enclosure filled with sound from a loudspeaker, the critical distance from the loudspeaker is that distance at which the direct (inverse square) sound level equals the general reverberant level. (See also reverberant field; inverse square.)

crosstalk—the signal of one channel, track, or circuit interfering with another is called crosstalk (from early telephone usage).

cue—(See foldback.)

damping—The introduction of a dissipative element into any resonant system. In electrical circuits, resistance provides damping. In an acoustically resonant structure such as a Hemholtz type absorber, glass fiber serves as a damping element. By damping, a resonance peak is reduced and broadened.

dB—(See decibel.)

dB (A)—A sound level meter reading made with a weighting network simulating human ear response at a loudness level of 40 phons.

dB(B)—A sound level meter reading made with a weighting network simulating the response of the human ear at a loudness level of 70 phons.

dB(C)—A sound level meter reading made with no weighting network in the circuit, i.e., flat. Decibels referenced to a zero-decibel sound pressure level of 0.0002 microbar.

dBm—Decibels referenced to a zero-decibel level of 1 mW in a 600Ω circuit.

dead room—(See anechoic room.)

decibel (db)—The human ear responds logarithmically and it is convenient to deal in logarithmic units in audio systems. The decibel is such a logarithmic unit, always referred to some reference level such as 0.0002 microbar for sound pressure, 1 mW in 600Ω in audio circuits. The smallest change in sound level the human ear can detect is 1 to 3 dB, depending on circumstances.

decode—To restore an encoded signal to usable form. (See also encode.)

delay—Digital, analog, or mechanical techniques may be employed to delay one audio signal with respect to another. Useful in sound reinforcement systems to compensate for sound transit times, and in recording for special effects such as phasing. (See also phasing; flanging; comb filter.)

delegation—Routing of input channels to output lines.

desk—A synonym for *audio control console* in audio systems, more common in British usage. (See also board; console.)

digital—Digital techniques are based on the on/off binary language of computers. Analog signals may be translated to digital signals by sampling at regular time intervals and noting the amplitude of each sampling pulse. Digital signals may readily be retranslated to analog form. (See also analog.)

distortion—Any change in waveform or harmonic content of an original signal as it passes through a device. This results from a deviation from strict linearity within the device. Distortion generates harmonics not in the original signal.

dividing network—An electrical network dividing the audible spectrum for efficient and faithful sound reproduction. In a three-way loudspeaker the dividing network sends only high-frequency energy to the high-frequency radiator (tweeter), only midrange energy to the midrange radiator, and only low-frequency energy to the low-frequency radiator (woofer).

doppler effect—A source of sound moving toward or away from an observer gives the observer the sensation of a changing pitch referred to as *Doppler shift*. The pitch increases as the source approaches, and decreases as it recedes.

dynamic range—All audio systems are limited by inherent noise at low levels and by distortion at high levels. The usable region between these two extremes is the dynamic range of the system, expressed in decibels.

echo—(See reverberation.)

effects, sound—The addition of recorded sounds for background or to achieve naturalness or dramatic effects.

effects, special—Signal processing to achieve a desired effect for novelty or to create a desired mood.

encode—Changing a signal in one way to achieve a given end with the expectation of applying a decoding step at a later stage. For example, certain noise reduction systems require encode/decode steps to achieve the desired result (See also decode.)

equalization—Adjustment of frequency response of a channel to achieve a flat or other desired response. Also applied to the adjustment of fre-quency response of the overall monitoring system, including the acoustics of the room.

erase—Magnetic tape having previously recorded signals on it must be erased before reuse. This is accomplished in recorders by a high-frequency current in an erase head over which the tape passes just before it reaches the recording head. Bulk erasers producing strong alternating magnetic fields erase rolls of tape prior to mounting on the recorder.

expander—An electronic signal processing device for increasing the dynamic range of a signal to restore a compressed signal to its original dynamic range.

fader—An adjustable resistance element in an electrical circuit to control the sound level (volume). (See also potentiometer; gain control; volume control.)

figure-8—A microphone directivity pattern resembling a figure 8 having good response front and back and nulls at the side.

filter—An electronic circuit useful for separating one part of the audible spectrum from another. A *high-pass filter* passes only the energy above a certain cutoff frequency, a *low-pass filter* only the energy below a cutoff frequency. A *bandpass filter* rejects energy below and above and passes only energy within a band.

flanging—An ethereal swishing, inside-out sound achieved by mixing a signal with the same signal slightly delayed. The name derives from an early method of achieving the effect with two tape recorders and slowing one by applying pressure to the flange of its supply reel. Commonly produced today by analog or digital delay devices. (See also fuzz; phasing; comb filter.)

flux—the lines of force of a magnetic field.

foldback—The signal fed to the headphones of the performer in the studio engaged in overdubbing. (see also overdub.)

free field—A sound field in which the effects of the boundaries are negligible over the region of interest.

frequency—The number of signal cycles occurring during each one-second period. Frequency is the physical measurement corresponding to the sensation of pitch. Audible sound falls roughly in the frequency range 20 Hz to 20,000 Hz.

fuzz—(See flanging.)

gain control—An adjustable resistance element in electronics for controlling signal voltages.

gating circuit—An electronically controlled circuit which, for example, cuts off a circuit when the signal level falls below a predetermined value.

Haas effect—When one is listening in a reverberant enclosure, the sound arriving at the ear within the first 35-40 msec is integrated by the hearing mechanism and interpreted as coming directly from the source. Sound arriving after this period is perceived as an echo or as random reverberation.

harmonics—A harmonic is any multiple of the fundamental frequency.

intermodulation distortion—If a nonlinearity exists in an amplifier, a signal component at one frequency will modulate a signal component at another frequency, creating new components which are called intermodulation (IM) distortion products.

inverse square—Sound pressure falls off inversely as the square of the distance from the source in the absence of all reflecting surfaces (such a condition is approached outdoors). (See also reverberation field; critical distance.)

isolation booth—A small enclosure associated with a recording studio in which an instrumentalist, vocalist, or narrator may be isolated acoustically from sounds in the studio. Visual contact is considered desirable.

jack field—Signal paths of console electronics are routed through jacks in the jack field. By plugging into these jacks the normal configuration of the console may be changed for unusual applications or for locating trouble.

lacquer—The master disc recording is cut in a lacquer coating on a very flat aluminum disc. The disc is often referred to as the *lacquer*.

LED—Light-emitting diode, a semiconductor device which emits light when voltage is applied.

level—The level of a quantity is the logarithm of the ratio of that quantity to a reference quantity of the same kind.

level indicators—Any visual device for indicating signal levels in the various channels of the console or tracks on the recorder. VU meters, dancing bars on a CRT screen, or stacks of light-emitting diodes may be used to indicate level. They may indicate instantaneous signal peaks or RMS (root-mean-square) effective values.

limiter—An electronic signal processing device by which the upward excursion of signal level may be limited to prevent overdriving of following devices.

linear—If the output of a device bears a constant ratio to its input, the device is said to be linear.

live room—A room characterized by reverberation resulting from unusually small amounts of sound absorption.

logic—the sequential and operation steps expressed in electronic circuits of the type required to accomplish a desired function.

mass law—The ability of a barrier to attenuate sound depends upon the mass of the barrier. Transmission loss computed from this simplified mass law may vary considerably from actual measurements.

master—A master type is the original tape on which is recorded the signals mixed down from the multitrack tape, contrasted to a copy or dubbing (rerecording) of the master tape. The master recorder is the machine on which the master tape is recorded. The master fader controls the level of all console output signals without disturbance of channel faders.

matrix—An electrical network; usually a large number of components of a given type, as resistors. With reference to quadraphony, the *matrix* is the decoding network that reconstitutes four channels from two.

microphone, contact—A special microphone affixed to a musical instrument in such a way that it responds primarily to the vibrations of the instrument rather than to airborne sounds. Also called *pickup*.

mid-side (Blumlein pair)—A combination of two microphones in one housing for stereo use, one having a cardioid (mid) and the other a figure-8 directivity pattern (side).

mixdown—The process of combining the several signals on a multitrack magnetic tape with appropriate levels, signal processing, and time relationships to give a complete performance in fewer channels than the master contains.

mixer—An electrical or electronic device capable of mixing (summing) two or more signals into a composite signal.

modulation noise—A type of noise generated in magnetic tape, the magnitude of which is proportional to signal level. In most cases the higher signal masks the increased noise but the fluctuating hissing noise produced by heavy bass signals can often be distracting.

monitor—The means for hearing and checking signals for control and evaluation. The name often applies to the loudspeakers in the control room.

monophonic (mono)—Recording and reproduction of sound by a single channel.

multitrack recording—Recording a multiplicity of audio track on magnetic tape. The number of tracks ranges from 2 to 40.

octave—The interval between two frequencies having a basic frequency ratio of 2:1.

omnidirectional—Having a uniform response to sound arriving from any direction, as in *omnidirectional microphone*.

operational amplifier (opamp)—An amplifier (usually an IC) requiring a modest number of exterior components to produce a wide range of amplifier characteristics.

overdub—In separation recording it is not necessary that all tracks be recorded concurrently. Individual tracks may be recorded or redone at a later time or even built up one track at a time. Synchronism is achieved through cue (foldback) signals of previously recorded tracks fed to the performer through headphones. To eliminate a time delay, such foldback signals are picked up from the record heads which are in sync with the track being recorded.

overtones—Overtones bear an octave relationship to the fundamental frequency. The overtones of 100 Hz occur at 200, 400, 800 . . . etc. Hz. Not to be confused with harmonics. (See also harmonics.)

panoramic potentiometer—An adjustable resistance network in an electric circuit by which the signal on a given channel may be positioned in the stereo or quad playback sound field.

panpot—(See panoramic potentiometer.)

phantom image—By phase and level adjustments the apparent source location in stereo or quad may be shifted between two loudspeakers with little relationship to the true source location. This apparent location of the source is called the phantom image.

phase—The time relationship between two signals.

phasing—The term applied to the proper connection of loudspeaker or microphone leads so that all elements are properly in phase. (See also flanging, comb filter.)

pink noise—A noise signal whose spectrum level increases 3 dB per octave. It is convenient to use pink noise with an analyzer having a bandwidth of a given percentage of the frequency to which it is tuned (e.g., 1/3 octave). (See also white noise; random noise.)

potentiometer—An adjustable resistance element in an electrical circuit by which magnitudes of voltages and currents may be controlled. (See also fader; volume control; gain control; attenuator.)

power amplifier—An amplifier designed to supply relatively large amounts of power to drive loudspeakers, etc.

preamplifier—An amplifier optimized for low

noise to amplify low-level signals such as those from microphones.

precedence effect—(See Haas effect.)

premixing—Employing an outboard mixer to mix signals from several related microphones before sending the combined signal to the main console. A device for overcoming the problem of limited input channels in the main console.

program amplifier—An amplifier used at intermediate signals levels between the preamplifiers and power amplifiers.

quadpot—(See panoramic potentiometer.)

quadraphony—The recording and reproduction of sound through four channels to give more spatial and ambient information than is possible with only two channels. The adjective form is *quadraphonic*.

random noise—An oscillation whose instantaneous magnitude is specified only by a probability function—useful in acoustic measurements.

release time—In signal processing devices actuated by signal level (e.g., compressors and expanders) the release time is a measure of the time required for the device to be restored to normal operation upon sudden removal of the actuating signal.

remix—(See mixdown.)

reverberation field—The reverberant sound or reverberation field in a room is that built up by sound which has undergone multiple reflections. The level of the reverberant field is essentially constant throughout the room. (See also critical distance; inverse square.)

reverberation—When any enclosure, recording studios included, is filled with sound and that sound is suddenly cut off, a finite length of time is required for the sound to reach inaudibility. This tailing off of sound resulting from multiple reflections from the boundaries of the enclosure is called reverberation.

reverberation, artificial—Artificial reverberation is commonly added to audio signals to simulate the ambient conditions of a large hall.

The delayed effect required in generating artificial reverberation may be produced in a reverberation chamber having hard, reflective surfaces, or by sending sound waves down a metal spring, or within a metal plate. Digital or other delay lines can be used in producing artificial reverberation as well as magnetic tape or discs.

rolloff—A gradual decrease in response of a circuit as contrasted to terms *cutoff* or *chopoff*, designating faster decrease in response.

saturation—In all magnetic tape there is a point above which the output is not proportional to the input. This is the region of magnetic saturation (to be avoided in recording).

screens—(See baffles.)

separation recording—The technique of fragmenting a musical group and recording each component with a separate microphone (or groups of microphones), a separate track on a multitrack recorder. Mixing these tracks in a later operation gives the final performance.

servo—A servo system is a device controlled by sensing the output. For example, let us say we want to control the speed of a motor. The motor may be driven by a servoamplifier controlled by a speed sensor attached to the motor shaft so that deviations from the desired speed produce error signals which compensate for the deviations. It is a feedback system.

shelving—Instead of a peak or dip in channel response near the high or low end of the audible band, an equalizer may also go up or down to a certain level and remain flat at that level. This flat region is called a shelf, and the circuits are referred to as *shelving*.

shift register—An integrated circuit of great complexity used for achieving time delay for audio use.

signal-to-noise—The number of decibels separating the signal level from the noise level of a channel, magnetic track, or electronic device.

slating—Recording voice identification signals on the magnetic tape at the beginning of a take.

sound absorption—Sound energy dissipated as heat in the interstices of fibrous materials or the fibers of flexural panels. The sound absorption coefficient represents that fraction of incident sound absorbed by the material. A coefficient of 0.22 means 22% of incident energy is absorbed.

sound level—A sound pressure expressed in decibels as a ratio to some reference level. In acoustics, the accepted reference level is 0.0002 microbar, which is close to the human threshold of hearing.

sound with sound—An amateur attempt at overdubbing. Requires a stereo recorder that permits playing of one track while recording on the other. Tracks can be combined successfully as headphone monitoring is used.

sound transmission class—A standard method of rating airborne sound transmission performance of a wall or floor—ceiling structure at different frequencies by means of a single number.

standing wave—The air in a room constitutes a complex acoustical system having many resonance points. For example, two parallel walls 20 ft apart are acoustically resonant at 28 Hz and multiples of 28 Hz. When sound from a loudspeaker excites this mode, nodes and antinodes of sound pressure, called a *standing wave,* result.

stereophonic—Recording and reproduction of sound through two channels to give spatial information, retaining essentially the positional information of the original performance.

synthesizer—A device for producing a wide variety of sounds useful for special effects, generating new-sound music, and imitating sounds of conventional instruments and recognizable noises (as clapping, whistling, etc.).

talkback—The facility by which the console operator can talk to those in the studio. Those in the studio can communicate with the control room over the normal microphone channels.

tape hiss—The electrical noise produced by the granularity of the oxide coating of the magnetic tape.

test tones—A test oscillator built into the console generates sine-wave tones of adjustable frequency for conforming console levels with recorder levels, checking frequency response,etc.

three-way loudspeaker—A three-way loudspeaker utilizes three separate radiators, one for high frequency, one for the midrange, and one for the low-frequency components of the signal. (See also dividing network).

transducer—Any element that changes one form of energy to another. Electroacoustic transducers change acoustic energy to electrical or vice versa. Microphones and loudspeakers are such transducers.

transients—A short high-amplitude variation in signal level. Short-lived impulsive bursts of sound pressure or voltage or current in electrical circuits.

transmission loss—As applied to sound transmission through partitions, baffles, or other sound barriers, transmission loss is measured by the number of decibels that sounds are attenuated in passing through the barrier.

treble—the energy of sound in the upper range of frequencies preceived by the human ear.

triamplifier—In the triamplification system, separate power amplifiers are used to drive the high-frequency, midrange,and low-frequency radiators in the loudspeaker; the dividing network is at low level before the power amplifiers. (see also dividing network; biamplifier.)

two-way loudspeaker—A two-way loudspeaker utilizes separate high- and low-frequency radiators. (See also dividing network.)

voltage-controlled amplifier—An amplifier whose gain can be controlled by varying a direct-current voltage. Used extensively in automated systems.

volume control—An adjustable resistance element in an electrical circuit to control sound level (volume).

VU—Decibels as indicated by the standard VU meter having standardized ballistic characteristics and a standard calibration based on 0 VU = 1 mW of power in a 600Ω circuit. Vocal or instrumental signals are highly transient in nature and the VU meter follows such changes in a standardized way.

wavelength—The distance a sound wave travels in the time it takes to complete one cycle.

white noise—A noise whose noise power per unit frequency is independent of frequency over a specified range. The spectrum of white noise measured with an analyzer having a constant bandwidth is uniform with frequency. (See also random noise; pink noise.)

X-Y microphones—A coincident pair of microphones with cardioid or figure-8 directivity patterns used for stereo pickup, arranged so that one picks up the left predominantly and the other the right.

Index

Index

319

naturalness, 84
network
    dividing, 151
noise cancellation, 133
noise gate, 213
noise reduction, 225
    companding, 234
    Dolby, 235
    electrical, 230
noise reduction system
    dbx, 236
noise reduction systems, 233
NP junction, 42
NPN transistor, 46

O

octaves, 250
Ohm's law, 18, 22
omnidirectional microphone, 123
omnidirectional pattern, 100
open microphones
    problem with too many, 265
outboard equipment, 174

P

P-type semiconductor, 42
panpot control, 174
parallel resonance, 35
parametric equalizers, 258
pattern interrelationships, 104
phantom power, 108
phase, 132
phase opposition, 87
pitch, 67
pitch contours, 68
plate reverberators, 205
PNP transistor, 47
polarity, 132
potential difference, 41
power amplifiers, 191
power factor, 25
power ratings of amplifiers, 191
power supplies, 194
powered mixers, 177
precedence effect, 74
preemphasis, 233
proximity effect, 106

Q

Q, 249
quantization, 304
quantizing the signal, 306

R

range
    dynamic, 209, 304
rarefaction, 2

reactive elements, 31
real time analyzer, 262
reverberation devices, 203
reciprocals, 24
recorders
    multitrack, 183
    typical, 291
recording
    multitrack, 203
recording formats, 287
rectifier, 44
release time, 212
reluctance, 18
resistance networks, 24
resistances in parallel, 24
resistances in series, 23
resonance
    parallel, 35
    series, 35
reverberation, 79, 174
reverberation chambers, 204
reverberator
    digital, 207
reverberators
    plate, 205
    spring, 205
reverse bias, 43
reverse polarity, 280
ribbon microphone, 122
ribbon microphones, 98
righthand rule, 20
RLC circuits, 34
rms, 30
room acoustics, 241

S

semiconductors, 41
series resonance, 35
Shure system, 269
sibilant control, 214
signal biased system, 92
signal processing
    audio, 209
signal quantizing, 306
silicon, 41
sine terminology, 30
sine wave, 2
sound
    audible, 241
    speed of, 3
sound fields, 80
sound perception, 63
sound processing equipment
    typical, 214
sound reinforcement, 79
    delays in, 221
sound reinforcement parameters, 90

sound reinforcement system, 9, 83
sound reinforcement system
    equalizing, 260
sound systems
    delay in, 91
    portable, 299
sound transmission, 9
sound waves, 1, 7, 10
spatial image, 204
spatial orientation, 72
specifications
    digital system, 307
spectrum, 69
speed of sound, 3
splicing, 295
spring reverberators, 205
stage monitors, 157
standing waves, 4
system equalizing, 249
systems
    digital, 307

T

tape recorder alignment, 297
tape recorder maintenance, 296
tape recording
    magnetic, 285
timbre, 69
time delay, 219
tone control, 249
torque, 18, 21
transistor
    junction, 45
    NPN, 46
transistor amplifier, 47
transistors
    field-effect, 48

U

understandability, 84

V

vectors, 33
velocity gradients, 9
VU meter, 58

W

wavefront shapes, 3
wavefronts, 5
    spherical, 4
wavelength, 3
wireless microphones, 109

Z

zener current, 45
zener diode, 44
zero levels, 61
zero response, 101

OTHER POPULAR TAB BOOKS OF INTEREST